THE
AUGUSTAN
MILIEU

LOUIS A. LANDA

THE
AUGUSTAN
MILIEU

Essays presented to
LOUIS A. LANDA

EDITED BY
HENRY KNIGHT MILLER
ERIC ROTHSTEIN
G. S. ROUSSEAU

OXFORD
AT THE CLARENDON PRESS
1970

Oxford University Press, Ely House, London W. 1

GLASGOW NEW YORK TORONTO MELBOURNE WELLINGTON
CAPE TOWN SALISBURY IBADAN NAIROBI DAR ES SALAAM LUSAKA ADDIS ABABA
BOMBAY CALCUTTA MADRAS KARACHI LAHORE DACCA
KUALA LUMPUR SINGAPORE HONG KONG TOKYO

PRINTED IN GREAT BRITAIN

PREFATORY STATEMENT

To Louis Landa, whose wisdom about the Augustan milieu has made the community of scholars his students, we should like to offer this volume. The essays that it includes come from that fortunate group of active eighteenth-century scholars with whom he has been associated—as colleague, as collaborator, as teacher. To honour him, each contributor has chosen a topic that should illuminate a different aspect of the relationship between the Augustan man of letters and his milieu. That milieu is in some cases represented by a literary legacy, like the techniques of rhetoric or parody; in some cases, by political or economic or scientific fact; in some cases, by the history of ideas. The programme for the volume, then, is eclectic, suggesting the range of Louis Landa's own work and interests; and, more important, trusting that its discrete and limited parts may give body to the large dim abstraction that the title names. The editors have resisted the urge to call for a narrower kind of unity, which would have shrunk the scope of the volume or have deflected the essays from that thoroughness, that responsiveness to immediate fact, to which Louis Landa's work and teaching alike have always given a just priority. We have tried instead (with apologies to Pope) to lend the inquiring scholar a microscopic eye, or at least a compound eye, for a complex age.

THE EDITORS

CONTENTS

Contents

I

ANNE GREENE AND THE OXFORD POETS

By JAMES SUTHERLAND

I

IT is unlikely that literary historians will ever recognize, or invent, a school of poets who could be described as the Sons of Cleveland; but between the years 1650 and 1660 the influence of John Cleveland must have been very considerable, more especially in the two universities. His poems were first collected in a volume called *The Character of a London-Diurnall, with several select Poems by the same Author*, and no fewer than seven further editions followed within the next twelve months. The year after the Restoration saw the publication of the twentieth edition; and although the demand then began to taper off, a twenty-fifth edition was published in 1687.[1] As a political satirist Cleveland had an obvious appeal for all those who detested the Good Old Cause and who had suffered under the Commonwealth; he expressed their sense of grievance and outrage, and he ridiculed effectively those whom they had learnt to hate. No doubt, however, many of his royalist readers would have appreciated him even more if he had said what he had to say more simply and less obscurely. It was at Oxford and Cambridge that his erudite wit, his atrocious 'clenches' or puns, and his bold catachrestical expressions were most admired—and not only admired, but imitated.

The lines from Cleveland's 'To Julia to expedite her promise,' which Johnson cited in his criticism of the metaphysicals[2] are typical of much of that poet's hit-or-miss writing:

> Since 'tis my Doom, Love's Under-Shrieve,
> Why this Reprieve?

---

[1] I take these facts from *The Poems of John Cleveland*, ed. Brian Morris and Eleanor Withington (Oxford, 1967). I am indebted to this excellent edition at some other points in this paper.

[2] *Lives of the English Poets*, ed. G. Birkbeck Hill (1905), i. 27.

Why doth my She-Advowson flie
Incumbency?

Here Cleveland plays upon the word 'doom', which means (*a*) fate
and (*b*) the sentence of the court passed on the poet by Love's
under-sheriff, Julia. The 'reprieve' she has granted him by still
holding out is a stay of execution for the man doomed or sentenced
to love her, but has little relevance to his being *fated* to love her:
Cleveland has simply dropped the first element in his pun. From
being Love's under-sheriff Julia is now abruptly transformed to
being the poet's 'she-advowson', where 'advowson' is wrested out
of its proper meaning, viz. 'the right of presentation to an ecclesiastical benefice or living', and is used to signify the living itself. An
incumbent is the holder of an ecclesiastical benefice, and incumbency is the position or office of an incumbent, or the sphere in
which he exercises his functions—here equated with the married
state. (Cleveland uses this metaphor again in 'Square-Cap', l. 37:
'And offers her money her Incumbent to be'.) But in this context
of consummation the poet almost certainly intended to draw a
sexual significance out of 'incumbency', which in its literal meaning
signifies 'the condition of lying or pressing upon something'.
(Cf. *OED* incumbent, *adj.* 1 : 'that lies, leans, rests, or presses with
its weight upon something else'.) Johnson's comment on the
thirteen lines that he quotes from Cleveland, 'Who would imagine
it possible that in a very few lines so many remote ideas could
be brought together?' enables him to restate his point that in
metaphysical poetry 'the most heterogeneous ideas are yoked by
violence together', and that 'nature and art are ransacked for
illustrations, comparisons, and allusions'.[1] What he fails to say,
since it does not suit his purpose, is that the whole poem is a
mockingly realistic variation on the traditional theme of 'Gather
ye rosebuds', as in Herrick's 'To the Virgins, to make much of
Time'. Cleveland is certainly not writing to Julia in the fashion of
Sir Charles Sedley, who, according to Rochester,[2] had

that prevailing, gentle Art,
That can with a resistless Charm impart
The loosest wishes to the chastest Heart:
Raise such a conflict, kindle such a *Fire*,

[1] *Lives of the English Poets,* ed. cit. i. 20.
[2] *Poems by John Wilmot Earl of Rochester* ('An Allusion to Horace'), ed. V.
de Sola Pinto (1953), p. 97.

Betwixt declining *Virtue*, and *Desire*;
Till the poor vanquish't *Maid* dissolves away
In *Dreams* all *Night*, in *Sighs*, and *Tears*, all day.

Nor can Cleveland be accused of perplexing the minds of the fair sex 'with nice speculations of philosophy, when he should engage their hearts and entertain them with the softnesses of love'.[1] Such an accusation would be beside the point, for the poet was not addressing himself to Julia and the fair sex in general: his audience was masculine and academic, the fellows, scholars, and commoners of the two universities, who had the necessary training and inclination to appreciate his intellectual gymnastics.

That Cleveland exerted a considerable influence on the minds of clever young university men in the 1650s may be seen from the sort of verse that issued from Oxford and Cambridge at this period. Much of it was the work of ingenious intellectuals who were not poets, but who (taught by Cleveland, and to some extent by Cowley) were able to produce something that looked like poetry, and that was capable of giving an esoteric pleasure to the initiated. Similarly, the verses written on the death of Lord Hastings by that young Westminster boy John Dryden (1649) are in the Cleveland–Cowley vein, and, however uncharacteristic of the later Dryden, are very much what we should expect in the circumstances, and at this point of time. For anyone who was called upon to contribute to a volume of *Lachrymae Musarum*, and whose own feelings were not deeply engaged ('What's Hecuba to him?'), the obscure and arcane style of Cleveland, with its elaborate tropes and clenches and learned allusions, offered a sort of concealment for absence or poverty of feeling. And the substitute for feeling was not so much thought arising naturally from the situation as *thoughts* 'invented' (in the old sense of 'come upon', 'found') in the course of allowing the mind to play around that situation and to search for something unusual and ingenious to say.

This unengaged intellectual decoration of a theme is well seen in an Oxford miscellany of 1651 entitled *Newes from the Dead*, which deals with the hanging at Oxford in December 1650 of a young woman called Anne Greene and her subsequent resuscitation by a number of physicians. To this miscellany some thirty Fellows and undergraduates contributed copies of verses, mainly

[1] *Essays of John Dryden* ('Discourse of Satire'), ed. W. P. Ker (1900), ii. 19.

in English, but also in Latin and French. If Anne Greene was the 'onlie begetter' of this anthology, nothing is known about who assembled it, or whether the individual writers were invited to send in their contributions. Most probably a number of the poems were written spontaneously and circulated about the University in manuscript, and others were later solicited to make up a collection. According to Thomas Warton[1], one of the moving spirits was Ralph Bathurst, at that time a Fellow of Trinity College, later a physician, and from 1664 President of Trinity. If Warton is right, several of the poems attributed to undergraduate members of Trinity College had been obligingly written by Bathurst; and if this is so, it may indicate that the various colleges had been invited to send in contributions, and that Bathurst was exerting himself for the greater glory of Trinity. Among the contributors were some who later became well known. They include Christopher (later Sir Christopher) Wren, then a Fellow Commoner of Wadham; Walter Pope, author of 'The Wish' and of a Life of Seth Ward (the Anne Greene story was an ideal one for Pope's facetious temperament); Anthony Wood, then a Postmaster at Merton College; Francis (later Sir Francis) Withins of St. John's, who became a Judge of the King's Bench; Joseph (later Sir Joseph) Williamson of Queen's, who was appointed Secretary of State in 1674; and Robert Sharrock, Fellow of New College and later Archdeacon of Westminster, a miscellaneous writer of some repute. One other name may be mentioned, Robert Mathew, Fellow of New College, if only because this was not his last contribution to Oxford poetry. In 1654 he contributed to a university miscellany of poems congratulating Cromwell on his peace with the Dutch; and in an anonymous satire on that miscellany he was ridiculed, fairly enough, as 'Cleavelandified Mathew'.[2] As we shall see, he was by no means the only 'Cleavelandified' Oxford poet of the 1650s.

II

There are three contemporary accounts of Anne Greene's ordeal. These are not equally reliable; but in the short narrative that follows I shall draw upon all three, for what matters here is the

---

[1] *The Life and Literary Remains of Ralph Bathurst, M.D.* (1761), pp. xv–xvi.
[2] *The Poems of John Cleveland*, pp. lxviii–lxix.

sensational impact that her execution made upon the Oxford of 1650–1.

(1) A Wonder of Wonders. Being a faithful *Narrative* and true *Relation*, of one *Anne Green*, Servant to Sir *Tho. Reed* in *Oxfordshire*. . . . *Witnessed by Dr. Petty, and Licensed according to Order.*

This is a prose pamphlet of six pages, dated on the final page 'Oxford Jan. 13, 1651', and subscribed 'Your obliged Servitor, W. Burdet'.

(2) A Declaration from *Oxford*, of Anne Green, a young woman that was lately, and unjustly hanged in the Castle-Yard; but since recovered, her neck set strait and her eyes fixed orderly and firmly in her head again: With her Speech touching four Angels that appeared to her when she was dead: and their strange expressions, apparations, and passages that happened thereupon, the like never heard of before. . . . London. Printed by I. Clowes. 1651.

Underneath the title there is a crude woodcut of a woman hanging by her neck from a gallows, with a man tugging at her ankles, and a soldier thrusting at her with the butt end of a musket. In the top left-hand corner Anne Greene is seen in a four-poster bed, with the words 'Behold God's Providence' issuing from her mouth. The London imprint shows that her remarkable story had spread far beyond the High in Oxford.

(3) Newes from the Dead. Or A True and Exact Narrative of the miraculous deliverance of *ANNE GREENE*, who being Executed at Oxford Decemb. 14 1650 afterwards revived; and by the care of certain Physitians there *is now perfectly recovered*. . . . Written by a Scoller in Oxford for the Satisfaction of a friend, who desired to be informed concerning the truth *of the businesse*. Whereunto are added certain Poems, casually written upon that Subject.

This was 'Printed by Leonard Litchfield, for Tho. Robinson. 1651'. The above title-page is that of 'The Second Impression with Additions' (i.e. additional verse contributions) which appeared later in the same year. According to Thomas Warton,[1] the prose narrative was the work of Richard Watkins, a Student of Christ Church, and afterwards Vicar of Ambrosden, near Oxford. Each of those three narratives contains some statements that are not in the other two, but *Newes from the Dead* is the most sober,

---

[1] *Life . . . of Ralph Bathurst*, p. 42.

and obviously the most reliable. The story that Watkins had to tell certainly needed no embellishment.

In the autumn of 1650, Anne Greene, then about twenty-two years of age, and 'strong, fleshie, and of indifferent good feature', was working as a domestic servant in the household of Sir Thomas Read, of Duns Tew in Oxfordshire. Sir Thomas, a notable man in his way, who had been High Sheriff of Oxfordshire, had a grandson called Jeffery, and this young adolescent of sixteen or seventeen succeeded in seducing the girl. Anne Greene (if she knew enough to understand her condition) found herself pregnant, and when in due course she gave birth to a child, either it was still-born or, as the prosecution was to contend, she smothered it. She made little attempt to conceal the birth; and, according to W. Burdet's account, one of her fellow servants 'ran shrieking out into the house, acquainting her Master and Mistriss with this sad accident'. When the facts became known she was carried before a Justice of the Peace. To him she admitted that she had been guilty of the sin of fornication, but she strenuously denied that she had murdered her infant. None the less she was indicted for the murder of her illegitimate child, tried before Serjeant Umpton Croke, 'who sat as Judge by a Commission of Oyer and Terminer',[1] found guilty by the jury, and duly sentenced to death. She was hanged at Oxford on Saturday, 14 December.

So far Anne Greene's story had followed a pattern that was only too familiar, and that was still common enough in the nineteenth century, when Matthew Arnold recounted the similar misfortunes of a 'girl named Wragg' whose infant was found strangled on 'the dismal Mapperly Hills'.[2] Anne Greene, however, has her small niche in history (and even in the *Dictionary of National Biography*) because of the totally unexpected sequel to her hanging.

Brought to the place of execution, she fell down on her knees (or so the author of *A Wonder of Wonders* would have us believe), 'humbly desiring God, that his Divine Majesty would be pleased to shew some remarkable judgement on her, for a signal and testification to the world of her innocency, which most miraculously was evidenced to her, to the great and wonderful admiration to all that shall either hear of or read these ensuing lines'.

[1] Robert Plot, *The Natural History of Oxford-shire* (1677), p. 198.
[2] Matthew Arnold, *Essays in Criticism*, 'The Function of Criticism at the Present Time', (London, 1889 edn.), p. 24.

After some words of repentance to the crowd gathered about the gallows and of forgiveness for her executioner, she was turned off the ladder, and left hanging by the neck for half an hour. In the meantime, in accordance with her own last request, her friends did all they could to shorten her sufferings—some, we are told, 'thumping her on the breast, other hanging with all their weight upon her legges; sometimes lifting her up, and then pulling her downe againe with a suddaine jerke, thereby the sooner to dispatch her out of her paine: insomuch that the Under-Sheriffe fearing lest thereby they should breake the rope, forbad them to do so any longer'. When the Sheriff was satisfied that justice had been done, the body was cut down, placed in a coffin, and conveyed to the house of Mr. Clark, an apothecary,[1] where some medical men were to dissect it.

It was at this point that someone heard a 'ruttle' in her throat; whereupon 'a lusty fellow that stood by (thinking to do an act of charity in ridding her out of the small reliques of a painfull life) stamped several times on her breast and stomack with all the force he could'. *Enfin Petty vint.* The lusty fellow was still doing his best to stamp the life out of Anne Greene when Dr. William Petty (the Professor of Anatomy, and afterwards more famous as Sir William Petty, the political arithmetician) and Dr. Thomas Willis (later one of the most celebrated medical men of the day) arrived on the scene. They too heard a 'ruttle' in her throat, and promptly set to work upon her. They were joined a little later by Ralph Bathurst and by Henry Clerke[2] of Magdalen College, and between them they slowly brought the unhappy woman round.[3] It is here that Richard Watkins is at his most convincing, for he avoids any sensational embroidering upon the return of Anne

[1] This could be Timothy Clarke (d. 1672), who graduated M.D. in 1652, and later became a physician in ordinary to Charles II. This identification seems the more probable, since he once proposed to the Royal Society 'that a man hanged might be begged of the King to try to revive him, and that in case he was revived, he might have his life granted him' (quoted in *DNB* from Thomas Birch, *History of the Royal Society*, ii. 471).

[2] M.D., 1652, and later (1672) President of Magdalen.

[3] Anne Greene's revival after being hanged was not unique. In 1705 one John Smith, later known as 'half-hanged Smith', was executed at Tyburn, but a few minutes later a reprieve came through for him and he was cut down. He received a free pardon, and continued his unsuccessful life of crime. For his subsequent misadventures see John Ashton, *Social Life in the Reign of Queen Anne* (1882), i. 215.

Greene from death to life, but concentrates his narrative on the various remedies applied by the doctors. The author of *A Wonder of Wonders*, on the other hand, tells us that Dr. Petty exclaimed that 'there was a great hand of God in the business', and he also asserts that when, after fourteen hours, the girl at last opened her eyes, her first words were: 'Behold God's providence, and his wonder of wonders.' The whole strange event, he believes, should be a lesson to all magistrates and courts of judicature 'to take special care in denouncing a sentence, without a due and legal process, according to the known Laws of the Land, by an impartial and uncorrupted Jury'. This last observation was clearly directed against Serjeant Croke, and perhaps also against Sir Thomas Read, who was thought to have pressed the charge unduly against the servant wench who had involved his family in unwelcome publicity. He is, no doubt, the 'great man' who 'moved to have her again carried to the place of execution, to be hanged up by the neck', but who was foiled by the indignant intervention of 'some honest Soldiers then present'. On the application of the Under-Sheriff Anne Greene was granted a reprieve.

Richard Watkins had gone out of his way to make it clear that she had not returned from the dead with any strange news. She had, he tells us, been carefully questioned by the doctors about what she remembered, but she could recall nothing at all of what happened during her execution, although 'about a fortnight after, she seemed to remember something of a fellow wrapt up in a blanket, which indeed was the habit of her Executioner'. It would be pleasant, he admitted, to be able to relate 'what fine visions the maid saw in the other world, what coelestial musick, or hellish howlings she heard; what spirits she conversed with; and what Revelations she brought back with her'. But there was nothing of the kind. Here Watkins seems to be glancing at the very different statement in *A Declaration from Oxford*; for in that much more popular account we read how Anne Greene 'being (as it were in a Garden of Paradice, there appeared to her 4 little boyes with wings, being four Angels, saying, *Woe unto them that decree unrighteous Decrees, and take away the right from the Judges that the innocent may be their prey.* Upon which words they vanished . . .' . Some seventeenth-century journalist was determined that on her return from the dead Anne Greene should recollect something more celestial than 'a fellow wrapt up in a blanket'. There was a

common form for such things: the public had legitimate expectations which must be satisfied. Whether Anne Greene had been talked into believing that she had really seen the four little boys with wings, or whether, as is more probable, the journalist had just made it up, we have no means to know. But there it all was in print, together with 'an excellent Prayer used by her morning, noon, and night, fit to be read in all Families, throughout England, Ireland, Scotland, and Wales'. Anne Greene was well on her way to becoming a saintly figure, almost a martyr. As if all this were not enough, Sir Thomas Read, described by Richard Watkins as 'her Grand Prosecutor', gave the whole episode a retributive climax by dying within three days of the girl's ordeal on the gallows. It is characteristic of *A Declaration from Oxford* that his death is made even more dramatic: Anne Greene, trying to remember what she could after being revived, alleged that 'she saw her chief enemy dead before her (which is observable, that within some hours after, Sir. Tho. Read died)'. Lust, murder, the gallows, resurrection, a heavenly vision, an omen of death, divine retribution: the story of Anne Greene had everything.

For the Oxford of 1650–1 it ended with her recovery at the hands of Dr. Petty and the death of Sir Thomas Read, but for the young woman herself it did not end until eight or nine years later. 'Being . . . perfectly recovered,' we are told by Dr. Robert Plot, 'after thanks given to God, and the persons instrumental in it, she returned into the Country to her friends at Steeple-Barton, where she was afterwards marryed, and lived in good repute amongst her Neighbors, having three Children afterwards, and not dying as I am informed till the year 1659.'[1]

III

The year 1650 was not an especially happy one for Oxford University. That traditionally loyal seat of learning had been shocked and saddened only a year before by the judicial execution —or, as royalists maintained, the judicial murder—of Charles I. Some of the Fellows and Heads of Colleges had been replaced by men more amenable to the new regime, and those who remained had to be careful what they said and how they behaved. But we are always apt to exaggerate the effect of public events on private

[1] *Natural History of Oxford-shire*, p. 199.

B

lives, and to assume that the shadow of history must inevitably darken the outlook of those who live in tragic and anxious times. So, perhaps, it does, but only intermittently. The English as a race have an ability to pick up the pieces and carry on, and the young certainly have great powers of recuperation. At all events, the execution of Anne Greene produced a small explosion of irreverent wit and high spirits among the undergraduates and at least some of the senior members of the University, which probably offered some sort of catharsis for pent-up feelings. Anne Greene having been hanged in good earnest was now to be hanged again in effigy, in the dispassionate and unconcerned verses of the Oxford wits.

The poems in *Newes from the Dead* vary in size from six to about forty lines. The writers share certain characteristics. They delight in puns, in paradox (to which, of course, this odd event was naturally suited), in a polysyllabic and learned vocabulary, metaphysical conceits, far-fetched allusions, and forced applications. Few of the poems are worth quoting in their entirety, since they rarely maintain a continuous argument, and are more concerned with stringing together their separate beads of wit; but the ambitious contribution of John Aylmer of New College (which I give complete) will show what he and his fellow poets were striving to do.

On the Death and Life of Anne Greene

What Cable-thread twin'd thee thy happy fate,
That it out-lasts thy own life's destin'd date?
Was thy Harmonious Soule strung so-so well,
As break it could not, stretcht to a Miracle?
5   Didst thou indent with Rigid Atropos
To los't a while, and then to quit the Losse?
As cast-off Habits, when hang'd by a space,
Regaine their Fashion and their pristine grace.
      Loe here's lifes *Gemini*, two life's in one!
10   Or th'same in'ts Tropicall Reversion!
Time after *Stylo novo* inchoated!
From the first Sun a Parely created!
A strange Appendix after *Finis* fixt,
Or *Funis* rather: Death and Life co-mixt!
15   A Posthume Act after Catastrophe!
Or Antedating of the Latter day!

Death's Puzler! Self-surviver! thy strange fate
Do's contradictions Legi[ti]mate.
Entwisted Miracles constellate here,
20   And complicated Wonders Co-insphere.
Thy uncouth Paradox Resuscitation
Tempts to beleeve, that from a pure Privation
Nature's propension signe's a free Regresse
To pristine Habit; tempts even to confesse
25   Plurality of Soules in One, since Thou
Can'st prodigally one to Death allow,
Another keep thy selfe; whilst both maintaine
Castor and *Pollux*-like alternate Reigne.
That Belgian Headsman, whose rare artfull hand
o   Could slice off heads, and they yet seem to stand,
Had he thee Execut'd, had sham'd his skill
When finding thee not dead, but living still.
Perillu's Torturing Engin had but bin
A very Bull, had'st thou first entred in.
35   Their Law would have some plea, were it to thee,
Who first the Malefactor Hang, then see
Wh're 'twere a just and equitable Cause,
Whether not consonant unto the Lawes.
     Strange *Sophister*! that grant'st to Destiny
40   The Premises, Conclusion do'st deny;
Dar'st yeeld to Suffer Death, but not to Dye.

Our poet begins conventionally enough with the thread of life
due to be cut by Atropos; but 'cable-thread' suggests also the
rope round the neck of the girl on the scaffold, as do 'strung' (3),
'stretcht' (4), and 'hang'd' (7). The simile of the cast-off clothes
(7–8) depends for its effect on our taking the body as the clothing
of the soul, in which case 'hang'd' has a double significance. The
poet now spurs his Pegasus. Anne Greene's twin life and life-
after-death are 'life's Gemini'; or, alternatively, they are the same
life 'in'ts Tropicall Reversion'. This last phrase clearly refers (or,
at any rate, seems to be intended to refer) to the sun reaching the
most northerly or southerly points of the ecliptic, and then turning or 'reverting' towards the equator again. Like the New Style
Gregorian calendar (11), time (= life) has begun again for Anne
Greene. A 'parely' (12) is 'a mate, or fellow, or companion', and
'sun' I take to be a symbol of life: her first life (before she was
hanged) is followed by a second life (now that she has been
brought to life again by the doctors). In the next line her life is

compared to a book, in which, although *finis* is normally the end, it isn't the end here, since there is an appendix (her resuscitation). The pun with *funis* (rope) is rather an adolescent joke, and I would like to believe that 'appendix' is not meant to carry a suggestion of 'append' = 'hang on' or 'hang'. 'Act' and 'Catastrophe' (15) refer, of course, to a stage play: the catastrophe (which normally comes in the last act) of the girl's death has here been followed by another act when she has returned to life. In the next line I take 'the Latter day' to be the Last Day, i.e. the day of resurrection. At this point I am tempted to call a halt, and to exclaim with Dr. Johnson, after a similar bout of exegesis: 'Of these trifles, enough!'

It seems likely, as I have already suggested, that some of the poems in *Newes from the Dead* had been circulating in Oxford colleges before the book appeared. I suspect that John Aylmer may have seen the contribution of a Fellow of his own college, J. Hutton, who referred to the resuscitation of Anne Greene as 'an ante-dated Resurrection'; although it is, of course, possible that Hutton stole this brilliant thought from his pupil. But when we also find the same thought struggling into birth in the poem of H. B. of All Souls, the resemblance seems too strong for coincidence:

> Straight from her Urne this Unchang'd Phoenix rose,
> Offspring Herselfe, and Midwife to her Throwes:
> And Antedates by this Mysterious Birth
> Her Resurrection: Borne again from Earth.

Among other coincidences of thought we may compare lines 21–4 and 39 of Aylmer's poem with Hutton's opening lines:

> Come Sophister, distinguish, you that call
> Restor'd Privation Supernaturall. . . .

(In Aylmer's poem 'Nature's propension' presumably means 'the inclination of Nature'; but since one of the meanings of 'propend' is 'to hang downward' he may once more be punning on Anne Greene's unhappy experience on the gallows.) More than one of the Oxford men play upon the word 'neck-verse' (the Latin verse set before anyone who pleaded benefit of clergy); and there is further play upon the gallows-tree becoming the tree of life. Several of the contributors are concerned with the question of whether the resurrected Anne Greene should be described as a virgin. John Watkins of Queen's College devotes his whole poem to this theme, ending with a hilarious pun:

> Mother, or Maid, I pray you whether?
> One, or both, or am I neither?
> The Mother dyed: may't not be said
> That the Survivor is a Maid?
> Here, take your Fee, declare your sense;
> And free me from this new Suspense.

To A. Spence of St. John's Anne Greene's execution was 'but a new prologue to Virginity'; and the heartlessly high-spirited John Mainard of Magdalen puns his way along to a similar conclusion:

> Sure Death abhorres the colour, all have seene
> That Death is blacke, and therefore loves no Greene:
> A happy colour, in what Praedicament
> Will the Logicians put this Accident?
> Shee had her Neck-verse; 'tis a currant signe
> Shee could not read, her verse was but a Line.
> Againe, upon this deed to set a crowne,
> Sh'ad been cut up, if not so soon cut downe.
> Read this, thou youthfull *Read*, and be afraid,
> Shee's a maid twice, and yet is not *dis-maid.* . . .

As one would expect in a body of verse produced by Oxford scholars, there is a frequent correlation between their academic studies and their poetical ideas. There is, for example, much classical allusion, most of it obvious (as to Orpheus and Virbius,[1] Ate, Clotho, Atropos, Minos, the phoenix rising from its ashes, etc.), but some of it less hackneyed (as in Aylmer's allusion to the brazen bull of Perillus). More interesting are the terms of logic and rhetoric which enter into their thought and expression, reflecting again the academic training of these young scholars, and no doubt offering them a satirical release from the jargon of the schools. In lines 3–4 of Mainard's poem above, a 'praedicament' is one of the ten categories or classes of predications formed by Aristotle, and an 'accident' (apart from the word-play) is 'a property or quality not essential to our conception of a substance'. Logical terms are scattered through Aylmer's poem, notably in the 'premises' and 'conclusion' of his second last line.

---

[1] Virbius: a name given to Hippolytus after he had been brought back to life by Æsculapius.

At the opening of Hutton's poem, already quoted, the word 'privation' is a term of logic, meaning 'the condition of being deprived of or being without some attribute formerly or properly possessed; the loss, or (loosely) the mere absence of a quality. Often called the negative or negation of the eighth Aristotelian category [or predicament], ἔχειν, *habitus*, the fact of having' (*OED*). The converse of 'privation' is therefore 'habit' (*habitus*): *OED* cites Abraham Fraunce, *The Lawiers Logike* (1588): 'The affirmative is called the habite, the negative the privation thereof.' Fortified by this information, we may now see why in Aylmer's poem (22–4)

> from a pure Privation
> Nature's propension signe's a free Regresse
> To pristine Habit.

Another of the poets already mentioned, A. Spence, gets away to an erudite start, also by calling upon his logic studies:

> Thou Sophister of Fate, that canst deny
> A faire dispute by an Amphiboly;
> Reade Hebrew-wise thy Necke-verse, make to be
> In thine own doom an *Infra-pollency*:
> Insertst no Negative, and yet canst state
> An affirm'd sentence Illegitimate. . . .

'Sophister' is here used for someone who employs false logic; 'dispute' can be either (1) debate, (2) logical argument; an 'amphiboly' is 'a sentence which may be construed in two distinct senses, an ambiguity'; 'negative' is a negative proposition in logic; 'sentence' is a statement (with a play on the sentence passed by a court of law); and 'illegitimate' is here used in the sense of being logically inadmissible. I confess to being baffled by the second couplet. If Anne Greene reads her neck-verse 'Hebrew-wise', she is, of course, reading it backward, and so reversing the normal order of things: 'pollency' is power, and an 'infrapollency' is presumably an inferior power, or possibly a power here below on earth. But what we are to understand from that I do not know. One can, however, see what John Evelyn had in mind when he complained that 'such as have lived long in Universities doe greatly affect words and expressions no where in use besides, as may be observed in Cleavelend's poems for Cambridge'[1].

---

[1] *Critical Essays of the Seventeenth Century*, ed. J. E. Spingarn, (1908–9), i. 312.

Not all the contributors tried to parade their erudition so insistently as Aylmer and Spence. Many were content to joke easily and cheerfully, or to make sarcastic comments on Sir Thomas Read and his grandson. It is a relief to turn to the more conventional wit of H. B. of All Souls, who concludes his poem with a traditional gibe at the medical profession, and a reference to the soldiers who intervened to save Anne Greene from being hanged a second time:

> For who can think her Guilty, whom the Tombe
> Does thus declare unworthy of her Doome?
> Whom Law, whom Physick could not kill, whose Date
> Souldiers Repriev'd, Three Committees of Fate?

IV

By the 1660s the reaction from such late metaphysical poetry as we have been considering was well under way. In the *Essay of Dramatic Poesy* Dryden sneered at Robert Wild, whose *Iter Boreale* offers a sort of popularized metaphysical verse; and quoting Horace's dictum in the *Ars Poetica* (70–2) that use and custom must control the poet's expression, he went on to say of Cleveland:

> The not observing this rule is that which the world has blamed in our satyrist, Cleveland: to express a thing hard and unnaturally, is his new way of elocution. . . . Wit is best conveyed to us in the most easy language; and is most to be admired when a great thought comes dressed in words so commonly received, that it is understood by the meanest apprehensions. . . .[1]

Some of the old rockets of metaphysical wit continued for some time to 'mount, [to] shine, evaporate, and fall' in Dryden's own poetry and in that of some of his contemporaries; but the new way of neo-classical writing and the growing conviction that wit is 'a propriety of thoughts and words'[2] soon changed the nature of English poetry.

Yet that change was less absolute than we sometimes assume: if a new sort of poetry was born, the mode of conception remained essentially the same. When Matthew Arnold said that the poetry of Dryden and Pope was 'conceived and composed in their

---

[1] Essays, ed. Ker ('Essay of Dramatic Poesy'), i. 52.
[2] Ibid. ('The Author's Apology for Heroic Poetry'), i. 190.

wits', whereas 'genuine poetry is conceived and composed in the soul',[1] he was saying something that has annoyed many modern admirers of neo-classical poetry, and that has provoked a good deal of indignant dissent. It has never been difficult to make fun of Arnold, and it is easy enough to point out that the second half of his statement is hopelessly vague: 'soul', a word much bandied about by the Victorians, gets us, critically, nowhere. But can we, and should we, dismiss with the same confidence Arnold's claim that the poetry of Dryden and Pope was 'conceived and composed in their wits'? and if we agree that it was so, need we assume with Arnold that their poetry is in that case *ipso facto* inferior?

As long as something called the 'soul' is thought of as superior to something called the 'wits', so long the admirers of neo-classical poetry will feel compelled to justify their admiration for it on other grounds than its intellectual brilliance. Yet much of the poetry of Dryden and Pope, and most of that written by Swift, seems to have its origin neither in emotion recollected in tranquillity nor in the depths of the unconscious; it is not recording some long-felt and deeply pondered experience, nor is it resolving some conflict. It is the work of a poet playing brilliantly around some theme on which his mind has focused, and over which it hovers and vibrates like a humming-bird above a flower. The kind of writing in which this sort of cerebral activity results is seen to perfection in the prologues and epilogues of Dryden. In so far as these differ (apart from their comparative brevity) from, say, *MacFlecknoe* and *Absalom and Achitophel*, the difference may be due to having to say something in the first case, and having something to say in the second. Behind *MacFlecknoe* and *Absalom and Achitophel* there lie, no doubt, varying degrees of experience and settled conviction. Even so, most of what went into these poems almost certainly entered the poet's mind for the first time in the act of composition. Much, indeed, of all Dryden's poetry appears to be the result of a spontaneous and unpremeditated association of ideas. How could it be otherwise, when so many of the poems he wrote were occasional, and sometimes written to order? Dryden sneered at Settle because he

faggotted his Notions as they fell,
And if they Rhim'd and Rattl'd all was well.[2]

---

[1] Matthew Arnold, *Essays in Criticism. Second Series* (London, 1888), p. 95.
[2] *The Second Part of Absalom and Achitophel*, 419–20.

Yet the difference between Dryden and Settle is not that Dryden didn't faggot *his* notions as they fell, but that his notions were held to a necessary relevance by the controlling power of a mind concentrating upon a theme. Given his poetical task—an epilogue for a new play, a funeral poem on Charles II or the Countess of Abingdon, a poem on the birth of a son to James II—Dryden (like Donne) had his central idea and dwelt upon it with intense concentration, but at the same time allowed his mind to fly off centrifugally in all directions, so that he could gather 'notions' to work out and elaborate that idea. Where the mature Dryden differed from Cleveland and the young poetasters of Oxford, and from his own immature self when he wrote the verses on the death of Lord Hastings, was in a greater willingness to reject the first idea that entered his head, and indeed to reject any idea at all that seemed to his considered judgement to depart too far from normal thinking and feeling. His mature judgement of poets like Cleveland and Cowley was that they 'could never forgive any conceit which came in [their] way; but swept like a drag-net, great and small. There was plenty enough, but the dishes were ill sorted.'[1] In his own poetry he aimed to retain the wit, but to sort the dishes by being selective. He aimed, too, to keep in touch with the common reader, and to construct a consecutive poetical argument which moved (and here he differs not only from Cleveland but from Donne) without abrupt transitions of thought and imagery from one point to another. Yet if Dryden's sort of poetry is not 'conceived and composed in the wits', it is hard to see how else it is composed. 'Only', as George III said to Fanny Burney on a different occasion, 'one must not say so! But what think you? . . . What? what?'

[1] *Essays*, ed. Ker ('Preface to *Fables*'), ii. 258.

2

DRYDEN'S CRITICISM OF SPANISH DRAMA

By JOHN LOFTIS

DRYDEN'S *Of Dramatick Poesie* is an essay in comparative literature, a learned and wide-ranging attempt to evaluate English drama of the first few years after the Restoration by comparing it with Greek and Roman drama of antiquity, Spanish and English drama of the late sixteenth and earlier seventeenth centuries, and French drama of the mid seventeenth century. It is an essay about dramatic theory, a speculative effort to arrive at an understanding of the nature of drama: about its relation alike to the external world and to the world of the spectators' imagination. The series of comparisons which comprise the essay are controlled by Dryden's desire to explicate problems confronting him as a dramatist, especially those having to do with dramatic language and with the construction of plots. Not unnaturally, the plays he had already written or was then writing determined some of the emphases and preoccupations in the essay, which shows throughout a speculative concern for first principles tempered by the experience of a very busy and successful dramatist.

If we look at his current and earlier work in drama, we can understand well enough why he should give attention in the essay to Spanish drama: especially to the contrasts between Spanish and French drama. He wrote *Of Dramatick Poesie* in its original form, it would appear, during 1665 and 1666, while he was at his father-in-law's estate at Charlton in Wiltshire, where with his wife he had taken refuge from the plague.[1] At about the same time he wrote *Secret Love*, his first two-part tragicomedy, and hence the prominence in the essay of considerations of

---

[1] For the chronology of his literary activities from 1664 to 1667 see Edward Niles Hooker and H. T. Swedenberg, Jr., eds., *The Works of John Dryden*, vol. i (Berkeley and Los Angeles, 1956), 260.

tragicomedy, notably discussions of the rapid alternation of scenes with contrasting emotional impact. He revised the essay and published it in 1668, the year in which his *An Evening's Love; Or, The Mock Astrologer* was acted, a play based in some measure on Calderón's *El astrólogo fingido.*[1] Looking back to the beginning of his dramatic career, we find other plays with components from Spanish literature, though it is invariably difficult to assess the nature of his Spanish borrowings. His second play, *The Rival Ladies* of 1664, is Spanish in locale and characters and has a plot that approximates a conventional one of the 'comedia'. Whatever the immediate source of the plot, it derives ultimately from Cervantes's novel *Las dos doncellas.*[2] His third play, *The Indian Queen*, a collaborative effort with Sir Robert Howard, has the complex background common to the heroic play, in which the French romances are conspicuous;[3] and yet the Peruvian locale and Incan exoticism are reminiscent of the conquistadors' narratives of adventure. So also his unaided *The Indian Emperour*, which much more than the earlier play draws on the historical accounts of the Spaniards, and indeed presents in telescoped form a dramatic version of Cortes's conquest of Mexico.[4] This much is certain. Dryden may also owe a more specific debt for the play to Calderón, to his *El príncipe constante*, to which *The Indian Emperour* bears a resemblance in several episodes and situations.[5] For *Secret Love* the sources and the more obvious literary relationships

[1] Dryden's sources for *An Evening's Love* are complex, and it is not certain that he borrowed directly from Calderón rather than merely through French intermediaries. In his Preface to the play he implies that he had read *El astrólogo fingido*:

[The play] was first Spanish, and called *El Astrologo Fingido*; then made French by the younger Corneille; and is now translated into English, and in print, under the name of *The Feigned Astrologer*. What I have performed in this will best appear by comparing it with those: you will see that I have rejected some adventures which I judged were not divertising; that I have heightened those which I have chosen; and that I have added others, which were neither in the French nor Spanish (in W. P. Ker, ed., *Essays of John Dryden* (Oxford, 1900), i. 145).

[2] John Harrington Smith, Dougald MacMillan, and Vinton A. Dearing, eds., *The Works of John Dryden*, viii (Berkeley and Los Angeles, 1962), 265–7.

[3] Ibid. 284–92.

[4] John Loftis and Vinton A. Dearing, eds., *The Works of John Dryden*, ix (Berkeley and Los Angeles, 1966), 306–14.

[5] N. D. Shergold and Peter Ure, 'Dryden and Calderón: A New Spanish Source for *The Indian Emperour*', *Modern Language Review* lxi (1966), 369–83.

are French, not Spanish;[1] and yet the tragicomical form of the play has more in common with the 'comedia' than with the neo-classical plays of the French.

Dryden's critical remarks imply that he had considered the dramatic theory embodied in the 'comedia', as when he writes in his Preface to *Albion and Albanius* (1685) in defence of that opera's three-act structure: 'For even Aristotle himself is contented to say simply, that in all actions there is a beginning, a middle, and an end; after which model all the Spanish plays are built.'[2] Yet notwithstanding the prominence of Spanish themes in his plays, the tone of his references to Spanish drama, in *Of Dramatick Poesie* and elsewhere in his writings, is ambivalent or depreciatory. He frequently criticizes the Spaniards for violation of neo-classical rules, as he does late in his life in his Preface to *A Parallel Betwixt Painting and Poetry* (1695), where he warns others 'not to make new rules of the drama, as Lopez de Vega has attempted unsuccessfully to do, but to be content to follow our masters, who understood Nature better than we'.[3] He had made a similar point more fully in *The Grounds of Criticism in Tragedy* (1679):

> As the action ought to be one, it ought, as such, to have order in it; that is, to have a natural beginning, a middle, and an end. A natural beginning, says Aristotle, is that which could not necessarily have been placed after another thing; and so of the rest. This consideration will arraign all plays after the new model of Spanish plots, where accident is heaped upon accident, and that which is first might as reasonably be last; an inconvenience not to be remedied, but by making one accident naturally produce another, otherwise it is a farce and not a play.[4]

This may reflect the greater rigidity of Dryden's neo-classicism in the years after Thomas Rymer had written. Yet even his spokesman Neander in *Of Dramatick Poesie* (1668) is critical of the 'irregularity' of Spanish plots, praising the French for improving them in their adaptations of the 'comedia'. In discussions of rhyme in drama he several times alludes to the Spanish precedent, and on one occasion at least, in his letter to Sir Robert Howard prefixed to *Annus Mirabilis* (1667), he implies that he had looked closely at the versification of the Spanish plays. This would mean that he

---

[1] Dryden, *Works*, ix. 334–44.
[2] *Essays*, i. 279.
[3] *Essays*, ii. 139.
[4] *Essays*, i. 208–9.

had studied the 'comedia' in the original language, and there is every reason to believe that he had indeed done so.[1]

The argument that Dryden made use of Calderón's *El príncipe constante* in writing *The Indian Emperour* is of central importance to an assessment of Dryden's knowledge of Spanish drama.[2] He wrote the play early in his career, presumably during the winter of 1664-5, and when it was produced in the spring of 1665 it had a success beyond that of any of his previous plays. So far as we know, Calderón's play had not been translated into either English or French by 1665, and thus if Dryden used it he must have read it in the original Spanish, in one of the several editions of Calderón's *Primera Parte*.[3] Thus, to assume that Dryden made use of *El príncipe constante* is also to assume that even before he wrote *Of Dramatick Poesie* he would have studied intensively one of Calderón's masterpieces in the original language, would in fact have studied it in a volume containing a number of Calderón's best plays. There is nothing impossible in the assumption : Dryden could read Spanish, and in at least two other plays, *The Mock Astrologer* and *The Assignation*,[4] he seems to have borrowed from Calderón. Nevertheless, I am not convinced that in *The Indian Emperour* he borrowed from Calderón,[5] and partly because of the difficulty of reconciling what he said about that dramatist in *Of Dramatick Poesie* (which he wrote in first draft soon after finishing the play) with a close knowledge of *El príncipe constante*.

His several references in the essay to Calderón and the Spanish drama suggest that his conception of the 'comedia', at that time at least, was largely bounded by the form of intrigue comedy then best known in England from Sir Samuel Tuke's *The Adventures of Five Hours*, an adaptation of *Los empeños de seis horas* (probably by Antonio Coello, but then thought to be by Calderón).[6]

[1] I have elsewhere presented evidence that Dryden could read Spanish: Dryden, *Works*, ix. 310; 'The Hispanic Element in Dryden', *Emory University Quarterly* xx (1964), 92–4. In this essay I referred briefly to the subject of the present study.   [2] Cf. Shergold and Ure, op. cit.

[3] On the publication of Calderón's plays see Edward M. Wilson, 'The Two Editions of Calderón's *Primera Parte* of 1640', *The Library*, 5th ser. xiv (1959), 175–91; and Shergold and Ure, op. cit.

[4] Cf. James Urvin Rundle, 'The Source of Dryden's "Comic Plot" in *The Assignation*', *Modern Philology* xlv (1947), 104–11.

[5] Cf. Dryden, *Works*, ix. 306–7.

[6] Allison Gaw, 'Tuke's *Adventures of Five Hours* in Relation to the "Spanish

It is scarcely necessary to add that this conception is inadequate to the variety and profundity of Spanish drama. Of the four interlocutors in *Of Dramatick Poesie*, it is Neander whose opinions coincide most closely with the opinions then held by Dryden, and making all allowances for the tentative and conversational nature of the essay we must think of Neander's criticism of the 'comedia' as in some measure representing a judgement by Dryden. The following would seem to be the crucial passage:

> But of late years Moliere, the younger Corneille, Quinault, and some others, have been imitating afar off the quick turns and graces of the English stage. They have mixed their serious plays with mirth, like our tragi-comedies, since the death of Cardinal Richelieu; which Lisideius and many others not observing, have commended that in them for a virtue which they themselves no longer practice. Most of their new plays are, like some of ours, derived from the Spanish novels. There is scarce one of them without a veil, and a trusty Diego, who drolls much after the rate of the *Adventures*. But their humours, if I may grace them with that name, are so thin-sown, that never above one of them comes up in any play. . . .
>
> I grant the French have performed what was possible on the groundwork of the Spanish plays; what was pleasant before, they have made regular: but there is not above one good play to be writ on all those plots; they are too much alike to please often; which we need not the experience of our own stage to justify. As for their new way of mingling mirth with serious plot, I do not, with Lisideius, condemn the thing, though I cannot approve their manner of doing it.[1]

Although this sounds as though Dryden had studied the 'comedia' appreciatively, it would nevertheless suggest that he shared the common Restoration notion of 'Spanish plots' as plays of love-intrigue and sword-play; and indeed nothing in *Of Dramatick Poesie*, spoken by Neander or anyone else, suggests that he had reached a more comprehensive estimate of the Spanish achievement in drama.

How much did Dryden know about the 'comedia', we may reasonably ask. The most important—and the most subtle— evidence turns on the use he made of it in his own plays (above all, his possible use of Calderón in *The Indian Emperour*), and this we cannot consider here. But his remarks in his critical essays warrant

Plot" and to John Dryden', in Allison Gaw, ed., *Studies in English Drama, First Series* (University of Pennsylvania, 1917), p. 23.

[1] *Essays*, i. 68–9.

the conclusion that, although he had studied Spanish drama in a comparatist's spirit of examining alternative approaches to the perennial problems of dramatic form, and had studied it, at least in his younger years, with a mind not fully convinced of the rightness of French neo-classical formalism, he nevertheless failed to perceive the magnificence of the Spanish artistic achievement. Dryden's criticism and dramatic practice alike prove that he had no doubt of Corneille's greatness.[1] The stature of Calderón—it would seem to me, the equal of Corneille's—receives no just critical acknowledgement from Dryden, whatever the facts about the sources of *The Indian Emperour*. His failing is, of course, explicable with reference to the assumptions of the age in which he lived. To chide him for not writing a just appreciation of Calderón —and Lope de Vega and other Spanish dramatists—is to criticize him for not possessing a literary discernment shown by no other Englishman of the seventeenth century.

If he failed to give the dramatists their due, he seems to have given the Spanish critics rather more than theirs. 'Dryden has assured me', Lord Bolingbroke told Joseph Spence many years after Dryden's death, 'that he got more from the Spanish critics alone than from the Italian and French, and all other critics put together.'[2] Presumably Dryden had in mind Lope de Vega's *Arte nuevo de hazer comedias en este tiempo*, to which he apparently refers in the Preface to *A Parallel Betwixt Painting and Poetry*, in a passage already quoted. In Lope's verse epistle he would have found an expression of restiveness with the dogmas of neo-classicism more intense than his own, even though Lope, like Dryden, was neo-classical in many assumptions.[3] Neander in *Of Dramatick Poesie* quotes Corneille's remark: 'Tis easy for speculative persons to judge severely; but if they would produce to public view ten or twelve pieces of this nature, they would perhaps

---

[1] Pierre Legouis, 'Corneille and Dryden as Dramatic Critics', in *Seventeenth-Century Studies Presented to Sir Herbert Grierson* (Oxford, 1938), pp. 269–91; Frank Livingstone Huntley, *On Dryden's 'Essay of Dramatic Poesy'* (Ann Arbor, Michigan, 1951), pp. 6–8; John M. Aden, 'Dryden, Corneille, and the *Essay of Dramatic Poesy*', *Review of English Studies*, n.s. vi (1955), 147–56.

[2] James M. Osborn, ed., *Joseph Spence. Observations, Anecdotes, and Characters of Books and Men* (Oxford, 1966), i. 317. For a valuable discussion of the background for this remark, see Huntley, pp. 3–6.

[3] Duncan Moir, 'Spanish Dramatic Theory and Practice', in M. J. Anderson, ed., *Classical Drama and its Influence* (New York, 1965), p. 196.

give more latitude to the rules than I have done, when, by experience, they had known how much we are bound up and constrained by them, and how many beauties of the stage they banished from it.'[1] Corneille's remark is in the spirit of Lope's essay, a successful dramatist's pragmatic appeal to theatrical experience in defence against theoretical criticism; and indeed Lope says much the same thing at greater length.[2] All this is consonant with one of the strains of Dryden's essay: a neo-classicism tempered by an appeal to experience in the theatre.

Lope read his verse epistle, the most systematic exposition of his theory of drama, to an academy in Madrid in 1609. The poem is conversationally organized and argued, and it includes few perceptions that cannot be traced to earlier critics; yet it is important because it articulates the critical theory of the dramatist who more than any other shaped the dramatic form. In overt statement Lope is deferential to the neo-classicists; he accepts many of their precepts and is apologetic about his departures from others, using the prudential defence that as a professional dramatist he had to please his audiences. But the tone of the essay undercuts the modesty of its explicit argument (and it has been well suggested that Lope in his oral presentation might have accentuated his irony with facial gestures),[3] with the result that his note of apology can scarcely be taken seriously. He was writing from a position of acknowledged eminence as Spain's leading dramatist, and, as Tirso de Molina later suggested, his deferential tone is perhaps to be attributed to a tactful modesty rather than to conviction.[4]

Lope's conception of the 'comedia' as embracing characters and situations which the neo-classicists divided between tragedy and comedy would seem to be relevant to Dryden's critical thought. As already noted, Dryden alludes in *Of Dramatick Poesie* to the 'comedia's' mixed nature. It is a complex dramatic form of great variety, sometimes taking the form of comedy and again that of tragedy, and generalizations about it are difficult; but it consistently avoids the rigid distinctions of characters, situations, and emotions considered appropriate to the separate genres that we find in the plays of the more severe neo-classicists. The 'comedia'

[1] *Essays*, i. 75–6.
[2] In H. J. Chaytor, ed., *Dramatic Theory in Spain* (Cambridge, 1925), p. 16.
[3] Otis H. Green, *Spain and the Western Tradition* (Madison, Wisconsin, 1965), iii. 274.   [4] *Los cigarrales de Toledo*, in Chaytor, p. 63.

differs in form from English tragicomedy and even from Shake-spearian drama with its frequent intermingling of characters and episodes of contrasting emotional impact, but it embodies some similar critical assumptions. The tragic and the comic should be mixed, writes Lope, appealing both to his experience in the theatre and to life. Lope does not have in mind, however, a two-part drama such as the form of tragicomedy which Neander praises in *Of Dramatick Poesie*, but drama with a single plot line.[1] That Dryden did not accept Lope's argument on this point we may be sure, from the example provided by his two-part tragicomedies as well as from his remarks in *Of Dramatick Poesie*. More than Lope, Dryden was influenced by neo-classical conceptions of decorum, and, paradoxically as it may seem to us, found in the double plot of tragicomedy a means of avoiding unseemly group-ings of characters, while yet attaining the pleasing contrasts and diversity of tragicomedy.[2] On this, as on most other topics, Dryden is more systematic than Lope, and a more severe neo-classicist; but he may well have welcomed Lope's support against such English critics as he represents fictionally in *Of Dramatick Poesie* in the character of Crites.

Did Dryden, in his tribute to the Spanish critics, have others than Lope in mind? Perhaps not: his essays do not include references to others by name nor passages that can easily be traced to works other than the *Arte nuevo*.[3] Spain had not, before Dryden wrote, produced critical work of sophistication com-parable to his own[4] (nor for that matter had England: we recall Samuel Johnson's denomination of him as the father of English criticism[5]). Other critics than Lope had anticipated Dryden's

---

[1] *Arte nuevo*, in Chaytor, p. 21.

[2] Frank Harper Moore, *The Nobler Pleasure* (Chapel Hill, N.C., 1963), pp. 43–5; Dryden, *Works*, ix. 334–6.

[3] It is suggestive of the limited knowledge in England of Spanish criticism that Gerard Langbaine in the Preface to *Momus Triumphans* (1688) mentions Lope de Vega alone among the Spaniards in a list of foreign dramatic critics.

[4] For accounts of dramatic criticism in Renaissance Spain see Alfred Morel-Fatio, 'Les Défenseurs de la comedia', *Bulletin hispanique* iv (1902), 30–62; and Moir, 'Spanish Dramatic Theory and Practice', loc. cit. Chaytor op. cit., provides a valuable selection of the critical texts. E. L. C. Riley, *Cervantes's Theory of the Novel* (Oxford, 1962), includes much that is relevant to the 'comedia', even though it is primarily concerned with prose fiction.

[5] Dryden, in G. Birkbeck Hill, ed., *Johnson's Lives of the English Poets* (Oxford, 1905), i. 410.

pragmatic appeal to theatrical effectiveness in opposition to neo-classical theory, and they had, more specifically, anticipated his reservations about the unities and some of his arguments in praise of tragicomedy. But such opinions were commonplace in the criticism of the Renaissance, and I would guess that Dryden at most gained from the Spaniards reinforcement in opinions that he already held.

W. P. Ker believed that Tirso de Molina's *Los cigarrales de Toledo* might have provided suggestions for *Of Dramatick Poesie*,[1] and the weight of Ker's learning compels us to consider the possibility. *Los cigarrales*, a miscellany of prose and drama published in 1624, includes a conversation piece in which gentlemen who have seen a performance of Tirso's own *El vergonzoso en palacio* discuss the 'comedia' with reference to the drama of antiquity. Tirso establishes an antithesis between a traditionalist, who criticizes the moderns for departing from the rules of the ancients, and a defender of Lope and his followers, an antithesis similar to that between Dryden's Crites and Neander. Tirso's defence of the moderns is more emphatic than Dryden's, and it is not so fully qualified by the suspension of judgement which in *Of Dramatick Poesie* results from the vigorous presentation of divergent opinion. Dryden's Neander has the final and strongest argument, to be sure, but he does not rout the opposition so completely as does Tirso's spokesman for the moderns, nor is his praise of Shakespeare and other English dramatists so free of neo-classical bias as is Tirso's spokesman's praise of Lope. Neander's admiration for Shakespeare is extravagant enough, but it is limited by a statement of his faults; and furthermore Neander isolates for extended praise Ben Jonson's *The Silent Woman*, a comedy that is neo-classical in form and spirit. On the other hand, Tirso's modern praises Lope as possessing sufficient authority to establish new rules for drama.[2] If less eloquent than Dryden's praise of Shakespeare as 'the man who of all modern, and perhaps ancient poets, had the largest and most comprehensive soul',[3] his praise of Lope is nevertheless bolder in its theoretical implications.

Despite the similarities between his own and Tirso's arguments and their common use of the dialogue structure, I see no reason for assuming that Dryden had read the earlier work. The dialogue

---

[1] *Essays*, i. xxxv–xxxvi.
[2] In Chaytor, pp. 62–3.
[3] *Of Dramatick Poesie*, in *Essays*, i. 79.

structure was as old as Plato and Cicero, and Tirso's literary opinions were common property.[1] Tirso, as I have said, was less systematic a neo-classicist than Dryden. In texture their arguments rarely resemble one another. The resemblance is most apparent in their separate defences of tragicomedy, and yet even on this subject there are significant differences, Dryden thinking of the form as having a double plot, and Tirso, like Lope before him, as incorporating in a single plot elements traditional to both comedy and tragedy. The strongest objection to Dryden's indebtedness is perhaps the simplest: *Los cigarrales* in comparison with *Of Dramatick Poesie* is casual and slight,[2] having none of the comprehensiveness nor logical and aesthetic rigour of Dryden's essay, which Dr. Johnson justly considered 'the first regular and valuable treatise [in English] on the art of writing'.[3]

At the time he wrote *Of Dramatick Poesie*, Dryden had reason enough for interest in Lope, his criticism, and Spanish drama: in particular for an interest in the contrast between the busy and complex plots of the Spaniards and the simpler and more neatly ordered plots of the French. This contrast, and a parallel to it in English drama (for there is an implied comparison of the Spanish to Renaissance English drama and the French to Restoration drama) provides a major theme in the essay. Which is preferable, Dryden asks through his interlocutors, a drama with a strong narrative line, with excitement, suspense, and bustle; or a quieter drama, largely dispensing with these qualities, which has in compensation emotional intensity and extended analysis of characters' minds?

Lisideius presents the case for the French:

Another thing in which the French differ from us and from the Spaniards, is, that they do not embarrass, or cumber themselves with too much plot; they only represent so much of a story as will constitute one whole and great action sufficient for a play; we, who undertake more, do but multiply adventures; which, not being produced from one another, as effects from causes, but barely following, constitute many actions in the drama, and consequently make it many plays.

But by pursuing close one argument, which is not cloyed with many turns, the French have gained more liberty for verse, in which they write; they have leisure to dwell on a subject which deserves it; and

[1] Cf. Chaytor, and Morel-Fatio, *passim.*   [2] Cf. Morel-Fatio.
[3] *Dryden, Lives of the English Poets*, i. 411.

to represent the passions (which we have acknowledged to be the poet's work), without being hurried from one thing to another, as we are in the plays of Calderon, which we have seen lately upon our theatres, under the name of Spanish plots.[1]

From the nature of Lisideius's criticism of Spanish plots and praise of the French, his endorsement of the unities follows as a logical correlative. Here, indeed, may be found a rationale for the unities of French drama more convincing to the modern mind than the argument on grounds of plausibility; the simplicity of action and restricted time scheme and locale of, say, *Cinna, Horace,* and *Polyeucte* provide aids to the depiction of passions and, conversely, barriers against the dispersal of the spectators' interest in a complex action. The pace of French classical drama, the time scheme in which dramatic time approximates elapsed time in the theatre, enforces extended analysis of characters' motives for action, and makes more difficult the substitution of interest in the resolution of suspense for that in the characters' response to the problems that confront them. If not the usual grounds for the defence of the unities in the seventeenth century, this argument for them as a means to a concentration on the essentials of drama has a certain continuing force, unlike the argument exploded by Samuel Johnson that the unities of time and place aid the spectator in his imaginative acceptance of dramatic action.[2]

Although the debate on the unities in *Of Dramatick Poesie* is not systematically referred to the contrast between Spanish and French dramas, it is steadily relevant to that contrast. Strict observance of the unities is difficult in a drama having a strong narrative line (though, as Neander notes, Tuke's *The Adventures of Five Hours,* the Spanish plot *par excellence,* conformed to them);[3] it leads to the French emphasis on character and motive rather than the Spanish emphasis on action.[4] And it leads also to a concentration on a single emotional state, of varying intensities to be sure, rather

[1] *Essays,* i. 59–60.

[2] *Mr. Johnson's Preface To his Edition of Shakespear's Plays* (London, 1765), pp. xxv–xxxi.

[3] Neander, speaking about Jonson's *The Silent Woman*: ' 'Tis all included in the limits of three hours and an half, which is no more than is required for the presentment on the stage. A beauty perhaps not much observed; if it had, we should not have looked on the Spanish translation of *Five Hours,* with so much wonder.' *Essays,* i. 83.

[4] Cf. A. A. Parker, *The Approach to the Spanish Drama of the Golden Age* (London, 1957), pp. 3–4:

than on a succession of contrasting states. Thus it is incompatible with many Spanish and English plays of the Renaissance.

As on most important subjects in the essay, Dryden is ambivalent about tragicomedy, damning it in the person of Lisideius and praising it in that of Neander. 'There is no theatre in the world has any thing so absurd as the English tragi-comedy'; says Lisideius, ''tis a drama of our own invention, and the fashion of it is enough to proclaim it so; here a course of mirth, there another of sadness and passion, a third of honour, and a fourth a duel. . . .'[1] And a moment later he explains the grounds of his objection: 'The end of tragedies or serious plays, says Aristotle, is to beget admiration, compassion, or concernment; but are not mirth and compassion things incompatible? and is it not evident that the poet must of necessity destroy the former by intermingling of the latter? that is, he must ruin the sole end and object of his tragedy, to introduce somewhat that is forced in, and is not of the body of it.'[2] English drama, not Spanish, is the target of this censure; and yet the criticism has an obvious relevance to the 'comedia', which does intermingle 'mirth and compassion'; and in the implied antitheses which comprise the structure of the essay this arraignment of tragicomedy becomes relevant to Spanish drama. At the outset of his defence of the English, in a passage quoted above, Neander takes into account a movement in French drama in the direction of Spanish practice, showing in doing so that Dryden was a remarkably well-informed reader of recent plays; and Neander expresses what we may take to be Dryden's own views on the subject, since they coincide with his current dramatic practice in *Secret Love*. His defence of tragicomedy, which has been described as the first important defence of it in English,[3] glances at Spanish

---

The generic characteristic of the Spanish drama is, of course, the fact that it is essentially a drama of action and not of characterization. It does not set out to portray rounded and complete characters, though certain plays may do so incidentally. Some of the misunderstanding from which the Spanish drama has suffered, more particularly the plays of Calderón, has been due to the regret critics have felt at the absence of fully developed lifelike characterization. We must, however, waive any preconceptions and accept the fact that the Spanish drama works on the assumption —which after all has the authority of Aristotle behind it—that the plot and not the characters is the primary thing.

[1] *Essays*, i. 57–8. [2] *Essays*, i. 58.
[3] Frank Humphrey Ristine, *English Tragicomedy, Its Origin and History* (New York, 1910), p. 169.

drama, but with a certain note of depreciation; and he praises the French for their improvements on the Spanish plots:

As for their new way of mingling mirth with serious plot, I do not, with Lisideius, condemn the thing, though I cannot approve their manner of doing it. He tells us, we cannot so speedily recollect ourselves after a scene of great passion and concernment, as to pass to another of mirth and humour, and to enjoy it with any relish: but why should he imagine the soul of man more heavy than his senses? Does not the eye pass from an unpleasant object to a pleasant in a much shorter time than is required to this? and does not the unpleasantness of the first commend the beauty of the latter? The old rule of logic might have convinced him, that contraries, when placed near, set off each other. A continued gravity keeps the spirit too much bent; we must refresh it sometimes, as we bait in a journey, that we may go on with greater ease. A scene of mirth, mixed with tragedy, has the same effect upon us which our music has betwixt the acts; and that we find a relief to us from the best plots and language of the stage, if the discourses have been long. I must therefore have stronger arguments, ere I am convinced that compassion and mirth in the same subject destroy each other; and in the mean time cannot but conclude, to the honour of our nation, that we have invented, increased, and perfected a more pleasant way of writing for the stage, than was ever known to the ancients or moderns of any nation, which is tragi-comedy.[1]

And thus at the same time that he defends qualities in Spanish drama which were then controversial, in qualified measure taking the Spanish side against at least the earlier French practice, he insists on the originality of the English invention of tragicomedy, denying its origin in any other country. This is an intelligible attitude if we distinguish between two qualities in tragicomedy: the double plot on the one hand, and the alternation of moods on the other. The former of these qualities was not present in Spanish drama, not at least in the manner of Dryden's plays; the latter was. Although some of the specifics of Dryden's praise of tragicomedy are thus irrelevant to his attitude toward the 'comedia', much of what he says about it is relevant, just as it is also relevant to his attitude to the English drama of the Renaissance.

Steadily in the background of Dryden's criticism of the 'comedia' is a comparison of it to English Renaissance drama, which also ignored the unities, had busy plots, and combined qualities

[1] *Essays,* i. 69–70.

of tragedy and comedy; and a differentiation of the 'comedia' from French classical drama, which with less incident gained more intensity—either of tragic or comic emotion—and more leisure for the detailed analysis of character and motive. Spanish and French drama sometimes represent in Dryden's writings a schematic antithesis: drama of action, exciting perhaps, but diffuse, and drama of character, sometimes tedious, but orderly and at best concentrated and moving. And this antithesis is broadly analogous to his conception of the contrast between the drama 'of the last age' and that of his own.

3

'DASHED AND BREW'D WITH LIES': THE POPISH PLOT AND THE COUNTRY PARTY

By MICHAEL MACKLEM

From hence began that Plot, the Nations Curse,
Bad in itself, but represented worse,
Rais'd in extremes, and in extremes decri'd,
With Oaths affirm'd, with dying Vows deni'd,
Not weigh'd or winnow'd by the Multitude,
But swallow'd in the Mass, unchewed and crude.
Some Truth there was, but dashed and brew'd with Lies;
To please the Fools, and puzzle all the Wise.
Succeeding Times did equal Folly call
Believing nothing or believing all.

NOTHING, it may be thought, could be more sensible than Dryden's cool account of the Popish Plot. No one is asked to believe the more extravagant accusations brought by the informers. No one needs to suppose, for example, that Queen Catherine did in fact conspire with Sir George Wakeman, the royal physician, to poison her husband. In any case, the Lord Chief Justice had the good sense and breeding to see that Sir George was acquitted on so gross a charge. But if Catherine herself was not guilty of treason, there were few in her own day who doubted that she kept bad company. Could anyone deny that the Catholics had been secretly planning to yoke the English people to the Church of Rome by murdering the King and crowning his brother James, the Catholic Duke of York? When the hour struck—when Pickering and Grove fired the powder in their pan, or when the four ruffians did their work at Windsor, or perchance when the royal physician gave the King too strong a drink—when the hour struck, 40,000 hidden Papists in the city of London alone were to rise by night and cut the throats of loyal citizens as they lay in their beds; Jesuits were to occupy every bishopric and archbishopric in the land (Oates could show you a list with the very names on it) and the Church was to repossess the lands and revenues it had been forced to surrender to the Crown, and to the loyal friends of the Crown, in the great days of King Henry VIII.[1]

England had been nourished on such tales for nearly a century and a half; for six generations Englishmen had exulted in a splendid hatred of Rome and His Imperial Majesty. Would Drake and Hawkins have ridden the western seas with such savage audacity if they had had no reason to rejoice in the discomfort of the King of Spain? Would the Elizabethan stage have glowed with life and beauty as it did if there had been no Armada? These tales of old were still remembered in 1678—indeed, they were to serve the pride of Englishmen for at least two centuries longer— but after almost twenty years of Charles II, a King more given to consider the interests of the Crown than those of the nation, a certain squalor had overtaken English policy. The Dutch wars were a shabby substitute for the flamboyant adventures of the Elizabethan seamen, and if Elizabeth had once refused the attentions of Philip II, Charles was now in the pay of Louis XIV. Having no Armada within living memory, the English were driven to invent one.

I

If the events of 1588 had served a national purpose and made national history, the events of 1678 were to serve the interests of a party. In the fall of 1678 the Whigs were as yet only a loosely knit group united by little more than their opposition to the Court. But they already had a leader in the Earl of Shaftesbury, who had been dismissed from office in 1674, and he had already

[1] It is fair to add that in *Absalom and Achitophel* Dryden went out of his way to make an appeal to those of moderate opinion. On other occasions he spoke more frankly of the desire of the country party to keep the Plot 'on foot, as long as possibly they can; and to give it hot water, as often as 'tis dying; for while they are in possession of this Jewel, they make themselves masters of the people'. Without 'such Artifices', indeed, their 'cause could not possibly subsist: fear of Popery and Arbitrary power must be kept up; or the St. *Georges* of their side, would have no Dragon to encounter'. See Charles E. Ward, *The Life of John Dryden* (Chapel Hill, 1961), pp. 162, 161.

seized on the essentials of a policy.[1] His immediate object was to exclude the Duke of York from the succession; beyond that, he apparently hoped to limit the royal prerogative and augment the effective control of the two houses over the day-to-day administration of government.

Whether or not Shaftesbury himself conceived of the Plot it is no longer profitable to inquire. Sir John Dalrymple remarked casually enough that Shaftesbury 'framed the fiction of the popish plot in the year 1678, in order to bury the Duke, and perhaps the King, under the weight of the national fear and hatred of popery'. He adds that when one of his friends in the upper house asked Shaftesbury how such a farrago of improbable nonsense could be passed off for the truth, the latter answered, 'the more nonsensical the better; if we cannot bring them to swallow worse nonsense than that, we shall never do any good with them'.[2] Shaftesbury himself made no bones about the part he played in the affair. '*I will not say*', he is said to have told a friend, '*who* Started *the Game, but I am sure I had the full* Hunting *of it.*'[3]

Witnesses soon learned what it was like to be hunted by the Earl of Shaftesbury. There was John Walters, one of the two men who discovered Sir Edmund Godfrey's body on Primrose Hill. He was first threatened by Shaftesbury and then fettered and handcuffed and thrown into prison for three days and nights. A few days later he was sent for by the Lords, and according to L'Estrange was taken by Shaftesbury '*into a* By-Closet', where he was promised a job shoeing the Earl's horses if he would accuse the Papists of Godfrey's murder. His companion, William Bromwell, was less fortunate. Shaftesbury told him that if he failed to accuse 'some *Great Roman Catholique*' he would be hanged for it; and in

[1] See J. R. Jones, 'Shaftesbury's "Worthy Men": A Whig View of the Parliament of 1679', *Bulletin of the Institute of Historical Research* xxx (1957), 232–41. Jones prints a list of the members of the House of Commons, with annotations by Shaftesbury. The original is in the Record Office, P.R.O. 30.24, Bundle VIa, piece no. 348.

[2] Sir John Dalrymple, *Memoirs of Great Britain and Ireland* (Edinburgh, 1771), pp. 43, 43 n. Dalrymple explains that 'Some papers I have seen convince me he contrived it, though the persons he made use of as informers ran beyond their instructions'. Unfortunately, he does not identify the 'papers', nor have they ever been found.

[3] Laurence Echard, *The History of England* (3 vols., London, 1707–18), iii. 460.

fact it was said he spent nine weeks in Newgate for his honesty. When Mary Gibbon testified that Godfrey had been in low spirits before his disappearance and so might be supposed to have taken his own life, Shaftesbury *'call'd to her, saying,* You Damn'd Woman, what Devillish Paper is This you have given us in? *Putting her upon her Oath to Declare who* Wrote *it; calling her* Bitch, *and other Vile Names, and Threatning her, That if she would not* Confess, *that Sir* John Banks, *Mr.* Pepys, *and* Monsieur de Puy *set her on to write that Paper, she should be torn to Pieces by the* Multitude; *Threatning her to have her Worry'd as the* Dogs *Worry* Cats, *insomuch that she fell into* Fits *upon't, and thought she should never have got home.'* There was a coachman named Francis Corral who, it was hoped, would implicate one of the popish lords in the murder of Godfrey. When he insisted that he knew nothing to the point, Shaftesbury told him he would have £500 if he spoke *'the Truth'*, *'The said Lord* Shaftesbury *laying down some* Mony *upon the* Table' as he spoke. When the coachman continued to stand his ground, the Earl lost his patience: 'We are the Peers of the Land', he cried, 'and if thou wilt not Confess, there shall be a Barrel of Nails provided for thee, to put thee in, and roul thee down a Hill.' The coachman answered simply, 'What would you have me to say, *my Lord?* I know nothing of the matter, would you have me to accuse other People, to bring them into the same Condition I now am?' 'Then thou shalt *Dye'*, Shaftesbury told him; whereupon the prisoner was taken back to Newgate, where he was kept in irons in the condemned hole. Twice more he was examined and still he refused to tell his captors what they wanted to hear. 'Thou art such a Peremptory Rogue', Shaftesbury told him, 'thou shalt go back to *Newgate,* and lye and Rot there a while. And then thou shalt be brought to be tryed at the Sessions, and then there will come enow against thee, and thou shalt be Hang'd. Hadst thou not better *Confess* the *Truth,* and have that *Mony,* then be brought before the Barr of the Judges, and be condemn'd to be *Hang'd ?'* When it became clear that no further use could be made of the man, he was sent back to Newgate once again to 'lye there and Rot', as his interrogator put it, and so apparently he did, for thirteen weeks and three days. When the man pleaded for his wife and children, he was told to let them starve.[1]

[1] [Sir Roger L'Estrange], *A Brief History of the Times* (London, 1687), pp. 100, 98, 101, 103, 105. When Mrs. Cellier tried to make use of this story

As often as not, Shaftesbury took a hand in starting the game as well. It is remarkable how often the informers who exposed the plot against the life of the King spoke also of attempts on the life of the Earl of Shaftesbury. Miles Prance, for example, had many friends who spoke to him openly of their intent to kill Shaftesbury. There was one Maddison who said as much to William Staley at the Cross Keys in Covent Garden (Staley was hanged and quartered at Tyburn in November of 1678). A man named Adamson met Prance at the White Post in Vere Street, and again at the Gridiron in Holborn, and on both occasions he told him that Shaftesbury deserved to die. Two of his other friends, Prosser and Bradshaw by name, told Prance that when the great day came Shaftesbury would be the first to be cut down. A certain Signor Francisco told the House of Lords that the Portuguese ambassador had offered him 50,000 pieces of eight to kill Oates, Bedloe, and Shaftesbury.[1] In January of 1680, a few months after Sir George Wakeman had been acquitted of attempting to poison the King, Sir William Scroggs, who had heard the case and so incurred the displeasure of the Whig managers, was accused by Oates of appearing drunk in public. Scroggs retorted that he had drunk once to the King and once to the Duke, which to a man of Oates's opinions might, he allowed, seem 'a cup too much'. Scroggs was by now disenchanted with Oates, whose evidence he had dismissed with contempt at Wakeman's trial. But Oates was still on good terms with Shaftesbury, for it was at Shaftesbury's that he had seen Scroggs in his cups. Indeed, Oates was a familiar figure in those quarters and that August he married Shaftesbury's niece, 'by his lordship's consent'.[2] It is remarkable that a man like

to discredit the Opposition, Corral and his wife hastened to deny it, but there is no more reason to suppose he was lying when he told the story than when he denied it.

[1] Historical Manuscripts Commission. Thirteenth Report, Appendix, Part VI (Fitzherbert MSS.), pp. 155–6; Seventh Report, Appendix, Part I (Verney MSS.), p. 479. Prosser was actually imprisoned. See *Calendar of State Papers, Domestic Series*, ? 13 Jan., 21 June 1679; *Journals of the House of Lords*, 20 Mar. 1679 (xiii. 467–8). See also H.M.C. Eleventh Report, Appendix, Part III (House of Lords MSS.), pp. 251–2. In the summer of 1680 Simpson Tonge told the King that from the beginning of 'the intrigue of this plot my father and Oates corresponded very much with Lords Wharton, Essex and Shaftesbury' (*Calendar of State Papers, Domestic Series*, Aug. 1680). It was Portuguese gold that was supposed to have induced Scroggs to acquit Sir George Wakeman.   [2] Ibid., 22 Jan. and 17 Aug. 1680.

Oates, altogether without means or social pretensions and possessed as he was of a singularly disagreeable person and figure, should have been able to prevail on a man in Shaftesbury's position to allow him to marry his niece. It is all the more remarkable that such a marriage should have taken place in view of the fact that Oates had more than once exposed his private life to public view: 'Mr. O—— was Try'd two Days ago for *Buggery*, and Clear'd: The next Day he brought his Action to the *King's Bench*, against his Accuser, being attended by the Earl of *Shaftsbury*, and other Peers, to the number of seven, for the Honour of the PROTESTANT CAUSE.'[1]

There was good hunting in Ireland too. In April of 1679—a few weeks after Scroggs drank to the health of the Duke of York in the company of Oates and Shaftesbury—the Earl of Ossory wrote to Ormonde in Ireland that Shaftesbury 'employs all manner of creatures to find him matter of complaint' among the Papists; in August he wrote to warn Ormonde that 'My Lord of Shaftesbury's emissaries are very busy in raising jealousies of your not being careful for the Protestant interest'. Ormonde wrote to Ossory the following April to report that Shaftesbury's agent had embarked that Sunday from Dublin 'with all his ten'. Shaftesbury, he added, would need 'much skill to make anything material out of their narratives and as much indulgence to make them creditable witnesses', for 'this kingdom has not been so quiet as it is at this instant these forty years'. However that might be, enough was made out of the narratives of these witnesses to bring Oliver Plunket, Archbishop of Armagh and Primate of Ireland, to the block.[2] They had hoped to bring down the Duke of York himself. One of Shaftesbury's agents was a man named Edward Joey ('a person that wthin these 10 dayes much frequents the Ld Shaftsburies') and Joey had offered to 'produce a person that has Letters of his R[oyal]. H[ighness]. own writeing to ye Earl of Tyronne to carry on the Irish plott'. Joey had caused one Gardiner to be examined in the matter of the Duke, and Gardiner was no

---

[1] The Earl of Rochester to the Hon. Mr. Henry Savile [1679], *Collected Works of John Wilmot Earl of Rochester*, edited by John Hayward (London, 1926), p. 263. Some years before Oates had been discharged from a chaplaincy for the same offence.

[2] H.M.C. New Series, Volume v (Ormonde MSS.), pp. 29, 184, 312. See also p. 94.

doubt the man who was reputed to have the incriminating letters in his possession. Evidently, however, he failed to produce them, for Joey was forced to alter his statement, after which Gardiner would not sign it.[1] Another agent was a man named Lewis—presumably the same William Lewis who in November of 1680 appeared at the bar of the House of Commons to denounce a plot to burn the fleet and murder the Earl of Shaftesbury. The following May, Lewis was working on an informer called Haines. He found that 'a little drink' made Haines 'free in discours'. Haines, as it turned out, was also in Shaftesbury's pay, for he told Lewis that 'Hee had bin lately wth my Ld. Sh. [and] goes today thither for to enq^r after monies to discharge his Lodgeings'.[2]

Nor was Shaftesbury above letting loose a few foxes of his own. On 18 August 1679, after almost a year spent in pursuit of his quarry, Edmund Warcup, a justice of the peace for the county of Middlesex, set down in his journal that 'the lord president [Shaftesbury] said that morning there was one bitter herbe in Mr Reades information spoiled the whole pot [of] porridge', adding that 'Reade must be reexamined & that left out'. A few weeks later Warcup met Oates in Fleet Street, 'coming from Shaftsbery'; Oates told him that 'Lord Shaftsbery would dally no longer; he would impeach the duke, against whome he had witnesses to prove high treason'.[3] In the event, the expectations of 'Lord Shafsbury and his gange'—as James called them[4]—were disappointed and nearly two years later, as we have seen, they were still hoping to prevail on creatures like Joey and Gardiner to discredit the Duke. By that time, however, at least fifteen men of humbler birth and station had been brought to Tyburn by the same means, to suffer for the advancement of the country party.

Shaftesbury was a party leader of cool and ruthless intelligence; he understood the mob and had a special flair for the effective gesture. There were, of course, the great occasions, occasions on which the Pope would be hanged or burned in effigy before the greedy eyes of the London populace. But no occasion was too

[1] Record Office, S.P. 29.415, piece no. 199.

[2] S.P. 29.415, piece no. 200. See *The Information of William Lewis, Gent.* (London, 1680).

[3] Keith Feiling and F. R. D. Needham, 'The Journals of Edmund Warcup, 1676–84', *English Historical Review*, xl (1925), 242, 244. The Warcup journals are printed in full, pp. 235–60.

[4] H.M.C. Fifteenth Report, Appendix, Part V (Foljambe MSS.), p. 123.

trifling or unimportant to be turned by dextrous management to the advantage of the cause. Not long before he was arrested, Edward Coleman, secretary to the Duke of York and a known Catholic, paid a visit to Woburn Abbey, seat of the Earl of Bedford. While there he took special pleasure in the gardens, and Lord Russell, the heir to the estate, became obsessed with the idea that if the Duke of York succeeded to the Crown Coleman would take possession of Woburn for his own use. Shaftesbury was careful to encourage this belief and never saw Russell without reminding him of what would happen if the Duke became king. Russell was from that time on a firm supporter of Exclusion. After the murder of Godfrey, Shaftesbury insisted that his wife, the Countess, carry a pair of pocket pistols in her muff, to defend her from the Papists. To be sure, she made no secret of her pistols, 'and most timorous ladies followed her fashion', as the Earl no doubt intended. The Earl of Ailesbury, who tells this story, remarked that the only person who profited from the anxieties of the ladies of fashion was the writer himself. He was obliged to pay an annuity of £1,000 out of his late wife's estate to the Countess of Southampton, but she grew so fearful of having her throat cut by Papists that she died of fright within a few months.[1]

II

News of the Popish Plot had set London on fire in September of 1678, when Oates first made his depositions before the council, seconded before long by Bedloe and Prance and the other informers. But no event wrought so powerfully on the public imagination as the disappearance of Sir Edmund Berry Godfrey, a popular magistrate with a well-earned reputation for hard work and honest dealing. Godfrey's body was discovered on 17 October near Primrose Hill and at once his death was blamed on the Papists.

History has singled out the murder of Godfrey as an act of uncommon violence and special significance. Actually, it was one of a number of similar incidents. On 22 November, a little more than a month after Godfrey's disappearance, a proclamation was published offering £200 for the discovery of the murderers of

[1] *Memoirs of Thomas, Earl of Ailesbury* (2 vols., London, 1890), i. 27, 29.

John Powell of London. It turned out, however, that Powell had not been murdered at all. He was found a few days later in the town of Worcester, in good health and spirits.[1] There was similar trouble the following spring in Dublin, where an 'officer of the Lord Mayor was assaulted at 11 at night in St. Nicholas' Street'; nor is it surprising to learn that the officer had been 'active with the Mayor to remove Masses', for which brave service to the Protestant cause he was 'in danger to be handled by Papists as was Sir E. Godfrey'.[2] The next year, in May, a justice of the peace from Lancashire, 'who had been very active against the Papists', was 'set upon by some ruffians, but we do not hear that he is dead'.[3] Three months later the Papists struck again, but in spite of their considerable experience in such matters they apparently failed to accomplish their purpose. A newsletter reported that 'Mr. Hughes, a vigilant prosecutor of the discovery of priests and Jesuits' estates', was 'set upon in Drury Lane and grievously assaulted by persons as yet unknown, so that his life is despaired of'.[4] That same summer an Irish Papist named Giles was tried for a criminal assault on John Arnold, a magistrate of stout Protestant sympathies, and sentenced to stand three times in the pillory at the mercy of the mob.[5]

But the murder of Godfrey was undoubtedly the most important of these incidents, if only because it furnished the model for the rest. The story of his disappearance and death is already familiar. The magistrate left his house in Hartshorn Lane on Saturday, 12 October 1678, and never returned. Five days later, on Thursday evening, his body was found in a ditch near Primrose Hill, two or three miles north of town. Godfrey had taken Oates's depositions concerning the Plot some time before and it was at once noised abroad—indeed, the rumour was on foot even before it was known that Godfrey was dead—that the magistrate had been killed by the Jesuits.

S[r] Edmund Godfrey [runs a contemporary account] hath been missing ever since Saturday-morning Last, and (though he appointed to dine at home) hath never been heard of since either by his Relations

[1] *Calendar of State Papers, Domestic Series*, 22 and 23 Nov. 1678.
[2] Sir George Rawdon to Viscount Conway from Dublin, ibid., 8 Apr. 1679.
[3] Ibid., 22 May 1680 (newsletter).
[4] Ibid., 17 Aug. 1680.   [5] See below, pp. 52-3.

or his Family: great jealousy is had of his being made-away by yᵉ Papists, he having taken Oats his first examination, & been very active since in prosecuting yᵉʳ discovery.[1]

The same night this was written, there was

news of his Corps being found among Bushes & Briers in a dry ditch (far out of the road-way) between Primrose-hill & St.-John's wood with his own Sword thrust through him: which was done by yᵉ bloody Murtherers to raise a suspicion of his having made-away, with himself; but upon full enquiry yesterday both by yᵉ Coroner's Enquest & some of his own Friends . . . a Verdict is found of his having been feloniously murthered by some unknown Persons; & those no common Highway-men or Foot-pads, he having a very considerable summ of Money (both Gold & Silver) found about him in his Pockets, as also his Watch, & Rings on his fingers. . . . He appeared upon search to have been strangled, & yᵗ with some other violence first, having some bruises on yᵉ Breast & Head, yᵉ Blood all settled in his Face . . . yᵉ impression of yᵉ cord about his Neck was also very evident, & a cross broad wound in his Breast besides that his own Sword was in, which was not at all bloody, nor (they say) his shirt neither: so yᵗ 'tis rationally supposed, yᵗ after he had been strangled some-where privately here about Town, they carried him out in yᵉ night, & thrust his Sword through him after he was cold.[2]

After the inquest, Godfrey's body was laid out for all to see and the shocking spectacle stirred up a frenzy of hatred and fear. Catholics in London went in danger of their lives. On the 31st a public funeral was held at St. Martin's in the Fields, where the sermon was preached by Dr. William Lloyd, the Vicar, standing in the pulpit between two great fellows, one on either hand, to protect him from the Papists. Lloyd spoke that day more truly than he knew: 'Who knows', he cried, 'but, in the end, it may prove a fatal blow to themselves [i.e., the Papists]? This . . . may occasion a fair riddance of all that Faction out of *England*.'[3]

The council at once published a proclamation offering £500 and a pardon to anyone who would discover the murder, and before many days had passed William Bedloe had provided a complete account of the killing, which, he said, had taken place at Somerset

---

[1] W[illia]m Gr[iffith] to Ben Coling[?wood] from Whitehall, 17 Oct. 1678, Lambeth Palace MS. 942.30, p. 24.

[2] Same to same from Whitehall, 19 Oct. 1678, ibid., p. 25.

[3] William Lloyd, *A Sermon at the Funeral of Sir Edmund-Bury Godfrey* (London, 1678), p. 42.

House, the London residence of the Queen.[1] A few weeks later he accused Miles Prance of being an accomplice and, after a taste of Newgate and an offer of pardon if he confessed, Prance sang to the same tune, though he had moments of doubt that compelled him for a time to deny the truth of his confession. On the strength of the evidence of Bedloe and Prance—supported by Oates who testified in general to the existence of a conspiracy against the life of the King—Robert Green, Henry Berry, and Lawrence Hill, three servants attached to the staff of Somerset House, were convicted of the murder and hanged on 21 February 1679.[2]

The death of these three innocent men was only the beginning. Already, on 26 November, a goldsmith named William Staley had been hanged and quartered after being accused of threatening to kill the King. Coleman was convicted of high treason the next day on the evidence of Oates and Bedloe, supported by a number of letters, which were exhibited to prove that Coleman had been in correspondence with Jesuits on the Continent. On 17 December Thomas Pickering and John Groves were convicted of conspiring to murder the King in St. James's Park and on the same day William Ireland was convicted of being an accessory. Pickering and Ireland were Jesuits, Groves a layman. All three were accused by Oates and Bedloe. Three months later, on 28 March 1679, David Lewis was tried and convicted of treason at Monmouth assizes for having administered the sacraments according to the usages of the Church of Rome. He was executed on 27 August, after refusing to purchase his life by confessing to the existence of a plot against the life of the King. That June Oates, Bedloe, and Prance, together with another informer named Stephen Dugdale, gave evidence at the Old Bailey against five Jesuits, Thomas Whitebread (Provincial of the Society in England), William Harcourt, John Fenwick, John Gavan, and Anthony Turner. All five were accused of attending a congrega-

---

[1] There is a record of Bedloe's confession in the British Museum, MS. Add. 11,055, fol. 245. See also Miles Prance, *A True Narrative and Discovery Of several very Remarkable Passages Relating to the Horrid Popish Plot* (London, 1679). The findings of the inquest were made public, so it was not too difficult for Bedloe and Prance to frame a story that more or less fitted the facts, though there were, as the Duke of York pointed out (Foljambe MSS., pp. 126–7), discrepancies between Prance's account of the murder and Bedloe's.

[2] See *Complete Collection of State Trials*, edited by William Cobbett (34 vols., London, 1809–28), vii. 159–230.

tion of their order at the White Horse Tavern in the Strand on 24 April 1678, at which plans were made to assassinate the King. In fact the Jesuits met at St. James's Palace, not at the White Horse, and the purpose of their meeting, which was an ordinary triennial congregation of the province, was to elect a proctor to be sent to Rome to take part in a general congress of the Society.[1] Oates at any rate could not have been expected to know where the meeting was held or what the delegates discussed, since he was at the time in residence at the Jesuit seminary of St. Omers in Flanders. Though Oates swore he had been present at the deliberations in London at the end of April, more than a dozen witnesses were called by the prisoners to prove that in fact he had not been away from St. Omers for more than a day at a time from December of 1677 until June of 1678, when he left the seminary.[2] There

[1] The minutes of the meeting were discovered some years ago in the College of Exatan in Holland. Forty senior Jesuits attended, including Whitebread, the Provincial, Harcourt (whose real name was Barrow), Turner, William Ireland, and David Lewis. See 'The Jesuit "Consult" of April 24th, 1678', *The Month*, cii (1903), 311–16. Pollock conjectures that Godfrey learned from Coleman that the meeting had been held at St. James's Palace and suggests that it was to prevent his disclosing this secret that the Jesuits had him dispatched (John Pollock, *The Popish Plot* (London, 1903)). But there is no evidence that Godfrey was in fact ever told, nor is there any reason to suppose that if he was told he would have used the information to the disadvantage of the Jesuits. An oblique reference to the meeting at St. James's was circulated in 1680 but it was not openly acknowledged until much later. See J. G. Muddiman, 'Mr. Pollock's "Popish Plot" Once More', *The Month*, cxliii (1924), [348]–52; *The Memoirs of Sir John Reresby*, edited by James J. Cartwright (London, 1875), p. 325.

[2] Though he is quite aware that the meeting took place at St. James's (in which case Oates, who thought it was held at the White Horse, obviously could not have been present), Pollock persists in disbelieving the evidence of the witnesses from St. Omers. His discussion of their testimony, which proceeds on the more or less unconscious assumption that everything a Jesuit says must *ipso facto* be false, is skilfully dissected by J[ohn] G[erard], in 'History "ex Hypothesi" and the Popish Plot', *The Month*, cii (1903), [2]–22. In the Cobbett edition of the *State Trials*, which Pollock used, there is an error of considerable importance. For the original, see *The Tryals and Condemnation of Thomas White . . ., William Harcourt . . ., John Fenwick . . ., John Gavan . . ., And Anthony Turner* (London, 1679), p. 48. Nor should it be forgotten that Oates was convicted of perjury on this very point when he appeared before Sir George Jeffreys at the King's Bench on 8 May 1685. On this occasion the court decided, after hearing several of the same witnesses and taking new evidence as well, that Oates had never attended the meeting and had, indeed, never left St. Omers. See *State Trials* ,x. 1079–1228. The next

were, however, a handful of witnesses who were prepared to swear that they had seen Oates in London at the time of the Jesuit congregation, and the jury believed them. All five of the accused were convicted of high treason and all were hanged and quartered on 20 June. Three weeks later Richard Langhorn, a Catholic attorney, was executed for being accessory to the deliberations at the White Horse Tavern. He had been tried at the Old Bailey the day after the trial of the five Jesuits, but his execution was delayed in the hope that he would accuse others to save his own life. Shaftesbury himself gave the matter his attention, according to a report received by Sir Joseph Williamson, Secretary of State: 'Certain it is that the Earls of Shaftesbury and Essex were with him several hours yesterday and this morning in Newgate.'[1] In less than a year fifteen men had been sacrificed to the cause and others, including Viscount Stafford and the Primate of Ireland, were to follow.

The question of who killed Sir Edmund Godfrey is of peculiar interest and importance because it holds the key to a further question: who were the authors of the Plot itself? At the time few would have hesitated to answer either question. In spite of the fact that the murder of Godfrey did irreparable damage to English Catholics—the disabilities imposed on them were not removed for a century and a half—public opinion was almost unanimous in laying the blame on the Jesuits. There were some, however, who were not so sure. Francis North, Lord Chief Justice of the Court of Common Pleas, was suspicious from the beginning that 'some divelish black purpose' lay behind the Plot. He suspected that the murder of Godfrey was a 'stratagem of those Execrable villaines who were the authors of this diabolicall Engin called the plott, And brought foreward to Retrieve a declining game'. The Catholics were not, as he pointed out, such 'stark fools' as to commit an act so injurious to their own cause. On the contrary, he believed, the whole 'Engin was drest up with designe to aid ye Exclusion of the D[uke of] York'. 'It could never be found out',

---

day (cols. 1227–1330) Oates was convicted of perjury in his testimony against William Ireland.

[1] *Calendar of State Papers, Domestic Series*, 19 June 1679. On 23 June Algernon Sydney wrote to Henry Savile: 'The earl of Shaftesbury hath been twice with him, but, as is said, hath as yet gained nothing from him' of importance (*The Works of Algernon Sydney* (London, 1772), Letters, p. 42).

he admitted, 'what persons lay behind yᵉ Curtaine, and managed this diabolicall machin.' But the truth, he saw, was to be found in the answer to one further question: *cui bono?* Who stood to gain most from the murder of Godfrey?[1] Burnet had no hesitation in attributing the long and sickening series of judicial murders to Shaftesbury, who, he says, 'drove them on in hopes that some one or other to have saved himself would have accused the duke [of York]'. The King was of the same opinion. Speaking of the examination and trial of Dr. Plunket, Burnet remarks that the 'witnesses were brutal and profligate men: yet the earl of Shaftesbury cherished them much: they were examined by the parliament at Westminster; and what they said was believed'.[2]

From that day to this, however, historians have been reluctant to believe that Shaftesbury or his friends could have been responsible for the death of Godfrey. But as it happens, there is no need to suppose Shaftesbury guilty of anything more—or less—than his customary skill in making use of others to serve his purpose.

Philip Herbert, seventh Earl of Pembroke, first attracted the attention of historians of the Popish Plot a generation ago, but even now comparatively little is known about him.[3] He was born in 1653 and became seventh Earl of Pembroke and Montgomery at the age of twenty-one. For nine years (he died at the age of thirty) he was notorious for drunkenness, brutality, and violence. In November of 1677, a little less than a year before Godfrey's disappearance, he wounded a man named Vaughan after a quarrel at Lockett's: 'yᵉ next morning [after the quarrel] my Lᵈ Pembroke sent, as it is reported, Mr Billinsly to let Vaughan know he was in drinke and to desire him to forget what had passed'. In later life Pembroke was seldom to be guilty of such pusillanimity as this, and unluckily Vaughan was not satisfied, but 'sent to my Lᵈ Pembroke to challenge him out'. So they fought 'in yᵉ moonshine behind Lockett's house', where 'Vaughan run my Lᵈ

[1] [Roger North], 'Current & Extempore Recollections of yᵉ late' Francis North, British Museum MS. Add. 32,509, fols. 47ᵛ, 50, 51ᵛ, 62, 62ᵛ. See also fol. 64.

[2] Gilbert Burnet, *History of his own Time* (2 vols., London, 1840), i. 310, 290, 331.

[3] See Muddiman, 'The Mystery of Sir E. B. Godfrey', *National Review* lxxxiv (1924), [138]–45. Pembroke is the villain in John Dickson Carr's *The Murder of Sir Edmund Godfrey* (New York, 1936, 1962).

Pembroke down'. But 'when he wase upon my L^d, my L^ds footman came and cut Mr Vaughan over ye hand soe y^t he was disabled, and, as soon as he was got up, my L^d run him into ye belly'.[1] Two months later, in January of 1678, Pembroke was sent to the Tower for 'Blasphemy, abuse of ye celebration of ye Sacrament of ye Lord's Supper, & other his Mis-demeanours (altogether unfitt to be named) towards ye Ld North's Chaplain & others'.[2] This is the only occasion on record on which Pembroke was accused of an offence of this kind, but the incident is part of a consistent pattern of coarse and aggressive behaviour. On the 30th Pembroke was released after the Lords had decided that the sworn testimony of a commoner was not sufficient to establish the guilt of a peer.

Just four days later he was in trouble again. On Sunday, 3 February, two men stopped in at Long's Tavern in the Haymarket for a drink. Pembroke was there before them and invited the newcomers to join him. After a time he and one of the visitors, a man named Henry Goring, fell to words. Pembroke's friends separated the two men and put Goring out of the room, whereupon his companion, one Nathaniel Cony, raised his voice in protest. Pembroke at once became enraged. He struck Cony in the face with such violence that he fell unconscious to the floor, where Pembroke kicked and stamped on him. A few days later Cony died.[3]

Before the issue could be brought to trial, another complaint against Pembroke was submitted to the House of Lords. On 5 February one Phillip Ricaut appeared at the bar of the upper house and stated that while he was taking leave of a friend in the Strand the previous Saturday, the Earl of Pembroke had come up to him and without provocation struck him with his fist in the eye, knocking him down in the roadway and falling on him 'with

[1] Charles Hatton to Christopher Hatton, 27 Nov. [16]77, *Correspondence of the Family of Hatton*, edited by Edward Maunde Thompson for the Camden Society (2 vols., London, 1878), i. 159.

[2] W[illia]m Gr[iffith], 'Memorables, Ecclesiastical & Civil, observed in ye year 1678', Lambeth Palace MS. 942.31, 3 Jan. 1678. See also *Lords' Journals*, 28 Jan. 1678, where it is recorded (xiii. 131) that Pembroke had been committed to the Tower 'for uttering such horrid and blasphemous Words, and other Actions proved upon Oath, as are not fit to be repeated in any Christian Assembly'.

[3] *The Tryal of Philip Earl of Pembroke and Montgomery* (London, 1679).

such Violence, that he almost stifled him with his Gripes in the Dirt'.[1] The Lords ordered that Pembroke be bound over in the amount of £2,000 to keep the peace for the space of a year. Meanwhile, proceedings were under way to bring him to trial for the murder of Nathaniel Cony. On 19 March the Lord Chancellor reported that a Grand Jury had found a true bill. The record of their findings was returned the same day by writ of *certiorari* and a day appointed for the trial. On 4 April Pembroke was duly tried by his peers in Westminster Hall. He was found guilty of manslaughter, whereupon he claimed benefit of clergy under the statute of 1 Edward VI and was discharged.[2]

Six months later Godfrey was found dead on Primrose Hill, his body bruised and beaten about the head and chest. That November, less than a month after Godfrey was buried, there was a new complaint against Pembroke. The Earl of Dorset told the House of Lords that on the previous Wednesday Pembroke had invited him to meet him at Lockett's, the same house in which Vaughan had been wounded in a quarrel the year before. As soon as Dorset appeared at Lockett's, Pembroke cried out that he had done him an injury and attacked him with his fists. He drew on Dorset, but before he could do worse the two men were parted by their servants. The next day Pembroke offered to apologize and was allowed to return to his estate at Wilton.[3]

It was nearly two years before Pembroke was heard of again. Then, one night in August of 1680 he was returning to London in a hackney coach. At Turnham Green the coach was challenged by the watch. Pembroke and his companions, who were thoroughly drunk, got out of the coach with swords drawn and advanced on the watchmen. In the ensuing scuffle two or three of the watch were wounded and one of them, a man named William Smeeth, later died of his wounds.[4] Pembroke could not claim benefit of

---

[1] *Lords' Journals*, 5 Feb. 1678 (xiii. 139).

[2] Ibid., 2, 6, 19, 22, 23, 26, 27 Mar., 4 Apr. 1678.

[3] Ibid., 27 Nov. 1678 (xiii. 384).

[4] See *Great and Bloody News, from Turnham-Green* (London, 1680) and *A True and Sad Relation Of Two Wicked and Bloody Murthers* (London, 1680). These two accounts are in essential agreement, though there are differences in detail. The author of the second pamphlet says that two other members of the watch also died of their wounds, but Pembroke's pardon mentions Smeeth alone. To quiet the town, some of Pembroke's friends got out what they called *An Impartial Account of the Misfortune That lately happened to . . .*

clergy a second time and his friends in the upper house were forced to take special pains to protect him from the penalties provided by the law for murderers. Twenty-four of the Lords, including the Duke of Monmouth and the Earl of Shaftesbury, signed a petition addressed to the King, asking that Pembroke be granted a pardon on the grounds that he had killed Smeeth 'upon a suddain Affray which by a vigorous construcion of Law may be murder'. The Lords pointed out that Smeeth's widow had given the Earl a release, whether at Pembroke's expense or at that of his friends we do not know. In any case, the pardon was granted under date of 10 June 1681 and on 4 July Pembroke was confirmed in possession of his estates, which on conviction would have been forfeit to the Crown.[1] Pembroke had voted against the Duke of York in the House of Lords and was no favourite with the King,[2] but he had married the sister of the Duchess of Portsmouth, and that no doubt stood him in good stead. Furthermore, he was on friendly terms with a number of the Whig Lords whom Charles could ill afford, despite the lavish promises of the King of France, to displease.

This was the man with whom Sir Edmund Godfrey was re-

Philip Earl of Pembroke (London, 1680). Their *Impartial Account* has little to say for Pembroke, however, except that Smeeth was insolent in his manner —he had been drinking (like Pembroke) and probably was. The author goes out of his way to deny a rumour then current that this was Pembroke's twenty-sixth killing. He insists—as if to show his lordship's singular fore-bearance—that Pembroke had killed only one man before. See also [B.R.], *Great News from Saxony: or, A New and Strange Relation Of the Mighty Giant Koorbmep* (London, 1680). John Aubrey tells of Pembroke's life at Wilton, where he kept '52 Mastives and 30 Grey-hounds, some Beares, and a Lyon, and a matter of 60 fellowes more bestiall then they' (*Brief Lives*, edited by Oliver Lawson Dick (London, 1960), p. 146).

[1] The original of the petition is in the Record Office, S.P. 29.415, piece no. 195. A draft pardon endorsed by Sir Robert Sawyer, the Attorney General, 'if his Majestye please to grant the Earles pardon upon the Petition of the said Peers this draught may passe', is in S.P. 29.415, piece no. 196. The patents of 10 June and 4 July 1681 are in C.66.3222, no. 1 and C.66.3223, no. 3.

[2] On 24 Dec. [1678], Lord Herbert wrote to his father, the Marquis of Worcester, to say that 'My Aunt Powis . . . tells me that my Lord Pembroke has so displeased the King by voting against the Prince after he had promised to vote for him, that it is impossible for him now to get the Custos Rotu-lorum's place' (H.M.C. Twelfth Report, Appendix, Part IX (Beaufort MSS.), p. 80).

quired to deal in the spring of 1678. For it was Godfrey who acted as foreman of the Grand Jury appointed to consider the indictment of the Earl of Pembroke for the murder of Nathaniel Cony.[1] Godfrey was a brave and conscientious magistrate who had already shown that he was not afraid of incurring the displeasure of the King himself in the performance of his duties. Nor did he shrink on this occasion from the displeasure of a peer. The Grand Jury returned a true bill and Pembroke was committed for trial in the House of Lords. It is significant that during the nine years of Pembroke's majority—a period during which he engaged in several quarrels, wounding a number of men and killing two—the Earl was brought to trial only once, and that at the instance of Sir Edmund Godfrey. Nor is there any reason to suppose that this fact was lost on either of the two men themselves. Godfrey for his part went abroad for several months and returned to England only a short time before Oates came to him with his depositions concerning a conspiracy against the life of the King.[2]

Oates first appeared before Godfrey on 6 September; on the 28th he appeared before him again and on the same day was examined by the council. Godfrey took no action on the strength of Oates's depositions, presumably because, having some acquaintance with Edward Coleman, he knew that Oates was lying. He told friends that 'Otes *is* Sworn, *and is* Perjur'd'.[3] None the less, he was extremely anxious lest he should come under suspicion for failing to take action against the several persons named in the depositions. Burnet noticed that he had grown 'apprehensive and reserved' and one day when they met in the street Godfrey said he was afraid of being 'knocked on the head'.[4] A few weeks later,

[1] The other members were Reginald Forster, William Bowles, Charles Pitfield, Thomas Robinson, Humfrey Wirley, James Dewy, William Hempson, and Thomas Harriott.

[2] Richard Tuke says that 'About the Year 1678. Having been by the constant Fatigues and Labours of his Business, reduced to a sickliness of Body, and Distempers growing upon him, he was advised by the *Phisicians* to go to *Montpellier* in *France*'. He took their advice and continued in France for some months. It was, Tuke goes on, 'not long after his return' that the Plot was discovered (*Memoires of the Life and Death of Sir Edmondbury Godfrey* (London, 1682), pp. 52, 53). Godfrey was certainly in London in February and March, while the Grand Jury was sitting, and if he was abroad for a period of several months shortly before Oates's story broke in September, he must have left town soon after Pembroke stood trial on 4 April.

[3] L'Estrange, iii. 187. [4] *History of his own Time*, i. 284.

when William Staley the goldsmith was indicted for treason,
Burnet, who knew the character of the principal witness for the
Crown, approached a number of the Lords in the hope of saving
the prisoner's life. Lord Hollis and Lord Halifax were willing to
listen, but 'the earl of Shaftesbury could not bear the discourse.
He said, we must support the evidence, and that all those who
undermined the credit of the witnesses were to be looked on as
public enemies.'[1] Was it this that Godfrey had feared: to be
looked on as an enemy of the people?[2]

Shortly before he left his house for the last time on Saturday
morning, 12 October, Godfrey was handed a message. He went
out soon after, no doubt intending to answer the message in
person, and was never heard from again. When his body was
discovered five days later, he appeared to have been strangled and
beaten to death. He had been wounded twice: there was 'a cross
broad wound in his Breast' as well as a clean thrust through the
heart and body, which had been pierced by his own sword. But
there was no bleeding from either wound, so it was evident that
Godfrey had not taken his own life.[3] Though there had been rain
and hail the night before, it was noticed by everyone present that
Godfrey's clothing was dry and his shoes perfectly clean. One
witness observed that the shoes had 'Seeds sticking to them, as if

---

[1] History of his own Time, pp. 287–8.

[2] According to L'Estrange, he told Mary Gibbon 'he was to be Hang'd,
for not discovering the Plot against his Majesty' (iii. 322). Oates, naturally
enough, told a different story. He testified during the trial of Green, Berry,
and Hill that Godfrey had told him a few days before his disappearance that
he had been threatened by 'several popish lords' for what he had done.
In point of fact, Godfrey had done nothing whatever to displease the
Catholics, and Oates came close to admitting as much when he said that
'others, who were well inclined to have the discovery made, did think that
he had not been quick enough in the prosecution, but had been too remiss,
and did threaten him, that they would complain to the parliament' (State
Trials, vii. 167).

[3] From L'Estrange's day to our own, those who wished to clear the
Catholics of suspicion have argued that Godfrey committed suicide. The
most effective exponent of this idea was Alfred Marks (Who Killed Sir Edmund
Berry Godfrey? (London, 1905)), who suggested that the bruises on Godfrey's
chest and face were the result of post-mortem hypostasis and the ring about
his neck nothing more than the mark of his collar cutting into the swollen
tissue. But such a theory wholly fails to account for the absence of bleeding
from the open wound, which can be explained only on the assumption that
the wound was made after Godfrey had died from other causes.

he had been in a Hay-mow'.[1] There were fresh marks of a cart in the soft ground and 'hay also was found scattered upon ye grass, with which they had either fed ye Cart-horse, or hid his Body in carrying it thither'.[2] If Godfrey had in fact walked from his house in Hartshorn Lane to Leicester Fields, where Pembroke lived, the previous Saturday (the streets were still dry then), if he had met his end after a savage beating, like Nathaniel Cony (who also was kicked and bruised about the face and chest), what more natural for his murderer, on recovering his senses, than to have his body taken away in a haycart to the edge of town and, after being skewered with his own sword to give the appearance of suicide, left lying in a ditch half concealed by the shrubbery?

However that may be, there was nothing more natural for a man like Shaftesbury, always ready to improve on an occasion to turn the passions of those less cool and less intelligent than himself to his own advantage, than to see in the brutal and mysterious killing of Godfrey a brilliant opportunity to raise the cry of Popery.

III

The death of Godfrey extinguished all doubts in the popular mind. Almost overnight it changed the political complexion of England. Within a few months general elections—the first since the Restoration—returned a Whig majority in the House of Commons. Shaftesbury was named Lord President of the Privy Council. The Exclusion Bill, which was the immediate objective of Shaftesbury and his party, was given first and second readings by the Commons in May. Parliament was prorogued, however, before the end of the month and dissolved a few weeks later. New elections in the fall strengthened the Whig position still further, but Parliament was not allowed to meet for more than a year. Meanwhile, Sir George Wakeman was acquitted, in July, on a charge of conspiring to poison the King. Six months later Sir Thomas Gascoigne, a man of eighty-five and too deaf to hear the evidence brought against him, was acquitted on a similar charge.

---

[1] *The Tryall of Nathanael Thompson, John Farewell, William Pain* (London: William Mason, 1682), p. 5. See also *The Tryall of Nathaniel Thompson, William Pain, and John Farwell* (London: Thomas Simmons, 1682), p. 21.

[2] Lambeth Palace MS. 942.30, p. 26.

A new incident was needed to arouse public opinion, inflame the popular imagination, and force the hand of the King.

An unusual opportunity presented itself when Justice Arnold came up to London in April of 1680 to appear before the council. Arnold (according to his own testimony) was on his way to the Devil Tavern between 10 and 11 o'clock on the evening of 15 April, when after crossing Bell Yard he was assaulted by three men just as he turned into Jackanapes Lane. They threw a cloak over his head and then attacked him with their swords. He was wearing a whalebone bodice for fear of the Papists, and he heard one of them say, 'Damme, he has armour on, cut his throat.' Before they could accomplish their purpose, however,—but not before they had given him a wound seven inches deep between his belly and his left pap, two wounds on his breast and two in his left arm —a candle was lighted in a house near by and a boy appeared with a link. Arnold cried out and his assailants ran off crying, 'Now, you dog, pray for . . . the soul of Captain Evans.'[1] Evans had been executed as a priest at Cardiff and the ruffians' taunt was taken to show that the magistrate had been set upon by Papists. Arnold had from the outset thrown himself eagerly into the task of rounding up and prosecuting Catholics. The previous summer he had been 'very active' in Gloucester and seized 'a vast quantity of Popish trinkets' of no small value.[2] The Earl of Ailesbury spoke of him with undisguised contempt as a man of 'violent and virulent temper, and no doubt a pensioner to the contriver of this plot, ever snarling against the ministry'.[3] He was certainly well known to Shaftesbury, with whom on more than one occasion he had worked over the evidence supplied by the informers.[4] Not long before, he had hounded David Lewis to his death for having exercised the functions of a priest of the Church of Rome, contrary to the statute of 27 Elizabeth I. Lewis was sentenced to be hanged and quartered. After being sentenced he was taken to London, where he was examined by Oates, Bedloe, Dugdale, and

[1] *State Trials*, vii, cols. 1130, 1137. The complete record of the trial is given in cols. 1129–62.

[2] Fitzherbert MSS., p. 18.

[3] *Memoirs of Thomas, Earl of Ailesbury*, i. 30.

[4] See 'Journals of Edmund Warcup', pp. 250, 252. It was Arnold who was to bring William Lewis to the bar of the House of Commons in November of 1680. Lewis told the members of a plot to set the fleet on fire and murder the Earl of Shaftesbury. See above, p. 38, n. 2.

Prance and offered his life on condition that he 'make some discovery of the plot'. When he professed his ignorance of the Plot and insisted that he was no conspirator but a priest—'and I bless the hour in which I was first called both unto faith and function'— he was returned to Uske, where he was executed a few weeks later.[1] Having failed to make effective use of the proceedings against Lewis, the authorities decided to do what they could with Arnold.

Arnold, as it turned out, was to have a rare opportunity of doing his friends a favour. On 9 July 1680—just as the public anger was cooling on the eve of the forthcoming trial of Lord Stafford—an Irish Papist named Giles was brought to trial at the Old Bailey for the attempted murder of the magistrate in Jackanapes Lane. He was directly accused by Arnold, who claimed to have recognized the prisoner by the light of the link. Giles produced witnesses to prove that in fact he spent the whole evening at the King's Arms. One of these, the chambermaid at the inn, testified that Giles went to bed between 10 and 11 o'clock, so he could not have been at that very time in Jackanapes Lane. Unfortunately for Giles, however, another witness for the defence, a man named Edward James, testified that he spent the whole evening from 9 until 12 with the prisoner in the kitchen. The discrepancy was accounted for inadvertently by one of the witnesses for the Crown. William Richmond first told the court a gaudy tale of how Giles had dipped his handkerchief in David Lewis's blood and then, having come to town that April, had asked where he might buy a good rapier—for Papists in those days were given to revealing their bloody intentions to anyone who would listen. He then explained that the chambermaid could not have seen Giles to bed soon after 10 because at that very time he, Richmond, was making love to her in Giles's own room. Presumably the maid put forward the hour at which she had seen Giles to bed because she wanted to avoid awkward inquiries as to what she had been doing earlier in the evening. But the court thought otherwise. Sir George Jeffreys told the jury that the evidence given by James and the maid was not to be believed, and the jurymen did their part by returning a verdict of guilty. Giles was sentenced to stand three times in the pillory and to pay a fine of £500.

[1] *State Trials*, vii. 259, 258.

Not everyone was satisfied with the case against Giles. Ailesbury said quite plainly that Arnold cut his own throat and then accused Giles to raise the credit of the Plot. With the death of Sir Edmund Godfrey still fresh in his mind, he remarked, 'you find one magistrate murdered by God knows who, and another laid hands on himself to carry on these base designs, and by these wicked artifices, the whole kingdom, I mean the foolish and unthinking part, believed all as gospel'.[1] The circumstances were investigated by the authorities and a minute of their findings is still extant. Part of this minute has been printed by Pollock.[2] The author obviously suspects that Giles was innocent. He makes note of the fact that though the lane was 'fouler at That time, then Ordinary', Arnold was found 'with a white Hatt upon his Head, no Dirt upon it, and his Cloths only Dirty, where he satt'. He points out that none of the neighbours saw anyone near Arnold, though there were link boys within a few yards of him and a woman who, as soon as he cried out, 'held a Candle from a window just over him'. If he was muffled with a cloak, 'how could he hear what the Ruffians sayd?' And if not, why could they not 'have stab'd the Knife into his Throte' or 'thrust him into his Belly, when they found the Sword would not enter his Bodyes [bodice]'? But the most telling part of the minute is contained in the last two paragraphs, which are omitted in Pollock's transcription. Since this remarkable passage does not appear to have been printed before, it is given here in full:

There's (one Ladd) a Milliner over against the Devill-Tavern in Fleetstreet [where Arnold said he was going when he was set upon], that observed three men wayting all that day over against the Temple-lane, which he took for Sergeants, till upon This Fact they became suspected for ye Assassins. This Milliner has described their Persons and Habitts, and still as any body is taken up, he is shew'd to the Milliner, to see if he knows him.

It is propounded that the Sheriffs of London may summon overnight all their Officers of that Quality to appear next morning; and that the Milliner may take a view of them, and declare upon Oath if he remembers any of those Officers to be the Persons. Now if it shall appear that these three men were City-Officers, and that they wayted There that day, upon their Duty; the Milliners Evidence will be then layd aside:

[1] *Memoirs of Thomas, Earl of Ailesbury*, i. 30, 31.
[2] Pollock prints what he calls the 'most important portion' of the minute, pp. 396–7. The original is in the Record Office, S.P. 29.413, piece no. 107.

whereas otherwise Honest men may be brought into great Scandall and Inconvenience, by beeing taken up, meerly for the Resemblance of those Persons.

It is very hard to believe that the three men who waited all that day for Arnold were constables. Certainly there were no constables near by when the assault took place, for Arnold had to be rescued by the link boys and the woman with a candle. Yet it is significant that unknown persons were observed to be waiting there and that they were three in number—for Arnold, who spoke of three ruffians, is unlikely to have known of Ladd and his evidence. These three men were in all probability the three men spoken of by Arnold. But who were they? Was Giles one of them? Clearly not, for each suspect was shown to the milliner, 'to see if he knows him'. Obviously, Ladd did not recognize Giles as one of the three, for if he had he would have been called as a witness against him. He did not recognize Giles and that is why his evidence was suppressed. Who then can the three strangers have been but the three ruffians who were set on to commit the assault on Arnold as part of a scheme to arouse public opinion by implicating some known Papist like Giles?

The trial of Giles came when it was badly needed and did a good deal to sustain popular excitement. At the end of the year Lord Stafford was found guilty of high treason and on 31 December he was executed. The following May Oliver Plunket was brought to trial at the King's Bench before Sir Francis Pemberton, who had taken Scroggs's place on the bench soon after the latter had imprudently allowed a jury to acquit Sir George Wakeman of conspiring to poison the King; Plunket was convicted and sentenced on 15 June and two weeks later he was executed. By that time, however, the Popish Plot had run its course. When Parliament finally did meet in October of 1680, the second Exclusion Bill was quickly passed through all three readings in the House of Commons, but was defeated in the Lords. Parliament was prorogued once again in January and later dissolved. A third Whig Parliament was elected and summoned to Oxford in March of 1681. But by that time Charles had completed arrangements with Louis XIV that made it possible for him to govern without Parliament, and the new session was dissolved after sitting for only a few days. Dissolution marked the end of Shaftesbury's influence in the country and the failure of his policies.

This sordid story of perjury, deception, and judicial murder would perhaps hardly be worth the telling if the Popish Plot had not become part of English folklore. For in the long run history is made not by facts but by what men think of them. And if Shaftesbury failed to exclude the Duke of York from the succession or to shift the balance of power from the King to the Houses of Parliament, as he had hoped, he succeeded in capturing the imagination of his own and later generations.

For more than two centuries memories of the Popish Plot served to nourish the pride of freeborn Englishmen, suspicious as they were of the Italian sun, the Latin temper and, at the centre of it all, the Church of Rome. Later historians might question the character of Titus Oates, and even of Bedloe, Prance, Dugdale, Lewis, and the rest; they might doubt the truth of many of their disclosures; their latent sense of guilt might (and often did) find an outlet in lavish execration of Sir William Scroggs, a judge of uncommon intelligence and evident sincerity, who for a time was deceived (like most of his contemporaries) by the informers and who, as soon as he began to see the truth, was relieved of his position on the bench. But few were prepared to recognize the Plot for what it was. There were exceptions. In his own day Burnet spoke of the informers as men driven by hatred and greed and led on by the Earl of Shaftesbury for the sake of political advantage. The King, perhaps because he was more familiar than most with the real state of relations between England and France, to say nothing of his own religious opinions, was never taken in. 'Being at the Duchess of Portsmouth's' one day late in 1680, Sir John Reresby found Charles 'very free in his discourse concerning the witnesses of the Popish Plot, making it clearly appear that several things which they gave in evidence were not only improbable, but impossible.'[1] Sir John Dalrymple bluntly asserted that the Whig leader 'framed the fiction of the popish plot in the year 1678, in order to bury the Duke, and perhaps the King, under the weight of the national fear and hatred of popery'. The Earl of Ailesbury was no less emphatic. 'The inventer of this sham plot', he recalled, 'studied how to

---

[1] *Memoirs of Sir John Reresby*, p. 191. See also p. 212. The King had the advantage also of knowing (p. 325) that the Jesuit congregation had been held at St. James's Palace and not at the White Horse, so it was clear to him from the beginning that Oates's story was a fabrication.

produce witnesses to swear to all he desired, and had a troop of ragamuffins at his elbow', by whose evidence he achieved his purpose.[1]

But men like Burnet and Reresby, Dalrymple and Ailesbury did not speak for their own or later generations. As recently as 1903 John Pollock published a full-dress study of the Plot purporting to prove the essential truth of Oates's story. As for Sir Edmund Godfrey, Pollock surmises that he had learned of the meeting at St. James's Palace and was murdered by the Jesuits for fear he would reveal the secret and embarrass the Duke of York. Though critics like Gerard and Muddiman pointed out some of the more disturbing of Pollock's errors and omissions, no attempt has yet been made to reopen the question and deal with it at length from a new and more meaningful point of view.[2] But as each new line of inquiry is followed up, however tentatively, it leads in the same direction. It is clear by now that the Popish Plot needs to be studied afresh, not for what it was supposed to be but for what it was, that is, a chapter in the history of the country party. Some things will never be known. Oates kept no record of his dealings with the opposition leaders, so no one can now say which of his accusations were his own and which were suggested to him by others. Everything we know of him suggests that he would have been a hard man to govern. His sense of his own importance grew and so did his evidence, which lost much of its credibility in the process. Bedloe and Prance appear to have been more amenable, though neither was careful to make his testimony concerning the murder of Godfrey wholly consistent with the testimony given by the other or with the evidence received at the inquest. But other things can be known, and that in some detail. It is possible to say without hesitation that the informers were hired; we know in most cases who hired them and in some cases how much they were paid. We know the kind of evidence that was wanted and the methods used to get it. We know what use was made of the evidence. In dealing with the central question of Godfrey's

[1] *Memoirs of Thomas, Earl of Ailesbury*, i. 29.

[2] This was written before the appearance in 1968 of K. H. D. Haley's new biography of Shaftesbury. Haley gives a sensible (if summary) account of the Plot, but though he admits that Shaftesbury was deeply involved he is not prepared to assess his responsibility or to consider the evidence in detail. Such an assessment has still to be made—and needs to be made.

murder, it is helpful to know that Godfrey was not the only magistrate said to have been set upon by Papists. There were several. One magistrate who was supposed to have been murdered by the Catholics was found alive and well the next day. Another was set upon in truth, but surviving evidence makes it unlikely that the prisoner convicted of the offence was in fact guilty of anything worse than being a Papist. As for Godfrey, we can at least say who did—and who did not—have an interest in his death, and who had the desire and the will to accomplish it. If we can never answer certain questions we can ask, and we can answer, others. We can begin to understand the real purpose and effects of the Popish Plot and we can see more clearly how—and at what cost—the Plot was made to serve the essential interests of a party.

4

SYMPATHY *V.* JUDGEMENT IN ROXANA'S FIRST LIAISON

By G. A. STARR

Roxana really begins with the story of a seduction, but this is preceded by the story of a disastrous marriage. In its humour and pathos alike, the account of Roxana's marriage to a fool has a biting grimness that resonates through her subsequent adventures : the opening note of poverty will give her later moments of brilliance and gaiety an undertone of anxiety, just as early abandonment and isolation will give her warmest attachments an air of transience.[1] Dramatic in themselves, these initial scenes introduce tonal and thematic patterns that persist throughout the book, yet their primary function, in my opinion, is to elicit our sympathy in preparation for later scenes that will put it to a severe test. However critical of Roxana he eventually induces us to become, Defoe's strategy is initially to gain her the strongest possible hold on our affection. Although at times he will appear to regard her as akin to Bunyan's Mr. Badman—a reprobate to be consigned to the Devil—he wisely avoids alienating us from her at the outset. If revulsion sets in too soon (or ever dominates our response completely), we are liable to stop reading, or at best read on with self-righteous detachment. *The Life and Death of Mr. Badman* illustrates the dangers of allowing readers to dissociate themselves even from thoroughgoing villains; Milton had known better, and so does Defoe.

The tale of a fortunate mistress is therefore ushered in with the preliminary tale of an unfortunate wife. Few scenes in Defoe's fiction are more graphic than the one in which Roxana, abandoned with five children and penniless, is discovered 'sitting on the Ground, with a great Heap of old Rags, Linnen, and other things

[1] A useful discussion of the 'fool husband' is to be found in Spiro Peterson, 'The Matrimonial Theme of Defoe's *Roxana*', *PMLA* lxx (1955), 166–91, esp. pp. 168–73.

about me, looking them over, to see if I had any thing among them
that would Sell or Pawn for a little Money, and had been crying
ready to burst myself, to think what I should do next'.[1] She is
visited by two of her husband's relatives, who 'when they saw . . .
how I look'd . . . and what a Condition I was in . . . sat down like
Job's three Comforters, and . . . cry'd as fast, and as heartily as I
did'.[2] We are led to commiserate by example, and the allusion to
Job helps to suggest both Roxana's innocence and her misery.
At the same time, it offers the first hint that her afflictions, like
Job's, herald a trial of constancy: painful in themselves, they are
still more malign in that they bring on temptation and break down
the power to resist it. Roxana's distress not only compels our
sympathy for a helpless victim of circumstances, but serves as a
necessary prelude—psychological as well as ethical—to the crucial
scenes that follow between her and her landlord.

In the *Review* we find a preliminary sketch of Roxana literally
floored with woe, but for the idea that probably inspired the first
forty pages of the book, we must turn to the *Athenian Mercury*.
The following case of conscience anticipates—in bare outline, it
is true, but with only minor variations of detail—Roxana's predicament up to the time she becomes the mistress of her landlord:

---

[1] *Roxana*, ed. Jane Jack (London, 1964), p. 17; all subsequent references
are to this edition. The 44th *Spectator* reports that an author 'who is fully
determin'd to break the most obdurate Hearts, has a Tragedy by him, where
the first person that appears on the Stage, is an afflicted Widow in her Mourn-
ing-Weeds, with half a Dozen fatherless Children attending her, like those
that usually hang about the Figure of Charity' (20 Apr. 1711; on the use of
children for pathetic effects in the drama of the period see Eric Rothstein,
Restoration Tragedy: Form and the Process of Change (Madison, 1967), pp. 153–4).

[2] *Roxana*, p. 17. In the *Review* Defoe had told the similar story of
a Poor Woman with three Children, her Husband gone from her to Sea, and whether
Alive or Dead, she knows not, absolutely without Employment, uncapable of
Labour, without Friends, without Help, and without Bread . . . Let any Father of
Children judge of this Case—Let them imagine they see the Poor Woman . . . sitting
on the Floor in Despair, and in all the Extremities of an Ungovern'd Rage, tearing
her Hair from her Head, and three little Innocent Babes crying round her for Bread;
let them consider her a Woman well Bred, well Taught, but Helpless and Friendless;
for my part, the Distress of it confounds my Pen (*Defoe's Review*, facsimile, ed.
Arthur W. Secord, 22 vols. (N.Y., 1938), i. 418).

Defoe concludes that 'God Almighty, whose Pity and Compassion is Infinite and Unbounded, . . . has made these Objects to Try the Temper and
Compassions of all his Creatures'; and with the same object of evoking compassion, the scene is recreated in *Roxana*.

*I'm a Gentlewoman of a small Fortune, and Married to a Man who . . .
left me with a Charge of Children, and went to another Country, without
making the least Provision either for them or me—Nor will his Friends look
on us, and I've been already very chargeable and troublesome to my own, who
are now grown as Cold as his: A Gentleman now Importunes me very much
to be his Mistress, who I know Loves me passionately, and will provide for me
and them. I desire your Advice what I were best do, Whether I must lay my
Children to the Parish; for Begging won't maintain us, and Stealing is as bad
as Whoring? Or how I ought to behave my self for I can find no Means, but either
to yield to this Temptation; or see my Children starve? I know I ought not to do
the least Evil that Good may come of it; but yet of two Evils, we must chuse the
least: An Answer to this would both oblige and quiet, your, &c.*[1]

Before examining Defoe's adaptation of it in *Roxana*, several
features of this query deserve brief comment. The writer is not
intent on finding support for a course she has already determined
on, but seems genuinely perplexed over the decision she faces; the
choice is not simply between good and evil, but between alterna-
tives that both dismay her; and there is no attempt to disguise
(from herself or from the Athenian Society) the moral implications
of granting the gentleman's suit. As we shall see, Roxana largely
preserves the same moral awareness in her dealings with her landlord, and although it later gives way to 'Lethargick' insensibility,
its presence at the outset is very important in shaping our attitude
towards her.[2]

---

[1] [John Dunton], *The Athenian Oracle: Being an Entire Collection of all the
Valuable Questions and Answers in the Old Athenian Mercuries* (2nd edn., London,
1706), iii. 350. For Defoe's debt to this journal see my article 'From Casuistry
to Fiction: the Importance of the *Athenian Mercury*', *JHI* xxviii (1967), 17–32.
On the topics of choosing a lesser evil to prevent a greater, and of doing evil
that good may come of it, see *Clarissa* (Oxford, 1930), ii. 262, 270.

[2] It may be helpful to show, by way of contrast, the kinds of obtuseness
and evasiveness which Roxana and her prototype in the *Athenian Mercury*
might have brought to their predicament. In Defoe's *Review*, for instance, a
correspondent informs the Scandal Club:

*I am a Young Woman, who have been highly Educated, and so Tenderly brought up by my
Parents, that since their Decease, with the Misfortune of a Bad Husband, who has left me, I
am altogether incapable of getting my Livelihood; and consequently am reduced to great
Streights: Now here lies the Case; I have Two Admirers, who equally promise to Assist me,
and Court me to keep them Company (I hope not Uncivilly.) The first is a Young Man that
I did truly Love before Marriage; the other a Person, whose Love is the firmest of the Two;
and (I am certain) would do the most for me; but then, on the other hand, I don't Affect him
with that Veneration as I do the former. Your Advice would be very acceptable in this case;
Whether I should please my self, in Obliging the former, without much Profit, (for I fear he'll
be but an Ordinary Benefactor;) or, reject him for the sake of the latter, of whom I have*

When the landlord first declares his 'more than ordinary Respect' for Roxana, and his intention to relieve her distresses, he insists at once 'I have no ill Design', claims that he is acting 'in meer Kindness', and alludes again in the same breath to 'so honest a Design as mine is' (26–7). But Defoe implies, as he had twenty years earlier in the *Review*, that it is naïve to suppose that a man can confer '*Considerable Favours*' on a young woman in an altogether '*Innocent way of Kindness*'. The landlord's protestations and his vocabulary of platonic courtliness arouse our suspicions, and the ensuing dialogues between Roxana and her maid Amy reinforce them.[1] 'I warrant you, Madam', Amy loses no time in suggesting, 'he'll ask you a Favour by and by.' 'Nay,' says Roxana, 'that's a hard thing too, that we should judge a Man to be wicked because he's charitable; and vicious because he's kind.' But Amy replies that 'there's abundance of Charity begins in that Vice, and he is not so unacquainted with things, as not to know, that Poverty is the strongest Incentive; a Temptation, against which no Virtue is powerful enough to stand out' (27–8). And within a few sentences Roxana is exclaiming, 'What, consent to lye with him for Bread?' Male pretensions and female ingenuousness thus give way, with astonishing but characteristic speed, before Amy's sprightly cynicism.

In his handling of Amy, Defoe puts to brilliant use the convention of the maid-confidante. In this scene Amy articulates and defends the position that Roxana ought to become her landlord's mistress. If Roxana herself were to propose such arguments, we might be impressed by her hard-headed practicality, but scarcely by her modesty or 'Virtue'; on the other hand, by making Amy

received *Considerable Favours, and that in an Innocent way of Kindness, which I can't promise my self the like from the other?* (*Review*, ii. 70–1).
This woman's situation initially resembles Roxana's, but it soon appears that she has no intention whatever of remaining in '*great Streights*', and only wonders which man to choose: her '*Case*' ignores (and her language of admirers and benefactors, civility and kindness, actually obscures) the moral issue involved.

    [1] Our suspicions might also be aroused by the memory of similar situations in the *Athenian Mercury*—e.g. that of '*A Gentlewoman that has a Husband who uses her* barbarously, . . . *having the Offer of a single Gentleman that will* maintain *her very well; Whether it be any* Sin to accept of his Kindness?' In response, the Athenian Society says that 'if by the *accepting his kindness*, be meant being *kind* to him again, then the Case is clear; and why all this fine clean Language to wrap up that broad Word WHORE?' (*Athenian Oracle*, i. 470).

their vigorous advocate, and by making Roxana just as vigorously repudiate them, Defoe can give the arguments their full force without the least jeopardy to his heroine. Although Amy concedes, for example, that 'it would not be Lawful for any thing else, but for Bread', she also exclaims, 'why nobody can starve, there's no bearing that, I'm sure', and reasons that 'Honesty is out of the Question, when Starving is the Case'. Roxana nevertheless insists 'I'd starve first', 'I'd die before I would consent', and concludes by observing, 'Hitherto I had not only preserv'd the Virtue itself, but the virtuous Inclination and Resolution; and had I kept myself there, I had been happy, tho' I had perish'd of meer Hunger; for, without question, a Woman ought rather to die, than to prostitute her Virtue and Honour, let the Temptation be what it will' (28, 29). Emphatic as this may be, it has been effectually forestalled by the preceding dialogue: Roxana may assert that her lofty principle is 'without question', but this is precisely what Amy has called in question. Neither author nor heroine need endorse Amy's arguments for them to do their work.

Variations on the same process mark the further dialogues between Roxana and both her landlord and her maid. We are given an elaborate series of extenuations for the deed she is about to commit, but because she does not plead on her own behalf, and is suitably shocked by the pleas that others provide for her, Roxana does not strike us as someone intent on rationalizing imminent mischief. The next time they meet, for instance, the landlord addresses her in the following style: 'Well, *Widow, says he*, so he call'd me, and so indeed I was in the worst Sence that desolate Word cou'd be us'd in . . .' (30). How innocuously this plea—for a plea it is—is introduced and justified! In the same spirit, Moll Flanders speaks of herself as 'a widow bewitched', with 'a husband and no husband', yet this line of defence is stronger in *Roxana*, simply because the heroine can let others suggest and expound it for her rather than urge it herself. 'He calls you Widow', Amy explains to Roxana, 'and such, indeed, you are; for as my Master has left you so many Years, he is dead to be sure; at least, he is dead to you; he is no Husband, you are, and ought to be free to marry who you will; . . . and tho' you cannot bring the Laws of the Land to join you together, yet . . . you may certainly take one another fairly' (36–7). The striking thing here is not that Amy is well versed in natural law, nor is it strange that Roxana refuses to be convinced. The inherent validity of Amy's argument matters almost as little as its source: the point is that Roxana gains our esteem whatever we make of it. Do we find it plausible? In that case Roxana is clearly its beneficiary, the more so for not having contrived it herself; we do not suspect her of manipulating our sympathies, since she is merely reporting Amy's opinion, from which she emphatically dissociates herself. Or do we find it specious? If so, Roxana anticipates us by labelling it 'Cant', 'Stuff', and 'Nonsense', and thus deflects our severity away from herself, towards her 'ignorant' and 'impudent Jade' and 'Slut' of a maid, whom she goes so far as to call 'a Viper, and Engine of the Devil' (40, 36, 38).

A similar ambiguity, which works in Roxana's favour however we look at it, marks the landlord's notion of his position. 'His Wife being gone from him, and refuses to lye with him, then he is a single Man again, as much as ever', Amy reports; 'he is of Opinion . . . that he may take another Woman into his Arms, provided he keeps true to the other Woman as a Wife' (37–8). Furthermore, he offers Roxana 'a Contract in Writing, wherein he engag'd himself to me; to cohabit constantly with me; to provide for me in all respects as a Wife'. Finally, he assures her that 'he took me not as a Mistress, but as his Wife', that 'it was clear to him he might lawfully do it, and that I was perfectly at Liberty', and (in a phrase that echoes Moll's words to Jemmy) that 'he had never deceiv'd me, and never would' (42, 43). What are we to make of this? Are we to conclude that 'there can be no question that Roxana was entitled to marry her landlord according to the laws of nature'; that 'this generous man' has 'tried his best in the face of an inhumane system of law'; and that, although Roxana 'upbraids herself for prostituting her virtue', Defoe 'would have exonerated her entirely'?[1] Or are we to conclude, as the Athenian Society had done when presented with the identical case, and as Roxana herself does about this one, that the man's written contract, and his conviction that a wife's misdeeds entitle him to remarry, are empty pretexts for adultery? It seems to me that Defoe deliberately leaves the question open. Few readers can have

---

[1] Maximillian E. Novak, *Defoe and the Nature of Man* (Oxford, 1963), pp. 102, 84; cf. 'Conscious Irony in *Moll Flanders*', *College English* xxvi (1964), 201, where Professor Novak states that Defoe 'regarded desertion as equivalent to divorce'.

given the landlord's brief such wholehearted assent as do Amy and Professor Novak; on the other hand, few readers can have dismissed it as summarily as does Roxana herself, who observes that 'we were to call one another Man and Wife, who, in the Sence of the Laws, both of God and our Country, were no more than two Adulterers, in short, a Whore and a Rogue' (43). What matters is that we find both sides of the argument sufficiently plausible to ensure that, whatever Roxana finally chooses to do, we shall not condemn her. Defoe is not intent on settling decisively the rights and wrongs of the question, but rather on making us see that it is a more complex and ambiguous question than we might have supposed, and that it would therefore be presumptuous of us to judge Roxana harshly.

Still another plea involves the notion of gratitude. 'O,'exclaims Roxana, 'let no Woman slight the Temptation that being generously deliver'd from Trouble, is to any Spirit furnish'd with Gratitude and just Principles' (35). 'By rewarding a person who has rescued her from death', observes Novak, 'she is following the laws of nature impeccably.'[1] Amy thinks so too, but Roxana herself is far more guarded: after initially suggesting (in the sentence just quoted) that the obligation of gratitude sanctions what she is about to do, she transfers the contention to Amy, and dissociates herself from it. Again Defoe skilfully enlists our sympathy for his heroine. If, on the one hand, we are inclined to dismiss the notion that gratitude overrides all sanctions against adultery, Roxana has forestalled our indignation by voicing it so emphatically herself. On the other hand, even if the argument is specious, Roxana's assertion of the fact by no means cancels its rhetorical impact. On the contrary, the gratitude motif remains psychologically effective despite—and even in a sense because of—Roxana's brisk dismissal of it as logically unsound.

If gratitude were Roxana's sole ground for granting the landlord's suit, her position would be shaky, for the plea will not bear very close scrutiny; nor will most of the others, if we stop to examine them. But she does not let us stop to examine them. She prevents this not only by the sheer pace of her narrative, but also by treating them as throwaways herself, dropping or explicitly repudiating each one in turn.[2] We can see this clearly if we turn

---

[1] *Defoe and the Nature of Man*, p. 117.

[2] An example of the 'throwaway' plea is the motif of love. 'I began',

from the question of gratitude to further, and perhaps stronger, points in her defence. I have suggested that an earlier scene, in which Roxana's two comforters discover her on the floor in rags and tears, is designed to prepare us for her later trial of constancy, and more specifically to make us sympathize with whatever she may be driven to do through lack of money and friends. This motif is resumed at a crucial point in her deliberations over the landlord's suit:

> I must do that Justice upon myself, as to say, I did what my own Conscience convinc'd me at the very Time I did it, was horribly unlawful, scandalous, and abominable. But Poverty was my Snare; dreadful Poverty! the Misery I had been in, was great, such as wou'd make the Heart tremble at the Apprehensions of its Return; and I might appeal to any that has had any Experience of the World, whether one so entirely destitute as I was, of all manner of Helps, or Friends, . . . could withstand the Proposal; not that I plead this as a Justification of

Roxana declares in the course of the courtship, 'not only to be much oblig'd to him, but to love him too, and that in a Manner that I had not been acquainted with myself' (35). But nothing more is made of this, except that Amy—to whom, as we have seen, ethically dubious but psychologically compelling arguments are regularly transferred—once observes to her mistress, 'you own you love this Gentleman, and he has given you sufficient Testimony of his Affection to you' (37). Of all the pretexts for doing what she is about to do, Roxana (and Defoe) evidently regard love as the very flimsiest. Later, when this man is murdered outside Paris, Roxana becomes more expansive: 'indeed, I lov'd him to a Degree inexpressible; and considering what Kindness he had shewn me at first, and how tenderly he had us'd me to the last, what cou'd I do less?' (54). Love is no longer an unsound motive to adultery, but a becoming response to generosity; therefore it can be frankly and fully acknowledged.

Another plea put forward only guardedly at the time, but given greater stress in retrospect, is that involving the Devil. Besides calling Amy an 'Engine of the Devil', Roxana says that her argument that the landlord 'had brought me out of the Hands of the Devil, by which she meant the Devil of Poverty and Distress, shou'd have been a powerful Motive to me, not to plunge myself into the Jaws of Hell, and into the Power of the real Devil, in Recompence for that Deliverance' (38). But it is only long afterwards that Roxana ventures to assign the Devil a decisive role, and asserts that all had been 'manag'd by the Evil Spirit' (201). Defoe seems to have recognized that, by ascribing too much to 'the Evil Spirit' at the time of the seduction, he would run the risk of putting Roxana at once in the full sway of the Devil, of thereby making her compliance too unequivocally evil, and hence of forfeiting some of our sympathy.

my Conduct, but that it may move the Pity, even of those that abhor the Crime.[1]

In this passage, it seems to me, the stress on 'dreadful Poverty' is important, but no more so than the disclaimers that precede and follow it. Indeed, Roxana's final words sum up the object of all the preliminaries to her seduction. Their appeal is not to some abstract sanction such as natural law, but to the immediate sympathies of the reader. The assent they seek is primarily emotional rather than theoretical, and their main strategy for obtaining it is to distinguish between 'the Crime', in itself admittedly abhorrent, and the special circumstances which afford, if not 'a Justification of [her] Conduct', at least grounds for pitying rather than condemning her. Roxana persuades us that the criminal cannot be equated with the crime—or, more generally, the doer with the deed. This casuistical aim accounts for her vehemence towards Amy's libertine views, and her repeated assertion that what she was about to do was 'unlawful, scandalous, and abominable'.[2]

That Roxana's tactics are psychological rather than logical can be further demonstrated from the very contradictions between her arguments. We have observed that she repeatedly claims to have seen through the specious glosses that Amy and the landlord put on the proposed liaison: insisting that ' 'tis in vain to mince the Matter', she labels them 'Cant', 'Stuff', and 'Nonsense', and eventually declares she 'sinn'd with open Eyes', 'knowing and owning it to be a Crime' (40, 43, 41). Nevertheless, she sometimes takes the opposite tack, and suggests that the eloquence of her interlocutors was a factor in her undoing. Amy 'had but too much Rhetorick in this Cause; she represented all those Things in

---

[1] *Roxana*, pp. 38–9; the Preface similarly points out that 'In the Manner she has told the Story, it is evident she does not insist upon her Justification in any one Part of it' (2).

[2] In this connection we should particularly note Roxana's insistence: 'my own Conscience convinc'd me *at the very Time I did it*'. Novak regards Roxana's self-criticism as the retrospective severity of a convert, and maintains that 'we must separate the penitent's judgment from the facts. At the time, Roxana has no concern with religion' (*Defoe and the Nature of Man*, p. 117). But it is essential to the distinction between agent and act that Roxana should be able to recognize the enormity of her action 'at the very Time'; and the clearest mark of her subsequent hardening in crime is precisely an inability to do so, a tendency either to persuade herself of the lawfulness of her misdeeds, or to let 'Lethargick Fumes' stifle her conscience altogether.

their proper Colours; she argued them all with her utmost Skill';
the landlord addresses Roxana 'in Words not to be answer'd';
and Roxana says of herself that she did not have her 'Sences' about
her, and that her 'Reason' was 'overcome' (39, 42, 38). Some
readers may find this inconsistency a symptom of muddle on
Roxana's part, and marvel at Defoe's subtle irony. Others may
see the muddle as Defoe's, and have sharp things to say about his
impoverished soul. Still others may ascribe it to mere carelessness,
and deplore the fact that Defoe wrote in such haste, with so little
forethought or revision. A fourth interpretation, sympathetic
towards both Defoe and his heroines, is that of Professor Sutherland, who (echoing Walt Whitman) says of Moll Flanders that she
has 'the inconsistency that comes from being alive; she lives for
the moment, and she changes with circumstances. Does she contradict herself? Very well, she contradicts herself.'[1] Roxana also
'lives for the moment', but in a somewhat different sense: what
she says from one moment to the next has as its constant object
—has as its primary, if not its sole, 'life'—a certain emotional
response on our part, and anything that serves to increase or
maintain this response is itself desirable. Sometimes what elicits
the required response will be the very opposite of what did so a
moment earlier; the factor that limits what can be achieved in this
line is weak rhetoric rather than faulty logic. Indeed, we ordinarily
object to logical lapses only when they obtrude themselves on us
through rhetorical lapses. What causes 'credibility gaps' is inept
propaganda, not lies and contradictions. Roxana's aim, like that of
a skilful politician, is to condition the public against blaming her
for what she and they both know is a dubious undertaking, and
to 'move the Pity, even of those that abhor the Crime'. To this

[1] Introduction to Riverside *Moll Flanders* (Boston, 1959), p. xv. I do not
wish to imply that the various suggestions just summarized (rather cavalierly)
are false, but merely that they do not exhaust the range of possible interpretations of Defoe's much-discussed inconsistencies. In his admirable
Introduction to *Colonel Jack* (London, 1965) Samuel Holt Monk remarks
that ' "Close reading" was not the vogue in the 1720's; the novel was not
written for critics; Defoe was writing at high speed, and the inconsistencies
not only in time but in many other details . . . would be unlikely to interfere
between the tale and its enthralled reader' (p. xxiii). All this is no doubt
true; nevertheless, through 'close reading' we can discover how Defoe's
very inconsistencies—or at least those under discussion here—help literally
to enthrall the reader, to make him willynilly Roxana's loyal, sympathetic
follower.

end she adopts positions which are logically clashing but rhetorically complementary.

Two final instances will further illustrate and confirm this. On the climactic day of his suit, Roxana's landlord must ride to town to do some business, but offers to return in three hours: 'we will make it a Wedding Supper, my Dear, *says he*, and with that Word, took me in his Arms, and kiss'd me so vehemently, that I made no question but he intended to do every thing else that *Amy* had talk'd of' (36). Roxana questions the word 'Wedding', but he promises to convince her that 'it is not so impossible as you make it'; when he has gone, Roxana says 'This kind of Discourse had *fir'd my Blood*, I confess', and asks Amy 'what will this all come to now? I am all in a Sweat at him' (ibid., italics mine). Soon afterwards, however, she refers to her impending seduction as a crime 'which I had but too much Inclination to commit; that is to say, not as a Crime, for I had nothing of the Vice in my Constitution; my Spirits were far from being high; *my Blood had no Fire in it*, to kindle the Flame of Desire'.[1] Logically, there is a direct contradiction here, but I do not think this lessens the effectiveness of either speech. After a long spell of friendless poverty Roxana is nearly overwhelmed by the landlord's sudden kindness, and by his insinuating words, which are ably seconded by Amy; in such a context, the first speech disposes us to sympathize with Roxana's frailty. Yet the second speech is equally an appeal for sympathy, and rests on the obvious assumption that Roxana's grateful sense of 'the kindness and good Humour of the Man', and her keen 'Dread of [her] own Circumstances', are less culpable motives than 'the Flame of Desire' for what she is about to do.[2]

---

[1] *Roxana*, p. 40; italics mine. Cf. the similar paradox in *Moll Flanders*, who says of the elder brother in the Colchester household 'His words, I must confess, fired my blood', and admits at various points to being 'fired', 'all on fire', and (rather bathetically) 'well warmed', but goes on to assert repeatedly that her looseness was owing to 'necessity', not to 'inclination' (World's Classics edn., ed. Bonamy Dobrée & Herbert Davis (London, 1961), pp. 26, 28, 29, and *passim*).

[2] Roxana says in the same vein that she was 'overcome with his Goodness to me', that she had 'scarce the Power to deny him any thing he wou'd ask', and that she was 'overcome by his Kindness' (34, 44; the words 'kind' and 'kindness' are repeated more than 25 times in as many pages). Roxana concludes these admissions of weakness by appealing to the reader to 'Pity humane Frailty, you that read of a Woman reduc'd in her Youth, and Prime, to the utmost Misery and Distress; and rais'd again, as above, by the

The point is that each speech has its local, momentary effect, and amidst all the other pleas for sympathy—some of them intrinsically specious, and as mutually contradictory as these two—the inconsistency goes unnoticed.

Defoe's treatment of the landlord involves similar contradictions, which make for the same effect. Roxana insists that the man is entirely sincere, if misguided, in thinking that their liaison amounts to a lawful marriage. The strategy in this is obvious: if the landlord were transparently a mere debauchee, it would be harder for Roxana to keep us from dismissing them as 'no more than two Adulterers, in short, a Whore and a Rogue' (43). What, then, are we to make of his guileless exchange with Amy? When he has proposed to become one of Roxana's lodgers, the two of them inspect the newly refurnished house: 'In the Room which was appointed for himself, *Amy* was doing something; Well, *Amy*, says he, I intend to Lye with you to Morrow-Night; *To Night, if you please Sir*, says *Amy* very innocently, *your Room is quite ready*: Well *Amy, says he*, I am glad you are so willing: No, says *Amy*, I mean your Chamber is ready to-Night, and away she run out of the Room asham'd enough' (33). By showing how the man's mind really works, such a *double entendre* tends to undermine his pretence of disinterested generosity; yet this is a 'most obliging Gentlemanly Man', 'the best-humour'd Man in the World', for whom Roxana eventually 'almost cry'd [her] self to Death' (45, 47, 54). Martin Price has spoken of Defoe's being 'particularly alert to unresolved paradoxes in human behavior': here Defoe has good rhetorical grounds for creating such a paradox and leaving it unresolved. By having things both ways, Roxana manages to suggest that whether her landlord's lofty protestations were genuine or spurious, the initiative was entirely his; her candour towards us helps to make it appear that if any element of duplicity was present, it was all on his side.[1]

unexpected and surprizing Bounty of a Stranger; I say pity her if she was not able, after all these things, to make any more Resistance' (34, 42; such 'admissions', we may note again, draw attention to the forces she has to contend with, rather than the gravity of her dereliction).

[1] *To the Palace of Wisdom* (Garden City, 1964), p. 267. Two further statements by the landlord are similar in spirit and effect to his exchange with Amy. At the very outset of the courtship, he admits to Roxana that 'he was under such Engagements that he cou'd not Marry me' (33), and after the seduction he acknowledges that 'it was true, in one sense, that he had two Wives' (47).

If what I have been saying tends to justify certain inconsistencies on affective grounds, it does not imply that every inconsistency in the episode is under full authorial control. On the one hand, inconsistencies may be due to inattention and haste: of this sort there are undoubtedly a great many in *Roxana*, as well as elsewhere in Defoe's writings. On the other hand, inconsistencies may be introduced deliberately to reveal the self-deception of a first-person narrator: such inconsistencies are a staple of the modern novel, and some critics claim that Defoe, too, constantly manipulates them with this object. The kind of inconsistency I have been discussing probably falls somewhere between these extremes—a matter neither of calculated irony nor of simple carelessness, but rather of leaving no stone unturned in the campaign to gain our sympathy for the heroine. Elsewhere in his writings, Defoe quotes approvingly the apostolic principle of being all things to all men so as to gain some, and a good bit of the inconsistency in what Roxana says of herself might be regarded as Pauline doctrine put into bizarre but effective practice.[1]

Roxana sums up this episode by saying that she yielded to her landlord 'not as deluded to believe it Lawful, but as overcome by his Kindness, and terrify'd at the Fear of my own Misery, if he should leave me; so with my Eyes open, and with my Conscience, as I may say, awake, I sinn'd, knowing it to be a Sin, but having no Power to resist' (44). The usefulness of this statement lies in its recapitulation not of the meaning but the method of all that precedes it. Perhaps the strongest palliative to everything Roxana does is her seeming refusal to palliate. By branding herself the chief of sinners, Roxana disengages her essential self, clear-sighted and unflinching, from the wayward creature beset by perplexity, frailty, and helpless passivity, whose misdeeds she must chronicle. At the same time, the refusal to palliate is only apparent, since

---

Both remarks are hedged with qualifications, but both render his sincerity questionable; the second one, for instance, tends to undermine Roxana's assertion that 'he either was before of the Opinion, or argued himself into it now, that we were both Free, and might lawfully Marry' (43; cf. also the diversions of the 'perfectly good-humour'd' landlord on the evening of the 'Wedding': 'he made the Girl so merry, that had he not been to lye with me the same Night, I believe he wou'd have play'd the Fool with *Amy* for half an Hour' (44)).

[1] See 1 Cor. 9: 22 and Defoe's *Letters*, ed. George Harris Healey (Oxford, 1955), pp. 42–3, 159.

Roxana employs most of the conventional devices of casuistry to 'move the Pity even of those that abhor the Crime'. The first part of this passage shifts from the overt fact of her yielding to the mental and emotional circumstances of her yielding ('not . . . deluded . . . but . . . overcome . . . and terrify'd'): quite apart from their intrinsic weight, the circumstances she amasses divert attention from what she has done to why she has done it, and thus lessen our abhorrence. The second part of the passage uses a different syntactical pattern to achieve the same effect, as a blunt admission is neutralized by the qualifying phrases that precede and follow it ('so with . . . and with . . . I sinn'd, knowing . . . but having'). Logically speaking, these phrases ought to aggravate the pivotal confession, but their actual effect is just the opposite. A fact is again obscured in a thicket of circumstance. The sentence offers a kind of grammatical paradigm for Defoe's treatment of the entire episode: there are two main verbs, 'yielded' and 'sinn'd', but they have been embedded in an elaborate series of adverbial phrases which serve to dissipate their force.

Roxana's parenthetical 'as I may say' also deserves brief comment. To speak of conscience as 'awake' hardly seems so bold a figure of speech as to require explanation or apology, yet she feels called upon to acknowledge this flutter of imagination. Why? Recent critics have had a good deal to say about the literal-mindedness of Defoe's heroes and heroines;[1] yet this quality scarcely accounts for the paradoxical effect of Roxana's 'as I may say'. This effect can best be determined by removing the parenthesis, and comparing the result with the passage as we have it: 'with my Eyes open, and with my Conscience awake, I sinn'd', *versus* 'with my Eyes open, and with my Conscience, as I may say, awake, I sinn'd'. On the one hand, the inclusion of 'as I may say' conveys an impression of scrupulous veracity, a firm determination to put things as plainly as possible. On the other hand, the insertion of these four words serves to lessen the impact of 'I sinn'd', by shattering the parallel construction and by shifting to the word 'awake' some of the stress that would otherwise fall on 'I sinn'd'. In other words, the parenthetical clause implies one

---

[1] The charge of literal-mindedness is argued vigorously by Robert Alter in an interesting chapter on *Moll Flanders* in *Rogue's Progress: Studies in the Picaresque Novel* (Cambridge, Mass., 1964). Cf. Ian Watt, *The Rise of the Novel* (London, 1957), pp. 26–30, 101–4.

thing but does quite another. What might in itself seem a touch
of rigorous precision serves not to sharpen or clarify, but to
soften and blur. We ordinarily think of *chiaroscuro* as a technique
for making essentials stand out boldly against non-essentials, but
Roxana sometimes clarifies non-essentials in order to tone down
disagreeable essentials.

Long after the liaison with her landlord is over, Roxana reviews
once again the factors that had led her to become his mistress:

I yielded to the Importunity of my Circumstances, the Misery of
which, the Devil dismally aggravated, to draw me to comply; for I
confess, I had strong Natural Aversions to the Crime at first, partly
owing to a virtuous Education, and partly to a Sence of Religion; but
the Devil, and that greater Devil of Poverty, prevail'd; and the Person
who laid Siege to me, did it in such an obliging, and I may almost say,
irresistible Manner, all still manag'd by the Evil Spirit; for I must be
allow'd to believe, that he has a Share in all such things, if not the
whole Management of them: But, I say, it was carried on by that
Person, in such an irresistible Manner, that, (as I said when I related
the Fact) there was no withstanding it: These Circumstances, I say,
the Devil manag'd, not only to bring me to comply, but he continued
them as Arguments to fortifie my Mind against all Reflection, and to
keep me in that horrid Course I had engag'd in, as if it were honest
and lawful.

But not to dwell upon that now; this was a Pretence, and here was
something to be said, tho' I acknowledge, it ought not to have been
sufficient to me at all; but, I say, to leave that, all this was out of Doors;
the Devil himself cou'd not form one Argument, or put one Reason
into my Head *now*, that cou'd serve for an Answer, no, not so much as
a pretended Answer to this Question, *Why I shou'd be a Whore now?*
(201.)

The first thing to note about this passage is that it occurs at a
point when Roxana is intent on ending another liaison; her
interest in the past is neither detached nor theoretical, but is
focused on the immediate, practical problem of discarding a man
whose temper has become 'fretful and captious', and whose
'capricious Humours' as a lover have grown 'surfeiting and
nauceous' (198–9). In other words, the passage is no more a disinterested essay at self-analysis than were her original comments,
at the time of her seduction; its object is rather to establish that
whatever grounds there were for her being a whore then, there
are none for her continuing to be a whore now. This is typical

of the entire book: moral, social, economic, and psychological reflections are seldom offered out of a desire on Roxana's part to fathom her own character and actions, or out of a desire on Defoe's part to reach a definitive assessment of her nature and behaviour. Instead, they are introduced mainly in order to shape our attitudes towards whatever Roxana has just done or is about to do.

In the process, Roxana's original commentary on her seduction is modified drastically. For instance, she now says that 'the Devil, and that greater Devil of Poverty, prevail'd': but this is to adopt Amy's view of the relative banefulness of poverty and the Devil, which Roxana had vigorously repudiated at the time. Nor, for that matter, had the Devil figured at all prominently among the forces ranged against her virtue. What, then, is the point of retroactively assigning the Devil a crucial role, as Roxana now does? Defoe wants to indicate in the strongest possible terms that she no longer has any excuse for being a whore, and therefore makes her assert that the Devil himself cannot justify it. This is simply a hyperbolic way of saying that the question '*What [am] I a Whore for now?*' is unanswerable. If even the Devil is incapable of rationalizing Roxana's continued whoredom, no further rationalizations are possible; the earlier occasion, on which the Devil could and did 'manage' everything—or so Roxana now alleges—is brought up by way of dramatic contrast. What accounts for the difference between the two stories is probably not that Defoe has forgotten what he wrote earlier, nor is it that he remembers perfectly and wants to show the heroine changing her tune for ironic purposes. It is rather that he has his eye here as always on the scene at hand, and does not let himself be inconvenienced by contradictory details contrived nearly two hundred pages earlier in the same *ad hoc* spirit.

Furthermore, what purports to be Roxana's final, authoritative judgement on the earlier episode is ambiguous in itself, and tonally at odds with the very remarks it summarizes. 'I acknowledge . . .', Roxana says, but her air of confession is offset by the substance of all that precedes it, and by the grammatical form of the qualifications that surround it: '*But* not to dwell upon that now; this was a Pretence, and here was something to be said, *tho'* I acknowledge, it ought not to have been sufficient to me at all; *but*, I say, to leave that, all this was out of Doors.' Characteristically, the relation between the parts of this sentence is not disjunctive; moral propositions in Defoe's writings are seldom mutually exclusive, so that actions are not evil *or* good, they are evil *but* good. Whatever the logical relationship between the members of her sentences, Roxana's repeated use of 'but' and 'though' as connectives allows her to have things both ways at the same time as she seems to be qualifying her assertions for precision's sake. Much has been written about the rambling looseness of Defoe's sentence-construction, but it is important to note that when it suits his purpose to do so, he uses strong connectives such as 'but' and 'though' to give his co-ordinate and subordinate clauses an air of consistency which their actual interrelationship does not bear out. (The frequent use of 'for' as a connective—twice in the passage just quoted—has a similar effect; it often implies a logical bond between propositions, similar to 'because', when in fact no such bond is present.) In short, what appears to be a *con*clusive statement turns out—as is so often the case in Defoe's writings—to be an *in*clusive one.

Enough has been said about the initial episode of *Roxana* to indicate what seem to be its leading aims and techniques. It could be objected that by focusing so intently on a single episode and its brief reprise, one does violence to the total structure of a book. An author's handling of a given passage is normally determined, after all, not only by the immediate responses he wants it to elicit, but by the role he means it to play in the book's larger design. This is perhaps less true of Defoe than of most later novelists, however, and the opening episode of *Roxana* merits the kind of attention given it here precisely because it is in so many respects a self-contained unit, the first in a series of discrete, mutually independent crises that make up the book. This episode, moreover, probably develops within itself as much depth or complexity as the book ever attains. New episodes generate fresh complexities, to be sure, but these do not make for greater depth, since they tend to supplant earlier ones, not to refine or resolve them. To substantiate these impressions, of course, would require a detailed discussion of subsequent episodes, which cannot be attempted here.[1] Our present concern is simply to have indicated

---

[1] These impressions are strongly suggested, however, by the initial episode itself. We have seen, for instance, that various complicating motives are assigned to agents outside the heroine: this portioning out of certain (baser)

that the story of Roxana's seduction is full of loose ends, but that many of these nevertheless have a common object, which they achieve with considerable skill—to 'move the Pity, even of those that abhor the Crime'.

motives to secondary characters conserves the total complexity of the episode, but externalizes conflicts that would otherwise take place within Roxana herself, and helps to explain why there should seem to be more paradox than profundity in her character.

5

SATIRE AND ECONOMICS IN THE AUGUSTAN AGE OF SATIRE

By JACOB VINER

THE invitation to contribute to a *Festschrift* in honour of my friend and colleague Louis Landa was very welcome to me. I was somewhat at a loss, however, as to a topic which would both have some relevance to Landa's interests and be within my competence, as an economist, to deal with. Shortly before the receipt of the invitation I participated in a symposium sponsored by Reed College on the Augustan Age of Satire, and in the process of preparing for it I did my first substantial reading of Augustan satirical texts and of what modern littérateurs have said about them. I decided that a reworked version of the lecture I gave at Reed College on some relations between Augustan satire and economics would come closer in relevance of subject-matter to Landa's interests than anything else I could do. That I lack the technical competence to deal in a sophisticated manner with satire as a literary genre I am fully aware. I have persuaded myself, however, that it is better that my topic should be dealt with by an amateur on the literary side than that it should not be dealt with at all. Although my conscience has been calmed, I confess that I would feel much better equipped to deal with my topic if my understanding of the nature of satire were nearly as good as Louis Landa's understanding of the complexities of eighteenth-century English economic thought.

My greatest difficulty in absorbing the professional literature on Augustan satire is in adjusting to the reverential tone with which much of it deals with satire, as if satire were in a realm by itself, above other literary genres; the satirists themselves, by attacking the persons, the classes, and the political, religious, and economic doctrines they abhor, damn these persons and doctrines and become in a way sanctified figures. In both respects, I grant, this attitude conforms with what the satirists regarded as the proper response to their efforts. Pope, for instance, certainly, and Swift probably, sincerely thought of satire, as employed by them, as a 'sacred weapon', used in 'Truth's defence', and 'sole Dread of Folly, Vice, and Insolence!'[1] Gilbert Highet says of the Augustan satirists that they operated in response to 'the urge to make fun of fools and scoundrels'.[2] I would not dream of questioning this, but I would insist that, like most humans, the satirists did not restrict the use of their aggressive talents to the lashing of rogues and fools. Satire, as far as I can see, has no greater magical power to purify its user, and no more visible tendency to be used only in the service of truth, beauty, and virtue, than poetry in general, or prose in general. I shall, indeed, argue later that an ancient doctrine especially prevalent among the saints, that the use of satire and its associated forms of wit should be left to the sinners, has often operated as a hindrance both to resort to satire by saints and to its effective use as an instrument of persuasion to righteousness.

For the economist *qua* economist what may most matter, and may be all that matters, in a satiric work is its actual influence, direct or indirect, on its audience, regardless of what may have been the intention or the hope of its author. This is fortunate for the economist, for it is generally easier to trace the actual influence of a particular satire than to penetrate the intention of the satirist.

Identification of the 'intention' of the satirist is primarily the task of the professional interpreter of texts. The record shows that in the case of satirical texts performance of the task encounters special difficulties, and often fails to result in a generally accepted resolution of these difficulties, even after centuries of effort. The satirist may have a bundle of intentions, not altogether harmonious, and he may even be unstable in his distribution of emphasis between his various intentions.

A satiric effort may be addressed to a particular audience to please or entertain it, or to arouse or strengthen its support of— or its hostility to—a particular cause or group or individual, or to provoke its audience and cause it discomfort. When Swift or Pope made the 'moneyed interest', or a particular Whig politician, or a particular group of Whigs, or Whiggery in general, the butt of his satire, how can one tell whether his primary objective was

---

[1] 'Epilogue to the Satires, Second Dialogue' (1738), *Works* (London, 1751), iv. 248.
[2] *The Anatomy of Satire* (Princeton, 1962), p. 305.

the pleasure to be derived from the exercise of his satirical skill, or the giving of pleasure to his Tory audience, or the giving of pain to the Whigs? A Grub-Street satirist, of course, might choose his victim with an eye to finding a paying audience. A satirist might make his audience his target, in the hope of reforming his hearers or readers by making them aware of their shortcomings, as a preacher may use satire to induce in the members of his congregation shame for their misdoings.

An intellectual satirist may satirize an occupation, or discipline, such as natural science, or law, or economics, or moral preaching, either to laugh its practitioners out of their obnoxious procedures or convictions, or to make it more difficult for them to obtain new followers. It is even conceivable that a satirist may have it as his major objective to hurt his target because of personal enmity, or desire for revenge for some previous affront, or as a phase of political warfare, or simply to find an outlet for his sadistic impulses. Only one thing seems to be exempt, or nearly so, from being satirized, and that is satire itself.

Defoe's *Robinson Crusoe* has been interpreted as a satire on capitalism, perhaps including some self-satire by the author as a complying member of a defective social system. There is no difficulty in principle in recognizing the possibility of deliberate self-satire. In this particular instance, however, I am by no means convinced by the evidence that has been gathered that there is a satirical element in *Robinson Crusoe* directed against capitalism, or against Daniel Defoe as a beneficiary thereof. One ground on which this interpretation seems to rest is that Defoe was trying to show how much an isolated individual could achieve economically without the aid of the economic market, and therefore how exploitative and unproductive was the well-paid machinery of capitalistic society. If this were a correct interpretation of Defoe's intention, he would have blundered as a satirist in giving Robinson Crusoe a rich hoard of capital, in the form of the cargo of the wrecked ship, to draw upon freely. In this important respect Defoe, by putting Crusoe in a situation where some capital goods are to him free goods, differentiated his environment from both that of the happy savage and that of the individual living in a capitalist community, and made Crusoe's situation more akin to that of the religious hermit who lives, in part at least, on the charity of those who toil and save in the market community.

Whatever the intentions of the satirist, to be effective satire requires both skill on the part of the satirist in pursuing his intentions and a not too unfavourable setting for their realization. Some intentions, if they are evident, can operate to make success difficult or unattainable. Some settings are inherently unfavourable for some or for all kinds of satirical intentions, and thus offer a barren field for the successful operation of satire. As an instrument of persuasion to action in a social cause, as a means of changing political attitudes or of helping or hurting a specific occupational or class group, satire thus has some inherent limitations.

Satire is a rhetorical genre which, as compared, say, with open and forthright exhortation, or with straight invective hurled at the enemy, or with positive argument, is peculiarly dependent on a high level of literary or verbal aptitude and sophistication on the part of its audiences, and on their possession in some measure of a sense of humour. It uses some degree of indirection, of paradox, of exaggeration, of distortion, or of disclosure of hitherto unperceived contradictions within established attitudes, as a method of changing the attitudes of its audiences. Some minimum degree of skill on the part of the satirist, together with some minimum degree of intelligence and verbal alertness on the part of the audience, will therefore normally be necessary if attitudes are to be changed upon exposure to the satire, instead of being left unmoved, or even being moved in a direction opposite to that intended by the satirist. Satire is a two-edged weapon; if misunderstood, the wrong edge may cut. If the satirist delivers his effort orally, he can use facial gestures, or modulations of his voice, to help make his intent apparent. If his tongue is at times in his cheek, he can let you see this visually and give you warning. Even then, however, he risks failure of communication if he occasionally shifts his tongue from one cheek to the other. In print, the words have to do the whole work, except for the knowledge or the notions the audience has of the record and the convictions of the author. Satire is thus not a suitable instrument for direct persuasion of a mass audience, and always needs a select audience.

Even for persons of a fair level of sophistication, satire often misfires. One main cause is that the audience it is addressed to fails to perceive when satire is intended, especially when the satirist—notably Jonathan Swift in *The Tale of a Tub*—mixes different modes in the same piece as an exercise in literary virtuosity, or where the audience recognizes that a satirical element is present but is mistaken as to the intended target. In such cases a country-cousin of satire, slanted and invidious invective directed at a frankly designated target, would probably be more effective as persuasion than elaborately wrought satire, and even straight and unshaped invective might do better still. Literary critics sometimes offer us allegedly sure signs of satirical intent, such as giving distorted or ridiculous names to the targets,[1] and this device has certainly been used occasionally by even the most august of the 'Augustan' satirists. I am old enough to be able to remember how effective it was on the modern vaudeville stage. It is still an effective weapon among children. It may well be, therefore, that, if distortion of names is not merely ridiculous but is directed to have some special satirical pertinence, it may be effective also for a higher-level audience. Swift and Pope must have thought so. Later, Dickens was to use this ploy indefatigably, but perhaps not without fatiguing his audience.

It is perhaps when satire is carried to its highest literary levels and is directed to an élite audience that the greatest risks of failure of communication may arise and may lead to the greatest possible amount of doubt, confusion, and misinterpretation. One of the chief literary achievements of the English Augustan Age was to substitute a plain and lucid English prose for the highly decorated and involuted, but no doubt also magnificent, prose of the previous century. I suspect that one of the literary explanations of the popularity of satire among writers in the Augustan Age was that resort to it enabled them to satisfy in their writing a nostalgia for obscurity, contrivance, impenetrability, while on the surface conforming to the new standards of lucidity and clarity. If they were at first unaware of the risks of failure to communicate that they thus ran, the painful experience which resulted often led them to a second attempt in order to repair the damage.

One writer, noting that 'there seem'd to be much want of a particular note of punctuation to distinguish irony, which is often so delicately couch'd as to escape the notice even of the attentive reader, and betray him into error', published a collection of other authors' poems, punctuated by dots above the ironic passages, as an example of the improvement this simple device would bring

---

[1] Gilbert Highet (op. cit., p. 275) remarks, 'Distorted or ridiculous names are always a sure sign of satire'.

to the interpretation of texts.[1] He apparently overlooked the possibility that an author might wish only his circle of like-minded friends, and not the rabble or the enemy, to perceive when he was serious and when waxing ironic or satiric. Swift, in a Preface added in 1710 to *The Tale of a Tub* to explain 'the Authors Intention' (a humiliating thing, I should think, for a satirist to have to do), said that some of the passages most objected to by readers 'are what they call Parodies, where the Author personates the Style and manner of other Writers, whom he has a mind to expose'. In the same year a minor writer, Joseph Trapp, with some overt indication that *The Tale of a Tub* was in his mind, ventured on more dangerous territory than parody, as a satirical device for calling attention to an enemy's flaws, by substituting for parody unaltered replicas of his target's texts. He did this to show that the tract he was attacking 'does not deserve to be answer'd. Or if it does, I will make the Author of it answer himself. . . . I will extract some of his remarkable passages, and lay them in more view before the eyes of the reader.'[2] I suppose this device could be designated 'enforced self-satire'. I have seen it used even in economics textbooks, where an incriminating passage is reproduced from some other book, but with an exclamation mark supplied by the author of the textbook to indicate that he was quoting with satirical intent, and not as a token of approval. Trapp, however, was not really content to rely on this maximum-risk device, which came perilously close to being analogous to a merchant's paying for the printing of his competitor's advertisements. Apart from selecting texts which may seem ridiculous only because they are wrenched from their contexts in an invidious way, Trapp provided tendentious labels for the reproduced texts, and he inserted, although without deceit, hostile comments into the heart of some of the extracts.

Francis Hare, later to be a bishop, in a satirical tract of 1714 pretended to be dissuading a devout young man of independent mind, in his own spiritual and material interest, from entering the ministry of the Church of England. Hare had been in controversy with the Church hierarchy, in part because of his allegedly Arian views. In this tract he warned prospective clergymen of the

---

[1] Edward Capell, ed., *Prolusions; or, select pieces of antient poetry* (London, 1760), Preface, p. v.

[2] Joseph Trapp, *Most Faults on one Side* (London, 1710), pp. 55–6.

pressure and the discriminatory economic treatment to which the lower clergy were subject unless they fully confirmed to the doctrinal views of the hierarchy. In eighteenth-century England this was strong meat. But Hare ended his tract by confessing that he himself regarded what he had written as 'a strange paradox' and 'a very wicked one' if read literally.[1] He presumably was seeking the benefits of satirical licence whilst guarding either his readers or himself or both from the consequences of failure to make clear that his text was not to be interpreted literally. The result for himself was that he was censured by the Lower House of Convocation of the Church of England for treating 'things sacred in a ludicrous and prophane manner'—that is, satirically.

Bishop Joseph Butler, in his *Analogy of Religion, Natural and Revealed, to the Constitution and Course of Nature*, 1736, used as a major argument in defence of revealed religion that the objections made by deists against revealed religion were applicable in like manner to natural theology. To some this seemed a dangerous line of argument, since it seemed to leave open to agnostics the retort that Butler had only demonstrated that Anglicanism and deism were in the same leaking boat. Lord Bolingbroke, as a deist, had been writing in radical manner and with great frankness against revealed religion and the organized ecclesiastical institutions which supported it, although he withheld publication of some of these writings during his lifetime. Edmund Burke, in *A Vindication of Natural Society*, 1756, one of his earliest publications, replied to Bolingbroke by adopting Butler's analogical mode of argument. Unlike Butler, however, Burke wrote satirically. He pretended to be defending 'natural society', or society without government, and to be attacking government. His intent was to demonstrate that the same kind of argument with which Bolingbroke attacked revealed religion could with comparable effectiveness be used to attack government. To show that, in part at least, he was directing his essay against Bolingbroke, and to show also that he was writing satirically, Burke parodied Bolingbroke's style and introduced some patently fantastic argument in derogation of government. It may be that Burke was also parodying Rousseau's primitivism.

Burke pictured current society under government as permeated

---

[1] Francis Hare, *The Difficulties and Discouragements Which attend the Study of the Scriptures in the Way of Private Judgment* (7th edn., London, 1716).

by war, by gross social inequality, inefficiency, corruption, and by encroachments on the natural liberty of the individual. In contrast he gave a romantically utopian picture of what society could or would be like in the absence of civil government. To some of Burke's readers, however, the satiric intent of the author in disparaging government in general was not apparent, and the description of government as it operated in the England of the time was not visibly fantastic. To these readers, and to all readers who were in no mood to have the existing political and economic *status quo* undermined even in fantasy, Burke's picture of society under government, including its economic aspects, was made too ugly, too realistic, and too plausible, to represent a successful use of the satirical technique. Within a year Burke brought out a new edition, with an added Preface explaining that his argument for natural society and against government was deliberately 'specious', that is, satirically intended:

The design was, to show that, without the exertion of any considerable forces, the same engines which were employed [e.g., by Bolingbroke] for the destruction of religion, might be employed with equal success for the subversion of government; and that specious arguments might be used against those things which they, who doubt of everything else, will never permit to be questioned.

Read literally, *The Vindication* was perhaps the most radical social essay published in the century after the time of the Commonwealth. Read literally, it was the first general formulation, at least in England, of the case for philosophical anarchism. It was later to be read as such by William Godwin, and was an influence on him when he was writing his *Political Justice*, the pioneer exposition of sincere English anarchism. *The Vindication* itself was reprinted by American anarchists in 1858 and in 1885. It was respectfully commented on by Rudolf Grossmann, a member of an anarchist sect of communists, in 1907 as a serious plea for 'natural society'. Grossmann interpreted Burke's later Preface to be intended 'as dust for the eyes of the stupid and the great'.[1] An American neo-liberal (or neo-conservative) in 1958 renewed the argument that *The Vindication* was sincere and not basically

---

[1] Grossmann wrote under the pseudonym of 'Pierre Ramus'. See Pierre Ramus, *William Godwin, der Theoretiker des kommunistischen Anarchismus* (Leipzig, 1907), pp. 10–11. See also F. E. L. Priestley, ed., William Godwin, *Enquiry concerning Political Justice* (Toronto, 1946), iii. 40, n. 40.

satirical, and gave some support to the idea that it should be included in the 'individualist camp', 'since there is no sign of enmity to private property as such in this work'.[1]

Another limitation on the effectiveness of satire as an instrument of persuasion was its common, though not necessary, association with humour, and in particular the constant danger that it might lead to laughter. At least from the time of ancient Greece to the eighteenth century laughter was somewhat on the defensive, on religious and on moral grounds. Its condemnation, however, like its occasional praise, was usually subject to reservations, and careful consideration commonly led to an intermediate final verdict as to its respectability. Thus Ecclesiastes 2 : 2, 'I said of laughter, it is mad; and of mirth, what doeth it?', but (ibid. 3 : 1 and 4) 'For everything there is a season, and a time for every purpose under heaven; . . . a time to weep, and a time to laugh'. Salvian in the fifth century preached: 'Let us laugh, Christians, but in a Christian manner.'[2] As late as the 1740s Edward Young, in his *Night Thoughts*, could write:

> Laughter, tho' never censur'd yet as sin,
> (Pardon a thought that only seems severe)
> Is half-immoral . . . (Night viii).

Shaftesbury early in the century had said in defence of ridicule, and especially of its good-humoured form, raillery, that capacity to withstand it was a good test of truth, and that truth could not be injured by it. This argument continued to be a topic for debate for a large part of the century, and many objected that Shaftesbury was unduly optimistic about the invulnerability of truth to ridicule and held that truth should not be put to this test. Some sensitive souls found repulsive on aesthetic grounds the close association of the sublime and the ridiculous that frequently occurred in satirical works.

Great sectors of the population of eighteenth-century England, for one or the other of these reasons, either must have been unreachable by satire of any subtlety or would not have reacted to it

[1] Murray N. Rothbard, 'A Note on Burke's *Vindication*', *JHI* xix (1958), 114–18. See, for a rejoinder, John C. Weston, ibid. 438. See also [John Ward], *Monthly Review* xv (1756), 18–22; and August M. Knoll, *Der soziale Gedanke im modernen Katholizismus* (Vienna, 1932), pp. 41–2, for other instances of literal interpretation of Burke's *Vindication*.

[2] Quoted by Jean Croiset, S.J., *Réflexions sur divers sujets de morale* (new edn., Paris, 1777), i. 137. (The first edition was not later than 1707.)

as the satirist intended or hoped. The sense of humour often necessary for the appreciation of satire is certainly not universally distributed by nature. Even if it were, cultural disciplines could suppress it, the disciplines of religious rigorism, of secular puritanism, of some occupational patterns of life, or of an educational system determined to put humour in its place. Where economic issues were involved, and where to achieve the intent of the satirist large numbers of men had to be directly influenced, satirical methods were therefore likely to be inadequate, or even to do more harm than good.

In relation to large groups, satire probably had more service to render as a lash administered as punishment for sin, or in the service of another smaller group, perhaps chiefly for the latter's entertainment, than as an instrument of persuasion or conversion of the large groups themselves. Moreover, the individual who recognizes that he is being made the target of satire may respond by resentment, where straightforward persuasion might have won him over.

I have found satire contending with satire on anything like an equal basis in only two areas: as an exercise appropriate to the literary arena, where the issues involved were primarily literary; and in the controversies between literary Anglicans and literary deists or freethinkers, where the satirists on each side could be skilled and could hope for sophisticated audiences and vulnerable, because sensitive, targets. This, be it noted, excludes the arena of economic debate, where this kind of sophistication would not ordinarily be present. Satire was thus an upper-class preserve in the main, with the satirists in the free or paid service of their social superiors, if they were not themselves members of a high social group. The upper classes, of course, however they are defined, were not a homogeneous group. They had their internecine quarrels and jealousies, in which satire could play an important role. But I have not succeeded in finding a clear-cut *English* instance in which a satirist, on an economic issue, was attacking a social group clearly higher than the one he belonged to or had been hired to serve. When Swift used satire to attack the *English* government on behalf of *Ireland's* manufactures or trade, he was acting, on principle and not for pay, on behalf of a group which was inferior in power and status to England, and on behalf of a 'national' issue on which he had a substantial sympathetic audience.

But when Swift attacked Irish landlords on behalf of the Irish poor, he was attacking the strong on behalf of the weak, and attacking a group higher in some senses than the one he belonged to. But one should always be prepared to accept Swift as an exception to many rules. I shall comment in a moment on a Scottish exception. But were there other exceptions? They can readily be found, no doubt, in France in particular, and in England itself in ages other than the Augustan. It may be that it was only in England, and only in the period 1660 to say 1760, that satire was widely practised and also usually had its darts pointed horizontally or downwards in the social scale, but not upward. This may be worth exploration.

My Scottish exception is John Witherspoon. He was a minister of the Kirk, of the orthodox and ardent Calvinist wing. The Moderates, or the 'enlightened' wing, a minority generally of higher social rank and superior education, and through their property and their connections possessing disproportionate legal control of church 'patronage', could determine in some significant degree who should occupy the pulpits of even ardently orthodox parish kirks. Church of Scotland affairs were the only area left to Scotland under the Union with England where the middling ranks of the people could exercise a vote on things that mattered to them or to Scotland as a whole, and only in the Assemblies of the Church could aspiring youth display its forensic talents before truly national gatherings. In this remnant left to Scotland of representative government, legal rights of membership in the Assembly and of presentation of ministers to the parish kirks which rested on grounds of heredity, of property, and of delegation of authority from London were an alien and oligarchical intrusion that was offensive even to some Scotsmen who, on purely religious grounds or on grounds of social affinity, were more at ease with the Moderates. In the constant tension between the orthodox and 'Popular' party, on the one hand, and the Moderates on the other, the Moderates, as also the few unaffiliated freethinkers, repeatedly subjected the orthodox to satiric jabs and pejorative labels, whose targets were not always expressly disclosed but were never unclear. To the Moderates, the orthodox Calvinists were 'enthusiasts', 'fanatics', addicts of 'superstition'.

As a lone exception among the orthodox Calvinists, John Witherspoon had the combination of capacities necessary to fight the Moderates with their own literary weapons. He was well educated, was skilful with his pen, and was either free from any moral aversion to the use of biting satire or in a righteous cause could keep that aversion under control.

In 1753, while a bitter controversy was under way in the General Assembly of the Church of Scotland between the Moderates and the Popular party, Witherspoon published anonymously, but with the authorship only sufficiently concealed to protect him from prosecution, a bitter tract, *Ecclesiastical Characteristics*, in which the religious beliefs, the personal character, and the patronage practices of the Moderates were subjected to severe satirical treatment. The tract created quite a storm, and Witherspoon felt obliged not long after to issue an 'Apology' for it in which he justified his resort to satire in the face of the long-standing tradition hostile to it and defended the severity of its tone. He claimed that 'A satire that does not bite is good for nothing. Hence it necessarily follows, that it is essential to this manner of writing, to provoke and give offence.' He appealed to instances of the use of irony in the Old Testament and to Pascal's attack in the *Provincial Letters* on the doctrinal laxity of the French Jesuit clergy as relevant precedents for his use of satire to expose the character defects of the Moderate clergy.[1] A modern, but clearly not 'Moderate', Scottish Presbyterian comments on *Ecclesiastical Characteristics* as follows:

> Its accuracy hit the Moderates in their weak spot—Their sensitiveness to ridicule. It exposed their gentlemanliness as sycophancy [to the powerful and the rich], their culture as paganism, their virtue as self-righteousness . . . satire won more friends for the evangelicals [the modern friendly term for orthodox Scottish Calvinists] than heated denunciation. The orthodox, hitherto armed with archaic weapons, equipped themselves with the modern armaments of their adversaries.[2]

I doubt, however, that Witherspoon had any satirical comrades among the orthodox in Scotland. Their lack of the types of literary skill required for effective satire, and the survival of doubt as to the respectability of satire, seem to have continued indefinitely

---

[1] John Witherspoon, *Ecclesiastical Characteristics* (1753), *A Serious Apology for the Ecclesiastical Characteristics* (1763), *Works* (2nd edn., Philadelphia, 1802), iii. 269–313.

[2] The Revd. A. L. Drummond, 'Witherspoon of Gifford and American Presbyterianism', *Records of the Scottish Church History Society* xiii (Glasgow, 1958), 191.

to bar the appearance of a second Witherspoon. There were among the orthodox some misgivings about Witherspoon's resort to satire even in a good cause: 'As one good soul expressed the doubt: "Alas! would it not have been better to have had recourse to prayer than to satire?"'[1]

Satire had an additional limitation as a tool of persuasion on an economic issue where the intended audience were sober-minded and intellectually scrupulous, and not seeking amusement. Such an audience would look for balanced presentation of pros and cons, for massing of argument and evidence even at the cost of dullness, for the avoidance of exaggeration and patent distortion. This is not the kind of audience nor the kind of rhetoric with which satire can feel at home.

I now venture to relate more concretely to the economic ideas, conditions, and institutions of our period the record of that period's satire, although my knowledge of that record, I regretfully confess, is rather sketchy. It seems clear to me that the satire which survives to later times, or is rediscovered in later times and then made much of by scholars, is mostly of two kinds; that which to later literary taste is aesthetically attractive, and that which to members of specific learned disciplines has important intellectual significance. I shall comment separately on these two categories, but first I have a remark to make on the relations between them. The number of satirists whose *satiric* writings are still studied and praised, both by professional students of literature for the literary effectiveness of their satire, and by philosophers, theologians, economists, political theorists, or other intellectuals, for their contributions to their respective disciplines, seems to be very small. Roaming over the last few centuries and the entire Western world, I can think only of Pierre Bayle, Pascal, Shaftesbury, David Hume, Montesquieu, Voltaire, and Edward Gibbon. Bernard Mandeville would seem to me to be eminently deserving of a place in this list, but for his literary and other admirers it is not his satirical technique that wins their applause. The leading literary student of Mandeville seems indeed to have managed to produce the one undisputedly great work on him without ever using the word 'satire'.

My list is no doubt an inexcusably short one, and even so some

[1] Varnum Lansing Collins, *President Witherspoon, A Biography* (Princeton, 1925), pp. 38–9.

G

may think it includes some very questionable names. But if it has any merit, two aspects of the list besides its brevity may be worth mentioning: it includes only British and French writers; and their satire was in each instance largely exercised on controversial issues in the field of religion, or of politics, or, as in the case of Voltaire, of both. This last point suggests to me that one of the reasons for resort to satire in a time when freedom of the press or of speech is far from complete is that it may be safer to wrap one's dangerous thoughts in a satirical shroud than to express them directly and openly. Of the writers I have listed, only one engaged in serious economic discussion in satirical form, and this again was Voltaire. His critique of the Physiocrats was one of the few major satirical achievements in the history of economic thought.

Like other satire, that with economic relevance may be directed against a person or group of persons, a social class, an occupation, a prevalent idea or pattern of behaviour, a learned discipline in its current state, a particular social institution, or the entire institutional structure of existing society.

It can be stated, with little need of qualification, that an outstanding aspect of literate and articulate England for the century from 1660 to 1760 was its contentment with its existing economic institutions and its absence of desire for significant change. As far as institutional reform is concerned, there was minor patching of the system of dealing with the indigent poor, and there was reconstruction of the barriers to foreign trade so as to reduce the weight given to fiscal or revenue considerations and to increase the weight given to mercantilist, or economic and strategic, considerations. Apart from this, nothing much happened in the way of economic-reform legislation or agitation. Although Parliament was incessantly busy legislating, and the volumes of statutes in force were getting fatter and fatter, no single statute can be cited in this entire century as marking an important change in the economic institutions of England, whether by way of destruction, repair, or innovation. What institutional change of consequence was going on was piecemeal, creeping, and largely spontaneous in the sense that it took the form of old legislation falling into obsolescence, and was made possible through parliamentary, judicial, or administrative inertia rather than by formal concerted action. This kind of institutional *status quo* conservatism, as distinct from reactionary conservatism striving to recapture by deliberate and concerted effort a lost Golden Age, or from organized pursuit of institutional innovation, was in matters of economic relevance at least as true of the heroes of Augustan satire as of the articulate public at large.

Once more I have to protect myself by making a qualification over Jonathan Swift. While I know of no important proposal he made for institutional economic change through legislation, it is clear that with respect to the jurisdictional relations of Ireland and England, and with respect to aspects of the Irish economy which only a free Ireland could change, he was an advocate of substantial change. But apart from this the Augustan satirists (as distinguished from the Grub-Street ones, whatever kinds of reform they may have yearned for or advocated) were not advocates of institutional reform by legislation, and, in effect, were not critics of the existing structure of economic and political institutions. They were, nevertheless, social reformers, if to be properly regarded as such it suffices that they were indisputably critics of the morals, intelligence, integrity, manners, marital relations, and religious convictions of the superintendents and janitors of these institutions, above all when the personnel happened to consist of Whigs, or at least of the wrong faction of Whigs.

Devoted to reform of individual morals, the Augustan satirists attacked zealously, and no doubt with just severity, all the Seven Deadly Sins. They also attacked some other sins that were perhaps not mortal, but only venial, that is, not very sinful sins, or only breaches of good manners. They were at times, moreover, systematically respectful of persons, as witness their somewhat automatic tendency to associate Whigs and sinfulness in politics, and dissenters and freethinkers and sinfulness in religious matters. They dwelt with traditional harshness upon the sin of avarice, but they tended to be most alert to its concrete manifestations when it took the form of ungentlemanly pursuit of money by 'moneyed men' and merchants, but not to find worthy of note the gentlemanly pursuit of power, status, or acres. Of a worthy landed family of ancient lineage, belonging to the class whom the Augustan satirists so admired and whom they regarded as alone fit to hold the reins of government, an anonymous contemporary satirist, probably of the Grub-Street variety, remarked: 'They ever let their love light where the land lay.' Again with the exception of Swift, satire seemed to find no appropriate target in avarice manifesting itself in rack-renting and enclosing landlords.

There is a deep and perhaps permanent cleft in social ethics in the economics profession, and in social thought in general, between those who think the reform of society must come through the moral reform of individuals and those who see it as realizable only by concerted community effort reforming social institutions to make possible a great society without necessarily transforming human nature. In between, of course, are a mixed lot of eclectics or pluralists or moderates who think some of both may prove necessary. The Augustan satirists definitely belonged to the first group. On this issue, the satirists seem to have been in complete harmony with the general opinion of the articulate classes of the England of their century; make men better men, and nothing else is required. The situation in France, on the other hand, was strikingly different; social criticism was there largely pointed at institutions rather than individuals.

I have not been able to discover whether in these matters Grub-Street satire had a substantially different set of targets. I can therefore venture no sweeping sociological generalization about the effect of the economic status and class affiliations of satirists on the things they choose to do and the manner in which they choose to do them. John Loftis has successfully demonstrated from an exhaustive study of the texts that as the years went by the authors of stage comedies in the Augustan period treated the manners and morals of the merchants with increasing sympathy. He attributed this to an increased respect for the merchant on the part of both the public and the dramatists, as the merchant rose in status and in affluence.[1] If, however, many of the comedy-writers belonged to Grub Street, and if their more august fellow writers correctly pictured Grub-Street writers as typically poor and mercenary, the simpler hypothesis would be that as soon as merchants came to the theatre in sufficient numbers the drama-tists would provide fare which would retain them as customers.

Persons who possessed or acquired wealth without deserving it were often subjected to satirical treatment, as for instance in Gay's *The Beggar's Opera*. This is sometimes interpreted by modern scholars as evidence that the satirists condemned on moral grounds

[1] John Loftis, *Comedy and Society from Congreve to Fielding* (Stanford, 1959).

a social system in which wealth was not distributed according to merit. This may be correct, but it does not follow, in the absence of more specific evidence, that the satirists hoped that their satire would lead to some institutional changes in the property system which would help to remove the abuse.

It was a fairly common doctrine of moralists, philosophers, and others that differences in merit between men were somewhat problematic, were not easy to determine in particular cases, and had no clear relation to social or class groupings. To base status on appraisal of merit, it was held, would make adjustment of the social hierarchy a matter of continuous turmoil, since there would never be general consensus as to the relative merit of particular individuals or social groups. But a stable social hierarchy was believed to be essential for political order and authority, and economic inequality was believed to be essential if there were to be incentives to enterprise. Shakespeare said in *Troilus and Cressida* :

> Oh, when degree is shak'd
> Which is the ladder to all high designs,
> The enterprise is sick, . . .
> Take but degree away, untune that string,
> And hark what discord follows. . . .

There is no reason to suppose that Shakespeare thought that 'degree' corresponded to merit, or should be made to do so. A long line of important thinkers, Pascal, Nicole, David Hume, Samuel Johnson, Adam Smith, and no doubt many others, agreed with Shakespeare on the importance of gradation, and of the 'subordination' it involved, and believed also that merit was too uncertain and controversial a basis to provide its foundation. They held, therefore, that factors more objective than merit must serve as the pragmatic criteria of social status, and they agreed that these must be birth and wealth, criteria not difficult to apply. Age was sometimes suggested as an additional criterion for status, one equally easy to apply objectively.

A satirist need therefore wish for no fundamental change in an existing society marked by gross economic inequality unassociated with merit, and yet at the same time with full consistency ridicule individuals who enjoy special advantages solely on account of birth, inherited wealth, or age, especially if these individuals display self-esteem. Reward without merit, taken by itself, could still be legitimately open to ridicule, the satirist could say, even if it could not be systematically eliminated without social disaster.

In the eighteenth century, apologetics for economic inequality flowed in a constant stream from the pulpits, the moral philosophers, and writers on economic matters, but apart from satiric jabs at particularly undeserving examples of privilege without merit very little was said on behalf of greater economic equality as a desirable and practicable goal. Apologists for the existing inequality of status refrained as a rule from claiming that there was corresponding inequality of merit, and on the contrary were often quite prepared to admit that virtue was more widespread among the poor than among the rich. Satire at the expense of the rich, on the stage, or in fiction, or in poetry or essays, could therefore have ample scope despite the fundamental conservatism of the satirist. Henry Fielding, for instance, in his two solemn economic tracts showed himself in full sympathy with the existing social structure, in which merit was not a prerequisite for privilege; in his novels, on the other hand, he freely satirized individuals who enjoyed privilege unassociated with merit.

It may be, as has been claimed, that it is an easy step from ridicule of social inequality not resting on differences in merit to advocacy of the legislative abolition of inequality or its conversion to a system of reward for superior merit. That step, however, was not taken, as far as I know, by any English writer, between 1660 and 1760. I have come across one possible exception, a poem in which ridicule of economic arguments used in defence of inequality is clearly associated with willingness to have the inequality removed by concerted social action. I withhold comment on the aesthetic merits of the poem, and although it seems to me to have an eighteenth-century flavour, it may quite possibly be a late nineteenth-century left-wing fabrication. Whatever its origin, it is social satire at the expense of class inequality, obviously carrying implications of the desirability of fundamental change, and is therefore alien to the general drift of genuine Augustan satire. I have the text, at second or third hand, from an 1890s song-book of the Independent Labour Party, an English Left-wing political organization which was the ancestor of the present British Labour Party.[1]

Now Dives daily feasted, and was gorgeously arrayed,

[1] *The Economic Review* viii (1898), 215.

Not at all because he liked it, but because 'twas good for trade;
That the people might have calico, he clothed himself in silk;
And surfeited himself with cream, that they might get the milk;
He fed five hundred servants, that the poor might not lack bread,
And had his vessels made of gold, that they might get more lead;[1]
And e'en to show his sympathy with the deserving poor,
He did no useful work himself, that they might do the more.[2]

Bernard Mandeville was a satirist of the Augustan period who is today commonly interpreted, by both literary experts and economists, as having intentions sharply different from those commonly attributed to him by his contemporaries. I think, nevertheless, that his contemporaries, without important exception, understood what he was after, and that Mandeville had no objection on ethical or religious grounds to the then-existing economic structure of society. He was ready and even anxious to concede that it did not meet traditional moral standards. But he did not genuinely regard this as an important objection. Standard morality, he believed, would if carried into practice bring economic disaster to society, and he had no righteous zeal for economic disaster. What Mandeville was satirizing was not the social structure itself, but the pretence of some of those who flourished under it that they themselves or the structure as a whole operated in harmony with the moral principles they professed. Secondly he attacked these moral principles themselves, and thirdly those who from a sentimental but genuine addiction to these principles advocated even minor changes in existing institutions to bring them nearer to what these principles demanded. What persons he found who did, in fact, advocate this kind of change of institutions I do not know. Mandeville alleged that the charity schools then being established were preparing the way for innovations of this sort, but the sponsors of these schools immediately and earnestly denied that they had any such reformist intentions.

While Mandeville repeatedly asserted his acceptance of the traditional code of ethics in its full rigour, he made every effort to

---

[1] 'Lead' here means pewter. In the late nineteenth century pewter was no longer the cheapest tableware.

[2] In *Speculation; Or, A Defence of Mankind, A Poem* (London, 1780), the lines on pp. 48–9 have a substantial resemblance, in theme and manner, to those quoted above. The poem was published anonymously, but its authorship has been attributed to Christopher Anstey (1724–1805), a Fellow of King's College, Cambridge.

demonstrate the disastrous consequences that would result if it should be generally carried into practice. Mandeville seems to shift back and forth between the role of the rigorous moralist who believes, but is convinced that living according to belief would bring an end to society, and the role of the intellectually honest rogue who regards conventional moral doctrine as a fit subject for laughter, but out of prudence, or to provide more fun for himself and his cronies, or to be more provoking to the professed moralists, whether they be genuine or hypocritical, chooses to do his laughing from behind a satiric veil. If the experts on satire were to analyse Mandeville's satirical procedure, I think they would find that it has some resemblance to the procedure of the young man who insisted on his right of admission in his ordinary street clothes to a masquerade ball restricted to those in costume, on the ground that he was dressed as a man dressed as a woman dressed as a man.

The overwhelmingly conservative tendency of English satire before the nineteenth century is illustrated by the use of the terms 'project' and 'projector'. By early in the seventeenth century it had become predominantly a derogatory term, applied indiscriminately to almost any proposal for innovation, whether in government, religion, industrial and financial procedures, or philanthropy. It carried implications of 'jobs', 'schemes', 'bubbles', 'illegitimate profit', or 'innovations', in presumptuous disregard of the sanctity of established traditions and ways of doing things. Occasionally someone would protest that 'projects' could be good as well as bad, especially when they constituted possibly useful inventions or processes in industry or agriculture. Samuel Johnson was one instance. But apparently almost no one can be cited before Bentham at the end of the eighteenth century who would praise in general terms receptivity to 'projects'. As pejorative terms, 'project' and 'projector' were part of the armoury of satire of the seventeenth and eighteenth centuries, and were frequently resorted to as convenient substitutes for objective argument. The term 'reformer' was in some degree also used pejoratively.

I have not been able to find a corresponding vocabulary available for use in support of proposals for change or for satiric thrusts against resistance to change. It is possible that systematic comparative study of the vocabulary of social satire in England and in France in the eighteenth century would be revealing, as indicating differences in the major targets of such satire in the two countries. I have found some bits of evidence, for instance, that when Continental writers wanted a term equivalent to the English 'project', used pejoratively, they adopted the English word. Some of the satires against 'projects' did have as their targets what we should now regard as frauds or wild schemes. But some of the proposals that were satirized would now be widely regarded as proposals for highly desirable innovations or 'reforms'.

I do not wish to give the impression, however, that I know of a vast English eighteenth-century satirical literature playing an important role in public debate of current economic issues. There may have been such a literature, but it has not come to my attention nor, as far as I know, been confirmed by the bibliographers.

One of the most widely debated and bitterly contested economic issues of the eighteenth century was Robert Walpole's 'Scheme' of 1733 to substitute excise taxes for import duties on wine and tobacco. I have found record of nearly one hundred separate tracts, a majority of them hostile, published in that year with this 'Scheme' as their central topic, and over the years I have examined perhaps thirty of them. In addition there were no doubt many broadsides and articles in periodicals. From the titles of the tracts and from what I know of their contents, it seems to me wholly improbable that satire was an important ingredient in the majority of them. I have found only four tracts, all hostile to the scheme, which were wholly or largely satirical in form.

I will comment on one illustrating some of the minor devices or tricks available in the repertory of an eighteenth-century satirist. The title of the tract is *The Origin and Essence of a General Excise: A Sermon preached on a very Extraordinary Occasion at a noted Chapel in Westminster*. That it was an actual sermon is pretence. It was probably a reply to an actual sermon preached at St. Paul's Cathedral by one of the Whig upper clergy in Walpole's political camp. It bore on its title-page, as the name of the author, Robert Viner, D.D. (or Vyner, or Winer, depending on the edition), in all probability a pseudonym playing on the 'wine' which was the subject of the excise scheme. As the text for the alleged sermon the author gave Luke 2 : 1 : 'And it came to pass, in those days, that a decree went out, that all the world should be taxed.' The satire was unfair, but by the usual standards mild, and it seems to me rather good fun though unlikely to have converted anyone.

The amount of satire I have found in our period which is of
economic relevance and which can be plausibly evaluated as
having exercised a substantial influence, positive or negative, on
the course of legislation is, as I have indicated, quantitatively
meagre. Satire, however, need not be directed at men, or at
actual proposals for legislation, or at political parties, or at
institutions. It may be directed at ideas, and such satire I shall label
as intellectual satire. If the ideas are economic ideas, are relevant
subject-matter for economic analysis, satire directed at them may
be important to economists, and may be important also, indirectly,
in affecting the receptiveness of politically significant persons to
specific legislative proposals and social trends.

It is part of the history, although often the unrecorded and
unanalysed history, of most intellectual disciplines that their procedures, tools, and findings have to face some amount of satirical
scrutiny, sometimes from within their own ranks, sometimes
from hostile outsiders. When a discipline, any discipline, introduces new tools of analysis, the pioneer sponsors of these tools
are liable to be over-enthusiastic as to their potentialities, and to
use them clumsily and naïvely. Such was the case with quantifica-
tion, or statistical procedure, as a tool of analysis in economic
thought and in demography. Under the label of 'political arith-
metic' it had its critics from its invention in the 1660s to well on
in the nineteenth century. Those of its critics who belonged to the
literary world were usually men of wider fame than its practitioners among the economists or elsewhere. In our period Swift,
Burke, and Defoe are notable as having treated political arith-
metic and its exponents satirically. In modern expert opinion
some of these criticisms had substantial justification. But the
critics were at fault at least in not realizing that the defects they
were laughing at were mostly the inevitable shortcomings of a
new technique, still in its infant stage but destined to have a great
future. In the cases of Swift and Burke the satire, taking the form
mainly of parody, was magnificent fun. It may conceivably have
done something to stimulate the political arithmeticians to improve on their performance.

I now call attention to another piece of intellectual satire, of
even more direct relevance to economic analysis, which was, I
think, technically successful from a literary point of view, and
which, as far as it went, was sound in terms of economic analysis,

but has not, as far as I know, received the attention of either students of Augustan satire or historians of economic thought.

There have always been objections to the introduction of new instruments or new processes in production which enable a given amount of product to be turned out with less expenditure of labour. The oldest basis of objection was religious: man had been sentenced to eat his bread in the sweat of his brow, and to evade this sentence by the use of machines was sinful; to use winnowing machines to winnow corn was impious because man thereby raised an artificial breeze, in defiance of God 'who maketh the wind to blow as He listeth'. In other words, the path to hell was paved with good inventions. Another basic objection rested on the economic argument or belief that labour-saving devices resulted in a reduction in the amount of employment available for the labour force *as a whole*. Finally, there was the objection from, or on behalf of, the particular sector of labour immediately affected that the demand for *its* labour was reduced or eliminated by machinery.

John Arbuthnot, a member of Swift's circle of friends, a wit, a physician, and a good mathematician, published an essay in 1716 entitled *The Humble Petition of the Colliers, Cooks . . . Blacksmiths . . . and Others*, in which he satirized the objections then current against labour-saving devices.[1] A process, he pretended, had been discovered whereby with the aid of burning glasses sunbeams could be substituted for coal in cooking, brewing, smelting ore, and so on. This would be damaging to all whose livelihood depended on the handling, mining, transportation, or use of coal. The petitioners therefore begged that Parliament should either prohibit or tax heavily the substitution of sunbeams for coal. This was good intellectual satire. It decided no issues, but if listened to it forced more profound analysis of the issues involved. A French economist of the middle years of the nineteenth century, Frederic Bastiat, a man with an exceptionally facile pen, who made up in the lucidity of his prose for what he lacked in profundity of thought, repeated in kind and in manner Arbuthnot's satiric technique for countering the popular objections to labour-saving processes of manufacture. Bastiat in translation, incidentally, had a large and appreciative audience in the United States. It is

[1] The *Petition* is reprinted in George A. Aitken, *The Life and Works of John Arbuthnot* (Oxford, 1892), pp. 375–8.

extremely improbable that Bastiat had ever heard of Arbuthnot, or had been indirectly influenced by him. For students of satirical technique, the incident may, however, be significant as showing that without plagiarism two identical flashes of satirical lightning may, at over a century's interval, hit an identical intellectual target.

Let me sum up briefly what I regard as my main findings as to the relations in England from 1660 to 1760 between satire and the course of English economic thought and economic history.

The century was one of continuous and profound complacency among the English upper classes with respect to the economic structure of English society. There were conflicts of attitude and policy within these classes, and satire had a role, though a minor one, in the conduct of controversy concerning these conflicts. Manners, individual morals, were freely lashed. But important institutions were left unscarred by satire. The bitter civil strife of earlier decades, involving extensive armed conflict for the last time in English domestic history, became after 1660 an unpleasant memory, which enforced rather than weakened underlying conservative attitudes averse to institutional change and to critical examination of existing institutions. Throughout the period I have been dealing with the great bulk of the people was, for all practical purposes, voiceless. A large portion of it was illiterate, probably a larger portion than in the previous century, when zealous Protestantism was striving to make accessible to every person, as essential to salvation, direct contact with the Word of God as revealed in the Scriptures. Satire itself was a difficult literary technique, requiring literary sophistication on the part of both its creators and its audience, and there was widespread aversion to its use, resting on traditional religious and moral considerations. Not one outstanding instance seems to have occurred of a sophisticate using satiric skills in the service of institutional change designed to make England a new Jerusalem, a happy land, for the great mass of the poor.

It would seem an appropriate task for literary critics and social historians to discover why, in ancient times, in the late Middle Ages, in eighteenth-century France, and in nineteenth-century England, but not in the Augustan Age of English satire, there were writers who resorted to the satiric lance as a weapon serviceable in promoting concerted action against the poverty, the misery, and the social degradation, of the depressed masses. In the otherwise rich recent critical and historical literature on English satire I find little emphasis on any of the points I have ventured to make, and no mention of some of them. Unless, as is quite possible, the adequate retort to this charge of neglect of an eminently suitable field for research should be that my acquaintance with the recent literature on English satire is in urgent need of broadening and deepening, there is for the literary experts some work awaiting their attention.

6

BISHOP BERKELEY AND TAR-WATER

By MARJORIE NICOLSON *and* G. S. ROUSSEAU

GEORGE BERKELEY, Dean of Derry—not yet Bishop of Cloyne —arrived in Rhode Island on 23 January 1729, and remained until shortly before he sailed home from Boston on 9 September 1731. He had come to the colonies in connection with his plan to establish in Bermuda a college for sons of English planters and for the education of Indians. During his residence on the mainland and in Newport he was marking time, waiting for confirmation of funds the government was supposedly assigning, which ultimately proved not forthcoming. In the late eighteenth and nineteenth centuries accounts of Berkeley's colonial visit came to be surrounded by various legends, one of which was that he arrived in Rhode Island by accident, because 'the captain of the ship in which he sailed could not find the island of Bermuda, and having given up the search after it, steered northward until they discovered land unknown to them, and which they supposed to be inhabited only by savages'.[1]

[1] This legend, which seems to have been persistent for many years, was repeated in these words by the grandson of one of Berkeley's closest Rhode Island associates, Wilkins Updike, *History of the Episcopal Church in Narragansett* (New York, 1847), p. 395. Alexander Campbell Fraser, *The Works of George Berkeley D.D.* (Oxford, 1871), iv. 154–8, disproved it from Berkeley's correspondence and other historical evidence. Rhode Island had been settled for a century, and Newport was an important cultural and trade centre, well known in England. Berkeley had chosen it deliberately. This visit was described in a letter from William Byrd to Sir John Percival. See Benjamin Rand, *Berkeley and Percival* (Cambridge, 1914), pp. 238, 244; other material about the period is in Rand, *Berkeley's American Sojourn* (Harvard Univ., 1932). In the most recent treatment of the American period, Alice Brayton, *George Berkeley in America* (Newport, 1954), p. 4, suggests that the stop in Virginia may have been made because two of Berkeley's travelling companions, Richard Dalton and John (later Sir John) James, both gentlemen of substance (who, she suggests, might have paid for the ship that made the crossing), wished to make a protracted visit there. Throughout this article we refer to the Luce and Jessop edition of *The Works of George Berkeley*, 9 vols. (London, 1948–57), as 'Luce and Jessop, *Works*'.

For the purposes of this study a more important legend which has been questioned is that Berkeley's acquaintance with tar-water came from the Narragansett Indians, on the mainland of Rhode Island; it may rather have come from South Carolinians. Such is the contention of Miss Alice Brayton,[1] who tends to discount Berkeley's interest in the Narragansett Indians as part of a sentimentalization of the 'noble savage' tradition, in which the distinguished Irish philosopher turns to the lowly Red Man for medical knowledge. According to Miss Brayton, Berkeley first heard of tar-water in the spring of 1730, when a violent epidemic of smallpox broke out in Boston and a stranger of Newport died of it. Among the Newport residents were several self-exiles from South Carolina, friends of Mrs. Berkeley, who used tar-water for their own protection and that of their slaves; they had learned the principle from Indians in South Carolina.[2]

Miss Brayton may be correct in her theory that Berkeley's knowledge of tar-water came from the South Carolinian *émigrés*, but she is probably not correct in discounting his interest in the Narragansett Indians. There is abundant evidence in Updike and other early historians of Berkeley's study of the Narragansetts both early in his stay on the mainland and later when, with the elder Updike, McSparran, and others, 'he repeatedly visited Narragansett . . . to examine into the condition and character of the Narragansett Indians'.[3] Since the proposed college in the

---

[1] Op. cit., pp. xiv–xv, 99–100.

[2] In the passage referred to above Miss Brayton says—without reference—that Berkeley mentioned South Carolinian Indians in connection with tar-water. We have not been able to locate the passage. In *Siris* (London, 1744), p. 4, he says: 'In certain parts of America tar-water is made. . . . This cold infusion of tar hath been used in some of our colonies, as a preservative or preparative against the small-pox.' On p. 9 he mentions 'the method used by our colonies in America, for making tar and pitch'. A. A. Luce, *The Life of George Berkeley, Bishop of Cloyne* (London, 1949), p. 200, says, in connection with the smallpox epidemic, that Berkeley 'heard that the Indians used tar-water as a specific preventive, though he did not actually meet it in use'. He does not indicate which Indians. One sentence in *Siris* (§ 115) leads us to wonder whether Berkeley had used tar-water in Rhode Island, perhaps at the time of the smallpox epidemic. He refers to 'my own manner of making it, and not the American; that sometimes makes it too strong, and sometimes too weak'. Unless otherwise stated, all references to *Siris* are to the reprinted London edition of 1744.

[3] Updike, *History*, p. 176. Alexander Fraser in his *Life* takes for granted Berkeley's interest in the Narragansetts, as does Luce, *Life*, p. 122, *et passim*.

Bermudas was in part for the education of Indians, it seems inevitable that Berkeley should have studied with care what he could learn of the mentality and other characteristics of the first Indians he had known.

Berkeley's knowledge of the Narragansett Indians is further shown in the sermon he preached on 18 February 1731, shortly after his return to London, before the Society for the Propagation of the Gospel in Foreign Parts.[1] Here he developed in some detail his observations on the condition of both Indians and Negroes in Rhode Island. He referred to the diminution in number of Indians, a result in part of wars and smallpox, but chiefly through the 'slow poison' of 'the Use of strong Liquors' taught them by their supposed masters. But we are here chiefly concerned with Berkeley's interest in tar-water.

I

The work in which Berkeley treated the subject was *Siris: A Chain of Philosophical Reflexions and Inquiries concerning the Virtues of Tar Water*, published in 1744. Until recently it was believed that *Siris* was not the original title but was added in later editions.[2] We now know that the first edition was that published in Dublin in March 1744, in which the title appeared. Berkeley considered *Siris* a contribution to philosophy, but the publisher of the first London editions realized that the introductory portion—the first 119-odd sections—describing a simple home-remedy specific for the prevention or cure of many diseases, would greatly attract general readers, particularly if the unfamiliar word 'Siris' were omitted and the stress seemed to be upon 'the Virtues of Tar Water'. Another indication of the publishers' lowering the work to the capacity of the general reader was the addition to the second Dublin edition (September 1744) of a 'Vocabulary of certain

---

[1] This, the only one of his sermons published during his lifetime, was printed at London in 1732. It may be found in *A Miscellany containing Several Tracts on Various Subjects by the Bishop of Cloyne* (London, 1752), pp. 215–35.

[2] This theory was generally accepted by Berkeley scholars until 1955, when E. J. Furlong and W. V. Denard published 'The Dating of the Editions of Berkeley's *Siris* and of his first Letter to Thomas Prior', *Hermathena*, lxxxvi (Nov. 1955), 66–76. Since six editions were published in 1744, the problem was inevitably complicated. Furlong and Denard show that the first edition was the Dublin one announced 20–4 Mar. 1744.

words not commonly understood'. Correct in their surmise, the publishers had a 'best-seller'. Six editions were sold out within a few months.[1]

For many years *Siris* continued to be regarded as a contribution to medicine rather than philosophy. With the exception of a few references considered below, it first began to assume philosophical importance in 1871 in Alexander Campbell Fraser's *The Works of George Berkeley, D.D.*[2] Fraser called it 'the curious and beautiful work of speculation in which he celebrated the new medicine'. Berkeley said that *Siris* had cost him more thought and research than any other work. Fraser adds : 'No one who examines its contents can be surprised to hear this. The book is full of fruit gathered in the remoter by-ways of science and philosophy.'

Fraser's estimate is shared by Professor John Wild in one of the most important twentieth-century treatments of Berkeley's philosophy.[3] Wild went even further than Fraser, challenging 'many of his modern commentators [who] have dismissed the *Siris* altogether as a senile aberration'. He devoted some fifty pages to a study of its ideas and their sources in early philosophy. Yet many modern readers have been perplexed by *Siris*, in part because of the first lengthy section, with its stress upon a simple household remedy for man and beast, the very part of the work with which most eighteenth-century readers stopped their reading. As recently as 1960 John Linnell declared :[4] 'If Berkeley had not written the *Siris*, his significant place in the history of philosophy would be what it actually is; if he had written only *Siris*, he would very likely have had little or no place in that history.'

An interesting example of a change in attitude may be seen in Professor A. A. Luce, Berkeley's most recent biographer, and co-editor with Professor T. E. Jessup of his *Works*. In 1936 he raised the question, 'Is there a Berkeleian Philosophy?'[5] and spoke of *Siris* as 'an old man's ramble through quack remedies to Elysian fields'. But in his biography,[6] published in 1949, his

---

[1] Perhaps at Berkeley's insistence, the title *Siris* was restored in the London edition announced on 30 Apr.

[2] op. cit. iv, p. 293.

[3] *George Berkeley: A Study of his Life and Philosophy* (Harvard Univ., 1936), p. 411.

[4] 'Berkeley's *Siris*', *The Personalist* xli (Winter 1960), 5.

[5] In *Hermathena* l (1936), 197.

[6] *Life*, p. 197.

treatment of *Siris* is sympathetic and understanding. He recognizes various reasons for the banishment from serious philosophy it had encountered:

> Tar is a black and sticky substance with none too good a name in letters, and the very idea of a bishop discarding his white lawn sleeves and handling it and extracting a nasty medicine from it is too much for our sense of gravity, and Berkeley's tar-water has become a jest. . . . No one objects to a laugh or two about it; Berkeley could see the funny side of it himself, and jokes his tar-drinking friends. But the joke has been carried too far; the whole affair has been treated as a craze, as a proof of unbalanced temperament and failing faculties, if not of a disordered mind. Serious biography must leave the comic aspect aside.

Professor Luce then shows how different the sections on tar-water seem in their historical perspective. Berkeley's tar-water, he rightly emphasizes, was no jest in his own day, except to a limited number. 'Thousands of sick and sufferers blessed his name. The apostles of old could heal the sick; a bishop in the eighteenth century could with perfect propriety make the attempt, and situated as he was Berkeley simply *had* to do so.' Luce's justification of the Bishop's activities reminds us of a quatrain, written in an eighteenth-century hand in the Princeton University copy of Berkeley's *Miscellany*:

> Who dare deride what pious Cloyne has done.
> The Church shall rise and vindicate her son.
> She tells us all her Bishops shepherds are
> And shepherds heal their rotten sheep with tar.

Luce calls our attention to the situation Berkeley faced when he began to administer tar-water to the Cloyne sick. The winter of 1739–40 was one of the most severe ever experienced, causing a famine. In Dublin there were nurses and doctors, even some hospitals, but in country districts there was no provision for the sick and poor, who inevitably turned to the clergy for aid. During the great frost Berkeley gave twenty pounds in gold to the poor each Monday. He and his wife ministered to their physical ailments with any medicines they could make. Sickness and plague followed upon the famine, and a severe epidemic of dysentery raged through Ireland and descended on Cloyne. Berkeley wrote to Thomas Prior on 8 February 1741[1] of cures he had

---

[1] *Letters* in Luce and Jessop, *Works*, viii. 249; see also 272–3.

been trying for the epidemic, and added: 'I believe tar-water might be useful to prevent (or to perfect the cure of) such an evil; there being, so far as I can judge, no more powerful corrector of putrid humours.' Some time during this period Berkeley began to experiment with the tar-water which in Rhode Island had proved effectual against smallpox. For a time he became a doctor on the one hand, a chemist on the other. A room in the episcopal residence was set apart for preparation of tar-water, and here he experimented on such matters as the stirring-time and the clarifying-time.[1] He had already read all that had been written about tar by the ancients, who knew its virtues though they did not use tar-water. Undoubtedly he kept himself abreast of anything germane to tar-water in the natural history of his own time.[2] When the violence of the plague and dysentery subsided and crops began to grow again, Berkeley had time to devote himself to the writing of *Siris*, and a little later to the tracts that followed it.

Among the controversies caused by even the earlier editions of *Siris*, the most immediate and the one that was to be of longest duration was that due to the opposition aroused among conservative members of the medical profession, to whom the new 'cure-all' seemed in a class with Joshua Ward's 'Pill and Drop', the

[1] E. J. Furlong in part determined the order of the various editions of *Siris* upon such internal evidence as these matters. See *Hermathena* lxxxvii (1956), 37–48.

[2] We had hoped to be able to determine more accurately than we can Berkeley's probable reading in contemporary natural science. A catalogue of the sale of his library by Leigh and Sotheby in 1796 is in the British Museum, but R. I. Aaron believes that many books Berkeley once owned are now missing. See his 'Catalogue of Berkeley's Library', *Mind* xli (1932), 465–75. Berkeley had left in America many of the books he had brought with him, which he had used in the writing of *Alciphron*. Of the forty-seven works to which he referred there, Aaron found only one in the catalogue. Among the approximately 1,000 books he gave or sent to Yale, ten were upon natural philosophy. These included the *Philosophical Transactions of the Royal Society* from its beginning to 1720. Twenty-five volumes deal with 'Anatomy, Physick, and Chyrurgery'. On this see Henry M. Fuller, 'Bishop Berkeley as a Benefactor of Yale', *Yale University Library Gazette* xxviii (1953), 1–18; Andrew Keogh, ibid. ix (1934), 1–25. J. M. Hone and M. M. Rossi, *Bishop Berkeley: His Life, Writings and Philosophy* (London, 1931), p. 236, describing Berkeley's involvement with tar-water, say: 'The library shelves were filled with books on medicine, mostly ancient and mediaeval.' They give no authority for the statement.

most popular nostrums of the preceding decade.[1] Of such opposition we shall hear more as we continue. Involved with this in many minds, not limited to the medical faculty, was the question whether the Bishop considered that he had found what alchemists had sought so diligently, the universal panacea. On this Berkeley spoke a number of times, most vigorously in *A Letter to Thomas Prior, Esq.*,[2] the sequel to *Siris*, published in Dublin in July 1744, while editions of *Siris* were still coming from the press:

The great objection I find made to this medicine is that it promises too much. What, say the objectors, do you pretend to a *panacea*, a thing strange, chimerical, and contrary to the opinion and experience of all mankind? Now, to speak out, and give this objection or question a plain and direct answer—I freely own that I suspect tar-water is a panacea. I may be mistaken, but it is worth trial: for the chance of so great and general benefit, I am willing to stand the ridicule of proposing it. . . .

. . . by a panacea is not meant a medicine which cures all individuals (this consists not with mortality), but a medicine that cures or relieves all the different species of distempers. . . .

After all that can be said, it is most certain that a panacea sounds odd, and conveys somewhat shocking to the ear and sense of most men, who are wont to rank the Universal Medicine with the philosopher's stone, and the squaring of the circle. . . . I do not say it is a panacea, I only suspect it to be so—time and trial will shew.

Other letters to Thomas Prior were published later, but we may leave them for a time to consider Prior's own contribution to the *Siris* controversy, *An Authentic Narrative of the Success of Tar-Water, in curing a great Number and Variety of Distempers.*[3]

Thomas Prior of Rathdowney had been a fellow student at Kilkenny College with Berkeley, who entered in his eleventh year; they remained close friends all their lives. Prior did not enter a profession, though he seems to have read law, but devoted himself to the remedy of public and social evils. He acted as Berkeley's legal agent, and was the founder and the Secretary of the Dublin Society. The *Authentic Narrative* was dedicated to Philip Stanhope, the fourth Earl of Chesterfield, in the hope

[1] See Marjorie Nicolson, 'Joshua Ward's "Pill and Drop", and Men of Letters', *JHI* xxix (1968), 177–96.

[2] In *Works*, ed. Alexander Campbell Fraser (Oxford, 1871), iii. 465–70.

[3] We have used the 'New Edition', London, 1746, published in Dublin and reprinted in London. The first edition had appeared earlier that year.

that he would find it a contribution to the public good. The work contained 'An Alphabetical Index of the several Distempers' which had been alleviated or cured by tar-water, and a remarkable list it is, of approximately 120 'Distempers', ranging alphabetically from 'ague' to 'wind', a few certified in only one instance, others many times. There are twenty-seven instances of the curing of coughs, twenty-one of scurvy, nineteen of asthma, eleven of the king's evil. Prior begins his pamphlet by discussing an advertisement that had appeared in the *Dublin Journal* for 3 July 1744, asserting that many patients in Stephen's Hospital had not benefited from tar-water. Upon investigation he found only six affidavits, and went on to point out in his narrative that the treatment had not been continued long enough. Most of the *Authentic Narrative* is devoted to brief case-histories of cure or relief by tar-water. These Prior had secured largely through advertisements in various periodicals. The most interesting one, which attracted widespread interest, as references to it show, was an affidavit, sworn to before the Mayor of Liverpool, by Captain Drape,[1] master of the ship *Little Foster* of Liverpool. On a voyage from Guinea to Jamaica he had carried over 200 Negro slaves, among whom 170 contracted smallpox. A passenger advised the master to give them tar-water. One who refused to drink it died; all the others recovered.

In addition to 120 testimonials, Prior included 'A Pindarique by the Right Honourable, L. C. J. M., inscribed to the author of *Siris*', and two anonymous sets of verses, which as we shall hear, were written by Berkeley. There is also an unsigned letter to the editor of the *General Evening Post* for 4 June 1744,[2] paying high tribute to *Siris*. This we mention because the author is one of the few eighteenth-century writers we have found who seems to have read *Siris* from beginning to end, and to have realized that it was much more than a disquisition on tar-water. Berkeley is praised as chemist, physician, philosopher, and divine. 'While he gradually leads me on from the simplest operations of nature, thro' the animal and vegetable world, up to the great author of both, I am charmed with my progress, and think I see in this *chain* of his, that golden one, which hung down to earth from

[1] He is so called by both Prior and Berkeley. In the *Gentleman's Magazine* his name is given as Draper.
[2] op. cit., p. 16.

heaven, as this by several links carries us up thither.' In the system of *Siris* the correspondent finds 'a principle of pure light', while in other philosophical systems he feels 'nothing but gravitation'.

Among those who seemed to forget that *Siris* was a philosophical rather than a medical work was its author. Most of the short remainder of the Bishop's life was devoted to tar-water. In 1744 he published *A Letter to Thomas Prior*, and in 1746 *A Second Letter from the author of Siris to Thomas Prior.*[1] Both are practical advice on the preparation and administration of the remedy, with a 'suspicion' that this is a panacea. Berkeley's last publication was *Farther Thoughts on Tar-Water*, which appeared in 1752.[2] He looks back happily on the remarkable increase in the use of tar-water: from Ireland and England it had spread throughout Europe. 'Many barrels of tar-water' were shipped from Amsterdam to Batavia. It was successfully used in the East and West Indies, and Berkeley had had accounts, by post and from travellers, of its widespread use in the colonies, 'particularly by those who possess great Numbers of Slaves'. For all practical purposes, tar-water had proved a panacea to man, woman, child, and beast. Other case-histories are quoted. So obsessed had the Bishop become with his American remedy, that he believed that tar-water always succeeds where Nature fails, offering among its successes such extreme examples as these: 'A Gentleman with a wither'd Arm had it restored by drinking Tar-Water. Another who, by running his Head against a Post, had a Concussion of the Brain attended with very bad Symptoms, recovered by drinking Tar-Water after other Medicines had failed. In my own Neighbourhood, one had lost the use of his Limbs by Poison, another had been bitten by a mad Ass; these Persons drank Tar-Water, and their Cure was attributed to it.' Bishop Berkeley had indeed found the universal panacea!

The effect of *Siris* was almost instantaneous. Tar-water warehouses were established in London and elsewhere. Advertisements for tar and tar-water appeared widely in periodicals. On 10 June 1744 William Duncombe wrote to Archbishop Herring:[3]

---

[1] In the British Museum copy these are attached to the 1746 *Authentic Narrative*.

[2] In *A Miscellany, containing Several Tracts on Various Subjects* (London, 1752), pp. 9–28. The most recent edition is in Luce and Jessop, *Works*, v.

[3] Quoted A. A. Luce, *Life*, p. 201.

'It is impossible to write a letter now without tincturing the ink with tar-water. This is the common topic of discourse both among the rich and poor, high and low; and the Bishop of Cloyne has made it as fashionable as going to Vauxhall or Ranelagh.' Luce says: 'A dispensary was opened in St. James's Street, London, by the "Proprietors of the tar-water warehouse", who published a tract professing to explain Berkeley's terms and giving instructions for making tar-water well. Lady Egmont took the remedy, and the Earl seems to have introduced it into Court circles. The Princess Caroline tried, and so did the Duke of Newcastle.'[1]

Some indication how quickly news of tar-water crossed the sea may be seen in a rare pamphlet, which, so far as we have been able to determine, is to be found only in the New York Public Library: *An Abstract from Dr. Berkeley's Treatise on tar water, with some reflexions therein. Adapted to diseases frequent in America. By a friend to the country* (New York, 1745). Dr. Saul Jarcho has shown that the author was Cadwallader Colden (1688–1776), 'the distinguished colonist physician, savant, and government official',[2] who contributed the papers anonymously to the *New York Weekly Post-Boy*, in which they constitute numbers 109–14, 18 February to 25 March 1745. In the articles Colden quoted a section of *Siris*, and followed it with twenty-seven paragraphs of discussion, on the whole decidedly finding for Berkeley. Dr. Jarcho says that in a fashion typical of the period, 'Colden's comments contain a great deal of reasoning and a very small measure of observation'. There is little question that the essays in the New York paper would have attracted a good deal of attention to the remedy that had proved so effective in Ireland. Within a year tar-water had come home to America.

II

Evidence of the popular interest aroused in England by tar-water may be seen by following some of the many references in

[1] Ibid.

[2] 'The Therapeutic Use of Resin and of Tar Water of Bishop George Berkeley and Cadwallader Colden', *New York State Journal of Medicine* iv (1955), 834–40. On pp. 834–5 Dr. Jarcho points out a fact Berkeley's biographers have not stressed, that in 1711 Berkeley had effectively used resin for the treatment of diarrhoea.

the *Gentleman's Magazine*. We deliberately choose this periodical rather than the *Dublin Journal*, still richer in materials, because that might be considered a prejudiced witness, since its printer and editor was George Faulkner, a close friend of Berkeley's, associated with him in various movements for the public good. The first mention of tar-water in the *Gentleman's Magazine* is in the number for January 1739 (ix. 36), remarkably early, since *Siris* was not to be published for five years. This is a short notice, 'A Receipt to make and use Tar-Water, for preventing Infection by the Small-Pox, and for a consumptive Habit'. The recipe is followed by a statement: 'By this Remedy several Persons in Charles Town, South-Carolina, where the Small Pox was lately very mortal, escap'd the Infection, though conversant with the Infected. . . .' The entry is referred to again in the issue for April 1744 (xiv. 193–6), in connection with a notice of the first London edition of *Siris*, which had recently appeared. 'The Virtues of [Tar-Water] have lately been set in so strong a Light, by an Author of the greatest Character for Learning, Penetration, and Veracity, that we should be negligent of our Duty to the Public, should we omit his judicious Observations.' The lengthy review is made up of extracts from the first third of *Siris*, sufficient to tell the reader how to prepare the water and to give him some idea of the many ills for which it was specific. One of the earliest reviews gives the reader no idea that *Siris* is a philosophical work, but limits its comments and excerpts to the medical section.

The issue for January 1745 (xv. 34) suggests that the publisher of the early London editions was correct in believing that the title *Siris* was not a good one, since the general reader would not understand its significance. An anonymous correspondent, writing to 'Mr. Urban', the editor, says that, because several of his acquaintance had been at a loss to understand the title, he will explain to the public that, according to 'Dionysius', Siris is the name given by Ethiopians to the Nile because of the darkness of the waters. 'Mr. Urban' adds an editorial note to the effect that Berkeley intended an allusion to the Greek word signifying 'chain'. The next number of the periodical contains a communication to the effect that members of the medical profession give warning that tar-water is dangerous in inflammatory cases, but the Bishop of Cloyne has written to one of the correspondent's acquaintance, insisting that the water had recently cured the Bishop's young

son of a fever. In the issue of March 1745 (xv. 163), the editors
quote from the *Dublin Journal* an account of the affidavit made by
Captain Drape about the Negroes on his ship who recovered
from smallpox, thanks to tar-water.

Beginning with the issue of June 1745 (xv. 317–19), we find
testimonials sent to Thomas Prior, who was collecting them for
his *Authentic Narrative*. One account that must have interested
readers was that of a woman, twice married, who never became
pregnant until she drank tar-water; the inquiring correspondent
learned that the husband also drank it. Many of the reports on
cures were picked up and used as advertising by the Tar-Water
Warehouse in Painter's Court, Bury Street, St. James's, which
announced 'Remarkable Cures perform'd by Tar-Water; collected
out of the "Gentleman's Magazine" to be had of the Proprietor'.
In issues of 1746 and 1747 readers were told that cures are not
limited to human beings; tar-water also cures various distempers
in animals. The magazine was obliging enough to publish a recipe
showing how to prepare it for cattle (xvii. 22). In March 1748
(xviii. 120), when there was 'cause to be apprehensive' about the
plague, the editors included an extract from Berkeley's treatise
indicating 'the usefulness of Tar-Water in the Plague'. In November 1748 (xviii. 485–6), 'Mr. Urban' is told that although 'our
college of physicians' has not yet seen fit to introduce tar-water
into the British Pharmacopoeia, the French have adopted it in the
Formules de Pharmacie.[1] Opposition of the medical profession to
tar-water was continuing, as is evidenced by a quotation sent to
the magazine in June 1749 (xix. 247) from *Reflections on Catholicons
or Universal Medicines*, by Thomas Knight, M.D., a lengthy tract
upon Berkeley's claims for his cure-all of which we shall hear
later.

Occasionally correspondents of the *Gentleman's Magazine*
launched into verse so far as *Siris* was concerned. The issue for

[1] Tar-water was later admitted to the British Pharmacopacia, and remained
in the Dublin list well on in the nineteenth century. In 'Bishop Berkeley and
his Use of Tar-Water', *Annals of Medical History*, 3rd Ser. iv (1942), 463–4,
Burton Chance says: 'In the latest practical United States Dispensatory two
or three columns are given to the chemical composition of the water, and
directions for its occasional employment.' Dr. Saul Jarcho, in his article on
Cadwallader Colden (p. 840), mentions its presence in 'the remarkable
pharmacopacia which was prepared for the French forces in the American
Revolution, and published at Newport in 1780'.

March 1745 (xv. 160), included 'SIRIS. A Vision'. In an elysian
garden, near a crystal fountain and a mossy grotto, the poet in
vision saw a nymph whose name proved to be 'Siris', the daughter
of Phoebus and Hygeia, whose 'dotal wealth' was her father's
skill and her mother's health. With water from the limpid stream
and tar from 'the wounded fir's disclosing side', she mixed a
draught which she bade the poet drink:

> her orders I obey'd,
> And quick as thought, felt all my anguish fled.

In more serious mood is a Latin ode 'To the Author of Siris'
(xxii. 472–3), together with a translation, in which Berkeley is
hailed among the great of all time:[1]

> There Newton, studious with extensive aim,
> And Boyle, the friend of man, my rev'rence claim:
> There great Hippocrates, with Syd'nham join'd,
> Share the sweet friendship of a kindred mind.

Most amusing among the verses are lines by one of the few contributors who seems to have read more of *Siris* than the introductory
section: 'On the Bishop of Cloyne's SIRIS, which, after treating
of the Virtues of Tar, enters upon the sublime Mystery of the
Trinity.' Since Tar and Trinity are indissolubly united, modern
Arians are urged to drink 'the juice of pines', because

> The *Irish* prelate's *Terebinthian* draughts
> Delude old *Antitrinitarian* thoughts.
> Swallow the julep of the *Norway tree*,
> You'll find the *three in one*, and *one in three*.
> How *orthodox* a *soup*! how glorious *pitch*,
> That cures *coughs*, *scurvy*, *heresy* and *itch*! . . .
> Ye *surgeons*, arm'd with lancets, cease to bleed;
> Ye *readers*, drop the *Athanasian* creed;
> Plain *tar*, by bishop *bless'd*, all art controuls;
> It *purifies* your *blood*, your *faith*, and *souls*.

Although 'Mr. Urban' was not aware of the fact, one group
of verses published by the *Gentleman's Magazine* in October 1744
had been written by Berkeley himself. On 3 September he had
sent them to Thomas Prior with the comment: 'The doctors, it
seems, are grown very abusive. To silence them, I send you the

---

[1] There is also a set of 'Verses sent to a Gentleman, on the Use of Tar-
Water' in the issue of Oct. 1757 (xxvii. 471).

above scrap of poetry, which I would by no means have known
or suspected for mine. You will therefore burn the original, and
send a copy to be printed in a newspaper, or the *Gentleman's
Magazine*.' The verses 'On *Siris* and its Enemies. By a Drinker of
Tar-Water' begin:

> How can devoted Siris stand
> Such dire attacks? The licens'd band,
> With upcast eyes and visage sad
> Proclaim, 'Alas! the world's run mad.
> The prelate's book has turn'd their brains,
> To set them right will cost us pains.
> His drug too makes our patients sick;
> And this doth vex us to the quick.'
> And vex'd they must be, to be sure,
> To find tar-water cannot cure,
> But makes men sicker still and sicker,
> And fees come thicker still and thicker.[1]

A scarcer set of Berkeleian verses, which appeared only in some
copies of *Siris*[2] in the second Dublin edition, suggest the scope
of *Siris* as a whole rather than that merely of the medical sections:

> Hail vulgar juice of never-fading pine!
> Cheap as thou art, thy virtues are divine.
> To shew them and explain (such is thy store)
> There needs much modern and much ancient lore.
> While with slow pains we search the healing spell,
> Those sparks of life, that in thy balsam dwell,
> From lowest earth by gentle steps we rise
> Through air, fire, aether to the highest skies. . . .
> But soon as intellect's bright sun displays
> O'er the benighted orb his fulgent rays,
> Delusive phantoms fly before the light,
> Nature and truth lie open to the sight:
> Causes connected with effects supply
> A golden chain, whose radiant links on high
> Fix'd to the sovereign throne from thence depend
> And reach e'en down to tar the nether end.

As another example of various poetic rhapsodies evoked by

---

[1] *Letters* in Luce and Jessop, *Works*, viii. 273–4.
[2] Luce and Jessop, *Works*, v. 225–6. Another poem of Berkeley's will be
found later.

Siris, we quote from 'Tar Water, A Ballad',[1] referred to but not quoted by the *Gentleman's Magazine* for January 1747. The verses probably appeared anonymously that month and sold for sixpence. They were written by a reader of Thomas Prior's *Authentic Narrative*, dedicated to Lord Chesterfield, and begin:

> Since good Master Prior,
> The Tar Water Squire,
>   Without being counted to blame,
> Vulgar Patrons hath scorn'd,
> And his Treatise adorn'd
>   With the Lustre of Chesterfield's Name.

The author also dedicates to Chesterfield his ballad, then passes to Berkeley and the virtues of the panacea:

> Then come, let us sing;
> Death, a Fig for thy Sting!
>   I think we shall serve thee a Trick;
> For the Bishop of *Cloyne*
> Has at last laid a Mine,
>   That will blow up both thee and Old Nick.
>
> Have but Faith in his Treatise
> Tho' you've Stone, Diabetes,
>   Gout or Fever, Tar Water's specifick;
> If you're costive, 'twill work;
> If you purge, 'tis a Cork,
>   And if old, it will make you prolifick.

It would seem that the ballad was later claimed by Sir Charles Hanbury Williams, ambassador to Russia and Saxony, and included in his *Works*.[2]

III

Hardly had *Siris* come from the press than pamphlets—replies and defences—began to appear. At least nine appeared during the

---

[1] *Tar Water, A Ballad, Inscribed to the Right Honourable Philip Earl of Chesterfield: Occasioned by reading a Narrative on the Success of Tar Water, Dedicated to his Lordship by Thomas Prior, Esquire.*

[2] *Works*, ed. Horace Walpole, Earl of Oxford (London, 1822), ii. 21–4. That volume also includes a short poem, 'On Charles Stanhope, Esq. Drinking Tar-Water'.

first year, 1744.[1] Some of these were written by medical men, largely inveighing against the entrance into their lists of a complete amateur, who, like John Wesley in *Primitive Physick* (1747), ventured to prescribe for many ills.[2] One was the work of an apothecary,[3] welcoming the new remedy—as apothecaries well might, with money flowing into their coffers—but suggesting changes in the recipe. At the opposite extreme is the most important scientific paper, that of Stephen Hales, which we shall consider presently. In addition is a small but interesting group of more 'literary' replies, naturally appealing more than the others to the literary historian. These we shall consider in some detail.

Most of the 'replies' of doctors we shall treat only briefly since they are largely repetitious. The first was chronologically the sixth paper in the war of words, appearing in July 1744: *A Cure for the Epidemical Madness of Drinking Tar-Water*, by T. R. M.D. This sixty-six-page pamphlet was the work of Dr. Thomas Reeve, whose chief claim to fame is that he was later President of the Royal College of Physicians for some ten years.[4] Reeve's basic position is that *Siris* is filled with errors because the author was ignorant of chemistry. He takes exception to many things, one of which is Berkeley's use of medical terminology. This section of his work may well have been responsible for the fact that the Dublin publisher of *Siris* added a glossary of terms to the edition that appeared in September 1744 and is found in some

[1] Alexander Campbell Fraser, *Works of George Berkeley*, ii. 355–7, listed twelve tracts in what he considered their chronological order. Earlier than that, an anonymous writer in the *Retrospective Review* i (London, 1853), 20–35, discussed a number of them, including *Anti-Siris*, *Siris in the Shades*, and the pamphlets by 'Risorius', Jackson the chemist, 'T. R.', 'Philanthropie', and Stephen Hales. Three others are mentioned, but so briefly that it is impossible to identify them. These are all largely passing comments and offer nothing in dating or identification.

[2] See G. S. Rousseau, 'John Wesley's *Primitive Physick* (1747)', *Harvard Library Bulletin* xvi (1968), 242–56.

[3] *Reflections concerning the Virtues of Tar-water*, published in June 1744, ascribed to H. Jackson, who is obviously an apothecary.

[4] Sir George Clark, *A History of the Royal College of Physicians of London* (Oxford, 1966), ii. 550–1, merely mentions that as President he proposed a candidate in 1754, and again mentions a resolution of thanks to him on his retirement as President in 1764. He seems to have had little stature ten years earlier when he wrote the pamphlet.

other editions. Even more than his errors in terminology, Reeve criticizes Berkeley's logic. Among the many virtues of tar-water, the Bishop had emphasized its cheapness in contrast with many expensive medicines. In that case, asks the physician, why did not Berkeley go the whole way with John Hancock and recommend the use of cold water only? This pamphlet was answered by one of the few doctors who ever spoke in Berkeley's defence, *The Bishop of Cloyne Defended; Or, Tar-Water Proved Useful, By Theory and Experiments. In Answer to T. R. M.D.*, which Fraser dated August 1744. The author identifies himself only as 'Philanthropos', but he was clearly a physician of some sort, since he uses medical terminology throughout and refers to various subjects in the history of medicine. He defends Berkeley's theory of the value of tar-water, though he criticizes him for overstatement and exaggeration of its virtues. Cannily he suggests that, while its use was undoubtedly justified in Cloyne, where the villagers were poor and underfed, better remedies are available to the English, who live more comfortably.

We shall omit discussion of a later pamphlet by a doctor,[1] and devote ourselves to the most interesting of the medical pamphlets, and the only one to which we know Berkeley's reaction. In June 1744 appeared an anonymous *Letter to the Right Reverend and the Bishop of Cloyne*,[2] rightly, we believe, attributed to James Jurin, M.D., Secretary of the Royal Society, later President of the Royal College of Physicians, important in the spread and development of inoculation techniques. Jurin had earlier written two replies to Berkeley on another subject.[3] The *Letter*

[1] Malcolm Flemyng, M.D., *A Proposal for the Improvement of the Practice of Medicine . . .* (Hull, 1748). The work is dedicated to Dr. Richard Mead. Flemyng was a well-known English physician, who later took part in the animal-spirits controversy with his *Nature of the Nervous Fluid; or, animal spirits demonstrated* (London, 1751); he also wrote a poem about hypochondria, *Neuropathia; sive de morbis hypochondriacis et hystericis . . .* (Hull, 1740).

[2] The rest of the title is: *Occasion'd by his Lordship's Treatise on the Virtues of Tar-Water. Impartially Examining How Far that Medicine deserves the Character His Lordship has given of it* (London, June 1744).

[3] In 1734 Berkeley had published *The Analyst: Or, a Discourse addressed to an Infidel Mathematician*. Addressed to Edmund Halley, this was an attack upon mathematics as Isaac Newton propounded it, and an analogical vindication of the mysteries of religious faith. Jurin replied, under the pseudonym of 'Philalethes Cantabrigiensis', in *Geometry no Friend to Infidelity* (London, 1734). Berkeley answered in *A Defence of Free-Thinking in Mathematics* (Dublin,

begins with a doffing of the hat in the presence of a Lord Bishop, but soon becomes an attack on Berkeley's attempt to bring 'again the whole Knowledge of Medicine to its Primitive Darkness to specific Remedies, and occult Qualities'. Jurin slyly makes clear that he is speaking of Berkeley's own opinions, 'not what you have copy'd from other Authors (which makes more than two Thirds of your Treatise)'. Jurin takes the Bishop's medical theories and opinions to be 'perfectly exalted above all Sense and Understanding'. Clearly the medical army is drawn up on one side of the field, and close to them in the Battle of the Books (there are vague echoes of Swift in some of Jurin's pages) are 'pernicious Wits', who have 'unmercifully *roasted* your Lordship'. 'I profess', says Jurin, 'I never hear a Horse-Laugh in a Corner of a Coffee-house, but I guess your Lordship is the subject of it.' We are told that a group of apothecaries, when their business was bad, had prepared a petition for the building of hospitals and alms houses, but suddenly finding their business 'prodigiously encrease', they turned their petition into an 'Address of Thanks' to 'your Lordship'. One wit after another is quoted[1] to indicate the laughter evoked by tar-water, but a single sample may suffice: 'Rot me, says another, and cocks his feather'd Hat with an uncommon Smartness, but the Author has serv'd his Medicine just as *Pope* serv'd him, by giving it every Virtue under Heaven, he had made all the World conclude it never had any.' To the paraphrase of Alexander Pope's line on Berkeley, Jurin adds a note querying whether Pope wrote sincerely, or whether it was true, as some thought, 'that he never praised any Body but with an Intent that the World should construe it into something more bitter than his severest Raillery'.

Jurin inveighs against Berkeley's misunderstanding and misinterpretation of the medical authorities to whom he has referred. The Bishop, he says, shows awareness that soap, opium, and mercury come closest to justifying the term 'universal medicine',

1735), and Jurin again in *The Minute Mathematician . . . a Defense of Sir Isaac Newton*, in the same year under the same pseudonym. In the *Letter*, discussed in our text, p. 8, Jurin asks ironically, 'What, I would ask him, may they not expect of one who can . . . improve upon Sir Isaac Newton?' The controversy was discussed by Alexander Campbell Fraser in his edition of Berkeley's *Works*, iii. 301–2.

[1] The quotations thus far have been from pp. 8–9; those that follow are from pp. 10–11.

though each has its limitations, but he puts in place of all of them his own universal panacea. The tone of the conclusion is bitter:

Why would a Man of the Bishop of Cloyne's Character throw by the Reverence and Good Will the World had to him and make himself so egregiously a Jest, by endeavouring to revive, against the Dictates of Sense, Science and right Reason, a Medicine which he knows was laugh'd out of the World more than Forty Years ago? . . . And to conclude in your Lordships own Way of Speaking: As Bishop of *Cloyne*, I *honour* and *respect*, but as a Physician, I *despise* and *pity* you.[1]

With the wits' gallery joining its forces to those of the medical fraternity, the *Letter*, like so much pamphleteering of the age, is a *mélange*, but it is far more interesting to the literary student than any other of the pamphlets written by doctors.

To this tract Berkeley made no public reply. However, on 19 June 1744 he wrote to Prior, enclosing a poem: 'Last night being unable to sleep for the heat, I fell into a reverie on my pillow, which produced the foregoing lines; and it is all the answer I intend for Dr. Jurin's letter.'[2] The verses follow:

> To drink or not to drink! that is the doubt,
> With *pro* and *con* the learn'd would make it out.
> *Britons, drink on!* the jolly prelate cries:
> What the prelate persuades the doctor denies.
> But why need the parties so learnedly fight,
> Or choleric *Jurin* so fiercely indite?
> Sure our senses can tell if the liquor be right.
> What agrees with his stomach, and what with his head,
> The drinker may feel, though he can't write or read.
> The authority's nothing: the doctors are men:
> And *who drinks tar-water will drink it again.*

[1] In the Houghton Library, Harvard College, is a group of pamphlets on the tar-water controversy, a number of which have never been catalogued. The index is in a nineteenth-century hand. The group includes all but three of the pamphlets listed by Alexander Campbell Fraser. In addition there is one bound with the Jurin letter, beginning at p. 17 of that work. This is an anonymous *Remarks on a Letter to the Right Reverend the Bishop of Cloyne* (London, July 1744). Intending a defence of Berkeley, the author answers Jurin point by point. This is a very dull piece of work. A 'justification' for a non-medical man's venturing to write on medicine is found on p. 19: 'The two great Names of Bacon and Boyle will be lasting Monuments, that the Knowledge of Physick is not confined to the Profession only.'

[2] A. A. Luce published the lines in *Letters* (Luce and Jessop, *Works*, viii. 271). He says (ix. 117) that he had been unable to find the verses in the *Dublin Journal*. Prior published them in his *Authentic Narrative*, p. 16.

From the point of view of the history of science, the most significant paper in the Berkeley controversy is that of Stephen Hales, *An Account of some Experiments and Observations on Tar-Water*, which was read before the Royal Society and published in December 1744.[1] Unlike the pamphlets discussed so far, this was not prepared as either attack on or defence of Berkeley, though it proved a most important defence. Hales was not concerned with the practical problems discussed by Berkeley of the making of tar-water and its administration to cure or alleviate many diseases. His was an attempt to analyse tar-water chemically, in order to learn wherein its undoubted curative properties lay. He discusses, among other things, experiments he had made upon tar from America, Norway, and Barbados. The paper is so highly technical that it has not the interest for the layman of some of Hales's other publications or of the man himself. Stephen Hales had read for holy orders at Cambridge and spent nearly all his life as 'the perpetual curate of Teddington', ministering to his parishioners. Actually he spent most of his time in scientific experimentation. His *Vegetable Staticks* of 1727 became a basic text in plant physiology, his *Haemastaticks* of 1733 a milestone in animal anatomy. Both were read by many laymen. He had become well enough known to the scientific world to be elected Fellow of the Royal Society in 1717. The Society awarded him its Copley Medal in 1739. He is known to many literary students through his acquaintance with Alexander Pope, since Teddington was a neighbour of Twickenham. The relation between pastor and poet was close enough for Hales to be one of the two witnesses to Pope's will. Pope referred to him twice in poetry, on one occasion as if he had recently been sketching 'parson Hales'. However, the Popean reference to Hales most frequently repeated is that in Spence's *Anecdotes*, in which Pope regretted that the good parson cut up animals, particularly dogs.

Berkeley replied to Hales in 'A Letter to Dr Hales', which appeared in the *Gentleman's Magazine* for February 1747, and was

---

[1] Several of Hales's papers and references to others appear in the *Philosophical Transactions*, but there is no mention of this one. Since it is long and highly technical, Hales apparently preferred to publish it as he did, *in toto*, rather than to have a digest made. It is very curious that there seems to be no reference to tar-water in the *Philosophical Transactions*. Two brief papers on tar were published at the end of the preceding century, xix (1695–7), 544; xx (1698), 291. These had to do only with methods of extracting tar.

also published by Berkeley, with a letter to Prior, as *Two Letters from the Right Reverend Dr. George Berkeley . . . to Thomas Prior . . . to the Rev. Dr. Hales.*[1] To the second edition of Hales's *Account* was added *A Letter to Dr. Hales Concerning the Nature of Tar*, by A. Reid, Esq.[2] Writing in 1747 he indicated that it had become the custom for the sick, particularly consumptives, 'to repair to the *Red-house* at Deptford as their last Resort' to drink 'the clear Liquor from the barrelled Tar, and be cured'. Reid warmly agreed with Hales on the importance of tar-water, but he offered some correction to Berkeley's recipes. Among the great of remote or recent past who, he thinks, would have approved tar-water, he numbered Pliny the Elder, Glauber, Van Helmont, Boyle, and Boerhaave. Berkeley had good reason to appreciate the agreement he found in Stephen Hales and his correspondent, in opposition to the various medical men who expressed their adverse views about tar-water.

By all odds, the most elusive of the pamphlets listed by Alexander Campbell Fraser proved to be *Reflections upon Catholicons, or Universal Medicines* (London, 1749), by Thomas Knight, M.D. It is not in the British Museum nor in libraries in Edinburgh, not in the Berkeley collection in Trinity College, Dublin, nor, so far as the good offices of Professor Lester Conner could determine for us, elsewhere in Dublin. We finally found a copy in the Bodleian Library. Because of its rarity we shall treat it in slightly more detail than some others. The author, a Fellow of the Royal College of Physicians, had earlier written another scientific-medical work, *An Essay of the Transmutation of Blood* (London, 1725), which stirred a controversy in the 1730s about the definitions and chemical composition of blood. In *Reflections upon Catholicons* Knight shows his familiarity with earlier controversialists, Prior, Hales, Reid, and 'Risorius', to whom he frequently refers. The main point of the pamphlet is that Berkeley's 'universal Catholicon', although beneficial at times, is not the panacea that its author and the apothecaries claimed it to be; for this reason the physician personally refuses to try it. 'Every Body', he says

---

[1] The entry in the *Gentleman's Magazine* is xvii. 64 f. *Two Letters* was published in London, 1747.

[2] Andrew Reid, who migrated to London from the Scottish provinces in 1720, edited a journal, *The Present State of the Republic of Letters*, and was a compiler for scientific subjects. He was responsible for the abridgement of the *Philosophical Transactions* of the Royal Society from 1720 to 1732, although he was not a member of the Society. He was also in charge of the abridgement of Newton's *Chronology*.

'takes Tar-Water, but that is not a sufficient Reason for me to take it; Custom is not a sovereign Law to judicious Persons, the Deluge of bad Example drowns the whole World; for not to follow the Fashion is look'd upon to be the worst Character a Man can have in this World.'[1] His basic criticism is expressed early in the work:

Hence it appears by experimental Observations and demonstrable Principles, that the Philosophical Reflections, and the Theory so artfully handled, setting forth the Virtues of Tar-Water, is no more than a bare Hypothesis, being not founded upon real but imaginary Principles; the fugacious, fine, active, acid, volatile Spirit, so bland and temperate, and the subtile aetherial Oil, which were to do the Feats, are lost, there remaining only in the Tar the grosser and less active Principles, the caustic Oil or Sulphur, and Salt corrupted and render'd alkaline by burning the Wood close cover'd up to make Tar.

Much of the pamphlet is devoted to a discussion of 'the acid Spirit' in tar. Here he shows himself abreast of recent trends in chemistry, since the 'universal acid' in the air was among the most frequently discussed chemical topics in the 1740s and 1750s.[2] As indications of this widespread interest we may note that Tobias Smollett mentioned the 'vague acid' (*acidum vagum*) briefly in his novel *Ferdinand Count Fathom* (1753), and that Henry Fielding made Tom Jones ask whether Sophia's illness midway in the chase was not caused by some 'unknown universal acid in the air'. According to Knight, a main reason why tar-water is not so efficacious as Berkeley claimed is that 'it is but reasonable to imagine, that if the acid Spirit in Tar-Water renders it cool and unnoxious', tar-water actually does nothing to the body but heat it, thus 'effecting its opposite'. 'It is a *Proteus*, which changes its Form every Moment, in assuming contrary Qualities answerable to the Occasion of those who take it.'

More readable than the pamphlets of medical men—with the exception of Dr. Jurin's—are the ones to which we now turn. On 24 July 1744 appeared *Remarks on the Bishop of Cloyne's Book Entitled Siris*, by Risorius, M.A. Oxon. The author has not been identified. This can hardly be called a 'literary' pamphlet, but it

[1] Our quotations are from pp. 106–7, 34–5, 66.
[2] See G. S. Rousseau, 'Smollett and the *Acidum Vagum*', *Isis* lviii (1967), 244–5.

was written by an amateur, not a doctor or scientist, since 'Risorius' shows little knowledge of medicine and frequently derogates doctors. He condemns the medical sections of *Siris* as 'a very rash and hasty Performance . . . by no means worthy of its learned, and reverend, Author.' He takes exception to Berkeley's implication that tar-water is a Catholicon, a universal panacea. As we continue through the six-part critique, tedious except when lightened by irony, we incline to believe that his basic criticism is that Berkeley is Irish, while 'Risorius' is a true-born Englishman. Tar-water, he declares, may conceivably be an excellent remedy when administered by 'the Bishop's masterly Hand', but may prove dangerous 'under the Management of the more Illiterate'. It is probably 'better adapted to the Climate of *Ireland* than to *English* Constitutions; in which Case, the prudent Part would be, to leave it entirely to the *Irish*, those Neighbours of the Bishop, who have the opportunity of applying immediately to his Lordship for advice. I am indeed persuaded, 'tis not *calculated to do good* to the *English*.'

Anti-Siris,[1] an anonymous pamphlet of some sixty pages, seems to have been the earliest of the replies to *Siris*, since it was published in May 1744. The epistolary style, while less literary, suggests the *Persian Letters* or Goldsmith's *A Citizen of the World*. A 'Foreign Gentleman', resident in London, wrote to his 'Friend abroad' that the 'continual fluctuations' and faddism he found in London in clothes and diversions, and in politics, was now paralleled in 'Drugs and Physick'. When he had first arrived in London, the current medical fad was '*Sugar*: and the Public swallowed it voraciously, till it had rotted half the Teeth in the Nation, and was supplanted by *Water*'. These were followed by Joshua Ward's 'Pill and Drop'.[2] But the popularity of all these pales into insignificance in contrast with the '*Nostrum* of *Tar Water*, lately come into general Vogue and Use here on the bare

---

[1] *Anti-Siris: Or, English Wisdom Exemplify'd by various Examples, But, Particularly, The present general Demand for Tar Water, On so unexceptionable Authority as that of a R——t R——d Itinerant Schemist, and Graduate in Divinity and Metaphysicks. In a Letter From a Foreign Gentleman at London, To his Friend Abroad.*

[2] The fashion for sugar is attributed in a note on p. 19 to 'Doctor *Slayer*, who wrote a learned Treatise on the Usefulness of *Sugar*'. The vogue of water is attributed on p. 22 to the Revd. Mr. Hancock, mentioned in a medical treatise above. Ward's nostrums are alluded to on p. 28.

Assertion of a Spiritual Q—k'. The 'Pill and Drop' were sold for much more than their Weight in Gold, 'while the B—p's Specific costs scarce anything'. Ward jealously kept his recipe secret; it is to the credit of the Reverend Quack that he publishes his. 'Anti-Siris' has his suspicions of the Bishop's reasons for his generosity, as we shall see.

The writer knows some true details of the Bishop's discovery of tar-water, although he is wrong about others. He is aware that Berkeley married just before crossing the sea and that his wife had taken a woman friend as her companion. He takes for granted, however, that Berkeley went to Bermuda and understands incorrectly that he returned to England in a year. He adds still another to the various legends that came to surround Berkeley's American sojourn:

[Joshua Ward] travell'd no farther than *Paris* in quest of Fame and Wealth, whereas his L——p went half Way to the *Antipodes* to seek for the Virtues of *Tar*; and 'tis not improbable but he would have gone all the Way, so intent was he to become famous and talk'd of, had he not luckily contracted an Intimacy with an *Indian,* whom he intended to convert to Christianity, who initiated the modern *Apostle* into all the *American* Arts and Sciences, and particularly into that Knowledge of *Tar*, which he now so generously communicates to his Fellow Subjects.[1]

The Anti-Sirian suggests that the Bishop's real purpose in publishing *Siris* was less to cure the bodies of men than to save their souls. His suspicions of Berkeley's motives go further:[2] 'It is pretty extraordinary too that he chose to publish his latent Poison, at so very critical a Conjuncture of the present, at a time when England is at war with France and that the *Pretender's* Son is within call.' *Anti-Siris* does not doubt that *Siris* will have political repercussions: 'The Call for this Commodity here must raise the Price in *Norway*, which will not only endear our Prince and Nation to the *Danes*, but will enable their King to help us against *France* without a *Subsidy*.' Indeed, the pine-growing Norwegians would reap a rich harvest, since the author computes that, if the demand for tar continues at its present rate, the consumption will amount to 29,784,569 pounds and $3\frac{7}{8}$ ounces. What Bishop Berkeley had initiated, he could not control.

By all means the liveliest and most interesting of the pamphlets

---

[1] Ibid., pp. 30, 34.   [2] Ibid., pp. 50–1.

is *Siris in the Shades*, with a sub-title, *A Dialogue concerning Tar Water; Between Mr. Benjamin Smith, lately deceased, Dr. Hancock, and Dr. Garth at their Meeting upon the Banks of the River Styx* (July 1744). No author is known. He was probably not a scientist, since there is nothing technical in the paper, and not a physician, since again the medical discussions are not in technical language. He may well have been a journalist; the style is lively and informal. Two of the characters may be readily identified, but the lately deceased 'Benjamin Smith' remains a mystery.[1] Dr. Garth is the well-known Samuel Garth, author of *The Dispensary* (1699), who had died in 1719. Less familiar to literary students, but known in the history of medicine, is John Hancock, D.D., Prebendary of Canterbury, whose name was mentioned in an earlier pamphlet. He was probably chosen for two reasons: like Berkeley, he was of the cloth; like him, too, he had come into fame and infamy because of his advocacy of a cure-all, cold water, the widespread use of which he recommended in his *Febrifugium Magnum* in 1722, at a time when there was fear of the plague. Hancock was mentioned by name in Defoe's *Journal of the Plague Year*, and two papers in the Hancock controversy were formerly attributed to Defoe.[2]

As the title implies, *Siris in the Shades* is a 'dialogue of the dead'. On the banks of the Styx Hancock meets Smith, who had died of 'a Burning Fever'. He blames his physician for not using the remedy recently discovered 'to cure all Diseases, and prolong a Man's Life to the Age of Methuselah'. If the medicine continues to be as popular as it was when Smith died, Charon may lay up his boat and take a holiday, since there will be no work for him. Smith praises tar-water, Hancock his own remedy, until they are at an impasse. When Dr. Garth appears, they refer the issue to him because he, they find, has read *Siris*. Smith learns to his surprise that books had been common in Hades until Pluto recently made an edict forbidding further traffic in them, since

---

[1] Various bibliographical aids we have consulted include only one work by a Benjamin Smith, *Method of Raising a Loaded Cart, When the Horse in the Shaft has fallen* (London, *c.* 1730). The only clue in the work itself is that Smith is 'a great mercury man'. Since the other speakers are given their own names, there seems no reason for disguising one of several 'mercury men' of the period.

[2] *Remarks upon Febrifugium Magnum; Flagellum, or a dry answer to Dr. Hancocke's wonderfully comic liquid book.* Both were published in 1722.

so many are now the work of free-thinkers. Pluto had been so impressed by all he had heard of *Siris* that he made an exception, and also released Tantalus from his punishment and ordered Dr. Garth to make tar-water and administer it to him. Hungry and thirsty, Tantalus drank it eagerly, but in three days it made him so horribly sick that he begged for his lake again.

With the arrival of Garth, Smith has more and more difficulty in his defence of Berkeley. The doctor tears his argument to pieces, showing how impossible it is—medically and logically—that the same medicine should be effective upon opposite conditions of hot, cold, moist, dry. Whoever wrote *Siris in the Shades* had read more of *Siris* than many of the readers we have encountered. Smith, newly arrived in the place of darkness, defends tar-water as embodying the *'luminous Spirit,* or the *solar Light'*.[1] Garth fails to understand how so many errors of fact could be made by a 'Person of his Lordship's Learning and Abilities, one that soars so high in Spirituals, and who can demonstrate the doctrine of the Trinity, by a necessary Chain of Reasoning, from the Virtue of *Tar-Water'*. He finally concludes that the sections on tar-water had been deliberately introduced by the Bishop to attract the attention of general readers to philosophy. ''Tis past a Doubt to me, that the Bishop's Book was writ with no other View, but to make Converts to his Philosophy; and that Tar-water was intended only for a Bait to draw worldly-minded People in to read it; or, as one may say, a Ladder, by which you may mount up to the Trinity.' His Lordship is not a quack, because 'the Book is not in Reality, a Treatise of *Physics,* but of *Metaphysics'*. It is conceivable that the author was the anonymous correspondent to the *General Evening Post,* mentioned above, one of the few who realized that *Siris* was a philosophical work. The letter was published on 4 June 1744, *Siris in the Shades* in July. Garth's last interpretation of *Siris* is somewhat similar to that in the letter.

We have largely concerned ourselves with pamphlets of the year of publication of *Siris,* mentioning a few later ones in notes, but the controversy continued for some years. Indeed, we find echoes of it thirty years later in a different connection. In 1776 William Hawes, a London apothecary wrote *An Examination of Mr. John Wesley's Primitive Physick* (London, 1776), blasting

[1] The quotations in this section are from pp. 12, 30, 33-5.

Wesley's remedies in general, but particularly his excessive prescription of tar-water in various ills. When Wesley prescribed it for 'St. Anthony's Fire', then a common disease, Hawes denounced the prescription on the grounds that tar-water is 'a very heating medicine'; later, when Wesley recommended the taking of tar-water as a cure for 'Old Age', Hawes again denounced him, as he did repeatedly in the paper. But we shall leave the pamphlet war, and turn in the final section of this study to consider the interest in tar-water of men—and women—of letters.

IV

The almost instantaneous effect of *Siris* may be seen in a letter of Thomas Gray's. The publication of the first edition in Dublin had been 20–4 March 1744; the first London edition was 'promised in a few days' on 30 March. Gray wrote to Thomas Wharton on 26 April:[1] 'oh Lord! I forgot to tell you, that Mr Trollope[2] & I are in a course of Tar-Water, he for his Present, and I for my future Distempers : if you think it will kill me, send away a Man & Horse directly, for I drink like a Fish.' Horace Walpole[3] wrote to Sir Horace Mann on 29 May 1744: 'We are now mad about tar-water, on the publication of a book that I will send you, written by Dr Berkeley Bishop of Cloyne. The book contains every subject from tar-water to the Trinity; however all the women read it, and understand it no more than they would if it were intelligible. A man came into an apothecary's shop t'other day, "Do you sell tar-water?" "Tar-water!" replied the apothecary, "why I sell nothing else!" ' Edmund Burke, a student at Trinity College, wrote to Richard Shackleton in July 1744:[4] 'I am sure Tar is the universal Medicine here notwith-

---

[1] *Correspondence of Thomas Gray*, ed. Paget Toynbee and Leonard Whibley (Oxford, 1935), i. 225. This is not a Warton of the poetic family, but Thomas Wharton, Pensioner of Pembroke Hall and student of medicine at Cambridge.

[2] Gray was Fellow of Peterhouse, Cambridge; William Trollope, Fellow of Pembroke, seems, from various of Gray's references, to have been a semi-invalid. He died in 1749.

[3] *Correspondence with Sir Horace Mann*, ed. Lewis, Smith, and Lam (Yale Univ., 1954), p. 452.

[4] *The Correspondence of Edmund Burke*, i, ed. Thomas W. Copeland (Chicago, 1958), 26.

standing the opposition of its Enemy's the physicians. Does anyone in your Villa, or Academy use it?'

Siris seems to have been the last book Alexander Pope ever read. His comment on it, to which we shall return, marked the approaching end of a friendship between Pope and Berkeley that had continued for over thirty years. Berkeley was not a Scriblerian, but he had been associated with the group during the period that he was a 'London Wit'. Swift he had probably known in Ireland.[1] It was through Swift that Berkeley received his appointment as Chaplain to the Earl of Peterborough, with whom he travelled on the Continent; probably through Swift that he began his association with Dr. John Arbuthnot, who rendered various services, and to whom it was due that one of Berkeley's letters found a place in the *Philosophical Transactions of the Royal Society*. Writing to Arbuthnot from Naples on 17 April 1717, Berkeley graphically described several ascents when Vesuvius was in eruption. Arbuthnot read the letter to the Society, and it was published in the records.[2]

When the younger Scriblerians, Alexander Pope and John Gay, were drawn into the charmed circle, Berkeley may well have felt even closer to them than to the seniors, since Berkeley and Gay were the same age, Pope three years younger. The group kept in touch with each other throughout their lives. Relationships among them have been discussed by their various biographers. We limit ourselves to Pope, since he was the only one who lived to read *Siris*.[3] His acquaintance with Berkeley had begun at least as early as 1713, since on 7 March of that year Berkeley mentioned in a letter to Sir John Percival that Pope had given him a copy of *Windsor Forest*.[4] Various letters to Pope from Berkeley,

[1] A. A. Luce in his *Life* of Berkeley discusses the relationship between Swift and Berkeley in detail, including that in Appendix II, pp. 232–3. The unexpected bequest of 'Vanessa' to Berkeley lies beyond the scope of this study.

[2] xxx, no. 354, pp. 709–13. It is also in Fraser, *Life and Letters*, and more recently in Jessop and Luce, *Works*, iv. 78–81. In *Philosophical Transactions* Berkeley's name is given as 'Edw.'.

[3] Swift was still alive, but his mental faculties were clouded.

[4] Benjamin Rand, *Berkeley and Percival* (Cambridge, 1914), p. 110. The Berkeley–Pope letters are in *The Correspondence of Alexander Pope*, ed. George Sherburn (Oxford, 1956). Professor Sherburn quotes (ii. 104 n.) a letter of Berkeley's written in 1721, when the plague threatened England, 'a preservative against the plague . . . the Jesuits bark taken as against the ague'. This prescription, Berkeley says, he had from Dr. Arbuthnot.

particularly during his Continental travels (1713–14, 1716–20), are extant.

All the Scriblerians followed with interest Berkeley's Bermuda project. Gay wrote to Pope in September 1725 that he had just seen their friend Dean Berkeley, who was most solicitous about Pope's health. 'He is now so full of his Bermuda's project that he hath printed his Proposal, and hath been with the Bishop of London about it.'[1] Joseph Spence included in his *Anecdotes*[2] a tale Lord Bathurst told Joseph Warton

that all the members of the Scriblerus Club, being met at his house at dinner, they agreed to rally Berkeley, who was also his guest, on his scheme at Bermudas. Berkeley having listened to all the lively things they had to say begged to be heard in his turn; and displayed his plan with such astonishing and animated force of eloquence and enthusiasm, that they were struck dumb, and after some pause, rose up all together with earnestness, exclaiming, 'Let us all set out with him immediately.'

In the same connection Spence also says that Berkeley liked to apply to the Bermudas Horace's description of the Fortunate Isles, in Epode XVI, 'and was so fond of this epode on that account, that he got Mr. Pope to translate it into English'. In October 1725 Pope lightly warned his friend Robert Digby that in another year he might 'carry you all with me to the *Bermudas*, the seat of all Earthly Happiness, and the new Jerusalem of the Righteous'.[3]

Berkeley went to America and returned, his scheme a failure, but tar-water in his mind. For a short time he remained in England, but when he was elevated to the see of Cloyne he

[1] *Correspondence*, ii. 324.

[2] In S. W. Singer's edition of the *Anecdotes* (London, 1964) the Bermuda accounts are on pp. 154–5. They are not included in *Observations, Anecdotes, and Characters of Books and Men*, ed. James M. Osborn (Oxford, 1966). The source was Joseph Warton, *Essay on Pope* (1782), ii. 204 n., where the same story is given verbatim, except that Warton said 'the members', rather than 'all'. If the story was true—Lord Bathurst often exaggerated in his stories— and if 'all' the members were present, it might have been during the summer of 1726, when Swift was back in England and when Berkeley's enthusiasm was at a peak, although Harley was by this time dead.

[3] *Correspondence*, ii. 330. In the 1735 edition of his Letters Pope added a note, calling attention to the fact that, just at the time he wrote, 'Dean Berkley' had developed his project of 'erecting a Settlement in Bermuda for the . . . Propagation of the Christian Faith, and of Sciences of America'.

returned to Ireland, there to spend almost all the rest of his life, there to develop tar-water and weave it into a philosophy. In the spring of 1734 Pope mentioned his 'strong inclination' to see the Bishop of Cloyne before his departure for Ireland. During the stay in London Pope presumably showed him the manuscript of *An Essay on Man*, since—again according to Spence[1]—Pope said: 'In the Moral Poem I had written an address to our Saviour, imitated from Lucretius' compliment to Epicurus, but omitted it by the advice of Dean Berkley.' In 1738 Pope published in his *Epilogue to the Satires*[2] the line of tribute to Berkeley we have heard paraphrased:

> Ev'n in a Bishop I can spy Desert;
> *Secker* is decent, *Rundel* has a Heart,
> Manners with Candour are to *Benson* giv'n,
> To *Berkley*, ev'ry Virtue under Heav'n.

Pope's final comment on Berkeley was in a letter to Hugh Bethel, characteristically undated, probably written in April 1744. 'I have had the bishop's book as a present', he wrote,[3] 'and have read it with a good deal of pleasure.' Undoubtedly Pope recognized *Siris*—of which he had probably received the first edition—as the work of philosophy it was, but there is little question that the medical sections would most have attracted his attention, since at that time his various physicians were desperately seeking relief for the condition they had diagnosed as dropsical asthma. Pope may have consulted them about the possibility of his taking tar-water, since he wrote to Bethel, who also suffered from asthma: 'my own doctors [have] disagreed with your Yorkshire Dr. Thomson, on the use of water in a dropsical asthma'.[4] Berkeley must deeply have regretted their decision, since Prior's alphabetical list included reports on the cure or alleviation of nineteen cases of asthma, three of dropsy, by the use of tar-water. Pope died without the universal panacea.

From Pope we pass to his once-adored, later-detested Lady

---

[1] In Singer's edition of Spence (1964), p. 103; in Osborn's, i. 135.

[2] *Imitations of Horace*, ed. John Butt (London, 1961), 316–17.

[3] Dr. Thompson (Thomson) is discussed at length in Marjorie Nicolson and G. S. Rousseau, *This Long Disease, My Life: Alexander Pope and the Sciences* (Princeton Univ., 1968), pp. 295–305.

[4] *Correspondence*, iv. 514.

Mary Wortley Montagu, who mentioned tar-water in her letters on three occasions, though one is a mere passing reference. On 24 April [1748] she wrote from Brescia to her husband, thanking him for volumes of Sir Charles Hanbury Williams's poetry, in one of which was the 'Ballad on Tar Water' that has been mentioned. [Bishop Berkeley's cure, she suggests, has taken the place of Joshua Ward's 'pill and drop' (which Williams had also satirized). She continued:[1]

Tis possible by this time that some other Quackery has taken the place of that. The English are easier than any other Nation infatuated by the prospect of universal medicines, nor is there any Country in the World where the Doctors raise such immense Fortunes. I attribute it to the Fund of Credulity which is in all Mankind. We have no longer faith in Miracles and Reliques, and therefore with the same Fury run after receits and Physicians. The same Money which 300 years ago was given for the Health of the Soul is now given for the Health of the Body, and by the same sort of People: Women and halfe witted Men. In the countries where they have shrines and Images, Quacks are despis'd, and Monks and Confessors find their account in manageing the Fear and hope which rule the actions of the Multitude.

Three years later she again mentioned the remedy to her husband:

Tar Water is arriv'd in Italy, I have been ask'd several Questions concerning the Use of it in England. I do not find it makes any great progress here. The Doctors confine it to a possibility of being usefull in the Case of inward ulcers, and allow it no farther merit. I told you sometime ago the method in this Country of makeing it the Interest of the Physician to keep the Town in good Health.

Those very satisfactory correspondents, Mrs. Elizabeth Carter and Miss Catherine Talbot, who seem to have read nearly all books published, mentioned tar-water to each other over a period of nearly a dozen years. Mrs. Carter first referred to it on 20 July 1744, some three months after *Siris* first appeared, experiencing some of the confusion of various later readers:[2]

I make no doubt but you have read *Siris*, as I have to no great purpose you will think, as I fairly confess I have no clear idea what one

[1] *The Complete Letters of Lady Mary Wortley Montagu*, ed. Robert Halsband (Oxford, 1966), ii. 397; 486–7; June 20 [1751].

[2] *A Series of Letters between Mrs. Elizabeth Carter and Miss Catherine Talbot, from the year 1741 to 1770 . . . in Two Volumes* (London, 1809). The two first references are i. 44, 46. It is interesting to find that during the 1740s and 1750s, Berkeley's son was one of Mrs. Carter's correspondents.

half of it means: what I can understand of it extremely pleases me, but possibly its being beyond the reach of my comprehension is the cause that some parts of the book appear entirely visionary, and more like the glittering confusion of a lively imagination, than any regular system of distinct reasoning.

She added: 'Pray what is your opinion of tar-water?' Miss Talbot replied on 7 September that, although she was considered the local 'quack', she had not yet ventured to try it on any of her neighbours, 'though by what I can learn of it, it is very good if properly applied'. The next sentence indicates that she was aware of some of the 'replies' to Berkeley we have considered: ''Tis very hard I think the good man, who published his opinion of it from no other notice than a general benevolence, should be so vilely abused for it, as he has been by various paltry scribblers.'

Two years later, on 1 November 1746, Mrs. Carter indicated that she had begun a course of tar-water:[1]

Have people utterly left off writing books? I have not heard of a new one this century, excepting one on the wonders of Tar-water. I thought the strong appetite to this medicine had been greatly worn off, and that folks now were universally agreed in the fashionable fury of drinking up the sea, an experiment perhaps much the less safe of the two. Tar-water being thus again in high repute, several of my acquaintance have persuaded me into a consent to drink it, though I depend but little upon its efficacy with regard to myself; however, as one ought to give a medicine fair play, I intend to persevere as far as a hogshead will go, before I pronounce that it does me no good.

Probably to her own surprise, Mrs. Carter found that the remedy suited her very well after she had persevered for some time 'with great resolution', since on 8 December 1746 she reported: 'I really think it has done me some good, for the first effect I perceived was that I could bear the sight of beef and pudding, and the next that I arrantly eat it, and upon the whole I am better.'[2]

That tar-water was considered a standard remedy, long after its novelty had ceased, is indicated by passing remarks between the two friends. Mrs. Carter, who had been away from her home in Deal, wrote on 21 May 1750 that she 'had a most formidable idea of being sick in a land overrun with physicians, and not like

[1] Ibid. i. 114–15; Miss Talbot mentioned her friend's new course briefly (i. 116).
[2] Ibid. i. 119.

Deal flowing with tar-water'. As late as 1755 she teased her friend, to whom, she declared, tar-water had become one of her two 'specifics'.

Henry Fielding tried every 'specific' known to his period in a vain attempt to regain health. He was attended for a time by the notoriously skeptical Dr. Thomas Thompson, the last of Pope's physicians, and then asked to be treated by tar-water, this move offering the measure of his desperation. Fielding's basic trouble, like Pope's, was diagnosed as dropsical asthma. In the last year of his life (1754) he was treated by Joshua Ward of 'pill and drop' fame, to whom he paid high tribute, although the treatments were ineffectual in what Fielding described as his 'weak and deplorable condition, with no fewer or less diseases than a jaundice, a dropsy, and an asthma, altogether uniting their forces in the destruction of a body so entirely emaciated, that it had lost all its muscular flesh'.[1] Defending Ward against the imputation of failure, Fielding went on to say that no one medicine could be a panacea for all ills, and continued:

But even such a panacea one of the greatest scholars and best of men did lately apprehend he had discovered. It is true, indeed, he was no physician; that is, he had not by the forms of his education acquired a right of applying his skill in the art of physic to his own private advantage; and yet, perhaps, it may be truly asserted, that no other modern hath contributed so much to make his physical skill useful to the public; at least, that none hath undergone the pains of communicating this discovery in writing to the world. The reader, I think, will scarce need to be informed that the writer I mean is the late bishop of Cloyne, in Ireland, and the discovery that of the virtues of tar-water.

I then happened to recollect, upon a hint given me by the inimitable author of the Female Quixote, that I had many years before, from curiosity only, taken a cursory view of bishop Berkeley's treatise on the virtues of tar-water[2] which I had formerly observed he strongly contends to be the real panacea which Sydenham supposes to be in existence in nature, tho' it yet remains undiscovered, and, perhaps, will always remain so.

[1] *The Journal of a Voyage to Lisbon* by Henry Fielding, ed. Austin Dobson (London, 1902), p. 27, and pp. 36–7 for the following passage.

[2] Fielding had in his library a copy of one edition of *Siris*, listed as 'Berkeley and Prior on Tar Water', 1744. See the 'Sale Catalogue' of his library in Ethel M. Thornbury, *Henry Fielding's Theory of the Comic Prose Epic* (Madison, 1931), p. 177.

Evidently Fielding re-read *Siris*—at least the medical sections—
to find that Berkeley considered tar-water effectual in dropsy.
After a brief period on a milk diet, he betook himself to tar-water,
dosing himself morning and evening with a half-pint. He had
earlier been tapped by surgical trochar for his condition. We
may let him continue the account:

> It was no more than three weeks since my last tapping, and my
> belly and limbs were distended with water. This did not give me the
> worse opinion of tar-water: for I never supposed there could be any
> such virtue in tar-water, as immediately to carry off a quantity of water
> already collected. For my delivery from this, I well knew I must be
> again obliged to the trochar; and that if the tar-water did me any good
> at all, it must be only by the slowest degrees; and that if it ever should
> get the better of my distemper, it must be by the tedious operation of
> undermining, and not by a sudden attack and storm.
> Some visible effects, however, and far beyond what my most sanguine
> hopes could with any modesty expect, I very soon experienced; the
> tar-water having, from the very first, lessened my illness, increased
> my appetite, and added, though in a very slow proportion, to my
> bodily strength.

Temporarily he showed improvement; when he was tapped again
the surgeon withdrew three quarts less than the previous time,
and Fielding bore the ordeal better than before, without faintness.
But his health had gone too far for improvement by any medicine,
and he started on his last journey, the voyage to Lisbon.

Throughout the eighteenth century—both before and after
the author's death—*Siris* remained largely a medical rather than a
philosophical work. From it William Cowper drew a figure that
has come to be associated with him rather than with Berkeley,
who wrote in *Siris* § 217: 'the luminous spirit lodged and
detained in the native balsam of pines and firs is of a nature so
mild, and benign, and proportioned to the human constitution,
as to warm without heating, to cheer but not inebriate'. Cowper
versified this idea in *The Task* (iv. 38–40):

> And while the bubbling and loud hissing urn
> Throws up a steamy column, and the cups
> That cheer but not inebriate wait on each . . .

Coleridge, who had gone through a period of Berkeley-enthusiasm
sufficient to cause him to name his second son 'Berkeley', showed

little admiration for *Siris* in a passage in his notebooks in which he said:[1]

> Much injury has been done to society by the naked *assertion* of Truths which have been repeated till at least they have [been] treated with contempt as old Paradoxes. Ex. gr. If Berkley instead of asserting that England could sustain three times its number, tho' it were encompassed by a brass Wall 50 cubits high, had written a treatise as long & eloquent as that which he squandered upon Tar Water & layed open the whole of the good, & all of the evil & delusion of Commerce, & artificial Wealth—my God, what a difference—

Professor D. J. Greene, in 'Smart, Berkeley, the Scientists and the Poets',[2] finds in Christopher Smart striking parallels to Berkeley, some of them in passages from *Siris*—though they are, of course, from the philosophical rather than the medical sections. The philosopher and the poet, he believes, were close together in their dismissal of both Newton and Locke. Whether the similarities between the poet and Berkeley were coincidental, or the result of 'influence', Mr. Greene does not know: 'What Smart's acquaintance was with Berkeley and his writings, I do not pretend to determine; I have found no evidence on the point. It may be that Smart arrived at all this independently or through some intermediary source. But the parallel in thought is striking.' William Blake owned a copy of *Siris*—one of the editions published at Dublin in 1744—and annotated it with marginalia.[3] It is significant that these do not begin until page 203—well after the long medical passages.

Since we have made no pretence of treating *Siris* as a work of philosophy, we shall not deal with writers of the nineteenth century, during which it ceased being a medical treatise. If, however, we may believe Pip in *Great Expectations* (1861), tar-water continued to be used. 'Some medical beast', he says, 'had revived tar-water as a fine medicine', and Pip is so frequently dosed with it by his sister that he is 'conscious of going about, smelling like a new fence'. We conclude with that modern

[1] *The Notebooks of Samuel Taylor Coleridge*, ed. Kathleen Coburn, (New York, 1957), i. 893. The note indicates that this was a 'garbled reference' to a passage in *The Querist*.

[2] *JHI* xiv (June 1953), 327–52. The passage quoted is on p. 343.

[3] *Poetry and Prose of William Blake*, ed. David V. Erdman (New York, 1965), pp. 562–4.

descendant of Berkeley, Smart, and Blake—William Butler Yeats. In his Introduction to J. M. Hone and M. M. Rossi's *Bishop Berkeley*, Yeats wrote:

... did he think that if he could stop all thought with his Utopian drug —what thinker has not felt the temptation—the mask might become real: he that cannot live must dream. Did tar-water, a cure-all learnt from American-Indians, suggest that though he could not quiet men's minds he might give their bodies quiet, and so bring to life that incredible benign image, the dream of a time that after the anarchy of the religious wars, the spiritual torture of Donne, of El Greco and Spinoza, longed to be protected and flattered. The first great imaginative wave had sunk, the second had not yet risen.[1]

The third sage in 'The Seven Sages' remarks:

> My great-grandfather's father talked of music,
> Drank tar-water with the Bishop of Cloyne.

In 'Blood and the Moon', in *The Winding Stair and Other Poems*, Yeats described his tower, with its 'winding, gyring, spiring treadmill of a stair', a figure that well describes *Siris*'s 'chain', leading the reader from tar-water to the Trinity:[2]

> I declare this tower is my symbol; I declare
> This winding, gyring, spiring treadmill of a stair is my
>   ancestral stair;
> That Goldsmith and the Dean, Berkeley and Burke have
>   travelled there . . .
>
> And God-appointed Berkeley that proved all things a dream,
> That this pragmatical, preposterous pig of a world, its
>   farrow that so solid seem,
> Must vanish on the instant if the mind but change its
>   theme . . .
> Everything that is not God consumed with intellectual fire.

[1] p. xviii.

[2] *The Variorum Edition of the Poems of W. B. Yeats*, ed. Peter Allt and Russell K. Alspach (New York, 1957), pp. 480–1.

7

STEELE, SWIFT, AND THE
QUEEN'S PHYSICIAN

By CALHOUN WINTON

THE last years of Queen Anne's life, the years between the
Sacheverell trial in 1710 and her death on 1 August 1714, were
so fraught with alarms and strife, so productive of charges and
countercharges, of tracts and pamphlets, of secret histories and
true relations, of memorials, petitions, and loyal addresses, that
the student of literature is sometimes inclined to dismiss the
substantive issues as so many fictions and to regard the prot-
agonists solely as rhetoricians practising their trade. Those prot-
agonists, it is true, were for the most part individuals of pungent
character who relished personal attack, and a surprising number
of them wrote effectively as well. The major professional propagandists, of course, did so: Jonathan Swift and Richard Steele,
Daniel Defoe and Mrs. Manley; their livelihood depended to a
greater or lesser extent on the quality of their work, and they
commented frequently and long on the events of those years.
Many of the principal characters, the Great People themselves,
wrote well too—and at length. Bolingbroke and the Duchess of
Marlborough, Walpole and Cowper, each of these left his own
testimony, striving to justify the particular position he took,
denouncing his rivals and applauding his friends. Because the
volume of evidence is very large, it is in fact less difficult to treat
the rhetorical techniques of the arguments than to analyse the
substance of those arguments.

But issues were raised of great moment, or at least so these men
and women believed. Almost all of them were uneasy about the
royal succession because, as they knew, their fortunes and perhaps their lives were in the balance. Nerves were on edge and
stayed on edge. The succession of the British monarchy was in
doubt, and those in the centre felt it important to guess in which
direction events would move. They were correct. Many who

guessed wrong were effectively excluded from public life for years to come; some, Bolingbroke and Ormonde, for example, thought their necks in danger and sought safety abroad. One may be as near certainty as possible in matters contrary to fact in asserting that if Bolingbroke had brought off his attempt to place James III on the British throne, life would have been correspondingly hard for the Whigs. At a time when it looked as if Bolingbroke might succeed, Steele, who was in a position to know, told his wife in confidence that civil war was inevitable.[1] Whig and Tory fashions in cosmetics, Tory and Whig claques for opera singers: these were amusing symptoms of the genuine pressure men lived under in that era, when the call to stand up and be counted was often sounded.

Not only did those involved feel that important issues were being debated as events moved on; they also assumed—and such occasions must be rare in human life—that they were able personally to influence those events. Again, unless one takes a rigidly deterministic view of history, they appear to have been right. At any rate, they were confident that they could alter the course of history and they worked day and night at the task. Since no one was sure of the true extent of the royal prerogative, it was held to be especially important to guide the Queen's opinions. The story of the Duchess of Marlborough's and Lady Masham's efforts in that activity is well known. Scarcely known at all is the story of Sir David Hamilton, one of the Queen's physicians, whose journal of her last years provides new information about the elbowing on the backstairs.[2] This essay will concentrate on two aspects of the journal which concern literary scholars: the succession negotiations and Swift's ecclesiastical preferment.[3] The succession negotiations, of course,

[1] *The Correspondence of Richard Steele*, ed. Rae Blanchard (Oxford, 1941), p. 299.

[2] The autograph journal, not in Hamilton's hand, is among the Panshanger MSS., Box 48, in the County Record Office, County Hall, Hertford, Herts. I should like to express my gratitude to the owner, Lady Monica Salmond, for granting permission to refer to and quote from the manuscript, and to the staff of the Record Office for expert and courteous assistance.

[3] Professor Henry Snyder of the University of Kansas has informed me that he intends to prepare an annotated edition of the journal. It is much to be desired. The existence of a manuscript table of contents to a longer version of the journal, among the papers at Blenheim (F-I-16), indicates that the

provided the principal issue for the Swift–Steele controversy of 1713–14, the seriousness of the situation being in general exaggerated by the Whigs and minimized on the Tory side. It appears that the Queen was sufficiently concerned about the Protestant Succession herself to undertake in the last weeks of her life private communication, by means of Hamilton, with the Elector of Hanover (later George I). This correspondence, unknown to Oxford and Bolingbroke, looked toward the exclusion of James Stuart. It also appears that Queen Anne personally opposed the ecclesiastical ambitions of Jonathan Swift.

Hamilton, who was born in Edinburgh about 1663, was the second of three sons of Isobell, third wife of James Hamilton of Dalzell, who had made his fortune by supplying Cromwell's army in Scotland. According to his own account, in a letter recommending himself to the continuing favour of George I, David Hamilton had studied medicine for several years in Leyden, had received a doctoral degree in medicine at Rheims, and had specialized in female illnesses in Paris, before returning to London to practice.[1] Elected a Fellow of the Royal Society in 1708,[2] he was knighted that same year. He was successively physician to Queen Anne and to Princess Caroline, as well as to many other ladies of high rank. He died in Kensington, 29 August 1721.

Although he was much sought after as a gynaecologist,[3]

Panshanger journal is a copy of parts of Sir David's original. At one time Hamilton evidently intended to publish the journal, whole or in part, for he writes in a letter (undated, but, to judge by the contents, about Oct. 1714) presenting his services to King George: 'Mon success a l'egard de la Reyne paroistra quand ie [ferai?] imprimer l'histoire de la maladie . . .' (Panshanger MSS., Box 48).

In quotations I have silently reduced all initial s's, except on proper nouns, to lower case, and have expanded the following scribal contractions: D^s to Duchess, Ld to Lord, My to Majesty, Qn to Queen, abt to about, cd to could, sd to said, shd to should, wch to which, wd to would, wth to with, wn to when, ye to the, ym to them, yn to then or than, yr to your, and yt to that. Otherwise all changes in orthography or punctuation are indicated by the use of square brackets.

[1] See letter described in n. 3 of p. 139. The entry on Hamilton in *DNB* is seriously inadequate. Unless otherwise indicated, biographical information in this essay is derived from Burke's *Peerage, Baronetage and Knightage*, s.v. 'Hamilton of Dalzell'.

[2] Elected 7 Apr. 1708. See *The Record of the Royal Society of London* (4th edn., London, 1940), p. 391.

[3] He was for many years physician to the Countess of Bristol, who

it may have been Hamilton's reputation for learned piety rather than his medical skill that attracted and retained the attention of the pious Queen. In 1701 he brought out a work of 665 closely printed pages, the title of which gives some indication of that middle path which Hamilton sought in all his doings: *The Inward Testimony of the Spirit of Christ to his Outward Revelation, In Opposition to the Deist, Socinian and prophane, Who deny both; To the Formalist, who deny his Inward; and to the Enthusiast, who deny his Outward Testimony to it.* Hamilton received the Queen's medical history in May 1703, and his regular attendance commenced, according to his statement in the journal, 'towards the latter end of the year 1708 . . .'.[1]

Like most others who decried faction in Queen Anne's day, Hamilton's moderation had its limits. His sympathies did not extend to those who supported Sacheverell or the Pretender, or to those who he believed supported the Pretender. He was, in short, a Whig. He was also a courtier, however, and he seems to have been sincerely devoted to the Queen. The journal is in part a defence of the Queen's conduct: 'I hope I may with the same Justice Vindicate Her Mind, & abstracting it from Impositions upon Her, & misguidings of Others. She had a Mind, & Inclinations therein Pious towards God, & to make all Her subjects Easie, instead of reproaching them, as they have done Her.'[2] The misguidings Hamilton mentions were performed, we learn from the journal, by those around the Queen in the service of Oxford and Bolingbroke. Oxford and Bolingbroke, of course, controlled the Court during the last four years of the Queen's life, and it is no small tribute to Hamilton's tact and agility that he managed to survive those years in place. He was but one of the Queen's physicians, and as the succession crisis intensified his private dialogue with the Queen was discouraged. To the very end, however, Hamilton played his cautious game, and during the last weeks of her life was entrusted with a personal

complained to her husband from Bath on hearing of Hamilton's death: '. . . 'tis a cutting stroak to one in my condition to loose the cheif (nay only) assistance I depended on to recover my ill state of health . . .'. The Countess survived another two decades, however. See the *Letter-Books of John Hervey, First Earl of Bristol* (Wells, 1894), ii. 178. I am indebted to Professor Bertrand Goldgar for this reference.

[1] MS., pp. 1–2. The journal is paginated and entries dated.

[2] MS., p. 69.

commission of great sensitivity, to open direct communication with her Hanoverian successor.

It has been known since the appearance of Archdeacon Coxe's *Memoirs of . . . Marlborough* in the nineteenth century that Hamilton acted as an intermediary between the Queen and the Duchess of Marlborough after the classic friendship had cooled.[1] He is not, however, to be regarded as a toady of Sarah's. Early in their relationship she wrote to him, 'Notwithstanding all the Ill People I have met with, I have an Opinion that you are an honest Man, & that you would not betray me, tho' our Acquaintance was purely accidental. I can see well enough your Partiality to Mrs. Morley [Queen Anne]. . . . You are her servant & that's a good reason to wish her well.' In many respects Hamilton and the Duchess pursued similar ends. For example, in an enclosure to the letter, intended for the Queen's eyes, she presents an opposition version of Harley's activities, arguing that he, using Mrs. Masham and the Duke of Shrewsbury, had forced the Queen to dismiss Sunderland, Godolphin, and Somers, and was at the time of writing (late 1710?) plotting, with the Sacheverell mob on his side, to proclaim the Pretender, who would feign conversion to the Anglican Faith.[2]

Here the Duchess sets forth, virtually complete, the general line of argument that Richard Steele, among the Whig pamphleteers, was to take in his political writings during the succession crisis of 1713–14, and that Jonathan Swift was to counter with his own propaganda version.[3] It is interesting to note that Swift

[1] William Coxe, *Memoirs of John Duke of Marlborough* (London, 1818–19), iii. 344. On the evidence of the journal, however, Coxe is mistaken in asserting that Hamilton 'owed his situation [as royal physician] to the interest of the duchess'.

[2] Sixth in a series of letters, this one dated 'Dec. 6th' [1710?], from the Duchess of Marlborough to Hamilton, copied at the end of the journal manuscript without pagination, in the same hand as the journal. The enclosure consists of the Duchess's running commentary on excerpts from *The Impartial Secret History of Arlus, Fortunatus, and Odolphus, Ministers of State to the Empress of Grand-Insula* (London, 1710), of which she observes 'in most particulars I know to be true'. This Whig tract is not to be, but often is, confused with the Tory *The Secret History of Arlus and Odolphus, Ministers of State to the Empress of Grandinsula* (London, 1710). The two tracts are, for example, merged into one entry (M183) in W. T. Morgan, *Bibliography of British History, 1700–1715*.

[3] See Bertrand Goldgar, *The Curse of Party: Swift's Relations with Addison*

apparently never realized that in the person of the Queen's physician he had a skilful and persistent antagonist within the inmost circle of influence, at work from the formation of the Tory ministry. In addition to conveying the Duchess of Marlborough's voluminous messages to the Queen, Hamilton was constantly prescribing his own form of political therapy, recommending books, sermons, pamphlets, and persons of the correct persuasion to his patient. The asseverations of impartiality in the journal wear somewhat thin, but he was not without ingenuity in covering his Whiggishness and fishing for information. In September 1710, for example, he showed her Dr. Samuel Clarke's *Now or Never*, and elicited the reply that Clarke (one of the Queen's chaplains and a forthright Whig) 'was a good man'.[1] '[And] upon shewing her the *Letter to the Examiner* & the *Essay upon Credit*, she said the Author was not *Davenant* but tho' she knew him, yet [must?] not discover him.'[2] During the same conversation, Hamilton reports, the Queen referred to Sacheverell as 'a foolish

and Steele (Lincoln, Neb., 1961), pp. 135–52; and C. Winton, *Captain Steele* (Baltimore, 1964), pp. 179–207.

[1] MS., p. 17 (22 Sept.). This pamphlet has never to my knowledge been ascribed to Clarke. For clarity's sake, the short title should be *Now or Never: An Answer*. I have used the Library Company of Philadelphia copy of Clarke's pamphlet (shelf-mark Up 6/2082; British Museum shelf-mark 4106, aa.3.[3]): *Now or Never: Or, A Project under God, To Secure the Church [and Monarchy] of England. In a Congratulatory Letter to the Right Honourable Lord D——, Upon his late Promotion: Answer'd Paragraph by Paragraph. By a well-meaning Tory, who is willing to clear the Church of England from Jacobitism* (London, 1710). Clarke's work is a Whig answer to the anonymous High Church pamphlet (Library Company shelf-mark Up 6/2082 A Godd): *Now or Never: Or, a Project under God, to Secure the Church [and Monarchy] of England. In a Congratulatory Letter to the Right Honourable Lord D——, Upon his late Promotion* (London, 1710). According to the *Union Catalog* of the Library of Congress, the Newberry Library also holds a copy of Clarke's pamphlet, which is erroneously ascribed to Charles Leslie (entry M375) in W. T. Morgan, *Bibliography of British History, 1700–1715*. The Library Company of Philadelphia copy of the original pamphlet which evoked Clarke's answer (and which, to judge it by style and content, could indeed have been written by Leslie) is, to my knowledge, unique. It is not noted in either the British Museum *Catalogue of Printed Books* or W. T. Morgan, *Bibliography*.

[2] The Queen seems to be equivocating. The *Essay upon [Public] Credit* was certainly written by Defoe (see *The Letters of Daniel Defoe*, ed. G. H. Healey (Oxford, 1955), p. 277), and the *Letter to the Examiner* has long been attributed on good evidence to Henry St. John, later Viscount Bolingbroke. See *The Examiner*, ed. Herbert Davis (Oxford, 1957), p. xxxiii.

man'. Hamilton was trying the ice. He was also working for positive results. As early as 23 September 1710 he contrived to let the Queen know that the clergy were afraid of the Pretender's coming in, without specifying which of the clergy. Throughout that autumn he laboured to secure the Queen's permission for a visit from the Duchess of Marlborough. The Queen, who was on her own part attempting to use Hamilton to recover the letters she had written to Sarah, signified that she preferred letters to a visit from her former confidante, 'because one can write ones thoughts as well as say them, especially its better in her, because when she speak[s] them it is always in Passion, which is uneasie to me'.[1] On this point, of readmitting the Duchess to her presence, Queen Anne was adamant.

By the latter part of 1711 Hamilton was forced to tread more cautiously, to 'keep Her self Quiet & me from being injurd . . .':

Is not what I have said demonstrated when I say, that if some Persons had been in waiting, however Her M——y inclin'd to speak to me, yet either the door must be left Open, or if that shut, I to stay no more than a Minute; whereas if others who had a Personal regard for me, had been then in waiting the door might be shut, and I stay without her Concern.[2]

The difference in treatment depended, that is, upon whether Lady Masham or the Duchess of Somerset was in waiting. Hamilton and Lord Cowper recognized that the presence or absence of the Whig Duchess, who had succeeded the Duchess of Marlborough as Groom of the Stole, was a matter of the highest importance; so, on the Tory side, did Jonathan Swift. The drama of the backstairs for the next several months is worth following closely.

If Bolingbroke's jest to Swift in August 1711 that the Queen had never heard of him was true at that time, it was certainly not true six months later.[3] By then Swift was well known to Queen Anne and his opportunities for substantial preferment from her hand were at an end. A lampoon on the Duchess of Somerset proved to be a grave miscalculation.

The violence of Swift's distaste for Elizabeth Percy, Duchess of Somerset, has often been remarked. In 1711 he had known her

---

[1] MS., p. 26 (5 Jan. 1710/11).

[2] MS., p. 37 (29 Dec. 1711).

[3] *Jonathan Swift: Journal to Stella*, ed. Harold Williams (Oxford, 1948), i. 327 (6 Aug. 1711).

for many years, since his tenure as secretary to Sir William Temple at Moor Park.[1] In those days the families used to exchange visits in good county style, between Moor Park and Petworth, seat of the Dukes of Somerset only seventeen miles away. No doubt Swift heard lurid stories of the red-haired Duchess's girlhood then; the unembroidered facts of her life were sensational enough. Left heiress of a large fortune when a child, by the death of her father the Earl of Northumberland, Elizabeth Percy won the attention of many suitors. She married the Earl of Ogle in 1679 and was left a widow, at the age of thirteen, by his death the following year. Thomas Thynne of Longleat, apparently successful in gaining her hand, was assassinated by the followers of another candidate, Count Königsmark. A few months later, in 1682, Elizabeth married Charles Seymour, Duke of Somerset. She was not then sixteen years old. Perhaps she slighted Sir William Temple's brilliant Irish secretary when she came to know him during the next decade; perhaps he felt that she had. In either case Swift was not the sort to forget. He was disposed, moreover, in later life to look back on those years at Moor Park with some rancour, as a period when opportunity had been lost to him because of the inattention of great men. Nevertheless, the main thrust of his dislike for the noble lady in 1711–12 was generated by politics. As in his quarrel with Richard Steele two years later, though personal disagreement may have been involved, the focus of difference was political. The presence so near the Queen of a woman known to be sympathetic to the Whigs seemed intolerable to many; Swift decided to take a hand in getting rid of her.

'I have written a *Prophecy*, which I design to print', he confided to Stella on 23 December. The next day he announced, 'My *Prophecy* is printed, and will be published after Christmas day; I like it mightily; I don't know how it will pass. You will never understand it at your distance, without help. I believe every body will guess it to be mine. . . .'

In truth *The W—ds–r Prophecy* must have made heavy going in the provinces, to those not familiar with the careers of Elizabeth Percy, Thomas Thynne, and Königsmark. According to the prefatory account on the broadside, the prophecy, written on parchment and enclosed in a leather case, had been discovered

---

[1] For an interesting discussion of those years see Irvin Ehrenpreis, *Mr. Swift and his Contemporaries*, rev. edn. (London, 1964), pp. 102–8.

near Windsor. It warned England to beware of '*Carrots* from Northumberland'.

> *Carrots* sown *Thyn* a deep root may get,
> If so be they are in *Sommer set*:
> Their *Conyngs mark* thou, for I have been told,
> They *Assassine* when young, and *Poison* when old.
> Root out these *Carrots*, O Thou, whose *Name*
> Is backwards and forwards always the same;
> And keep close to Thee always that *Name*;
> Which backwards and forwards is allmost the same.
> And *Englond* wouldst thou be happy still,
> Bury those *Carrots* under a *Hill*.[1]

Swift hoped an attentive London reader would know that the Duchess of Somerset had carrot hair and that Lady Masham was born Abigail Hill, and would also recognize that the poetic manner was like that of Swift's earlier poem, *Prediction of Merlin*. In his exuberance he apparently did not realize the inflammatory nature of his hint that the Groom of the Stole was a poisoner. This was strong stuff, even if the line was interpreted only metaphorically as denoting a poisoner of counsel.

When Swift called on Lady Masham at noon on Monday (26 December) she urged him not to let the broadside be published. '[S]o I writ to the printer to stop them', Swift reported to Stella, adding, however, that they had 'been printed and given about, but not sold'. It is questionable whether Swift exerted himself to suppress the poem; he was in any case not successful. The next day the printer brought 'dozens a piece' of the broadside to a meeting of Swift's Society; two more editions appeared, whether authorized or pirated. Swift was proud of the poem. 'People', he wrote, 'are mad for it.'

Some people. By late January 1712 Dr. Hamilton had cast his clinical eye over the poem. He read it as an obvious attempt to dish the Whigs, and promptly rushed off to urge that the Queen should keep the Duchess of Somerset in place. The Queen expressed her desire and intention to do so. On the 26th Lord Cowper told Hamilton that he should prepare the Queen for Tory endeavours against the Duchess, 'in which they had already

[1] *The Poems of Jonathan Swift*, ed. Sir Harold Williams (Oxford, 1958), i. 145–8. Words here italicized are roman in the original; all others black letter there.

begun, by the Windsor Prophecy. . . . The Duke [of Somerset]
knew it to be a design to Lessen her, & to make her fall a sacrifice
to Mrs. Masham, because Swift was notoriously Employ'd by the
Ministry.' This conversation with Cowper took place on a Saturday. Hamilton set about his task on the following Monday,
28 January.

> . . . I told her Majesty what had pass'd between the Duchess of
> S[omerse]t & my Lord C[owpe]r; & what had pass'd between my
> Lord C[owpe]r & me, on Saturday, & also of their Fear, least the
> Queen should be turn'd from Her, because this day they had been
> endeavouring to bespatter Her by the Windsor Prophecy, & so
> might go on to do so still. She said, that woud have no Influence on
> her, to turn Her respect from the Duchess. I told her that upon my
> saying the same, I was answer'd that it had happen'd so, between Her
> Majesty & others.

Hamilton alludes here to the Duchess of Marlborough's fate.
The interchange illustrates Hamilton's tact and audacity in
intrigue. He always tried the ice before venturing far from shore,
but when it was firm he would take a mile. By this allusion he
hoped not only to ascertain the shape of the Queen's feelings
about the Duchess of Somerset, but, as a bonus, as it were, to
secure timely hints about the Queen's state of mind regarding
Sarah. He got what he sought: 'She said, that that was owing to
the Duchess of M[arlborough]'s own Temper & Carriage, & she
was sure, she would never meet with any such thing from the
Duchess of Somerset.'

Next day, 29 January, Hamilton arrived, bearing his copy of
The Windsor Prophecy. The Queen refused to examine it, but
Hamilton had already performed his mission: the Duchess of
Somerset was secure in her place and Queen Anne had acquired
a sufficient distaste for the *Prophecy* to decline seeing it. Hamilton
informed his patient that all he aimed at was 'maintaining her
health & quiet of mind . . .'. He was not without skill in other
areas as well.

The following day the physician came down with a fever which
prevented his attendance on the Queen for two weeks. In the
meanwhile William Graham, Dean of Wells, had died, creating
a vacancy in the hierarchy which Swift felt himself entitled to
fill by virtue of his fidelity to the Ministry. On 5 February he
had written to Oxford: 'I most humbly take leave to inform your

Lordship, that the Dean of Wells dyed this morning at one oClock; I entirely submit my good Fortune to your Lordship. . . .'[1] For months reports persisted that Swift would be awarded the benefice, and there is no doubt that he wanted it. During the summer of 1712 Stella wrote to congratulate him on the appointment, rumours having reached Dublin. Swift replied testily that he heard 'not a word of it; thô the Town is full of it, and the Court always giving me Joy and Vexation'.[2] Eventually the deanery went to Dr. Brailsford, once chaplain to the Duke of Newcastle.

Sir Charles Firth believed that John Sharp, Archbishop of York, intervened some time between January and April 1713 to prevent Swift's appointment.[3] Sharp may have intervened, but there was no need to do so. The decision had been made: the deanery of Wells was not to be Swift's. By 15 February 1711/12 Hamilton was sufficiently recovered from his fever to attend the Queen. 'She discoursed of Dr. Swifts Character. He was good for some things she said But had not dispos'd of that Benefice to him, nor woud not.' In the autumn, when no one had been appointed and, as has been observed, rumours were flying, Hamilton brought up the subject once more, to make certain she had not changed her mind. '[U]pon my saying it was talk'd that Dr. Swift was to be Dean of Wells, she said it was false. . . .'[4]

Although Swift's aspirations for ecclesiastical preferment in England had been choked off—quite unknown to him, of course, —opportunities remained in Ireland. On 23 April 1713 he was able to write to Stella that the Queen had signed all the warrants 'among which Stearn is Bp of Dromore, & [the] D[uke of] Orm[on]d is to send over an Order for making me Dean of St. Patricks'. He was installed as Dean of St. Patrick's on 13 June 1713, at the order of Ormonde, the Lord Lieutenant.[5] Hamilton had also been trying to prevent this appointment, but with less success. The journal entry for 22 December 1712 reads: 'I told Her Majesty she was teaz'd to preffer Dr. Swift, & said that in conversation I did not contradict it, because such a report look'd

---

[1] *The Correspondence of Jonathan Swift,* ed. Sir Harold Williams (Oxford, 1963–5), i. 288.

[2] *Journal,* ed. Williams, ii. 552 (7 Aug. 1712).

[3] 'Dean Swift and Ecclesiastical Preferment', *RES,* ii (1926), 12.

[4] MS., p. 45 (9 Sept. 1712).

[5] Louis A. Landa, *Swift and the Church of Ireland* (Oxford, 1954), p. 74.

well on her side, & it made it look the better that their Teazing did not make her yeild.' After Swift's appointment had been ordered, the Queen explained the transaction to Hamilton. 'She Discours'd of Dr. Swifts being a Dean in Ireland, Saying that all the Deanerys in Ireland were of the Lord Lieutenants gift, but the Bishopricks of Hers. I told Her most knew that she was pressd to prefer him, & it was Honourable to Her as a Pious Queen, to refuse it.'[1] A few days afterwards, on 1 May, he told her 'how few knew that Swift was preferrd by the Duke of Ormond & not by Her, but that I had remov'd the Mistake where I went, by what she told me Her self'. We may be sure. The following week he was still at it. 'I told Her how lucky it was that she told me the Deaneries in Ireland were not in her Gift, for Neither Lord Kingston nor Lord Harvey knew it till I acquainted them.'[2]

Later, Swift was to accuse Archbishop Sharp of blocking his preferment and Oxford himself of failing to press his promotion. It is clear, however, from the evidence of Hamilton's journal, that an Irish deanery in the gift of the Lord Lieutenant was the best Swift could hope for, because of the Queen's opposition. It appears, too, that *The Windsor Prophecy* was the immediate cause of offence. Swift sensed this, for in 'The Author upon Himself', written in 1714, he speaks of 'S[omerset]'s Reproaches'.

> From her red Locks her Mouth with Venom fills:
> And thence into the Royal Ear instills.
> The Qu—— incens'd, his Services forgot. . . .[3]

He never, however, understood Hamilton's active part in the frustration of his ambitions.

During those years before the death of the Queen, when Swift was seeking preferment, the succession was, as all the world knew, a subject of paramount concern in British politics. A vast body of partisan writing on the topic of the Queen's health appeared, with the effect that the Queen has since generally been

[1] MS., p. 56 (25 Apr. 1713).
[2] MS., p. 57. These noblemen were Baron Hervey of Ickworth, created Earl of Bristol on 19 Oct. 1714 (the father of Alexander Pope's acquaintance); and the Earl of Kingston, brother of Lady Mary Wortley Montagu, or perhaps their father Evelyn Pierrepont, Marquess of Dorchester created Duke of Kingston-upon-Hull in 1715.
[3] *Poems*, ed. Williams (1958), i. 195.

portrayed, particularly in popular accounts, as a chronic invalid in an advanced state of decrepitude. Hamilton's journal presents a different picture. In 1710 he recorded the fact that her menstruation 'happend to her as if she had been but 20 years old . . .'.[1] His diagnosis of the Queen's final illness lies in the area of what would today be termed psychosomatic medicine: he theorized that her troubles were brought on by psychological pressure from those around her, especially during her menstrual periods. The Tory advisers 'teazed' her during those periods and ultimately brought about her death. Her only complaint, Hamilton asserts, was a 'sharpness in her blood . . .'. During her last years 'a succession of disquiets happen'd' that weakened her resistance to the sharpness, which was 'translated upwards upon the Nerves, & Brain'. All the stories of her supposed ailments, other than this one, '*were utterly false* & the Effect of a lying Corrupt spirit. . . . How many have mention'd to me a Monstrous description of Dropsical swelling, of her Majesty's limbs & Elsewhere; when I have been Vindicating Her Constitution, as without any Tendency to it, & Tho' Her Royal Body, when Dissected declar'd the truth thereof. . . .'[2]

Be that as it may, the evidence of Hamilton's journal reveals that he was not above pressing his sovereign from time to time himself, when it was a question of gathering information about the Queen's opinion on the succession. On 10 August 1710, only two days after Godolphin had broken his White Staff, and the Tories had begun to come in, Hamilton was asked by the Queen 'what was talked'. He replied 'that they talk'd of her Majesty's Inclinations to the Pretender'. A sort of informal interrogation went on year after year, with Lord Cowper apparently the chief source of questions. Hamilton reported to the Queen (11 October 1712): Cowper 'told me that Things look'd as tho' the Pretender was design'd, & all in Places, who are for him':

Oh fye says she, there is no such thing. What do they think I'm a

[1] MS., p. 5 (11 Feb. 1710).

[2] MS., pp. 68–9, entry undated, following that of 29 July 1714. Comment on the validity of Hamilton's diagnosis is beyond my competence, but it may be worth noting that Bothmar, the Hanoverian envoy, reported after presenting his credentials in late June that he found the Queen paler than he had seen her for three years: quoted in Wolfgang Michael, *Englische Geschichte im achtzehnten Jahrhundert* (Berlin & Leipzig, 1921–37), i. 344.

Child, & to be imposed upon [?] . . . I said to Her, I was sure Her Majesty was not in the Pretenders Affair, & that I hop'd she would live long to Prevent it. I challeng'd my Lord [Cowper?] for not waiting oftener on your Majesty to show his Affection & his being of no Party. To which she said he was as much so as any man. If he Visited your Majesty often they would say he was a going of[f], giving her an instance of their report of Mr. Steele as such, upon his going two or three times to my Lord Oxford. I have endeavour'd to impress Mr. Steele with an Assurance of your Majesty's not being in the Pretenders Interest. He said if he thought that, he would goe home & sleep sounder than he had done for many nights.[1]

One wishes for more visions like this one, of Steele returning to Bloomsbury Square to a well-earned rest, secure in the knowledge that his Sovereign was no Jacobite. Unfortunately, this is the only direct reference to Steele himself that I have found in Hamilton's journal, but it demonstrates that they were acquainted, and that on at least one occasion he supplied Steele with information about the succession. There is no reason to think that this was the only occasion.

For example, Steele published *Guardian* no. 128 on 7 August 1713, the celebrated issue with the epigraph *Delenda est Carthago* which demanded the demolition of Dunkirk. This was the opening shot in a propaganda battle that lasted until the Queen's death the following year. Three days after the publication of the *Guardian* Hamilton arrived for a session with the Queen: 'Visiting the Queen at Hampton Court, discours'd about the Address to demolish Dunkirk, & the book call'd the History of the Parliamt, telling Her how it look'd well in Her Majesty, to know such things, in Order to know the Mind of Her People. . . .' The 'History of the Parliamt' refers, presumably, to Sir Robert Walpole's *A Short History of Parliament*, written 'partly to refute Swift's *Conduct of the Allies* and partly to strengthen the whig case at the forthcoming election [of 1713]'.[2]

Although Hamilton pronounced the Queen 'fine and well' on 16 October 1713 she became seriously ill during December. Hamilton's political sentiments must have been known by then,

[1] The reference is to Steele's consultation with Oxford about a lottery scheme. See Steele's *Correspondence*, ed. Blanchard, pp. 59–60.
[2] J. H. Plumb, *Sir Robert Walpole: The Making of a Statesman* (London, 1956), pp. 183–4.

to some at least. 'No Opportunity of Private Discourse, the rest of the Phisitians generally going in with me . . .', he writes on 17 February 1713/14. On the 25th of the month he tells of observing to the Queen:

I see some danger, in staying long with Your Majesty, both of Disquiet to You, & making me the object of suspicion & Malice, & so of Hindering me, of serving your Majesty. . . . I'll therefore be Cautious till some time is over. To which she reply'd she could not but be satisfy'd with everything I did, because I could have no End of my own, but only her Health & Quiet, & said she lik'd my present Caution.

About April 1714 word of Bolingbroke's and Oxford's negotiations with the Pretender leaked to the Whig leadership. This was no doubt the news which inspired Steele's prediction to his wife of civil war. Although James Stuart refused to change his religion in return for the throne of England, no one but Bolingbroke and Oxford could know this, and no one at all but James himself could be certain that he would stick to his resolution. As a countering force, the Whigs moved to have the Electoral Prince (later George II) over to England to take his place in the House of Lords as the Duke of Cambridge. Steele, among others, greeted the motion with public approbation, outlining the benefits to be expected in the second number of his new periodical, the *Reader* (24 April 1714). The Tory press vigorously opposed the Prince's coming, and so, in the beginning, did the Queen, telling Hamilton about 7 April: 'She was extreamly griev'd about the Talk of some of the Family of Hanover's coming over. . . . She would give any security for the succession if they would not let any of that Family come over. . . .'[1]

By the end of July she had changed her opinion, according to Hamilton. On the 23rd of that month he secured permission from Lady Masham for a visit to the royal patient, using as his excuse that he wished to seek preferment for a friend. He records in his journal a remarkable interview. The Queen had found, he writes,

that the many things which she [I?] had suggested were true, particularly her subjects Fear that she was for the Pretender [;] when she had been talkd of to be at the head of the Protestant Religion, should she be an Instrum[en]t of Ruining it in Her Own Kingdoms [?] But she

[1] MS., p. 61. Two entries, for 7 and 8 Apr., are run together at this point and there is an obvious lacuna in the manuscript.

had been dealt insincerely with & teaz'd to do many Things ag[ains]t her own Inclination, particularly That, of turning my Lord Godolphin Out, remembering me of what I had said to Her. . . . This discourse melted me to that Degree, that Lady Masham was surpris'd to see me come out with such a Violent heat, & ask'd me if the Queen had refus'd the Petition, to which I answer'd No, but my bashfullness always makes me come out from the Queen in such a Colour.

An even more remarkable interview took place on 27 July, the day on which Oxford was dismissed, and on which it seemed that Bolingbroke had triumphed. Hamilton had been given a letter from the Elector of Hanover by an emissary, to show to the Queen. The Queen directed Hamilton to convey the information to the Elector

That the Changes she was ab[ou]t to make, shoud not injure him, nor lessen Her friendship to him unless he was the Cause of it himself, by Personal Ingratitude, & that if he would write to Her upon this Her Profession of friendship, she would Immediately answer it with Her own hand, without the knowledge of any of Her Ministry, & desir'd that his writing might be without the knowledge of any of his.

On the pretext of seeing his son enrolled at the University of Leyden or Utrecht, Hamilton was to leave immediately for the Elector's Court.

Then asking Her of my Errand thither she told me it was to settle a sincere Friendship with the Elector, & that all occasions of Jealousie might be remov'd. . . . Her own letter & what History I could give him of my self would secure me of his Confidence to Open to me & to Write to Her. For He was to ask leave to come Over to pay a Visit to Her for three or four weeks by which Means he would have entire satisfaction, & she Quiet, she resolving to put it upon him to make Changes.[1]

'She told me', Hamilton records, 'Lord Oxford would be out that night, & upon telling Her that Bolingbroke was said to get the staff, she said No.'

[1] Hamilton's account is given some corroboration by his letter of 10 Dec. 1714 to Mary Countess Cowper (Panshanger MSS., Box 48). There he states that he was not only the Queen's physician but also her friend, as exemplified by the trust she gave him before her death 'to write to Schulemberg about the King which Letters the Baron [Bothmar?] says the King saw'. Presumably Hamilton would not have risked lying, inasmuch as Lord Cowper could easily have verified his story at Court.

This was Hamilton's last private interview with the Queen. The next day her illness returned, and on 1 August she died, or, as Hamilton put it in a rare burst of metaphor, 'Death succeeded, the Preventer of all future projected Thoughts.' His journal contains material of high interest to the political and constitutional historian. The student of literature, too, is given illuminating glimpses here and there of the real life behind the documents he reads. Jonathan Swift had a resourceful foe in the Queen's entourage, of whom he was unaware; Steele and the Whig propagandists a reliable friend. If Hamilton's journal is to be credited, by the end of her life the Queen herself had been won over to the Whig version of history.

8

GULLIVER'S TRAVELS AND THE OPPOSITION TO WALPOLE

By BERTRAND A. GOLDGAR

MODERN commentators have never taken very seriously Gulliver's declaration, 'I meddle not the least with any Party'. Every student of Swift is familiar with the interpretations of the political allegory proposed by Sir Charles Firth, A. E. Case, and others. But how was the book received in contemporary political circles? The question is of special interest when we realize that the publication of the *Travels* on 28 October 1726 predated by only six weeks the opening of a new propaganda campaign against the administration of Walpole, a campaign managed by Swift's friends Bolingbroke and Pulteney, and signalled by the appearance of a new journal, the *Craftsman*. Indeed Sir Robert's latest biographer speaks of Swift's book as 'one of the most remarkable and virulent satires ever to be written against Walpole', and John Loftis terms it one of the 'propagandistic triumphs' of the Opposition.[1] On the other hand, we have been assured by other scholars that Swift's fears about its reception were groundless, that the fictional framework of the satire was so diverting that the book gave no offence, and that Swift spoke sincerely when, five years later, he claimed never to have offended Walpole.[2]

Nor, in settling such a question, are the celebrated letters from Swift's friends helpful. Much of the correspondence concerning

---

[1] Firth, 'The Political Significance of *Gulliver's Travels*', *Proceedings of the British Academy*, ix (1920), 210–41; Case, *Four Essays on Gulliver's Travels* (Princeton, 1945), pp. 69–97; J. H. Plumb, *Robert Walpole: The King's Minister* (London, 1960), p. 104; Loftis, *The Politics of Drama in Augustan England* (New York, 1963), p. 94.

[2] See W. A. Eddy, *Gulliver's Travels: A Critical Study* (Princeton, 1923), pp. 193–4; Case, pp. 105–6; Sir Harold Williams, ed., *Gulliver's Travels: The Text of the First Edition* (London, 1926), p. xxviii; Herbert Davis, ed., *Prose Works of Jonathan Swift* (Oxford, 1939–68), v. xv–xvi.

the publication or reception of the *Travels* is couched either in
mysterious terms or in friendly banter, and sometimes contradictions appear which are difficult to reconcile. Swift, concerned
about hurting his own person or fortune, had sought a printer
willing to venture his ears; but Pope, a few weeks after its
publication, reported that no 'considerable man' was very angry
at the book, so that Swift 'needed not to have been so secret upon
this head'. At the same time he was amused to observe 'that
countenance with which it is received by some statesmen'.
Both Pope and Gay agreed that the book was thought to be free
from 'particular reflections', but Swift wrote from Ireland that
'the general opinion is, that reflections on particular persons
are most to be blamed', and he clearly felt he had angered the
Ministry.[1] None of this is particularly revealing about the re-
actions of the political world to a book which, despite changes in
the text by its cautious London printer, might well have seemed
a precursor to Bolingbroke's and Pulteney's new journal of the
Opposition.

   Much more fruitful in determining the extent and nature of
that reaction are comments in political journals, 'keys', newspapers, and pamphlets in the first five years following the publication of the book, and it is these I now wish to examine. For
the sake of convenience this evidence may be divided into three
groups: comments which dwell on the 'particular reflections',
or which assume Swift to be associated with the Opposition;
indications that even by its genre as a 'general' satire *Gulliver's
Travels* had political overtones; and examples of the manner in
which the opponents of Walpole capitalized on Swift's book by
quotation and imitation. There was, to be sure, little hint of this
reaction in the first month after the appearance of the *Travels*.
But the evidence indicates that, whether Swift wished it or not,
his book was received almost at once as a decidedly political
document, and was both understood and used as a contribution
to the political journalism of the Opposition.

   In the month immediately following its publication there was
much to support Pope's contention that no men of consequence
were angry at the book. The manner in which the *Travels* 'for their
Variety of Wit and pleasant Diversion' became 'the general

   [1] *Correspondence*, ed. Sir Harold Williams (Oxford, 1963), iii. 102, 181,
182, 189, 208.

Entertainment of Town and Country' is well known; harle-
quinades, Lilliputian odes, scandalous memoirs of the Court of
Lilliput—all helped to make Lemuel Gulliver as popular a topic
of town conversation as Mary Tofts the Rabbit Woman, about
whom 'Gulliver' himself wrote a pamphlet.[1] As Gay indicated
to Swift on 17 November, even the more serious criticism tended
to be philosophical rather than political; the Revd. James Hume,
in a letter written apparently soon after *Gulliver* was published,
condemned the fiction as 'improbable' and the satire as too
general to be useful, but made no reference to any possible
political significance.[2] Indeed, during November the world of
political journalism itself seemed more diverted than vexed by the
book. *Mist's Weekly Journal*, a paper usually able to turn anything
(even the Rabbit Woman) against the government, merely
imitated Swift's satire to ridicule the 'Kingdom of Philology'—
not without a few gentle hits at Swift himself; whereas the
violently Whiggish *Weekly Journal or British Gazetteer* was content
to print a whimsical letter to Lemuel from his brother Ephraim
Gulliver, and the *London Journal*, another supporter of the Government, made incidental references to Gulliver's adventures in language either neutral or favourable.[3] Thus, whatever the private
views of 'people of greater perspicuity', as Gay termed them, public
criticism in the political world was for the moment disarmed.

However, the political neutrality of Swift's book was not
destined to last. Even during November keys and pamphlets
exploiting its political meanings were probably already in preparation. On 5 December the *Craftsman* began its long career
of ridiculing Walpole's Ministry, and from that moment the
political atmosphere became increasingly bitter. By the spring of
1727 no literary work with possible political implications could
hope to escape close scrutiny, especially when its author was known
to be on good terms with Bolingbroke and Pulteney. From the
beginning its political allusions were obviously understood;
the delight in the book expressed by the Oxford Tory Dr. Stratford and the exiled Jacobite Francis Atterbury was no doubt
matched by a corresponding displeasure in those statesmen whose

[1] *Parker's Penny Post*, no. 146 (28 Nov. 1726); see Eddy, pp. 193 ff.
[2] *Correspondence*, iii. 183; B.M. Add. MSS. 29, 477, fols. 87–8.
[3] *Mist's*, no. 83 (19 Nov. 1726); *Weekly Journal*, no. 81 (26 Nov. 1726);
London Journal, no. 381 (12 Nov.) and no. 283 (26 Nov. 1726).

faces Pope enjoyed watching.[1] Yet it was only after the inauguration of the *Craftsman* and the beginning of a newly invigorated journalistic war that these implications became politically useful. It is instructive to note that Abel Boyer, who serialized excerpts from *Gulliver* in his *Political State of Great Britain*, categorized the work as a 'Romantic Satire' in his November issue and as a 'Political Satyr' in his issue for December. As befitted his journal, Boyer emphasized the political passages by capital letters and other devices, but apart from suggesting that the Flying Island represents the Royal Prerogative he made no interpretations of specific symbols; indeed he argued that the 'Allusions and Allegories . . . are for the most part so strong, so glaring, and so obvious' that no explanation is necessary. Nor did he accuse Swift of political malice or of alliance with the Opposition, though he did identify the author as his old friend 'the *Examiner*'.[2]

But in these same months, December and January 1726/7, others were less reluctant to draw the *Travels* into political disputes of the moment. The *Craftsman* itself, though it was soon to praise the book obliquely, refrained from interpreting specific allusions in the way it was later to do with *The Beggar's Opera*. Instead, no. 14 (16 January) engages in mock disparagement of the modern tendency to turn serious things into ridicule, as exemplified by *Gulliver's Travels* and *An Enquiry into the Reasons for the Conduct of Great Britain*, the latter a defence by Bishop Hoadly of the Government's management of foreign affairs. In fact, the *Craftsman* remarks ironically, the *Enquiry* is only a servile imitation which might better be entitled '*Gulliver* turn'd Statesman'. Actually, 'Caleb D'Anvers', author of the *Craftsman*, had little need to point to specific allusions in Swift's work, since several other writers had been busily undertaking that task. In the first weeks of December appeared three books written to satisfy the demands of those who, like Swift's friend Erasmus Lewis, were 'dayly refining' and seeking the key.[3] Each of these volumes deserves to be considered separately.

[1] H.M.C. *Portland*, vii. 445–6; Atterbury, *Epistolary Correspondence*, ed. John Nichols (London, 1783–90), iv. 75–6, 84.

[2] xxxii (1726), 460, 477, 515; xxxiii (1727), 27.

[3] *Correspondence*, iii. 179. Approximate dates of publication indicated here and elsewhere are based on newspaper advertisements or the *Monthly Catalogue*.

The first is the series of four separate keys by 'Signior Corolini del Marco', published by Curll. These are of some interest because not only is Flimnap identified with Walpole but Reldresal (as Case has suggested) with his brother-in-law Viscount Townshend; the identifications refer, however, only to the rope-dances in Part One and to the description of a chief minister in Part Four, and no effort is made to explain a consistent allegory. Curll's writer also explains the satiric jibes at the Orders of the Garter, Thistle, and Bath; understands the 'conspiracy' against Gulliver to represent the 'sufferings' of the late Earl of Oxford; equates the physician in the academy of political projectors with Walpole; and sees references to the South Sea Bubble everywhere.[1] When these keys were issued in one volume as the *Travels . . . Compendiously Methodized*, they included a frontispiece showing Flimnap with his wand, looking short, fat, and curiously deformed —probably meant to be taken as Walpole—and a poem called 'Verses Writ in the Blank Leaf of a Lady's *Gulliver*, as it lay open, in an Apartment of St. James's Palace'. The verses tell us that despite the remote nations Lemuel visits, the 'Secret' is to be found only in Court, where Magna Charta is ignored, judges play at ombre, bishops are subservient to statesmen, senators purchase places, and vice triumphs: 'See Wagers laid who come shall next in Play | And read your *Gulliver* both *Night* and Day.'[2] Nowhere, however, do the keys suggest that Swift's book is designed for an immediate political purpose, and some of the 'interpretations' they contain should perhaps be attributed to the difficulties which Curll himself was having with the Government at just this time.[3] At best, these pamphlets were merely a flimsy effort to capitalize on a work which had caught the popular imagination; they deserve the contempt with which they were received by Boyer and others when they first appeared.

Of much more serious import is a tract called *A Letter from a Clergyman to his Friend*, also published in December, which indeed has the manner of a typical response to an anti-government pamphlet. The writer conceives of *Gulliver's Travels* as a primarily

[1] *Lemuel Gulliver's Travels . . . Compendiously Methodized* (London, 1726), key to Part One, pp. 13, 26; key to Part Three, p. 23; key to Part Four, pp. 16–17.

[2] Sig. [A4].

[3] See Ralph Straus, *The Unspeakable Curll* (London, 1927), pp. 101–20.

political document intended to breed disharmony and 'create a Dislike in the People to those in the Administration', a design especially vile 'in such a Juncture as the present'. Moreover, he hints that Swift is united with others in this incendiary plot, as he warns that 'there is no honest Man among us but would contribute the utmost in his Power to bring the Author, and *those concerned with him* to exemplary Punishment'.[1] Gulliver's description of English parliaments is objected to, but the *Letter* centres its attention upon Swift's insult to the 'Family and Person of the greatest Man this Nation ever produced'. Oddly enough, it is Swift's description of Flimnap as 'morose' that particularly enrages the writer, who promptly unleashes four pages of impassioned panegyric of Walpole as 'amiable to all', 'the Delight of his Royal Master, and the Darling of the People', the preserver of the peace of Europe, and the wise statesman on whose great pattern future ministers will grow wise. But only ridicule of such a man could be expected from Dr. Swift, who now caps a career of irreligion and chicanery by 'leading People into Disaffection and Disloyalty who are committed to his Care for right Information'.[2]

The charge made in the *Letter* that *Gulliver's Travels* was written to support the Bolingbroke–Pulteney Opposition appears also in a third pamphlet published in December, *Gulliver Decypher'd*. This book, once erroneously attributed to Arbuthnot, heaps abuse on 'Peter, Martin, and Johnny' (i.e., Pope, Swift, and Arbuthnot), while at the same time it pretends to vindicate the 'Rev. Dean' who has been accused as the author of the *Travels*: 'A Third Reason why this Book cannot be the worthy D——, is the many oblique Reflections it is said to cast upon our present happy Administration, to which 'tis well known how *devoutly* he is attach'd and affected.'[3] Gulliver, he admits, is no traitor, 'tho' every Body says that he is disaffected'. And this disaffection the writer lays squarely at the door of Swift's friends in the Opposition. It is inconceivable, he argues ironically, that the Dean

[1] (London, 1726), p. 9. Italics mine.

[2] pp. 15–18, 21.

[3] (London, 1726), p. 10. On the authorship of this pamphlet see the comment by Sir Harold Williams in *Prose Works*, ed. Davis, vol. xi. p. xxii n.; it may also be noted that this piece was among the group of attacks collected and annotated by Pope; see *The Rape of the Lock*, ed. Geoffrey Tillotson (London, 1940), the Twickenham edition, ii. 393.

would act so contrary to the dignity of his character 'merely to gratify a little Party Malice, or to oblige a Set of People who are never likely to have it in their Power to serve him or any of their Adherents'. Moreover, he quotes the King of Brobdingnag's reflections on the management of the treasury and standing armies (both commonplace topics of the Opposition), and then comments in terms that allude to the new and surprising alliance of Tories and dissident Whigs:

Every Body knows, that all this has been a common *Jacobite* Insinuation . . . but, to our great Surprize, it is of late, very frequently in the Mouths of a quite different Set of People, discarded Courtiers some call them, of whom we may truly say—*No King can govern, nor no God can please.* For unless they are concern'd in the Administration, nothing goes right.[1]

Elsewhere, however, this tract praises the wit of the *Travels*, concluding, mildy enough, that the book is the production of two or three men of talent 'who think sufficient Regard is not paid to their Merit by those in *Power*, for which Reason they rail at them'.[2] Yet even this last remark seems to respond to the charge of the decay of letters under Walpole, a motif soon to be common in Opposition propaganda.

In the light of pamphlets such as the three just described, it is small wonder that the Gulliver of a spurious sequel (February 1726/7) complained of having been slandered with politics.[3] None of these tracts, of course, provided a reading of the *Travels* as a consistent political allegory, but that such efforts were being made is perhaps indicated by a somewhat mystifying piece published in May 1727, called *Pudding and Dumpling Burnt to Pot.* This work, attributed to Henry Carey, purports to provide a key to the allegory of *A Learned Dissertation on Dumpling* (1724?), said here to be by Swift, but actually by Carey himself.[4] Not only is Swift the author of the *Dissertation*, claims Carey, he also has written it in allegorical form to vindicate the character of Sir Robert Walpole in his struggle against the 'Misrepresentations of an enraged and disappointed Party': 'In a Word, the whole

[1] pp. xii, 30, 38.
[2] p. 45.
[3] *Travels . . . by Captain Lemuel Gulliver, Vol. III* (London, 1727), p. 3.
[4] Ascribed to Carey by F. T. Wood, 'An Eighteenth-century Original for Lamb?' *RES* v (1929), 442–7.

Dissertation seems calculated to ingratiate the D—n in Sir * * * Favour.'[1] Carey sounds almost serious in his strictures against the writers for the Opposition, but *Pudding and Dumpling Burnt to Pot* is primarily a joke at Swift's expense, and a typical satire on political allegorizing; the second edition contains an appendix proving that 'Namby Pamby', Carey's parody of Ambrose Philips, is actually a true account of the siege of Gibraltar. That contemporary readings of *Gulliver's Travel* are at least partly in Carey's mind is shown by the fact that in his Preface he ridicules Curll's *Keys*, 'Keys which *Gulliver* himself could never have found out'. To demonstrate that Walpole is Swift's hero in another work would seem doubly amusing to those familiar either with the keys or with *Gulliver's Travels* itself. And perhaps it is not too far-fetched to suggest that when Carey criticizes 'Swift' for skipping about chronologically from reign to reign in the historical allegory of the *Dissertation*, he is reflecting the difficulty which even some modern commentators have encountered in making a consistent allegory out of the *Travels*.

By the spring of 1727, when Carey's hoax was published, extended political commentaries on the *Travels* had ceased to appear, but they were being replaced by an increasing number of attacks on Swift and on *Gulliver* in the paper war between opposing factions. He was, of course, thought to be contributing to the *Craftsman*, though there is no evidence that he did so—he had declined Pulteney's gambit as early as September 1726. But when he returned to England in April, it was to a political climate described by Bolingbroke as 'boisterous' and by Pope as 'very warm, and very angry'.[2] In the journalistic battle the chief source of anger was the series of pamphlets by Bolingbroke called the *Occasional Writer*, appearing in February and March. One of Bolingbroke's motifs in the first of these papers is that the Ministry is remiss in rewarding the 'brightest talents'; as might be expected, the *Answer* from a ministerial defender alluded sarcastically to Swift's career under the Tory administration in 1710–14. Similarly, other replies to the Bolingbroke pamphlets drew in Swift ('your Friend *Gulliver*'), and, on one occasion, Pope ('a *Coadjutor* of yours, who carries a *natural Pack* on his Shoulders').[3] One such

[1] (London, 1727), pp. 28–9.
[2] *Correspondence*, iii. 199, 201.
[3] *The Occasional Writer Numb. I. With an Answer Paragraph by Paragraph*

attack, ridiculing a Latin motto used by Bolingbroke, quotes the motto from Persius (*Sat.* ii. 73–4) used in advertisements of *Gulliver's Travels*; it is, he says, more venerable, but it has been 'pre-engag'd by a Friend; and He the only Author who for chaste *Decency*, and severe *Veracity*, has a better Title to it than your self'.[1] Even Boyer's *Political State*, which, it will be recalled, had earlier reacted to the *Travels* with neutrality if not with approval, now angrily pointed to both Swift and *Gulliver* in its efforts to counter the effect of Bolingbroke's *Occasional Writer*. It was no doubt this kind of thing that Swift had in mind when he complained to Sheridan on 13 May of the 'Beasts and Blockheads' hired to write for Walpole, and which, as Davis points out, helped to inspire his own 'Letter to the Writer of the Occasional Paper'.[2]

Swift's 'Letter' was worked out in collaboration with Bolingbroke, but, for reasons not entirely clear, remained unpublished. Yet its appearance, even with his name, would have done no more than confirm suspicions already raised by *Gulliver's Travels* about his share in the Opposition. Throughout 1727 and 1728 attacks on Swift and sometimes specifically on *Gulliver* continued to appear in pro-government newspapers and in separate volumes, accusing him of disaffection and linking him with Bolingbroke and Pulteney.[3] Some of these, it is true, were simply in reaction to the appearance of the Pope–Swift *Miscellanies*, and were, on the surface, non-political; Smedley's *Gulliveriana* (1728), for instance, is surprisingly free of the usual political smears. But the more general view in the circles around Walpole was probably expressed in a political pamphlet appearing in May 1728, where Swift is accorded a central place in the Opposition. The following passage is intended to be the judgement of a future historian on the 'insolent Faction' headed by Pulteney :

This Gentleman was at the Head of the Faction; and assisted by several Persons of Wit; but they were chiefly Men of desperate

(London, 1727), p. 8; *An Answer to the Occasional Writer No. II* (London, 1727), p. 9; *British Journal*, no. 231 (25 Feb. 1726/7).

[1] *A Letter to the Occasional Writer, on the Receipt of his Third* (London, 1727), pp. 22–3.

[2] Boyer, xxxiii. 149; *Correspondence*, iii. 207; *Prose Works*, vol. v, p. xiv.

[3] See *British Journal*, no. 257 (26 Aug. 1727); *The Flying Post* for 4 Apr. and 11 May 1728; *Like will to Like* (London, 1728), pp. 31–2; *Worse and Worse* (London, 1728), p. 10; and *An Essay upon the Taste and Writings of the Present Time* (London, 1728), p. 8.

Fortunes, or worse Characters; the most noted of these were an attainted Lord, who had before sacrificed his Interests with all Parties, and an *Irish* Dean, who, though one of a happy Genius, and some Learning, was such a debauched immoral Man, that whatever was known to come from him was of no Weight with the people.[1]

Why Swift should be singled out for a place of honour in the councils of the Opposition is not made clear; perhaps the writer merely had in mind Swift's well-known friendship with Bolingbroke, but, perhaps too, he recalled the image of Flimnap and Reldresal cutting capers on a tightrope.

Swift may have been right in supposing that personal satire was what his book was most blamed for, but there can be little doubt that many of the general themes of the *Travels* were well suited to the purposes of the Opposition. The broad indictment of human folly and corrupt institutions in Parts Two and Four (usually held to be of little political interest) was soon to be echoed in the flood of pamphlets and papers attacking Walpole. Gulliver's emotion at considering how the native virtues of English Yeomen 'were prostituted for a piece of Money by their Grand-children, who in selling their Votes, and managing at Elections have acquired every Vice and Corruption that can possibly be learned in a Court',[2] is hardly distinguishable from the passion expressed in scores of *Mist's*, *Craftsman*s, and tracts in 1727 and 1728. Even Swift's attack on war suited immediate partisan needs, for until the signing of the Preliminaries of Paris in May 1727 the Opposition press carried on a vigorous campaign against what they pretended to believe was Walpole's war policy. Again, the marks of a bad administration listed in the *Craftsman* for 24 June 1727 would have seemed familiar enough to readers of *Gulliver*: a desire for mystery in handling public affairs, the corruption of Parliament, a vein of 'Luxury' throughout the land, the manufacture of fictitious plots or conspiracies, the corruption of the law, and the failure to base preferments on virtue and merit. The last item, the promotion of the unworthy, was one of the most frequently reiterated motifs in the Opposition press, and one evidently near to Swift's heart; it appears in the *Travels* less often than one might expect, but the fact that 'Wit, Merit,

[1] *Remarks on the R——p—n of the H—— of C——ns to the K——g* (London, n.d.), pp. 28–9.
[2] *Gulliver's Travels: The Text of the First Edition*, ed. Williams, p. 279.

and Learning' are not yet rewarded was singled out by Gulliver in his letter to Sympson nine years later as an example of the failure of his book to produce effects—but then neither had the 'Courts and Levees of great Ministers' yet been 'weeded and swept'.[1] In connection with this theme it is amusing to note that *Mist's Weekly Journal*, no. 107 (6 May 1727), voiced the typical complaint that rope-dancers, singers, and posture-masters can expect to make their fortune in Walpole's England, but an 'Architect, a Mathematician, or a Poet, comes not here for Preferment'; in the same issue Mist included as a news item Swift's arrival from Dublin, 'where his Absence is as much regretted, as his Presence here is pleasing to the Learned and Ingenious, who will have the Opportunity of his entertaining Conversation'.

Even in the most general sense, as an indictment of human corruption and the degeneracy of the age, *Gulliver's Travels* was useful to those who opposed Walpole, especially since this indictment is coupled with a recognizable portrait of the Prime Minister and with a partisan viewpoint on such issues as standing armies or a national debt. It is noteworthy that the *Craftsman*, though it refrained from capitalizing on 'particular reflections', praised the *Travels* soon after its publication in terms which showed its appreciation of the political value of 'general' satire. No. 20 (13 February 1726/7), attacking the decay of letters under the Walpole ministry, concludes with this ironic passage:

I hope these dissatisfy'd, repining Spirits will at last allow that, however other parts of Learning may have been neglected and despis'd, yet no *Encouragement* has been wanting to *satirical* Writings; and if they do not soon produce some excellent pieces of this kind, I think they will be fairly left without any Excuse, and I shall be willing to give them up to all the Severity of the Patrons of the *Antients*.

Indeed, we have had some very good specimens of this sort of writing already publish'd; *one* of which seems to lash mankind in too severe and general a manner; however, as there is a great deal of *Wit* in that book, so I am sorry to say, for the Sake of human nature in general, and of my own Country in particular, that, I am afraid, there is *too much Truth in it*.

The Government press, of course, shared none of this enthusiasm for satiric writing; in fact, as time went on, political writers tended

---

[1] *Prose Works*, ed. Davis, xi. 6.

to associate 'satire' with the Opposition and 'panegyric' with the forces of the administration.

But to understand why 'general' satire, in particular, should be offensive to defenders of the Government we must review a related theme which was repeated countless times in political writing of the day: the responsibility of the head of state for the health of the body politic, and the consequent tendency for morally diseased leaders to 'infect' an entire kingdom. As the *Craftsman* puts it, when corruption is placed 'on the Pinnacle of Power, in the very Heart of a first *Minister*, it will no longer be contained within any bounds; the Contagion will take and spread, and the whole Country become infected'.[1] Swift himself, at Bolingbroke's suggestion, makes much of this 'transference' in his 'Letter to the Writer of the Occasional Paper', and the medical metaphor in which it was usually expressed is carried to its literal extreme by the 'Ingenious Doctor' in the School of Political Projectors in Lagado, who cures public diseases by applying private remedies to politicians. Curll's *Key*, incidentally, rather perversely finds that this doctor suggests 'a country Practiser (near Lynn Regis, in Comitatu Norfolciae) who is a much greater Adept in this Science' (i.e. Walpole),[2] and the 'universal Resemblance between the Natural and the Political Body' was doubtless responsible for the frequency with which Walpole was satirized in these years as a quack doctor.

It was by a reversal of this traditional motif that general satire which laid bare the defects of existing institutions could have political implications. If something is rotten in the State of England, we must seek the source, if not in the King, then at least in his Chief Minister. It may be helpful to recall a poem by Swift which exploits this idea for the purpose of ridiculing Edward Young. 'Satire the Last' (1726) of Young's *The Universal Passion* was dedicated to Walpole, and included a passage which shows Young is aware that satirizing a 'flood of *British* folly' while simultaneously praising those in power may seem a bit paradoxical. He addresses Sir Robert directly:

> Nor think that Thou art foreign to my Theme;
> The *Fountain* is not foreign to the *Stream*.

[1] No. 86 (24 Feb. 1728).
[2] *Travels . . . Compendiously Methodized*, key to Part Three, p. 23.

How all mankind will be surpriz'd, to see
This flood of *British* Folly charg'd on thee?[1]

His escape from this difficulty is to argue, not too convincingly,
that the folly of the English is the bad effect of a good cause, the
success of their rulers in making Britain a land of wealth and
peace. Swift, however, mocks the inconsistency of separating
fountain from stream; 'On Reading Dr. Young's Satires' (written
1726) reminds Young that he cannot have it both ways; either
the satire is false or the dedications to those in power are hypocritical:

> If there be Truth in what you sing,
> Such Godlike Virtues in the *King*,
> A *Minister* so filled with Zeal
> And Wisdom for the Common-Weal. . . .
> If this be Truth, as you attest,
> What *Land* was ever *half* so *blest*? . . .
> For, such is good Examples's Pow'r,
> It does its Office ev'ry Hour,
> Where *Governors* are good and wise;
> Or else the truest Maxim lyes:
> For this we know, all antient Sages
> Decree, that *ad exemplum Regis*,
> Thro' all the Realm his *Virtues* run,
> Rip'ning, and kindling like the Sun.

But, Swift continues, let us suppose your satiric depiction of
Britain is an accurate one:

> Or take it in a diff'rent View;
> I ask, if what you say be *true*,
> If you allow the present Age
> Deserves your *Satire's* keenest Rage; . . .
> If these be of all Crimes the worst,
> What *Land* was ever *half* so *curst*?[2]

It is small wonder that Young judged *Gulliver's Travels* to have
little wit 'of that Kind which I most like'.[3]

---

[1] *The Universal Passion. Satire the Last* (London, 1726), p. 1; in later editions
Satire the Last became Satire VII of *The Love of Fame*.
[2] *Poems*, ed. Sir Harold Williams (2nd edn., Oxford, 1958), ii. 391–2.
[3] In a letter of 21 Feb. 1726/7, printed by Richard Tickell in *Thomas Tickell
and the Eighteenth-Century Poets* (London, 1931), pp. 126–7.

Certainly, papers and journals supporting the Government were as aware as Swift that satires broadly indicting the degeneracy of the times were by implication specifically indicting the Court and the Ministry. The *London Journal*, for instance, accuses the *Craftsman* of depicting all things as corrupt merely to libel Walpole : '. . . because he is in Power, all things are out of order; *Nature* and *Providence* are but *just safe*, and scarce left unarraigned; For *his sake*, the *whole Nation* hath been abused; Corruption and Degeneracy universally charged.'[1] The *Craftsman* had, indeed, been requested by one of its readers to show how 'generally depraved' the present age has grown, how corruption has spread through all orders and professions, so that it is not surprising to find the *London Journal*, in other issues, ridiculing those who write 'Satyrs upon the Age', who proceed from the mistaken assumption that 'Men are by Nature bad' merely to prove that 'Men in Power are ill Men'. Another of Walpole's propaganda organs, the *Free Briton*, also complains that 'Nature in general has been painted all Black, and Government in particular decry'd like a Pestilence'.[2] Sometimes, too, these diatribes against 'false Philosophy' were accompanied by panegyrics on the honesty, sobriety, and wisdom of the English people. But however 'philosophical' the air of these discourses, they all end by attacking Opposition leaders or defending the administration.[3]

Such, then, are the ways in which 'general' satire like that in the second and fourth parts of the *Travels* could be linked with the political opposition. Sometimes, though infrequently, such attacks pointed directly at Swift's book. Thus the *British Journal* for 29 April 1727 printed, without acknowledgement of source or author, an essay by James Arbuckle which had appeared in the *Dublin Journal* in March.[4] Here we find the usual disparagement of those satirists who murmur against the age and who even depict mankind as less excellent than the brutes; given the date, that the allusion is to Swift seems fairly certain. The essay supplements

[1] No. 627 (31 July 1731).

[2] *Craftsman*, no. 161 (2 Aug. 1729); *London Journal*, no. 502 (15 Mar. 1728/9), no. 565 (30 May 1730), no. 606 (13 Mar. 1730/1); *Free Briton*, no. 5 (1 Jan. 1729/30).

[3] Indictment of 'general' satire on purely literary or philosophical grounds was common enough; see my essay 'Satires on Man and "the Dignity of Human Nature" ', *PMLA* lxxx (1965), 535–41.

[4] Printed in Arbuckle's *Hibernicus's Letters* (London, 1729), ii. 397–405.

the attack with an optimistic appraisal of the age: are not commerce and learning flourishing? Have not increased trade and riches made Britain a nation of peace and plenty and not, as some claim, of 'Luxury and Prodigality'? The political turn to what begins as a literary-philosophical comment would be unmistakable to a contemporary reader. Even more pointed is a passage in a short-lived Government paper called the *Senator* (1728). In the second issue of that journal its author begins with a defence of the integrity of Parliament, rails at those who would spread discontent with the administration, and advances to this general conclusion:

To attack Government, to debase Humane Nature, and to undermine Society, is the whole Secret of Popular Writing. The Delicacy of Satyr, the old Attick Poignancy, are no longer studied. Dullness pointed with Malice passes very well for Wit; and he that is revenging his own private Misfortunes upon the publick Tranquility, is to all Intents and Purposes, *A Patriot*.

That the writer has *Gulliver's Travels* particularly in mind is indicated by the following issue, where a letter supposedly from a reader complains that the *Senator*'s first two papers have been insufficiently specific: 'You . . . have glanc'd your Resentment rather against the Immoral Sentiments of *Gulliver* and the Political Sophistries of *Cyrus*, then against the much more dangerous, tho' perhaps at the same time much lower Malice of the *Craftsman*.'[1]

Swift himself seems to have recognized that even the 'general' satire of the *Travels* could be accused of having political implications, for in his poem *The Life and Character of Dr. Swift* (written 1731) he juxtaposes the charge that he offended Walpole with the charge that his satire reveals scenes of evil:

> But, why wou'd he, except he *slobber'd*,
> Offend our *Patriot*, Great Sir R——,
> Whose *Councils* aid the Sov'reign Pow'r,
> To *save* the *Nation* ev'ry hour?
> What *Scenes* of Evil he unravels,
> In *Satyrs*, *Libels*, *lying Travels*![2]

Swift's defence here is, of course, to cite the moral end of his satire; but perhaps more appropriate to the theme we have been

---

[1] No. ii (13 Feb. 1727/8); no. iii (16 Feb.).
[2] *Poems*, ii. 548.

examining is his ironic disclaimer in the 'Letter to the Writer of the Occasional Paper': 'Supposing times of corruption, which I am very far from doing, if a writer displays them in their proper colours, does he do any thing worse than sending customers to the shop? Here only, at the sign of the Brazen Head, are to be sold places and pensions: beware of counterfeits, and take care of mistaking the door.'[1]

In the period 1726–31 there are a few notable instances of yet a third way in which *Gulliver's Travels* proved helpful to the Opposition: by summary, quotation, and imitation. Thus the *Craftsman*, no. 218 (5 September 1730), asserts that the principal journalistic device of the Government papers is evasion: 'This Rule is admirably explain'd by that ingenious Traveller, Captain *Lemuel Gulliver* where he gives his Master the *Houyhnhnm* an Account of the *Lawyers* of a certain Country.' And there follows a summary of that section of the *Travels*. A more interesting example of the method of adapting Swift in an Opposition paper, however, occurs in *Fog's Weekly Journal*, no. 96 (25 July 1730). This essay first strikes a pseudo-literary note; *Gulliver's Travels*, claims the writer, has suffered unduly from the tendency of guilty men to take innocent remarks as a personal affront:

> Thus, if a Writer animadverts upon some fashionable Piece of Roguery, many a Man whom the Author never thought of understands the whole Satyr to be leveled at him. . . .
>
> It is for this Reason, perhaps, that some People feel a Satyr in Captain *Gulliver's* Travels, while the Rest of the World can read them over and over, without finding the least Sting in any Part.
>
> I am one of those that can discover no latent Meaning, and yet conceive there is good Instruction to be gather'd from many of those singular Remarks he makes upon the strange Regions he visited.

After this ironic passage, so reminiscent of the ballad 'When you censure the age' in *The Beggar's Opera*, *Fog's* proceeds to quote lengthy excerpts from Gulliver's visit to Glubbdubdrib. In the passages quoted Swift is attacking the corruption of Parliament, the base methods by which men become great and wealthy, the preferment of the unworthy, the corruption of a kingdom by luxury, the selling and buying of votes, and so on—all themes, of course, which readers of *Fog's* would at once apply to Walpole,

---

[1] *Prose Works*, v. 97.

despite *Fog's* claim that Swift is merely giving us an instructive account of past ages. The whole essay is convincing testimony to the ease with which the *Travels* were read politically, as well as to the obvious similarity between Swift's techniques and the necessarily oblique methods of Opposition propaganda. The following month (in no. 101 for 29 August 1730) *Fog's* again quoted a long passage from Part Three of the *Travels*, this time on the usefulness of fabricated plots and the arbitrary methods of deciphering political messages. Though on this occasion *Fog's* failed to identify the *Travels* as his source and referred to Swift merely as a 'modern Author', the use of such excerpts in an Opposition journal may help to explain why Swift, the following year, singled out Part Three as the section of the *Travels* likely to be 'Offensive to a *Loyal* Ear'.[1]

Imitations of the *Travels* for political purposes arose naturally enough from the recognition that in both form and content such a satire was admirably suited to the needs of writers who must attack their opponents indirectly. Even the Government writers succumbed to the temptation. *A Cursory View of the History of Lilliput* appeared in August 1727, by which time it was becoming obvious that Opposition hopes of supplanting Walpole after the death of George I were to come to nothing. This pamphlet, in the guise of describing Big-Endians, Tramecksans, and the like, gives a history of English politics from the Reformation to the accession of George II, a history which ridicules the Opposition for their false expectations, which assumes all Tories are Jacobites, and which even suggests allegorically that Queen Anne conspired to bring in the Pretender. It is dull stuff, but it reflects, I think, the degree of understanding with which the political allusions in the *Travels* must have been read, for the *Cursory View* is apparently designed to turn the tables on Swift by using the symbols of his political allegory to exult over a Walpolian triumph and mock his friends. 'Gulliver's' knowledge of human affairs must be limited, says the author, since the heir to the Crown did *not* have a hobble in his gait (that is, the Prince of Wales did not lean toward the opponents of Walpole, as events have shown).[2] On the Opposition side, too, *Gulliver* was subject to direct imitation. Thus *Craftsman* no. 150 (17 May 1729) conflates Swift and Montesquieu in a 'Persian Letter', in which Gulliver tells

[1] *Poems*, ii. 550.   [2] (London, 1727), p. v.

the traveller Rica of a strange land fallen upon evil days because its public funds have been intrusted to 'Shamgrigg' (Walpole). But the best example of a full-fledged imitation of the *Travels* for political satire is *A Voyage to Cacklogallinia* (August 1727), by 'Captain Samuel Brunt', who has travelled to a land of giant cocks and hens. Though there are a number of objects of derision here, the book in my view is almost certainly intended primarily as an attack on the administration.[1] The prime minister of Cacklogallinia, 'Brusquallio', clearly corresponds to Walpole in every physical and spiritual detail. The satiric method, however, is an interesting variation on Swift's. In his conversation with Brusquallio, modelled on Gulliver's conversation with kings and masters, Brunt paints a glorious picture of English life, while the prime minister cynically reads him a lesson on power politics and government by corruption. The political bitterness of this imitation of the *Travels*, like the excerpts quoted in Opposition journals, must have strengthened the impression of Swift's satire as a 'party' document.

It is, indeed, easy to understand why in the *Letter to Sympson* added to the *Travels* in 1735 Swift makes Gulliver complain of the 'Libels, and Keys, and Reflections, and Memoirs, and Second Parts; wherein I see myself accused of reflecting upon great States-Folk . . .'[2] How, he protests, could what was said so long ago and at such a distance be applied to 'any of the *Yahoos*, who now are said to govern the Herd'? Yet such applications were constantly made. Far from being received merely as an inoffensive romance, the potential of *Gulliver's Travels* as partisan propaganda was recognized, exploited, and attacked in the first five years of its history; by both its 'particular reflections' and its 'general' satire it could easily be viewed as a contribution to the campaign of the Bolingbroke–Pulteney Opposition. There is no reason to think Swift was particularly pleased by all this. Though his own relations with Walpole are another, and more complicated, story, it may be said that in the summer of 1727 he might have been embarrassed by anything of his which could be

---

[1] In her edition for the Facsimile Text Society (New York, 1940) Marjorie Nicolson is interested mainly in the satire on the South Sea Bubble and in the place of this volume in the tradition of 'voyages to the moon'. See also the review by James Sutherland, *RES* xvi (1940), 476–8.

[2] *Prose Works*, xi. 6–7.

construed as a libel on the Court.[1] Moreover, as he coldly informed the Abbé Desfontaines, his book was not written for only one city, one province, one kingdom, or even one age, since the same vices reign everywhere.[2] But, whatever Swift's feelings on the matter, the evidence shows that those *Travels* intended to mend the world were also of some service to an immediate political cause with which he was fully in sympathy.[3]

[1] See the comment by Herbert Davis, *Prose Works*, vol. v, p. xiii.

[2] *Correspondence*, iii. 226.

[3] Research for this essay was supported by a grant from the American Philosophical Society.

9

SWIFT AND THE ATTERBURY CASE

By EDWARD ROSENHEIM, JR.

ON 16 May 1723 (O.S.) the House of Lords passed, on its third
reading, a Bill to 'inflict pains and penalties' upon Francis Atterbury, Bishop of Rochester and Dean of Westminster. The charges
brought against him were lengthily stated, but basically alleged
that he was a leader in a treasonable conspiracy, involving invasion, insurrection, and the restoration of the Pretender to the
throne of England. The 'pains and penalties', again stated in
detail, took full effect on 18 June 1723, when the 'late' Bishop,
deprived of 'any office, dignity, promotion, benefice, or employment in England', aged sixty and in wretched health, left his
native country for an exile on the Continent that terminated
only with his death, nine years later.[1]

Swift's reaction to these events takes satiric form in at least
two places. The more famous of these is the concluding section
of Chapter Six, Book Three, of *Gulliver's Travels*, which describes
Gulliver's encounter with one of the 'professors' in Lagado's
school of political projectors. Here, it will be recalled, Gulliver
inspects his host's description of a project for discovering 'Plots
and Conspiracies' by a species of copromancy, and then helpfully
offers his own account of practices in 'the Kingdom of *Tribnia*,
by the Natives called *Langden*'.[2] In this society, which is overrun

---

[1] An account of Atterbury's hearing, along with related materials, will be
found in *A Complete Collection of State Trials and Proceedings for High Treason
and Other Crimes and Misdemeanors . . .*, ed. T. B. Howell (London, 1809–26),
xvi. 323–695. I hereafter refer to this volume as *State Trials*.

[2] *The Prose Writings of Jonathan Swift*, ed. Herbert Davis (Oxford, 1939–68),
xi. 190–2. I employ this edition, hereafter called 'Davis', for my references to
the text of *Gulliver's Travels*. Davis's text, based on that of the Faulkner
edition of 1735, provides a version of the section on plots which is less
'cautious' than that of earlier editions (see collation, ibid., pp. 311–12).
In its earlier printed form the text contained, in addition to a shorter, less
explicit list of 'cypher' specimens, a 'hypothetical' account of the plot-ridden

by witnesses and informers, we see how secret codes can be deciphered, acrostics can be used to convey 'political Meanings', and such a message as '*Our Brother* Tom *has just got the Piles*' can be perfectly rearranged into '*Resist,—a Plot is brought home—The Tour.*'

A second literary product of Swift's response to the Atterbury affair is the clever poem called 'Upon the horrid *Plot* discovered by Harlequin the B— of R—'s French *Dog*'.[1] First published in Faulkner's edition of Swift's *Works* in 1735, these verses deride the use, by Atterbury's enemies, of facts concerning a dog allegedly sent to the Bishop, and, expanding on the conceit that the dog has thus served as a 'witness', go on to assail the various 'dogs' in human form who have victimized the unhappy prelate.

For several reasons, the student of Swift may find it useful to examine the main facts surrounding the prosecution of Atterbury. Certain published comments upon Swift's allusions to the case have, in the first place, fostered some misconceptions. These questionable interpretations may well attest Swift's satiric success by reflecting the 'version' of the case implicit in his fanciful account. But fully to grasp the character of his satiric invention, we should understand the historical actuality which served, as it were, as its genesis. Moreover, some familiarity with the Atterbury case, both as it was conducted in Parliament and as it was argued 'out of doors', may suggest to others, as it has to me, that the Bishop's prosecution and punishment are reflected both more closely and more extensively in *Gulliver's Travels* than has generally been recognized.

The attack upon Atterbury comprises only one strand—although the most sensational one—of a complex enterprise by which the Walpolites, through the exposure of a Jacobite invasion planned for the year 1722, 'helped to restore a little of the popularity of the government'.[2] The Jacobite plot itself survives as an authentic but almost farcical project, doomed from its outset by faulty communication, internal dissension, insufficient financing,

---

kingdom. Thus, in place of the anagrams on Britain and England (themselves, I believe, a deliberately childish mockery of deciphering techniques), Gulliver offers his suggestions as to what might be done, 'should I happen to live in a Kingdom where Plots and Conspiracies were . . . in Vogue . . .'.

[1] *The Poems of Jonathan Swift*, ed. Sir Harold Williams (2nd edn., Oxford, 1958), i. 297–301.

[2] J. H. Plumb, *England in the Eighteenth Century* (London, 1950), p. 61.

and, not least, by the well-informed vigilance of the Walpole Government. As Andrew Lang has put it, 'The year 1722 saw a long train of gunpowder explode without harming any one except the Jacobites who laid it.'[1]

Although the 'explosions' had begun several months earlier, Atterbury himself was arrested and confined to the Tower on 24 August 1722. Here he remained for the ensuing nine months, under circumstances which, while doubtless uncongenial, may or may not have warranted the bitter complaints he was to make before the House of Lords.[2] On 11 March 1722/3 the Bill of attainder against him was ordered into the House of Commons, before whom, however, as a member of the Upper House, he refused to be tried.[3] Accordingly, it was in the Lords that the Bill was introduced for its first reading on 6 May. Of the ten days' debate that followed there are abundant records. Only a verbatim account of the examination of witnesses is lacking, and the arguments by counsel, together with the speeches of various peers, seem to preserve all important elements of the case which each side advanced.[4]

The trial was conducted in a climate of opinion that accepted the conspiracy as a formidable reality. Its putative seriousness had been recognized the previous October, when Parliament suspended habeas corpus for a year, and when the King himself,

[1] Andrew Lang, *A History of Scotland from the Roman Occupation* (London & Edinburgh, 1907), iv. 337.

[2] *State Trials*, xvi. 490–1; *The Speech of Francis Late Lord Bishop of Rochester at the Bar of the House of Lords on Saturday the 11th of May, 1723....* (London, 1723), p. 3. Atterbury's alleged mistreatment while in confinement was exploited by his defenders and denied by his enemies. The Bishop's most recent biographer implies that he suffered largely because of the hostility of Colonel Williamson, deputy-lieutenant of the Tower of London. See H. C. Beeching, *Francis Atterbury* (London, 1909), pp. 285–9.

[3] *State Trials*, xvi. 426, 434–6.

[4] In addition to *State Trials*, the Atterbury hearing is reported in detail in *Cobbett's Parliamentary History of England from the Norman Conquest in 1066 to the Year 1803* (London, 1811, etc.), viii. 97–353. Speeches before the Lords for both the prosecution and the defence were printed shortly after the hearing, and will here be cited where relevant. There is also in the British Museum (Add. MS. 34,713) a series of notes taken throughout the hearing by the Lord Chancellor (Macclesfield). These are of value chiefly in confirming the accuracy of the published reports—although they are also important in indicating the extent and general tenor, if not the precise details, of Sir Robert Walpole's testimony before the House of Lords.

addressing both Houses of Parliament, spoke of massive prepara-
tions abroad, grave dissensions at home, and the need for 'an
entire Union among all that sincerely wish well to the present
Establishment'.[1] Within a month of the King's address legal
prosecution began with the trial of one crucial figure in the plot—
Christopher Layer, a somewhat disreputable lawyer and inveterate
Jacobite. The record of Layer's trial makes it clear that he had
visited the Pretender in Rome and had subsequently attempted to
recruit disaffected soldiers for the proposed insurrection.[2] A
detailed plan for the seizure of the Tower and other key positions
was found among his papers. More significantly, for those seeking
the true Jacobite leaders in England, he was found to be in
communication with such suspects as Lord North and Gray and
Atterbury's old pupil, Charles Boyle, now Earl of Orrery (both
of whom, like Atterbury, were already under arrest).

Layer was found guilty and condemned to be drawn and
quartered, but this melancholy event was delayed for many
months, while a Committee of the House of Commons probed
exhaustively into the affairs of Layer and all those apparently
connected with him. The Committee's report, issued on 1 March
1722/3, is a document of seventy-six folio pages, accompanied
by some 350 additional pages of 'appendixes' which reproduce
letters, depositions, and examination proceedings.[3] Between
them, the report and the appended materials provide virtually
all the evidence on which the Government reconstructed the

---

[1] *His Majesties Most Gracious Speech to both Houses of Parliament on Thursday
the eleventh day of October, 1722* (London, 1722), p. 7.

[2] Layer's trial is fully reported in *The Whole Proceeding upon the Arraignment, Tryal, Conviction and Attainder of Christopher Layer Esq for High Treason
in Compassing and Imagining the Death of the King, 1722* (actually Jan. 1722/3).
(I shall hereafter refer to this document as *Layer Trial*.) Layer's biography in
the *DNB* (xxxii. 304) is almost entirely based on a biased and unsympathetic
pamphlet, *A Faithful Account of the Life of Christopher Layer . . . by a Gentleman
of Norwich, his School-Fellow* (London, 1723), but the account of his pleading at
his own trial suggests that he was, at least, a shrewd and resourceful lawyer.

[3] The Committee of the Commons was chaired by Pulteney and included
such Whig stalwarts as Walpole and Spencer Compton (*State Trials*, xvi.
323). Its report is titled *A Report from the Committee Appointed by Order of the
House of Commons to Examine Christopher Layer and Others*. I shall refer to it as
the *Committee of Commons Report*, and, as the 'Appendixes' contain a number
of independently paginated sections, I shall employ its system of numbering,
within sections designated by letter, to refer to specific documents.

details of the plot. Moreover, they offer such grounds as then existed for assigning Francis Atterbury a central role in that forlorn enterprise.

To the dispassionate student those grounds are less than impressive. Sir Keith Feiling has observed that the evidence against Atterbury, 'though not (as it is now) decisive, was enough to send him into exile for life'.[1] It was enough, chiefly because the action against the Bishop (and against two other defendants, George Kelly and John Plunket) took the form of a legislative Bill rather than a judicial proceeding, and was patently guided more by a concern for national security than by a strict desire for justice. The prosecution itself admitted that the evidence against the Bishop 'was not all of it strictly legal . . . according to the ordinary Course of Justice', and argued that the Lords were 'not tied to the Rules of Westminster-Hall'.[2]

In all the massive materials presented for the Lords' consideration there was no incriminating document in the Bishop's hand, no deposition as to words directly spoken by him, no suspect communication directly mentioning him by name. Although Atterbury's guilt is clear today, its establishment in 1723 indeed called for extraordinary efforts.

One such effort centred largely upon the figure of George Kelly, a venturesome non-juring parson,[3] who had been arrested, interrogated, and released before Atterbury's own commitment. (He was subsequently re-arrested and, as a co-defendant with Atterbury, tried and convicted.) Apart from treasonable activities of his own, Kelly was accused of having served as agent and amanuensis for the Bishop of Rochester, and the case against the

---

[1] Sir Keith Feiling, *The Second Tory Party, 1714–1832* (London, 1938), p. 19. Atterbury's complicity in the Jacobite plot became entirely clear with the publication of *The Stuart Papers Printed from the Originals in the Possession of Her Majesty the Queen*, ed. J. H. Glover (London and Edinburgh, 1847). That correspondence reveals that from 1715 until his death in 1732 Atterbury was in the service of the Pretender.

[2] *The Replies of Thomas Reeve, Esq; and Clement Wearg, Esq; in the House of Lords, The Thirteenth of May, 1723. In Behalf of the Bill to inflict Pains and Penalties on the late Bishop of Rochester* (London, 1723), p. 2.

[3] *DNB* xxx. 350. Kelly appears to have been an engaging person (Andrew Lang made him the hero of a historical novel, *Parson Kelly*, published in 1900) and was something of a favourite during the confinement which followed his conviction—and which is supposed to have terminated with his escape.

Bishop rested, to a great extent, upon establishing the latter fact.

Kelly persistently denied having served Atterbury in any capacity. The prosecution, therefore, was forced to rely heavily on hearsay evidence, from questionable quarters. It consisted chiefly of depositions taken from a disreputable figure named Philip Neynoe, who was drowned while escaping from custody before he could even appear at the Layer trial.[1] To this was added the even less persuasive testimony of Andrew Pancier, a former lieutenant of dragoons, who swore that 'one Skeen' had provided him with extensive details of the conspiracy, including the part played by Atterbury. Skeen, however, categorically denied the story under oath, and became, in fact, a minor bulwark for the defence, not only by asserting that Pancier had tried unsuccessfully to bribe him, but by swearing that Neynoe had confessed to him that his own story had been concocted entirely at Walpole's instigation. Thus the prosecution was ultimately able to make little use of the depositions from the dead Neynoe and the unsavoury Pancier. On the contrary, the use of 'informations' from such shabby sources played into the hands of Atterbury's defenders, both during the hearing itself and in the pamphleteering that accompanied and followed it.[2]

A further ineffectual effort by the prosecution involved two letters, addressed to Atterbury and signed by Charles Halstead, a sea captain who was alleged to have sailed to Bilbao ('Bilboa') on an abortive mission to return the exiled Duke of Ormonde to England.[3] Actually, these were brief requests for appointments with the Bishop, purpose unspecified, but natural enough for a man who was a tenant under Atterbury's bishopric. Their substance,

[1] *Committee of Commons Report*, Appendix, E-8 to E-11. Neynoe's character was so dubious that even Bishop Willis, one of Atterbury's fiercest antagonists, confessed that he 'did indeed . . . always think him to be a Knave'. See *The Bishop of Salisbury's Speech in the House of Lords upon the Third Reading of the Bill to Inflict Pains and Penalties on Francis (late) Bishop of Rochester. The 1st of May, 1723*, p. 6.

[2] *Committee of Commons Report*, Appendix, D-1, D-2; *The Defence of Francis, Late Lord Bishop of Rochester at the Bar of the House of Lords by William Wynne Esq; One of his Lordship's Counsel* (London, 1723), p. 35; *Replies* of Reeve and Wearg, pp. 6–8. The last source contains the prosecution's admission that Neynoe's evidence was 'only hearsay as to the Bishop of Rochester' but adds that 'it's being true or false won't affect this case.'

[3] *Committee of Commons Report*, p. 39, Appendix, AA-12, AA-13, D-8, D-9.

therefore, did little to strengthen the prosecution's case. On the other hand, their place of seizure was gleefully noted—and eventually immortalized—by one of the Bishop's sympathizers. For it was these two inconsequential documents which, so the report ran, had been triumphantly discovered, by the Government officers, in the episcopal close-stool![1]

It is probable that Atterbury's opponents recognized the weakness of this kind of evidence, and it is thus not surprising that their chief arguments centred upon a third collection of documents. These were the letters that involved, among other things, the celebrated 'lame dog', and though somewhat complicated and highly circumstantial, they were far more damaging than the depositions of the informers or the non-committal notes found in the close-stool.[2] The basic documents in this instance were three letters, largely in cipher, dated 20 April 1722, which had been intercepted by clerks in the post office, who swore they were in the hand of George Kelly. Drawing upon professional experts in deciphering, and upon keys found in the papers of alleged conspirators, the prosecution maintained that the letters were addressed, respectively, to the Jacobite General Dillon, the Earl of Mar, and the Pretender himself, while their contents referred transparently to the proposed invasion. The signatures on the letters are, again respectively, 'T. Illington', 'T. Jones', and '1378' —the last being interpreted by the experts to stand for the letter 'R'. These three letters, moreover, were offered in evidence along with additional correspondence among the suspected Jacobites, from which it is clear, even to today's objective reader, that 'Jones' and 'Illington' are the same person—and a person deeply involved in the enterprise with which the letters are uniformly concerned.

But the task of the prosecution was to prove that 'Jones' and 'Illington' referred to the Bishop of Rochester, and for this purpose the letters appear remarkably—indeed suspiciously—useful.[3]

---

[1] *Committee of Commons Report*, Appendix, D-45.

[2] The three critical letters are discussed at length in the *Committee of Commons Report*, pp. 40–8, and are included in its Appendix as items D-10, D-11, and D-12. Additional correspondence relied on to identify Atterbury as author of the three incriminating documents is likewise in the Appendix, items D-13 to D-28. The letters are also reproduced in the *Stuart Papers* (Glover), at pp. 11–15 of the appendix to that volume.

[3] The possibility that the letters were deliberately contrived to implicate Atterbury has given rise to controversy that cannot be appropriately discussed

They contain, in the first place, references to the whereabouts of Jones (or Illington) on specific dates—on some of which he is 'in town' and on others 'in the country'—and these coincide perfectly with Atterbury's reported movements between Westminster and the episcopal residence at Bromley. Various allusions in the letters further make it clear that Jones–Illington was suffering seriously from gout during the period of the correspondence and that his wife, after a long illness, died during the final week in April. And Atterbury, a chronic victim of gout, had sustained a particularly crippling attack in late April, while his wife had died, on 27 April, after a protracted illness.

But neither gout, bereavement, nor time-tables attained the prominence in the case which was achieved by the dog, Harlequin. The correspondence plainly reveals that such an animal had been sent from France as a gift for Jones (or Illington), but had injured its leg in transit and was therefore not delivered to Jones–Illington, to the latter's 'great Tribulation'.[1] In this case, the link with Atterbury was supplied by a Mrs. Barnes, a former landlady of George Kelly, who deposed that a dog, injured on the trip from France, had indeed 'been left to her to be cured by Mr Kelly', who informed her that 'the said dog was for the Bishop of *Rochester*'.[2]

The counsel for the Bill against Atterbury, suspending their insistence on other proofs, asked with heavy irony, 'Is there no other Person who was in Town on the seventh of *May*, out of Town on the tenth and fourteenth, in Town on the fifteenth, whose Wife died the Week before the thirtieth of *April*, he himself then ill of the Gout, to whom a Dog was sent from *France* by the name of *Harlequin*, that broke its Leg, and was brought to Mrs. *Barnes* by Mr. *Kelly* in order to be cured?'[3]

Damning as such a question appears, it had been concocted from little more than hearsay evidence and some highly irregular procedures. The three letters attributed to the Bishop were copies —the originals having been intercepted at the post office, but

here. Beeching (pp. 285–9) summarizes the speculations of his predecessors and suggests that not only Mar (whose duplicity seems quite probable) but also George Kelly served as Walpole's agents in 'framing' the Bishop. The latter conjecture appears entirely unsupported.

[1] *Committee of Commons Report*, Appendix, D-20.

[2] Ibid., Appendix, E-4.

[3] *Replies* of Reeve and Wearg, p. 19.

eventually sent on to their addressees (obviously to elicit the forthcoming damaging replies). The letters were alleged to be in Kelly's hand by clerks who had seen, but not retained, specimens of Kelly's writing months earlier. More astonishingly, the experts, on whose skill at deciphering the Lords relied almost entirely for the substance of the letters, refused to answer any questions concerning their methods, because this might 'tend to discover the art or mystery of decyphering'—a refusal cheerfully sustained by the House.[1] As for the circumstantial details of the letters themselves, they acquired their overwhelming particularity only if the Harlequin story could be believed—and to support its truth there was only one bewildered woman's account of something she had been told by one man.

The defence assailed this patchwork structure repeatedly and at great length, but the case against it is nowhere better stated than in Atterbury's own words:

> Shall I stand committed before your Lordships on such an Evidence as this? The Hearsay of an Hearsay; a Party dead, and that deny'd what he said; by strange and obscure Passages, and fictitious Names in Letters; by the Conjectures of Decypherers, without any Opportunity given me of examining and looking into the Truth of their Decyphering; by the Depositions of Post-Office Clerks about the Similitudes of Hands; their Depositions made at distant Times, and without comparing any one of the Originals; by a strange Interpretation of them, for nothing more, I am perswaded, can be made of the Arguments, than what is call'd the intercepted Correspondence.[2]

The Bishop himself somewhat vitiated this statement by accompanying it with arguments that invoked his character, position, sufferings, and achievements, and by declaring, in effect, that he had been 'framed'.[3] His defenders, however, concentrated almost exclusively upon the frailty of the case against him. Neither of his two counsel, Sir Constantine Phipps and William Wynne, spent much effort in positive attempts to dissociate their client from the plot. Instead, after elaborate protests at the 'extra-legal' character of the proceedings, they hammered persistently at the circumstantial evidence and attentuated inferences upon which the prosecution relied. And, in the final

[1] *State Trials*, xvi. 497.
[2] *The Speech of Francis Late Lord Bishop of Rochester*, p. 14.
[3] Ibid., p. 6.

stage of the proceeding, the Duke of Wharton, in a vigorous defence of Atterbury, openly dismissed 'arguments against attainder', and declared that the 'Harlequin' documents were the 'Great and only Foundation remaining to support this Bill'.[1]

The colourful questions that dominated the hearing before the Lords assumed even greater prominence in public discussion of the case—and that discussion was abundant. From their outset the Government's movements against the plotters appear to have been widely known.[2] As the King's October address suggests, the danger of the plot was, if anything, exaggerated for the benefit of the public. Reports of major proceedings, from Layer's trial in October to the final 'replies' against the Bishop the following May, were printed and circulated by parliamentary order. Walpole's enemies, on the other hand, vigorously counter-attacked, denouncing the Government's activities, in a phrase of the day, as 'a plot against the people'. Neither faction had forgotten the Sacheverell affair, a precedent which offered hope to the Tories and a warning to the Whigs. The latter seem to have recognized, in particular, that the imprisonment of a High Church champion would prove highly unpopular with many of the clergy. Within a month of Atterbury's arrest there appeared a *Letter to the Clergy of the Church of England*, shrewdly designed to justify that event in the eyes of clergymen of all political faiths.[3] For a more general

---

[1] *His Grace the Duke of Wharton's Speech in the House of Lords on the Third Reading of the Bill to Inflict Pains and Penalties on Francis (late) Lord Bishop of Rochester. May the 15th, 1723*, p. 12.

[2] In June of 1722, within a month of Kelly's arrest and two months before Atterbury's, letters from William Stratford to Edward Harley reported details of the 'Harlequin' story with considerable accuracy; see H.M.C. *Portland*, vii. 326, 328, 330. Stratford, while he personally hated Atterbury, was certainly no intimate of the Walpolites, and his knowledge of these facts suggests that, at a very early date, they were being widely circulated.

[3] *A Letter to the Clergy of the Church of England, On Occasion of the Commitment of the Right Reverend the Lord Bishop of Rochester to the Tower of London* (London, 1722). The anonymous 'Clergyman' who is announced as author of the tract is identified as Zachary Pearce (himself to become Bishop of Rochester at a later date) by John Nichols in *Literary Anecdotes of the Eighteenth Century*, iii. 111. The pamphlet at once elicited a published reply, the anonymous *Spirit and Conduct of Several Writers . . . concerning the Commitment of the . . . Lord Bishop of Rochester*, a work which, despite its manifest artlessness, appeared in at least two editions. Bids for the sympathy of the clergy continued to be prominent in Whig literature—as, for example, in a series of

audience, Ambrose Philips's play, *Humfrey, Duke of Gloucester*, extolled the virtues of active patriotism and held up the dreadful spectacle of a corrupt prelate (Beauford, Bishop of Winchester, as performed by Cibber). To insure that the message got across, a separate *Introduction* to Philips's tragedy was published, and the Whig journal, *Pasquin*, devoted its entire issue of 6 March 1722/3 to an 'application' of the play to contemporary circumstances.

The controversy appears at its most intense, indeed, in the pages of the periodical journals. On the Walpole side a number of these publications were almost entirely given over to the Atterbury affair, both during the period of the Bishop's imprisonment and for months after his departure into exile. During the spring and summer of 1723 such papers as the *British Journal* and the *Weekly Journal; or British Gazetteer* furiously assailed the Bishop in issue after issue. Of the 110 numbers of *Pasquin*, which were published between 28 November 1722 and 26 March 1723/4, seventy-four are principally or exclusively devoted to similar attacks, while in many other issues, letters and news-items seem designed to keep the affair before the public.

Of the assaults upon Atterbury, none was more prominent than that of Benjamin Hoadly, at the time Bishop of Hereford, though soon to be translated—in the series of such moves that followed the trial—to the see of Salisbury. Hoadly, whose violent doctrinal differences with Atterbury (and, indeed, all of High Church persuasion) had begun decades earlier, appears to have remained silent during the hearing in the House of Lords, but his subsequent writings survive as perhaps the most effective of all replies to the Bishop's defence. In thirteen letters, published under the name of 'Britannicus' in the *London Journal*, Hoadly conducted a close and savage analysis of Atterbury's widely publicized speech before the House, and pointed out—persuasively, it must be admitted— that the Bishop's line of argument would hardly have been adopted by a man who was, in truth, innocent.[1]

letters addressed specifically to clergymen in the *British Journal*, nos. 31–4 (20 Apr. to 11 May 1723).

[1] Letters by 'Britannicus' attacking Atterbury's speech appeared in the *London Journal* between 13 July and 5 Oct. 1723. A similar series, under the same pseudonym, had attacked George Kelly's defence in seven issues of the periodical between 25 May and 6 July. These series are both included in 110 letters, all signed 'Britannicus', that are reprinted in Hoadly's *Works*, ed. John Hoadly (London, 1773), iii. 3–395. If, indeed, Hoadly was the writer

Not surprisingly, in view of the dangers of defending alleged Jacobites against the Government, pro-Atterbury periodicals were neither so numerous nor so outspoken as those which pressed the Walpolite case. *Mist's Weekly Journal; or Saturday's Post*, to be sure, obliquely but unmistakably mocked the proceedings against the Bishop well through the summer of 1723.[1] But Atterbury's most daring journalistic defence was provided by that strange character, Philip, Duke of Wharton, whose grotesque career achieved a ·moment of rare integrity during his spirited advocacy of the Bishop's cause before the House of Lords. Following the hearing, Wharton kept his dangerous view of the matter before the public in the pages of his journal, the *True Briton*, in most of whose seventy-four numbers the alleged injustice of the proceedings receives virtually exclusive attention.[2]

Just as it was in the Whig interest grossly to exaggerate the Jacobite threat, so the principal strategy of the *True Briton* was to treat the plot as an illusion and its prosecution as a disgraceful farce. For this purpose such central ingredients in the case as the lame dog, the decipherers, and the plainly disreputable witnesses lent themselves well to ridicule. The comic possibilities inherent in the Harlequin evidence had appeared even to the unfortunate Atterbury, who, speaking in his own defence, observed that his enemies 'perhaps, are not much in the wrong to think, that one intercepted Dog should be of as much use as ten intercepted Letters'.[3]

of all of the 'Britannicus' letters—which appeared with regularity in the *London Journal* between Sept. 1722 and Jan. 1724/5—he was certainly among the most energetic and vehement of the Government's journalistic spokesmen.

[1] As a rule, Mist's periodical discussed the issues involved in the prosecution of the plot in a rather general, though obviously pointed fashion, confining its direct attacks to Atterbury's journalistic enemies rather than the Government or the House of Lords. Thus on 1 June 1723 it deplores 'Conspiracies' by the State, carried on by 'Persons in *Power* and *Trust* with a Prince', while on 15 June (no. 242) it offers a farce called 'The Metamorphosis or *Harlequin Cato*', in which the writer who, under the name of Cato, had written letters against the Bishop in the *British Journal* is fiercely lampooned.

[2] The *True Briton* ran from 3 June 1723 to 14 Feb. 1724/5. Robert J. Allen has argued that the liveliest writing in the journal was the work not of Wharton but of Oldisworth; see his 'William Oldisworth: the Author of the *Examiner*', *PQ* xxvi (Apr. 1947), 159–80.

[3] *The Speech of Francis Late Lord Bishop of Rochester*, p. 8.

These potentially ludicrous aspects of the affair were exploited by Atterbury's sympathizers in ways which often anticipate Swift's use of them in *Gulliver's Travels*. The 'decyphering' lent itself to elaborate mockery—particularly since, in the language Swift was to use, it involved 'a Set of Artists very dexterous', whose undisclosed secrets had the power to send men to death or exile. With a straight face, *Mist's Weekly Journal* published ridiculous correspondence in cipher and, in adjacent issues, lengthy and sober accounts of oracles and divination.[1] Less circumspectly, the *True Briton*—in a manner remarkably like that of Swift's 'Our Brother Tom' gambit—'decyphers' an innocuous document in order to yield a sinister meaning. The entire issue of 28 June 1723 is devoted to showing that a '*Latin* epistle from Doctor Freind to Doctor Mead'—an authentic document, dealing with the smallpox[2]—is actually, when deciphered, a 'barefaced impudent attack upon our Excellent Constitution'. Employing a few such assumptions as that 'by Variolae' the Doctor 'means *Government*', the article produces, by elaborate puns and parallels, a 'proof' whose accuracy is, like that of Swift's anagram, a chief source of its humour.

An even more ambitious satiric enterprise in the *True Briton* is an extended allegory, said to be recovered from an ancient Spanish manuscript, in which the Bishop of Tortosa is grotesquely persecuted by a Walpole-like Don Ferdinando, who is aided by a servile and villainous coterie of bishops.[3] Here, as elsewhere in the Tory literature, the Harlequin evidence is wildly lampooned, as Don Ferdinando preaches a congratulatory sermon to a congregation of spotted dogs and asks, '*Ye* dear inimitable Creatures, *could I ever have excommunicated the Bishop of* Tortosa *without you had deposed* Heresy *against him?*'[4]

---

[1] See, in particular, issues between 22 June 1723 (no. 243) and 17 Aug. 1723 (no. 251).

[2] *Johannis Freind ad Celeberrimum Virum Ricardum Mead, M.D. de Quibusdam Variolarum generibus Epistola* (dated 30 Mar. 1723). The work is actually dated from the Tower—in which Freind was confined as a suspected Jacobite plotter—and the *True Briton* mockingly cites this fact as clear proof of the doctor's guilt, for which the 'decyphering' provides mere supplementary support.

[3] *True Briton*, no. 15 (22 July 1723); no. 16 (28 July 1723); and no. 55 (9 Dec. 1723).

[4] Ibid., no. 55 (9 Dec. 1723).

To this kind of ridicule, the Walpolite journals did not, as a rule, reply in kind. The plot, they implied, invited anything but levity, and they did their best to discountenance what one journal called 'the indefatigable Endeavour of several Persons and Papers, to reflect upon and ridicule the late Conspiracy'.[1] *Pasquin*, it is true attempted a whole repertory of satiric performances—including several rather feeble adaptations of the *True Briton*'s papers on the Bishop of Tortosa—but the Whig journal's undisguised truculence and the heavy-handed directness of its regular attacks on Wharton convey a far stronger impression of blunt bad temper than of humorous disdain. Indeed, one of its issues is given over to a denunciation of various forms of political satire, while in another the author announces that he has been forced to drop 'the Style of *Pasquin*' in order to make it clear that the most recent *True Briton* 'has injudiciously and outrageously offended against every Person in the Kingdom'.[2]

Although ridicule was thus an important and effective weapon for Atterbury's defenders, there was one aspect of the case which they viewed with open anger. This was the systematic and acknowledged employment of paid informers, whom the Bishop's allies represented as not only contemptible in themselves but as the sinister agents of scheming superiors. Although, in the House of Lords, the evidence of the informers had appeared almost ludicrous and had, indeed, backfired upon the prosecution,[3] it raised questions which were not allowed to die. Throughout its career, the *True Briton* persisted in its denunciations of what, in the final issue (17 February 1723/4), Wharton called 'Treason against the People'.

Swift's recipe for manufacturing plots (particularly in the 'hypothetical', as opposed to 'Tribnian', form that it takes in early editions of the *Travels*) is interestingly anticipated in the second number of Wharton's journal (10 June 1723). Here the author suggests that if 'hereafter, a corrupt and Wicked Administration

---

[1] *Weekly Journal; or British Gazetteer*, no. 44 (3 Aug. 1723).

[2] *Pasquin*, no. 38 (27 May 1723); no. 51 (26 July 1723).

[3] Even in the Whig press there is evidence that the informers caused some embarrassment. Thus 'Cato' writes, 'I will freely own that many Things have been done which cannot be justified; some, perhaps, ignorantly, many ambitiously, and others, it is to be feared, traiterously, to help the Conspirators by provoking the People and by rendering the Administration odious' (*British Journal*, no. 31, 20 Apr. 1723).

should intend the Subversion of the State', the task can best be executed 'by forming of a Sham-plot' in which 'Proper Tools would be set to work'. Throughout the summer of 1723 the *True Briton* referred repeatedly and scathingly to informers and false 'evidences', and its issue of 25 November (no. 51) recurs to this topic in a manner of particular interest to students of *Gulliver's Travels*. For we recall that the very first of the Utopian 'Laws and Customs' described in Chapter Six of the 'Voyage to Lilliput' calls for the savage punishment of false informers. And the *True Briton* likewise insists that informers should be viewed as major criminals if their evidence proves false, and that 'there should be a wholesome Law made, that *Transportation*, at least, should be their Punishment'.

In his satiric reflections on the Atterbury case Swift was able to include topics and, in a broad sense, strategies that had emerged prominently in both the legal and literary defence of the Bishop. It is not hard to understand why Swift had taken no immediate part in that defence. Apart from the writing of *Gulliver's Travels*, there were, in 1722–3, more pressing concerns to occupy the Dean of St. Patrick's—not least, the rising storm over Wood's coinage. Although Swift and Atterbury had been closely associated during the *Examiner* period and their relationship appears to have remained congenial throughout the Bishop's lifetime,[1] there appears to be no reason for the latter's making special claims on his friend's loyalty or talent. Swift's reaction to Atterbury's plight seems, indeed, to have been marked by a kind of wry disgust at his prosecution rather than by any profound dismay at his sufferings.[2]

[1] The latest surviving letter from Swift to Atterbury is dated 18 July 1717 and attests to a continuing, if not intimate, friendship; see Swift's *Correspondence*, ed. Sir Harold Williams (Oxford, 1963–5), ii. 278–80. On at least two occasions during his exile, in 1728 and 1731, Atterbury sent the Dean literary items which he thought would be of interest; see John Nichols, *The Epistolary Correspondence . . . of the Right Reverend Francis Atterbury* (London, 1783–90), iv. 167, and *The Correspondence of Alexander Pope*, ed. George Sherburn (Oxford, 1956), iii. 247.

[2] On 9 Oct. 1722 Swift writes to Robert Cope, 'Strange revolutions since I left you: a Bishop of my old aquaintance in The Tower for treason, and a doctor of my new acquaintance made a Bishop' (Swift's *Correspondence*, ii. 434). The new acquaintance was Theophilus Bolton, who had been made Bishop of Clonfert.

Moreover, unlike Pope, but quite like the majority of Atterbury's other defenders, Swift has left little indication of belief in the Bishop's actual innocence.[1]

On the other hand, there can be no doubt about Swift's basic sentiments toward the affair or about the features of the case which most aroused them. As the King's address made clear, the plot had been exploited, if not actually trumped-up, to consolidate support for the Hanoverians and the Walpole Ministry. Throughout the proceedings the Whigs had played (to hostile eyes) their accustomed parts—the Privy Council and Committee of the Commons as inquisitors, their paid agents as false witnesses, their allies among the Lords as partisan, autocratic judges. In particular, the bishops in the House of Lords acted in a way which could confirm Swift in one of his deepest aversions.[2] Only one bishop—Swift's friend, Francis Gastrell, then Bishop of Chester—joined those Lords who dissented from the Bill against Atterbury.[3] Richard Willis—whose efforts were shortly rewarded by his translation from the see of Salisbury to that of Winchester—attacked Atterbury in a heated speech, which, despite its excesses and inelegances, was quickly published.[4] Wake, the Archbishop of Canterbury, had, from the outset, urged the exposure of the plot, which, in a published address to the King, he described as the 'Depths of Satan' and a 'Mystery of Iniquity'.[5] And, as we have seen, Hoadly, in the grateful role of 'Britannicus', was the

---

[1] Pope's apparent complete belief in Atterbury's innocence and his somewhat naïve testimony at his friend's hearing are well known and are made especially clear in three letters which he wrote to the Bishop during April and May of 1723; see *The Correspondence of Alexander Pope*, ii. 166–70. In what is primarily a persuasive study in attribution, Maynard Mack notes the singular depth of conviction and affection expressed in Pope's letters to Atterbury at this time; see his 'Letters of Pope to Atterbury in the Tower', *RES* xxi (Apr. 1945), 117–25.

[2] Swift's strained relations with the English bishops are carefully discussed by Louis A. Landa in *Swift and the Church of Ireland* (Oxford, 1954), pp. 180–8.

[3] *State Trials*, xvi. 462.

[4] *The Bishop of Salisbury's Speech in the House of Lords upon the Third Reading of the Bill to Inflict Pains and Penalties upon Francis Bishop of Rochester. May 15th 1723.*

[5] *To the King's most Excellent Majesty, The Humble Address of the Archbishop, President of the Concovation of the Province of Canterbury; the Bishops and Clergy of the same Province in Convocation Assembled on Wednesday the Thirty-first Day of October, 1722* (London, 1722), p. 3.

conspicuous leader of the journalistic assault upon his erstwhile brother-bishop.

Beyond the fact that the enemies of Atterbury were likewise those of Swift, there were aspects of the affair that, whatever the personalities or politics involved, were calculated to arouse the Dean's indignation. These included the solemn reliance upon the deposition of shoddy informers, the highly circumstantial evidence, the Lords' complacent acceptance of the experts' arcane decipherings, and, not least, the professions of piety, patriotism, and benevolence which accompanied every stage of the attack. Despite the debate that continues to rage around Swift's 'ultimate' beliefs, it seems safe to say that the proceedings against Atterbury must have offended him quite as much upon moral as upon political grounds.

Swift's reaction to the case was not only unequivocal but, it would seem, well-informed. A letter, written by Swift to Robert Cope in October 1722, reveals that he was abreast of relatively detailed aspects of the movement against the plot, and that he had read that early attempt to justify Atterbury's imprisonment, the *Letter to the Clergy of the Church of England*. We know that he 'saw', and at least intended to borrow, Wharton's defence of Atterbury before the Lords.[1] More significantly, his poem 'Upon the horrid Plot discovered by Harlequin' reveals a familiarity both with the main aspects of the affair and with certain personalities whose roles were relatively minor and are only briefly recorded in the voluminous materials surrounding the Parliamentary hearing.

Thus, though the deposition and death of Philip Neynoe (Swift calls him 't'other Puppy that was Drown'd') were notorious, and though 'Curr *Plunket*' was tried and convicted under the same Bill as the Bishop, Swift mentions other figures who had a far less conspicuous part in the proceedings. Among these is the witness 'Skean', who, while he played a modest role in the hearing itself, is almost totally ignored in the pamphleteering that surrounds the trial. Even more obscure is '*Mason* that abandoned Bitch'. She served merely as the custodian of incriminating papers, alleged to have belonged to Christopher Layer, and her brief testimony is not even mentioned in the published records of the debates before the House of Lords, appearing only in the massive appendixes to the *Report* of the

[1] Swift's *Correspondence*, ii. 436; iii. 10.

Committee of Commons. Her 'bitchiness', moreover, does not emerge *vis-à-vis* Atterbury, but seems to have consisted of sexual promiscuity and an understandable evasiveness on that score—qualities that are revealed nowhere in the materials of the *Report*, but are to be inferred only from the cross-examination conducted during the trial of Christopher Layer.[1]

(I must parenthetically admit to some bewilderment over the 'Harlequin' poem's castigation, as 'dogs', of figures who were, at worst, innocuous, or, as in the case of Skeen—whom Swift calls a 'Whelp'—who actually were helpful in Atterbury's defence. It is possible that the poem reflects a reading of the Atterbury materials that was superficial, confused, or imperfectly remembered. Thus Swift may have been aware only of Skeen's reported disclosure of the plot, and not of his subsequent robust denial and counter-attack; he may have confused John Plunket—who, though stupid, was resolute in declaring his own innocence and that of the Bishop—with one Mathew Plunkett, an ex-sergeant who appears in a minor but authentic role as an informer; he may have seen, and been amused by, the examination of Mrs. Mason, and then unwittingly substituted her name for that of Mrs. Barnes, whose deposition concerning Harlequin, while guileless, was so damaging to the Bishop. I am inclined, however, to feel that Swift, somewhat like Wharton, was concerned exclusively with the case against Atterbury, and hence indifferent to the fates of the other suspected Jacobites, except as they affected the Bishop. From this standpoint, indeed, it may well have appeared desirable to dissociate Atterbury from the 'rabble' suspected with him—especially from those whose guilt was relatively plain or who, like Plunket, had produced correspondence, if not testimony, to implicate the Bishop.[2] One can well believe that, apart from the loyal and intelligent Kelly, Swift's concern for Atterbury's cause did not extend to the motley herd of career-Jacobites, turncoats, fanatics, and drifters whom the Government had rounded up.)

[1] *Layer Trial*, pp. 64–9, 109–11; *Committee of Commons Report*, Appendix, B-19.

[2] In his speech before the Lords, Wharton argued that, precisely because the letters attributed to Atterbury employed a cipher found in Plunket's possession, they could not have been written by the Bishop, who would have had nothing to do with 'so insignificant a wretch as Plunket' (*His Grace the Duke of Wharton's Speech*, p. 14).

The relevant passages of *Gulliver's Travels* reflect a sound understanding of the facts in the Atterbury case and of the strategies employed in the Bishop's defence, but both are transformed by Swift's literary powers into satiric conceits, with an autonomous power to delight us. This is especially true of Swift's initial conceit —the ingenious if repellant prescription for discovering plots by the inspection of the suspects' ordure. The solemn annotations of some editors tend to imply that the documents allegedly discovered in the Bishop's close-stool occupied a prominent place in his hearing, and that Swift, accordingly, is here lampooning a central feature of the affair. In fact, as we have already indicated, the two letters played a very minor and ineffectual part in Atterbury's prosecution, and their hiding-place none at all. In all the mass of documents assembled by the Committee of Commons I have found the close-stool mentioned only once—and then, transiently and peripherally, in a sympathetic account of the Bishop's arrest.[1] In all the other documents surrounding the conspiracy I have discovered only one further reference to the close-stool—but this is in a paper which we know Swift saw, namely, Wharton's speech before the House of Lords.[2] Here the reference is again only incidental, but it could well have served as the germ—though only the germ—of Swift's 'large paper of instructions for discovering plots and conspiracies'. If, as is entirely possible, the very minor episode of the close-stool did inspire that extravagant 'project', then it testifies to Swift's sharp eye for scatological possibilities and his magnificent talent for developing them. And it testifies as well to the power of his satiric invention to transcend the facts which have engendered it. The permanent suggestion that Swift has conveyed is that his formula for divining treason lay in some unjustifiable invasion of the Bishop's privacy and an insupportable interpretation of whatever was found there.

Unlike the prescription for copromancy that precedes it, the colourful list of 'mysterious Meanings' reflects more closely than is often recognized particular details of the Atterbury affair. At the same time, I suspect the list as a whole conveys an impression which—as is entirely proper to satire—obscures certain actual circumstances attending the Jacobite ciphers. Unless my

---

[1] *Committee of Commons Report*, Appendix, D-45.
[2] *His Grace the Duke of Wharton's Speech*, p. 5.

own experience with Swift's 'specimens' is unusual, they suggest that Atterbury's enemies attached ludicrous and indefensible meanings to ordinary, innocent correspondence which they had seized. What we must remember, however, is that the correspondence among the Jacobites themselves is actually loaded down with codes and ciphers, pseudonyms and initials, to such an extent that it would achieve a kind of puerile, Tom-Sawyer quality, if we were not aware of the life-and-death reality which it reflects. Atterbury's own Jacobite letters, as we now know, are no less dependent than the others upon these devices. As their editor observes, 'Almost every letter contains cant names for persons and things; and portions of each are written entirely in cypher.'[1] The captured papers reproduced in the *Report* of the Committee of Commons include no less than nine elaborate 'keys', involving words, letters, and numbers, and several of them contain more than 500 items.[2]

A glance at most of the suspected letters themselves will further dispel the notion that they were innocent correspondence. In most instances they contain, beside quite obvious pseudonyms, such inconsistencies, repetitions, triviality, and sheer nonsense that it is often impossible to regard them as serious communications. It is significant that, although both Atterbury and his counsel repeatedly challenged the integrity of the professional decipherers, they at no time denied that codes and ciphers were used in the correspondence, nor did they even suggest that the true substance of the letters could be found in their apparent meaning.

Swift's famous list, of course, involves some delightfully artful name-calling, but it also includes several items which closely reflect particulars of the Atterbury affair. Of these, the best known is the equation of a 'lame Dog' with 'an Invader'—but it has given rise to some curious misinterpretations. There is no point in tracing the history of the misleading annotations, except to say that they persist in recent, generally excellent, editions of the *Travels*.[3] But it may be useful to point to one specimen—that found in A. E. Case's distinguished study, *Four Essays on Gulliver's*

---

[1] *Stuart Papers* (Glover), Preface, p. ii.

[2] *Committee of Commons Report*, Appendix, BY-1, C-50, C-51, C-52, F-11, H-34 to 39, I-14.

[3] In the most recent edition of *Gulliver's Travels* I have seen—that of Peter Dixon and John Chalker (Harmondsworth, Middlesex; Penguin Books,

Travels (Princeton, 1945)—if only because Professor Case is ordinarily so authoritative that we tend to accept his information without question. It was alleged, says Case (on page 92 of his book), 'that the Bishop and his correspondents used the name of the Bishop's lame dog Harlequin as a symbol for the Pretender: hence the inclusion . . . of '*a lame dog*, an *Invader*'. But the prosecution used Harlequin only in the manner I have described: he was never employed as a code-symbol, for the Pretender or any one else. It is possible that Swift intended, by a kind of satiric synecdoche, to imply that the affair of Harlequin was blown up into a symbol for the entire Jacobite conspiracy. I find more amusement in the notion that here Swift is suggesting that the French dog was, himself, an 'invader' in a sense—just as in the 'Harlequin' verses he is treated as a 'witness' who has earned a place at Court. However one interprets Swift's joke, the fact is simply that the dog's name was never believed to convey any hidden meaning.

Another item in Swift's list deserves mention, since its specific reference to the case against Atterbury is not generally noted. This is the translation of 'the Gout' into 'a high Priest'—a matching which seems to lack both humour and significance unless understood in the context of the Atterbury affair. For, we recall, the identification of the Bishop as 'Jones' or 'Illington' depended critically on the fact that both Atterbury and his alleged fictional counterparts were reported as being seriously ill with the gout during the period of the incriminating correspondence. Here, then, in an almost literal sense, the gout—or at least a sufferer from it—was made to identify the 'high priest', who was thus doubly its victim.[1]

A similarly pointed reference can, I think, be detected in Swift's equation of 'an empty Tun' with 'a General'. As a generic characterization of military leaders, Swift's epithet does not appear particularly apt or characteristic, and one is accordingly

---

1967)—a note tells us: 'Much of the evidence against Atterbury was based on intercepted letters which were supposed to refer to plots under feigned names, and references to a lame dog called Harlequin were made to appear particularly sinister' (pp. 357–8).

[1] While the Bishop's gout figures repeatedly in the circumstantial reasoning of the prosecution, its central importance is nowhere more strongly emphasized than in the *Replies* of Reeve and Wearg, especially at p. 4.

tempted to search for a more particular target. Marlborough comes to mind at once, but that 'Mighty Warrior' had died in the summer of 1722, was in no way notable in the prosecution of the plot, and was not conspicuously tun-like. A far more promising candidate is William, first Earl Cadogan, once Marlborough's most trusted subordinate and his successor, in 1722, as Commander-in-Chief of the Army. Cadogan achieves prominence in the history of the plot not only as active commander of the troops who, in the spring of 1722, encamped in Hyde Park, but because his contemplated capture was an important step in the conspirators' plans, and his name, indeed, was included in the Jacobite codes.[1] Moreover, his hatred for Atterbury is supposed to have given rise to his suggestion that the Bishop should be 'thrown to the lions', and to have elicited from Atterbury a doggerel response that, among other things, indicates why the phrase, 'an empty Tun', was particularly applicable to the General:

> Ungrateful to th'Ungrateful man he grew by,
> A big, bad, bold, blustering, bloody, blundering booby.[2]

The *DNB* confirms the fact that Cadogan was an unusually large man, whose career included enough inept misadventures—including indictment by the Commons for embezzlement in 1717 —to warrant the charge of stupidity in the characterizations produced by both Atterbury and Swift.

Literary deciphering can itself be pushed too far, and we should not read into Swift's specimens any greater particularity of reference than the text, or its historical context, seems to invite. Since, however, the Gulliverian encounter we are inspecting had its origin in the Atterbury affair, it is possible that other of Swift's epithets, though plainly quite applicable to general institutions, involved a dimension of special relevance to the events of 1722–3. Thus the 'Committee of Grandees' ('a Chamber pot'),

---

[1] *Committee of Commons Report*, p. 20; Appendix, B-11, BY-1, I-14. Relevant facts concerning Cadogan's career will be found in the *DNB* viii. 182–7.

[2] The 'Ungrateful man' is Marlborough, who, in his old age, was supposed to have been coldly treated by Cadogan. The episode involving Cadogan's cruel remark and Atterbury's response is recounted in Beeching's *Francis Atterbury* (p. 285). Pope's very measured 'character' of Cadogan, in a letter to Bethel in 1726, is explained by Sherburn on the ground of the General's 'attitude toward Atterbury' (*The Correspondence of Alexander Pope*, ii. 386).

whatever else it brings to mind, can certainly apply to that hand-picked group of powerful Whig leaders who formed the special Committee of the Commons, submitted the exhaustive, damaging *Report*, and live, in the irony of Swift's verses, as 'the secret wise Committee' which 'interrogated' the dog Harlequin.[1] The equation of the 'Close-stool' with 'a Privy-council' continues the references to the Bishop's toilet with a rather childish pun, but we also recall that a select committee of the Privy Council undertook the initial, fundamental interrogation of all of the suspected plotters. Even the linking of 'the Plague' with 'a standing Army' —expressing an aversion to this Whig policy that also appears in Gulliver's discussions with the Brobdingnagian king and his Houyhnhnm master—had a direct topical application. In the spring of 1723 the Government was rejoicing in the nation's deliverance from both the plague that had attacked France and the threatened Jacobite invasion from that country—the latter having been partly forestalled, in effect, by the metaphorical 'plague' of a fully mustered standing army.[2] Whether or not these, and perhaps additional, applications reflect Swift's primary intention, they suggest, at least, that for many of the innocuous looking items in Swift's code we can find particular exemplification in the history of the Jacobite conspiracy.

The delightful anagram involving '*Our Brother* Tom' is ingenious not only in its perfection but as a parody of the style to be found in the correspondence of the conspirators. The 'jargon' of these letters is anything but romantic in its feigned topics, and reports or inquiries about personal health are a staple of

[1] It is true that Swift expressed disdain for the Government's 'secret committee' of 1715; see his letter to Chetwode in June of that year in the *Correspondence*, ii. 175. Any application made by his readers in 1726, however, would almost certainly have been to the widely publicized committee of 1722–3.

[2] Thursday 25 Apr. 1723 was proclaimed a day of public thanksgiving for the nation's preservation 'from that Dreadful Plague with which the Kingdom of France was lately visited'. On the following day *Pasquin* (no. 29) published a poem (attributed, by generally responsible manuscript annotations in the British Museum files of that journal, to Nicholas Amhurst) in which the spread of the plague is compared to the progress of an army. In its concluding lines King George is hailed as conqueror of both plague and plot, since Heaven,

> For *Brunswick*'s Sake, preserves the faithless Age,
> From *Popish* Zeal, and Pestilential Rage;
> Against both Foes at once our Cause maintains,
> Guards us from sudden *Death*, and breaks the *Plotter*'s chains.

these communications—as is the use of such appellations as 'brother' and 'cousin'.[1] Equally commonplace are the names under which the conspirators concealed their identities, and familiar Christian names and homely surnames predominate in both the 'keys' and the letters themselves. 'Tom' is, in fact, reported—early in the Committee of Commons *Report*—as the code-name for the Duke of Ormonde.[2]

Swift's 'translation' of the code-message contains something very like a crux in its concluding words, 'The Tour'. A. E. Case has explained the phrase as follows:

It is not accident that while the 'a' in this message is a lower-case letter, the 'T' of 'The' is a capital. 'The Tour' is a signature. During part of his exile in France Bolingbroke requested his friends to address him as M. Le Tour. A grammarian would point out that 'la tour' is a tower; a tour is 'le tour'; but Swift apparently did not regard this as a serious objection. Perhaps, too, he did not wish to abandon what he felt was a very appropriate anagram.[3]

Because Professor Case's explanation survives, in part at least, in recent, excellent, editions of the *Travels*,[4] I think we should recognize the difficulties it raises. Bolingbroke's use of the name 'La Tour' is supported by only one reference—a letter to Charles Ford in January 1722.[5] The correspondence neither of Pope nor of Swift refers to this pseudonym, although the latter refers several times to Bolingbroke's adoption of the name 'Charlot'.[6]

---

[1] Extracts from the correspondence that are cited, for purposes of their own, in the *Replies*, of Reeve and Wearg (p. 20) provide specimens of the conspirators' style, e.g.: ' 'Tis said Hore is laid up with his old Distemper, Hobbert is pretty well recovered'; 'Mr. Hore is laid up, and so is Jemison with the Gout'; 'I saw your acquaintance Crow two days ago, who deliver'd me a Present from my Cousin Jones; I am really much concerned for this Lady's State of Health.' Comparable examples can be found in the *Commons Committee Report*, Appendix D-29, D-32, E-46, E-47, E-54 to E-57, and E-60.

[2] *Commons Committee Report*, pp. 6–7.

[3] *Four Essays on Gulliver's Travels* (Princeton, 1945), pp. 91–2.

[4] e.g., *Gulliver's Travels and Other Writings*, ed. M. K. Starkman (New York and London, 1962), p. 189. Mrs. Starkman recognizes that 'The Tour' may refer to the Tower, but echoes Case in asserting that it 'is a signature' and identifying Bolingbroke.

[5] Case cites *Letters of Jonathan Swift to Charles Ford*, ed. D. Nichol Smith (Oxford, 1935), p. 236.

[6] The Swift–Ford correspondence reveals this; ibid., pp. 65, 68, 80, 83, 93. See also Swift's *Correspondence*, ed. Williams, at ii. 219, 407.

If Swift is really referring to Bolingbroke, his allusion would, at the most, have been recognized only by a very small 'in-group'. Moreover, there is no reason to believe that in 1723, or assuredly in 1726, Swift would have so centrally employed his friend's name in the apparatus of a mock-Jacobite communication. Bolingbroke had left the Pretender's service early in 1716, and his subsequent efforts to regain favour with the English Government resulted in his pardon in May 1723. Swift's use of his name as the 'signal' of a Jacobite document would, even if intelligible, have been inappropriate and, indeed, malicious.

If 'The Tour' is, in fact, supposed to be someone's signature, a far more probable candidate can be identified. This is the Pretender himself. The *Stuart Papers* reveal that 'M. La Tour' was actually one of the code-names by which 'James III' was known in the Jacobite correspondence of 1715 and 1716.[1] But this identification, although, I think, far more tenable than Professor Case's hypothesis, presents some of the same difficulties. 'M. La Tour' is only one of forty-six code-names which a single volume of the *Stuart Papers* assigns to the Pretender—and I can find no reason to believe that it was made public until their publication in the nineteenth century. If Swift had somehow known of this particular pseudonym, his use of it in 1726 would, again, have been understood by almost none of his readers.

But for those readers, their attention drawn to the Atterbury case by the passage on 'plots' as a whole, there would have been little difficulty in grasping a reference to the Tower—even if the word were simplified (or Gallicized) in spelling. In the records of the proposed Jacobite invasion the 'first Matter projected to be done' is the capture of the Tower of London, a fact conspicuously included in the allegations of the prosecution.[2] Whatever more specific meaning, if any, the term was intended to convey—and it might have been mentioned as a rallying-point, a military objective, or a password—it would have served to a contemporary reader as a hallmark of the Jacobite conspiracy of 1722. The capital 'T' which led Professor Case to identify 'The Tour' as a

---

[1] H.M.C. *Calendar of the Stuart Papers . . . at Windsor Castle* (1902–23), ii. 554, 575.

[2] *Commons Committee Report*, p. 1. See also Appendix, BX-20 of that document, *Layer Trial*, p. 152, and repeated references during the hearing as reported in *State Trials*, xvi. 323–695.

signature might also have been used to signify a substantively, if not grammatically, complete phrase. It is even possible that the message was to be seen as 'dated from' the Tower. Correspondence from Jacobite suspects in custody there had been seized, and figured so prominently in the prosecution, by virtue of its place of origin, that the 'suspicions' attaching to any letter from the Tower, were elaborately mocked in the *True Briton*'s exercise in 'decyphering'.[1] In any case, the hypothetical M. La Tour would have meant very little to the majority of Swift's readers, while, for those of them even moderately familiar with the history of the plot, the Tower would have had immediate significance.[2]

If the allusions I have been discussing are authentic, they imply an audience that was reasonably well versed in the principal facts and issues surrounding the prosecution of Atterbury. I believe it is safe to assume that Swift had such an audience, for the Atterbury case, as we have seen, aroused intense feeling, produced voluminous discussion in print, and hinged critically on highly colourful and conveniently 'non-technical' features.

Such readers, more perhaps than those of our own time, would likwise have been sensitive to whatever passages, elsewhere in *Gulliver's Travels*, seemed to reflect upon the Atterbury affair. I shall not, in these concluding paragraphs, insist that Swift 'must have had in mind' the Atterbury case whenever a passage seems relevant to that event. I suggest, however, that some of the institutions and practices which his satire appears to assail in quite general terms find immediate and telling exemplification in the circumstances of the Bishop's prosecution. If the original readers of *Gulliver's Travels* were, in these instances, inclined to make

---

[1] *True Briton*, no. 8 (28 June 1723).

[2] I am indebted to a reader of this paper for a suggestion that greatly increases the likelihood that Swift's eighteenth-century readers would have associated 'Tour' with 'Tower'. The two words were homophones, as suggested by Bysshe's grouping them under the same vowel sound (*A Dictionary of Rhymes*, p. 30, appended to *The Art of English Poetry* (4th edn., London, 1710)). The *OED*, moreover, records the indifferent use of both spellings in reference to a lady's false hair-piece during the early eighteenth century (*Tour*, sb. 1, 4). Thus, if the passage were read aloud by Swift's contemporaries, the suggestion of a tower would have been virtually unavoidable.

topical 'applications'—and most readers of contemporary satiric works are so inclined—then the Atterbury affair came most readily to hand.

I have, for example, already referred to the prominence of Swift's prescriptions concerning 'informers' in the laws of Lilliput. His hatred of the breed is made clear at a number of other points—one of which, the 'defiance' of the Lilliputian informers, Clustril and Drunlo, has been long, if not definitely, associated with the activities of Neynoe and Pancier.[1] In each of four separate Swiftian 'catalogues' of abominable callings or practices, false witness, subornation, and perjury are conspicuously included— the last of these being Gulliver's climactic list of 'natural' vices in the diatribe against pride that concludes the Fourth Voyage.[2] Swift's aversion to informers was not limited to those who participated in the proceedings of 1722–3—his treatment of Thomas Prendergast, mentioned in the 'Harlequin' poem, makes this clear—but in the quarter-century preceding *Gulliver's* appearance no specimens were as conspicuous as the unlovely crew who deposed against Atterbury. If, in effect, we look for actual informers who could have given rise to Swift's wrath, we shall find our most prominent and historically immediate possibilities in the record of the Jacobite prosecutions.

Professor Ehrenpreis has effectively argued that the First Book of *Gulliver's Travels* is 'largely an allegory of English political history from 1708 to 1715', but urges that this fact should not 'limit its meaning'.[3] Thus, while the narrative centre of the First Book has its principal analogue in the events surrounding the Treaty of Utrecht, no reader denies that it also satirically represents features of the Court of George I and the Walpole Ministry —that the caperings of Flimnap or the aspersions on a corrupt, sycophantic court cannot, and need not, be forced into the history of the fallen Harleyites. I should therefore suggest that a relatively sustained passage in the First Book derives its chief satiric implications from the Atterbury case. This is the account of the 'great *Lenity*' by which it is decided that Gulliver is to be blinded and starved to death, and which is reaffirmed by the Emperor

---

[1] The passage appears at p. 65 in Davis. Case (*Four Essays on Gulliver's Travels*, p. 80) associates the Lilliputian informers with Neynoe and Pancier.

[2] Davis, pp. 199, 252, 276, 296.

[3] Irvin Ehrenpreis, *The Personality of Jonathan Swift* (London, 1958), p. 84.

himself, who 'after the Court had decreed any cruel Execution, either to gratify the Monarch's Resentment, or the Malice of a Favourite . . . always made a Speech to his whole Council, expressing his *great Lenity and Tenderness, as Qualities known and confessed by all the World*'.[1]

Gulliver's 'merciful' punishment, we recall, is required because (in the words of his anonymous, sympathetic informant) 'his sacred Majesty, and the Council, who are your Judges, were in their own Consciences fully convinced of your Guilt; which was a sufficient Argument to condemn you to death, without the *formal Proofs required by the strict Letter of the Law*'.[2] In the italicized phrase, echoes of the Atterbury trial have been recognized by editors; the statement is, in fact, a remarkably close—and quite undistorted —paraphrase of the 'reasoning' by which the Bishop's hearing under a legislative Bill, and on evidence 'not strictly legal', was, as we have seen, justified by the 'Council who were his Judges'.[3]

I should argue that the extended account of the Lilliputians' 'lenity', of which the passage I have just discussed is a part, points with comparable particularity to the Atterbury affair. It is true that, as some editors have pointed out, the treatment of the defeated Jacobite leaders in the uprising of 1715 was described, not without some reason, as merciful. But whatever memories of that professed clemency may have lingered in partisan minds would only have been revived and exacerbated by the much more recent—and egregious—professions of Atterbury's enemies.

Swift himself, soon after the Bishop's imprisonment, reacted with furious sarcasm to the praise of the King's merciful policies that he found in the *Letter to the Clergy of the Church of England*. To Robert Cope he wrote: 'It is a wonderful thing to see the Tories provoking his present majesty, whose clemency, mercy, and forgiving temper, have been so signal, so extraordinary, so more than humane, during the whole course of his reign, which

---

[1] Davis, p. 72.

[2] Ibid., p. 71.

[3] Counsel for the prosecution offered technical arguments to support the legislative rather than judicial principles that obtained in the hearing before the House of Lords. It was the Bishop of Salisbury, however, who played into the hands of Atterbury's adherents by making such assertions as that 'no Government can subsist, if there be not a Power in it, to change, to abrogate, to suspend, or dispense with its Laws, as Necessity or Conveniency shall require' (*The Bishop of Salisbury's Speech*, p. 4).

plainly appears, not only from his own speeches and declarations, but also from a most ingenious pamphlet just come over, relating to the wicked Bishop of Rochester.'[1] Some of Atterbury's most implacable assailants professed a pious concurrence in the lenity of his punishment—thus both flattering the mercy of the monarch and his servants, and, at the same time, implying that the Bishop's 'pains and penalties' were much less severe than they properly might have been. Thus Willis, the Bishop of Salisbury, despite the venom of his speech against Atterbury, applauded the Lords for 'giving so full and fair a hearing and . . . making the Penalties so much less than the Crimes deserve'. Their Lordships, he was sure, would always 'be ready to stand by, a Wise, and a Good, and a Merciful Prince; and . . . defend him against all Treasons, and Traiterous Conspiracies whatsoever'.[2]

In his prorogation speech, ten days after Atterbury's conviction, the King, expressing his delight in the Lords' verdict, conformed entirely to Swift's ironic characterization. After dwelling on the conspiracy in its full horror, he went on to say: 'And yet it is with Pleasure I reflect, that the Justice of Parliament had been so temper'd with Mercy, that even Those, who are resolv'd to be dissatisfied, must acknowledge the Lenity of your Proceedings, and will be at a Loss for any Pretence to Complain, so few Examples having been made, and the Penalties inflicted by the Bill, falling so much short of the Punishments due for the same Crimes by the Common Course of the Law.'[3] Here was new justification for the dubious legality of the proceedings against the Bishop. In the language of the Lilliputians, the 'strict Letter of the Law' had, indeed, been ignored, but only to allow full exercise to his Majesty's 'great Lenity and Tenderness'.

Gulliver, we recall, decides to escape from Lilliput rather than to stand trial. The reason for this decision, he tells us, is that 'having in my Life perused many State-Tryals, which I ever observed to terminate as the Judges thought fit to direct; I durst not rely on so dangerous a Decision, in so critical a Juncture, and against such powerful Enemies'. In Swift's own life there had been 'many State-Tryals', but none so recent, or so

---

[1] Swift's *Correspondence*, ii. 436.

[2] *The Bishop of Salisbury's Speech*, p. 10.

[3] *His Majesty's most Gracious Speech to both Houses of Parliament on Monday the Twenty-seventh Day of May, 1723*, p. 3.

well calculated to justify Gulliver's decision, as that of the Bishop of Rochester.

In the first three Books of the *Travels* Gulliver rarely offers the kind of direct, damning assessment of his own society that so notably marks the 'Voyage to the Houyhnhnms'. One point at which he does so, however, is in his account of the spirits who are summoned for him in Glubbdubdrib, where he professes being 'chiefly disgusted with modern History'.[1] From this experience he learns how 'prostitute Writers' have ascribed to villainous sorts of men those virtues which, in fact, they most conspicuously lacked—including, we note, the attribution of 'Truth to Informers'. He had discovered, he goes on to say, how 'many innocent and excellent Persons have been condemned to Death or Banishment, by the practising of great Ministers upon the Corruption of Judges, and the Malice of Factions'.

At least one of Swift's contemporary readers found that the passage pointed clearly to the events of 1722–3. In a 'Key' to *Gulliver's Travels*, produced in 1726 by one 'Signor Corolini', and more notable for its admiring summaries than for its explication of particular allusions, the author devotes one of his rare 'glosses' to the sentence on the fate of 'innocent and excellent Persons'. 'Now here', he says, 'I am sensible that the present Disaffected in *England*, will immediately apply the Cases of an executed Barrister, banished Bishop, and an imprisoned Priest.'[2] The cases can only be those of the executed attorney, Layer, the banished Bishop of Rochester, and the imprisoned 'Parson Kelly'. To the 'disaffected' of 1726—and Swift was surely among them— the sins and sinner of modern history were to be found in the Walpole Government, and appeared most openly in the prosecution of the Jacobite conspirators.

A powerful motif of alienation and exile recurs throughout *Gulliver's Travels*. It transcends all reference to particular outcasts and prisoners, and, in my own view, can best be explained only

---

[1] Davis, p. 199.

[2] *A Key, Being Observations and Explanatory Notes upon the Travels of Lemuel Gulliver. By Signor Corolini, a noble Venetian now Residing in London* (1726). The *Key* appears to have been published by Curll, if not, as its author's pseudonym might suggest, actually written by him; see Ralph Straus, *The Unspeakable Curll* (London, 1927), pp. 116, 280–1. The British Museum copy of this work consists of four independently paginated letters addressed to Swift. The passage I quote appears in the third of these, at p. 27.

by the facts of Swift's own life. In the light of these facts, however, Swift's sympathy for Atterbury's cause and his hatred for the Bishop's enemies can be seen both as political and, in one sense, deeply personal. When Swift, replying to Pope's expression of similar sentiments, writes of his 'Infelicity in being so strongly attach'd to Traytors (as they call them) and Exiles, and State Criminals', he is speaking both of his fate and of his predilections.[1]

Most of the recent abundant critical discussion of *Gulliver's Travels* has focused upon questions of meaning and motive, largely as they emerge from the Fourth Voyage and Gulliver's adventures among the Yahoos and Houyhnhnms. This emphasis is only natural, for it remains in the power of that strange myth to 'vex the world' for which it has a continuing, painful relevance.

But *Gulliver's Travels* is also addressed to a smaller world, limited in territory and time to the British Isles of Swift's day, and peculiarly vulnerable to his satire because of specific men, events, and institutions. It is a world in which, for Swift, political structures and practices assume great importance, and it is, in this fundamental respect, a foolish, cruel, and dishonourable world. In Swift's indictment of his own society the Atterbury affair provides an important target, because, in the prosecution of the Bishop, there were displayed precisely those political vices which Swift most hated—perjury, bribery, sycophancy, cruelty, and, not least, the abuse of power by ill-trained peers and self-serving prelates.

Gulliver's Travels is, to be sure, 'above' mere political pamphleteering, but this is so, not because Swift disdains the particulars of political controversy, but because he exploits them in his pursuit of graver, more persistent problems of human belief and conduct. If, for today's reader, the book is a timeless assault on pride or hypocrisy or ingratitude, it also remains a record of Swift's response—angry, artful, and immediate—to the manifestation of these sins in the Hanoverian world.

---

[1] Swift's *Correspondence*, ii. 464.

IO

JONATHAN SWIFT AS JUPITER: 'BAUCIS AND PHILEMON'

By ERIC ROTHSTEIN

WE do not know the tone of Swift's voice when he mentioned, as he 'was often wont to', 'that in a poem of not two hundred lines ['Baucis and Philemon'] Mr. *Addison* made him blot out fourscore, add fourscore, and alter fourscore'.[1] Most modern Swiftians have thought that he might well have been disgruntled, since hindsight could show him that the 'accomplished "Baucis and Philemon"' was 'better before Addison had passed over it his smoothing chamois leather'.[2] I am not about to take issue with those critics who regret Swift's changes: the original version (which survives incomplete in manuscript) opens with an infectious verve that the revised and published version never approaches. If we grant this, the question remains why the man who had written, and was to write, with such gusto could be prevailed upon to scratch much of it away. The answer, one may hope, lies in the poem itself, seen in its historical context. After all, Addison presumably won Swift over with reasonable arguments rather than sheer force of personality: although affable, Swift was not what James would call 'of a docility'. Nor could he be wooed by smoothness or primness for their own sakes.

A look at some of Swift's revisions in 'Baucis and Philemon' will support this last assertion. For example, 'Old Sermons' that the original version called 'Chang'd' are now 'Vampt' 'in the Preface and the Text' (M 178, P 128).[3] The new participle is more

---

[1] Quoted from Delany's *Observations*, in *The Poems of Jonathan Swift*, ed. Harold Williams (Oxford, 1937, Second Edition, 1958)—hereafter designated '*Poems*'—i. 88.

[2] Bonamy Dobrée, *English Literature in the Early Eighteenth Century, 1700–1740* (Oxford, 1959), p. 67.

[3] The two versions of 'Baucis and Philemon' are printed in *Poems*, i. 90–5 and 111–17. I have inserted parenthetical line references into the text, designating the first version, extant in manuscript, as 'M'; the published version as 'P'.

vivid, technically precise, and suggestive of the patchwork super-
ficiality that makes Philemon's new status as a parson absurd.
Similarly, Swift turns to a precise, almost technical term in describing the bedstead as 'Compact of Timber' instead of the
original 'Compos'd of Timber' (P 102, M 148). The etymology
(*com* & *pangere*: to fasten together) and the everyday connotations
of 'compact' give the reader a more definite sense of the actual
bulky object; while the special force of the Latin roots—picked
up by surrounding 'Metamorphos'd' (M 150, P 104) with
'Ancestors' and 'antient' rather than the manuscript version's
'Grandfathers' and 'former'—reminds one that 'Baucis and
Philemon' is an Ovidian imitation with a mock-heroic flavour.
The diction sharpens the incongruity of the bed's becoming a
pew to 'lodg[e] Folks dispos'd to Sleep'. Swift obtains visual
immediacy and descriptive precision once again by changing the
couplet about the flyer, or regulatory apparatus, of the roasting-
jack that turns into a clock: in the original version (133–4) the
flyer 'now stopt by some hidden Pow'rs | Moves round but twice
in twice twelve Hours', while in the revision (73–4) it, 'slacken'd
by some secret Power, | Now hardly moves an inch an Hour'.
Here a specious local effect—the play on 'twice' through the
repetition—disappears in favour of a subtler rhythmic slowing
down, which is (as the 'twice' is not) the point of the line. The
new first line sounds more coherent and much more specific than
the old; 'secret', too, picks up the two meanings of mechanical
and spiritual concealment better than 'hidden'. Such revisions
indicate that Swift rewrote the poem thoughtfully and sensitively,
and that he did not by any means abandon energy or vividness
in rewriting. Addison's arguments, if these changes are consistent
with them, clearly aimed at more than imposing an educated
delicacy upon raffish verse.

Each of the three revisions just mentioned not only makes the
poetic language more precise but also works to integrate the
given passage with the larger interests of the poem. To the degree
that the examples are representative, they suggest that Swift's
motives for revision proceeded in good part from his sense of
'Baucis and Philemon' as an entirety. And since the dialectic of
Augustan criticism commonly begins with intention, with the
effect of a work as an entirety, Swift and Addison presumably
began there too when they talked over possible changes. The

least flexible such intention, perhaps, is that of topicality, which dominates all but two of Swift's other extant poems written between the end of 1693 and the autumn of 1710. But 'Baucis and Philemon' seems to be without topical references. It joins 'Verses Wrote in a Lady's Ivory Table-Book' and 'The Description of the Morning' as poems whose effect is in no way occasional, whatever their genesis may have been. Thus the local references in 'Baucis and Philemon' change in different versions of the poem: 'Rixham' (the Welsh town of Wrexham) in the original version becomes a Kentish village in the revision, while Hills's pirated edition confides to us that Swift is talking about 'the Parish of *Chilthorne*, near the County Town of *Somerset*', Bristol.[1] Nor would the actual destruction of a pair of yews, such as those that Swift's old couple become, have been likely to suggest this Ovidian imitation. In Ovid the two become an oak and a linden, not yews.

Scholars have mentioned a different and more likely sort of topicality, that Swift may have inverted the legend in reaction to Dryden's genial and rather sentimental adaptation of it in his *Fables*. Whether or not Dryden told Cousin Swift that he would never be a poet, Swift's attacks on Dryden in *A Tale of a Tub* and *The Battel of the Books*, both written only a few years before the first version of 'Baucis and Philemon' (1706), leave no doubt of his animus, particularly in relation to Dryden's versions of the ancients.[2] He might well have found the 'Baucis and Philemon' especially offensive, for Dryden had emphasized a tender idealization of the rustic couple. In the *Metamorphoses*, for instance, Philemon simply drops a pittance of sooty pork into his kettle:

> . . . furca levat ille bicorni
> Sordida terga suis, nigro pendentia tigno:
> Servatoque diu resecat de tergore partem
> Exiguam; sectamque domat ferventibus undis. (viii. 647–50)

Dryden's translation of this passage (D, 62–9) supplies a 'good old *Philemon*', speaks of a 'Chine' instead of a 'filthy chine' of bacon ('sordida terga'), and assures us that the scanty portion that Philemon cuts was 'a large Portion of a little Store, | Which for

---

[1] Hills's edition is quoted in *Poems*, i. 111 n.

[2] Relations between Dryden and Swift are most comprehensively discussed by David Novarr, 'Swift's Relation with Dryden, and Gulliver's *Annus Mirabilis*', *English Studies* xlvii (1966), 341–54. Novarr mentions several scholars who trace Swift's 'Baucis and Philemon' to Dryden's.

their Sakes alone he wish'd were more', and which he plunges in
the pot 'without delay'.[1] Later, Philemon in Dryden's poem asks

> that neither she
> With Widows Tears may live to bury me,
> Nor weeping I, with wither'd Arms may bear
> My breathless *Baucis* to the Sepulcher. (D, 173–6)

Ovid's old man merely asks the gods to let him and his wife die
at the same time 'nec conjugis unquam | Busta meae videam;
neu sim tumulandus ab illa' (viii. 708–10). Swift might well have
been contemptuous of Dryden's soft-hearted tamperings, enough
so to have been prompted to choose this subject for irreverent
treatment.

To pursue the genetic influence of Dryden further than this
general suggestion, however, would be unjustified. Neither version of Swift's poem parodies Dryden's typical or striking turns
of phrase. Although Swift objected to Dryden's triplets,[2] nine
of which appear in the *Fables'* 'Baucis and Philemon', neither
version of Swift's poem mocks them. And his revision, by making
his poem formally more self-contained, actually decreases the
possibilities for an allusive lampoon. Finally, Addison could
not have advised the changes that were made if he believed that the
poem was to be a satire on Dryden. 'When a Hero is to be pulled
down and degraded', he was to write in *Spectator* 249, 'it is done
best in Doggerel.' The burlesquing of an established ideal, such
as Dryden's old couple, would have demanded more colloquialism
and odd rhyming, not less. In short, Dryden's 'Baucis and Philemon', like Ovid's original, contributes only a climate of expectation for Swift. While its excesses sharpen the effect of Swift's
incongruities, it does not bear the immediate brunt of the attack,
any more than Virgil and the Vulgate bear that of *The Dunciad*.

[1] Ovidian quotations come from Nicholaus Heinsius's text, which was
standard after 1661, and was used in all three of the important annotated
Ovids—those of Schrevelius, Cnipping, and Crispinus—between 1661 and
the composition of Swift's poem. Passages from Dryden, line references to
which I have marked 'D', come from *The Poems and Fables of John Dryden*, ed.
James Kinsley (Oxford, 1962), pp. 641–6.

[2] In a letter to Thomas Beach, written in April 1735, Swift calls the triplet
'a vicious way of rhyming, wherewith Dryden abounded, and was imitated
by all the bad versifiers in Charles the Second's reign'. *The Correspondence of
Jonathan Swift*, ed. Sir Harold Williams, iv (Oxford, 1965), 321; see also his
letter to Pope, 28 June 1715, *Correspondence*, ii (Oxford, 1963), 176.

The poem which Addison and Swift discussed is not a burlesque, but a realistic and comic imitation of Ovid, in an idiom that stands at a reasonably consistent tonal distance from its Ovidian source. Satiric attention is focused upon the subject-matter rather than upon literary modes. For this reason the questions of rhetoric posed by Swift's revisions can be answered only by considering the rhetorical advantages of his imitating Ovid.

Since medieval times the Ovidian tradition had involved allegory and moral commentary. While both ebbed during the seventeenth century and sank to low tide during the eighteenth, both would have been very much a part of Swift's sense of Ovid's accomplishment. Familiar books, from the sober sermons of Isaac Barrow to Urquhart's Rabelais, would have informed him of the relations, actual or supposed, between Ovid's stories and the Bible's. Scholars to whom he might turn maintained that pagan myths, including Ovid's, were 'reflections of the Hebrew patriarchs in a cracked and dusty mirror', and their journalistic counterparts undertook to inform the public that—in the words of *The British Apollo* (1708–11)—'the *heathens* in and before *Ovid*'s time, borrowed many things from those [Scriptural] oracles of truth'.[1] One of the Ovidian tales referred to the Bible was that of Philemon and Baucis, as Duryer notes in his French translation of the *Metamorphoses* (1684):

> Quelqu'un a dit que cette Fable de Baucis & de Philemon enseigne que l'hospitalité, & la frugalité sont des choses agreables à Dieu. L'Escriture Saincte nous en rend aussi tesmoinage en nous apprenant que des Anges revestus d'une forme humaine ont souvent conversé avec les hommes; Et ie ne sçay si cette Fable n'a point esté composée sur l'histoire Saincte aussi bien que beaucoup d'autre, comme nous l'avons déja fait voir.

---

[1] See 'The Being of God Proved from Universal Consent' in *The Works of the Learned Isaac Barrow, D.D.* (3rd edn., London, 1716), i. 92; Rabelais's 'The Author's Prologue to the First Book'; Don Cameron Allen, *The Legend of Noah* (Urbana, 1963), pp. 83–4; *The British Apollo* (3rd edn., London, 1726), iii. 747–9. If authors sacred and profane, learned and popular, accepted so strict a form of allegory as an equation between Ovidian and scriptural stories, one can imagine how extremely common were other sorts of allegorical interpretations. Among Swift's literary acquaintance in particular, a consciousness of allegorizations of Ovid is shown by Parnell and Garth (as we are reminded by Douglas Bush, *Mythology and the Renaissance Tradition in English Poetry* (New York, 1963), pp. 255–6), along with Prior, Addison, and Pope.

The most commonly mentioned biblical parallel to the story of
Philemon and Baucis was the story of Lot. If Swift read about
his old couple in an edition of Cnipping's Ovid, or one of
Farnaby's, he surely would have seen a note of Farnaby's that
refers to several Church Fathers who accepted the relation between Ovidian and biblical floods, and which goes on to say:

> Dixi ad v. 211 lib. I adumbratum esse illum descensum Jovis sub
> mortali specie in Arcadiam ex historia quae habetur Genes. cap. 18.
> Quod hic clarius liquet, ubi sub persona Jovis & Mercurii hospitio
> exceptorum a Philemone & Baucide, quos illi deduxerunt in montem
> postquam ulti fuissent viciniae improbitatem, urbe & regione in lacum
> versa repraesentatur historia Lothi 19 cap. Genes.

If he saw this note, Swift could understand why the Philemon and
Baucis of Dryden—who used Cnipping's text—are told 'nor once
look backward in your Flight' (D, 146), a command that has no
counterpart in Ovid and no function in Dryden's poem, except
as a reminiscence of the story of Lot. Swift might also have learned
of the parallel between the Greek and Hebrew couples from
George Sandys's notes to his translation of the *Metamorphoses*, or
have inferred it from Matthew Poole's great compendium of
biblical commentaries, the *Synopsis Criticorum*, where one finds
that the story of Lot brought to Grotius's mind the Ovidian
passage in which Philemon and Baucis climb their mountain to
watch their churlish neighbours drown. Further evidence of the
popularity of this interpretation comes from Matthew Prior,
whose 'Observations on Ovid's *Metamorphoses*', composed some
ten or fifteen years after Swift's poem, discusses parallels between
the Bible and the *Metamorphoses* at some length, and remarks that
'Jupiter and Mercury coming down to Baucis and Philemon has
a great deal of the Angels being entertained by Lott'.[1]

---

[1] P. Duryer, *Les Metamorphoses d'Ovide, traduites en François* . . . *avec des
explications sur toutes les fables* (Lyon, 1684), pp. 804–5. Farnaby's note is to
Met. viii. 624, where he gives numerous patristic referencs to support his
linking of Ovid and the Bible. Dryden's use of Cnipping's Ovid, and of
specific annotated texts of other classical authors, is illuminatingly discussed
by J. McG. Bottkol, 'Dryden's Latin Scholarship', *Modern Philology*, xl (1943),
241–54. Sandys's commentary on the story of Baucis and Philemon occurs in
the folio editions of his *Ovid's Metamorphosis. Englished, Mythologiz'd, and
Represented in Figures by G. S.*; while the annotations were no longer being
reprinted during Swift's lifetime, the earlier editions were certainly available
to him—the 1640 folio, for instance, was in Congreve's library. See John

One effect of the reiterated connection between this pair of Ovidian and biblical stories was that, when allegory or moral reading was broached, special attention was given to 'Baucis and Philemon', along with such quasi-scriptural myths as Deucalion's flood or the sacrifice of Iphigeneia: it became a recurrent example, surrounded by what I earlier called 'a climate of expectation'. Even men who did not accept at face-value any elaborate moral reading of Ovid were aware of the arguments of men who did, including the arguments relating to this myth. Among the group of conversant skeptics should be counted the young Joseph Addison, who translated and annotated a number of episodes from the *Metamorphoses*. Here he casts a jaundiced eye upon such commentators as Alexander Ross, who 'discovers in him [Ovid] the greatest mysteries of the Christian religion, and finds almost in every page some typical representation of the world, the flesh, and the devil', along with other men who 'have employed themselves on what never entered into the poet's thoughts, in adapting a dull moral to every story, and making the persons of his poems to be only nicknames for such virtues or vices'. Addison shows himself acquainted not only with these critics but also with the historical and grammatical commentators; he ends by approving Daniel Crispinus's conservative edition *ad usum Delphini*. What Swift might not have known about the allusive potentialities implicit in an episode from the *Metamorphoses* Addison could have told him.[1] In this context it becomes

C. Hodges, *The Library of William Congreve* (New York, 1955), p. 77, item 428. For Grotius's reference see Matthew Poole, *Synopsis Criticorum Aliorumque Sacrae Scripturae Interpretum et Commentatorum*, i, Pars Prima (Utrecht, 1684), 178. Prior's comments are to be found in *The Literary Works*, ed. H. Bunker Wright and Monroe K. Spears (Oxford, 1959), i. 666. See also Anthony Blackwall, *An Introduction to the Classics* (3rd edn., London, 1725): 'The Fable of *Baucis* and *Philemon* is nothing but the Relation of *Lot* and his Wife, vary'd by the Licentiousness of *Poetical Fancy*' (p. 82). Another evidence of this habit of mind is pointed out by Wolfgang Stechow, who shows that Continental painters of the seventeenth century treated the Supper at Emmaus as an analogue to the story of Baucis and Philemon—'The Myth of Philemon and Baucis in Art', *Journal of the Warburg and Courtauld Institutes* iv (1940–1), 103–13.

[1] *The Works of Joseph Addison*, ed. Henry G. Bohn (London, 1906), i. 141–2. Swift's personal library included at his death two Ovids, an incunabular Regis edition and an Elzevir of 1679—items 623 and 156 in the sale catalogue reproduced by Sir Harold Williams, *Dean Swift's Library* (Cambridge, 1932). Neither edition would have included the sort of annotation that we

quite clear why Swift was interested in submitting his Ovidian poem for Addison's judgement, stylistic and conceptual.

The 'Baucis and Philemon' that Swift and Addison considered, if it was substantially the same as that in the extant manuscript, might be divided into five parts: the account of the two vagrant 'saints' and their nasty reception in the village, their reception by Baucis and Philemon, the revelation of their divine powers, the metamorphosis of the house, and lastly, the metamorphosis of Philemon. Probably the poem also included, like the published version, accounts of the metamorphosis of Baucis, the final transmutation of the couple into trees, and a conclusion—we do not know. Of the five parts where the original and printed versions can be compared, only the first two show significant changes. Odd rhymes, like the splendid mendicant cry, 'Good People, | My Comrade's Blind, and I'm a Creeple' (M 15–16), vanish from the beginning. So do the bawlings, the threats to 'fling the P— pot on your head' (M 38), and the other loud hostilities that menace the two saints before they find a haven with the old couple (M 14–46). 'Two Brother-Hermits', Swift originally wrote, 'Came to a Village hard by Rixham | Ragged, and not a Groat betwixt 'em'; the later version is dry by contrast: 'Disguis'd in tatter'd Habits, went | To a small Village down in *Kent*' (M 9–10, P 9–10). These are the revisions that, for obvious reasons, have drawn most critical fire. One ought to consider them, however, in the light of the one revision in the second section of the poem, Swift's elimination of the lines (M 61–70) that describe Philemon and Baucis feeding their saintly visitors. In the printed version the narrative passes directly from Philemon's cutting the bacon to the famous self-replenishing jug, leaving out the serving of bacon fritters on earthenware, Baucis's hearty 'Eat, Honest Friends', and Philemon's getting his wife's consent to broach their kilderkin of home-brewed beer. The omission of these lines is the more striking since the passage as it stood approximated a section of Ovid's tale: Swift surrendered a specific

have been noticing, and it may hypothetically be that Swift did not buy an annotated Ovid because he found that some of the notes imposed on his credulity. My point is not, of course, that he accepted allegorical readings of Ovid, but that, like the other literate men of his time, he was familiar with them—from school, from reading, from his acquaintances—and that they formed a necessary background for his poem.

allusiveness here, just as he surrendered local strength and vivacity in the beginning of the poem. Assuming that the two kinds of revision are consistent, we are led to conclude first, that Addison's advice had wider aims than to chasten 'Baucis and Philemon'; second, that Swift and Addison must have discovered some sort of disparity between the beginning of the poem, as Swift first wrote it, and the sections that toy more specifically with the Ovidian theme of metamorphosis. These latter sections remained largely unaltered, and, as we shall note, forced retrospective changes for consistency of idiom and theme.

Addison seems to have seen, and to have brought Swift to see, that the direction of 'Baucis and Philemon' should be determined by the imitation of Ovid through inversion. This mode of inversion, as I have suggested, is not verbal, or the sort of narrative parody that plays with a sequence of events, but ideological. Ovid's Laelex introduces the original story with a point in mind, to rebut the impiety of Ixion's cynical son by proving that 'quicquid Superi voluere, peractum est' (viii. 612–19). Late Renaissance commentators, as we have seen, grafted this exemplum upon a biblical trunk. Lot's rescue from the fleshpots of Sodom reinforced the Providential moral already explicit in Ovid, and broadened its ethical base. From this twin tradition Swift drew the methods and themes of his imitation: contemporary (Christian) application of the myth; the defining of spiritual identity through material change—disguise, relocation, and metamorphosis; and finally, Providential justice. The first of these three is presupposed by the imitation of Ovid; the development of the second is the formal procedure of the poem; the third becomes the poem's ironic point. Together they make up the 'intention' of Swift's 'Baucis and Philemon'.

The first section of the poem, up to the metamorphoses of house and couple that begin at line 51, may serve to illustrate Swift's treatment. He starts, as does the literate reader, with a recognition that Ovid's mythic world thrives on an ambiguous temporality. The divine lingers immanent within the mundane, while transitory objects are exalted to the borders of eternity. This is true in at least three separate ways. As a narrative, the typical Ovidian tale deals with a mortal who comes in contact with the gods—actual gods, the persistent metaphoric force of Cupid, the *numina* of fountains and forests—and as a result of that contact changes into a being at once natural and timeless. Morally, if one reads the mythic histories as did the late Renaissance commentators, each story embodies universal meanings, discovering within the temporally located event some sort of eternal axiom. Finally, if scriptural truths are implicit within the Ovidian myths, still another sort of ambiguous temporality develops, that of typological extension. By transposing the Ovidian story to a more modern England, Swift permits himself to increase the pressure of these implications. He deliberately increases it again by referring the legend to saints' lives: hagiography sees the timeless lurking in a man's present, and the meaning of a holy man's life lurking in our present. Given this context, Swift immediately begins so play with it. The title of the poem prepares the reader to take 'antient Times' in the first line as referring to a classical story, while 'saints' in the second shifts the time to, say, the Middle Ages. Later, the familiar location, 'a small Village down in *Kent*', and the use of '*Goody*' (10, 24) lead the wary reader to suspect what in fact is about to happen, a blurring of time to provide an ersatz universality for Swift's little history. By line 94 a reference to '*English Moll*' will have brought the tale at least to the Renaissance, and then, with the talk of '*Dissenters*' and '*Right Divine*', to a vague Tory present. There is to be no specific indication of time until the end of the poem, when we learn that some of this has happened during living memory (165-6). Even then the datable event is not the wondrous exaltation of the old couple but their eventual anti-Ovidian return to the world of transience, when they are metamorphosed once more at the hands (or hatchets) of their spiritual successors in the parsonage. The grim inverted metamorphosis can be placed in time; Swift leaves the playfully ironic one on the level of the unreal.

While Swift lays this train of references, he also disclaims responsibility for the truth of these 'facts'. His account is 'as Story tells' (1) and 'as Authors of the Legend write' (6), obscure authorities to compare with Ovid's Laelex, who can say that he himself has seen the metamorphosed oak and linden twine. The effect of Swift's disclaimers is not to secure verisimilitude in the manner of an 'objective' Cervantes or Fielding, but rather to encourage the reader's suspicions. This process begins with 'Saints', a name that would remind Englishmen either of Puritan fanatics or of Catholic impostors. As in *A Tale of a Tub*, whichever one chooses makes little difference, for both are associated with a hypocritical spirituality, proceeding from and degenerating into materialism. Puritanism and Catholicism, in other words, provide one made-to-order inversion of the simultaneously material and numinal Ovidian tale. Swift increases suspicion by presenting mortals 'Taking their *Tour* in Masquerade' (8) instead of Jupiter and Mercury. The frivolous associations of 'Masquerade' immediately taint the central theme of metamorphosis, while the incongruity of 'Saints by Trade' (7) equates sanctity with livelihood—as does 'the Strolers Canting Strain' (11)—so as once more to confuse the material and divine.

Within this carefully prepared context, the famous self-replenishing jug, that token of a perpetuity that supersedes the transient, has no symbolic significance. Whereas Ovid describes the humble dinner being sedulously prepared by the old couple, and thereby sets up a natural contrast to the jug's divine abundance, Swift offers only six lines of rather general description, in no way stressing the poverty of the couple or the meagreness of their fare: Ovid's Philemon boils a 'partem exiguam' of bacon, Swift's 'freely from the fattest Side | Cut out large Slices to be fry'd' (26–7). The flattening of the rhetoric deprives the miracle of its narrative energy and leaves it simply a material fact. Logically, then, Swift's Baucis and Philemon should react materially to it, as they do in the revised version, looking to see if the candles are burning blue—i.e., to see if a sulphurous spirit is present[1]—while Ovid's should react, as they do, with adoration of the gods.

At this point Swift makes two tactical omissions. Ovid's version of the myth first shows the newly discovered gods rescuing a goose that Baucis and Philemon try to sacrifice for dinner, and then moves to the broad panorama of the churlish village inundated while the cottage of the old couple grows into a temple. A model of general justice thus follows a model of beneficence

---

[1] See John Brand, *Observations of Popular Antiquities*, ed. Sir Henry Ellis (London, 1842), iii. 94. The reaction of Sunday gamblers to a supposed devil in Charles Johnstone's novel *Chrysal, or the Adventures of a Guinea*, ii. ch. xvii, suggests that blue-burning candles were specifically related to diabolic spirits. If so, the material reaction of Swift's old couple becomes still funnier, and the need for the visitors' soothings more explicable: 'Good Folks, you need not be afraid, | We are but *Saints*, the Hermits said' (43–4).

that extends even to dumb creatures, and both prepare the reader to accept the metamorphoses of Baucis and Philemon with proper reverence and sense of achieved order. Swift, preparing something quite different, drops the goose, disposes of the neighbours with insouciant speed, and sweeps to the metamorphosis of the cottage. Here he embellishes the scene at great length in a manner that imitates Ovid's frequent superabundance of fancy and wit. But in expanding to fifty-six lines what Ovid here had summarized in two and a half, Swift drowns any sense of wonder in a flood of bizarre description. Furthermore, the miracles of alteration are pinchbeck, for the furniture of Swift's couple maintains its worldly nature despite the ingenious magic of the saints; as Mandeville wryly put it, 'some Shew of Resemblance is kept in the Changes'.[1] The old kettle, since it becomes the church bell, is nominally bell-shaped, but in this church of theirs it remains very much an overturned kettle 'with the Upside down, to shew | Its Inclinations for below'. With a 'Superior Force' holding it up and upside down, its heaviness mechanically repealed, the unhappy kettle or bell hangs from the joist in 'Suspence'—both literal suspension and psychological frustration of its desire for a return to material normality (57–64). As a clock, the roasting-jack shows solicitude about its old charge, the meat, of which it is now dispossessed. The marvel of its transmutation is sapped by Swift's exclamation over a mock paradox, that an increase in the number of its inner wheels has slowed its motion.[2] The longings of the kettle, the separation of jack and meat, and the slowing of the jack all make metamorphosis not grace but privation.

As Swift mentions a human, the lazy cookmaid (83), his description of the metamorphosis takes a new tack, satire. The chair

---

[1] *The Fable of the Bees*, ed. F. B. Kaye (Oxford, 1924), ii. 33–4.

[2] The visual precision of Swift's imagination in making a jack become a clock will be evident if one looks at the drawing of a turnspit of 1684 in Marjorie and C. H. B. Quennell, *A History of Everyday Things in England*, ii (London, 1919), 109. Weight-driven, regulated by a fly-wheel or balance-wheel, fitted with a heavy winding-drum and differential gears—this jack looks very much like the movement of a 'lantern clock', a type that remained exceptionally popular into the early eighteenth century. Because the lantern clock sat at eye-height or lower, on a table or mantel, and because it was made so that the sides could be swung open to reveal the mechanism, the general appearance of its wheels and spindles must have been a familiar enough sight to any of Swift's readers.

changes into a pulpit, presumably to yield the same trifling talk as before. Patriotic and maudlin ballads, which suddenly 'look abundance better, | Improv'd in Picture, Size, and Letter' (97–8), become blazons of the genealogy of the Twelve Tribes, but—by parallel with the other dubious metamorphoses, in which there is 'small Change' (87), as well as by the implications of the stress on their outward appearance—popular myth and sacred history seem pretty much interchangeable. The 'Order' of the pictures and the tribal 'Heraldry' that they present remain an order without meaning. What Swift has done is to move from the material disposition of objects, dull and heavy objects like kettles and roasting-jacks, to the moral disposition of the piety practised in the house. This rhetorical movement makes it inevitable not only that Philemon and Baucis should share, but also that their spiritual natures should seem to be deduced from, the irredeemably material natures of their household goods.

The climax to this satiric descent, a parody of the ascent from the mundane in Ovid, comes with the bed that changes into pews, 'Which still their antient Nature keep; By lodging Folks dispos'd to Sleep (105–6). The genial hospitality that had been the old couple's great virtue now falls into irony. Swift matches this fall by the order of his description. Where in the manuscript version he counts on simple agglomeration to produce his reductive effect, merely by piling cumbersome and incongruous particulars upon one another, he here sets out the new parts of the church in descending order: roof and steeple, bell and clock, pulpit, buckets, pictures, and pews. From the rising of the roof at the beginning of this section, as matter supposedly turns to serve the spirit, the reader progresses through a series of comic disillusionments, dropping to the material once more, and ending with that most material of activities, 'Sleep'.

Sleep epitomizes sloth, an inertial force that vitiates the energy of change, and that therefore connects the poetic themes of materialism and temporality. In the world of sloth, perpetuity comes about not through divine metamorphosis but through the intransigence of matter. Swift's original version had already incorporated this idea connotatively, through the slowing of the jack, the crawling of the groaning chair, the frustration of the bell (*née* kettle), as well as the accommodativeness of the new pews. In the published poem he altered the striking but over-energetic

'The heavy Wall went clamb'ring after' to 'climb'd slowly after' (M 94, P 54), giving up a local incongruity for an effect of retardation. Similarly, whereas Philemon's chair had crawled like an insect (M 106), it now crawled like 'an huge Snail' (P 86), as Swift made his image visually exact, prosodically imitative, and connotatively useful to the whole poem. The snail is doubly appropriate for Philemon's pulpit, in fact, for its proverbial connection with sloth was enhanced by its being thought to be a blind beast.[1] In the midst of this sluggish, aimless little world, the sanctity of troth does not last long. The Ovidian myth turns on the keeping of faith by Baucis and Philemon, with each other and with the gods, as the gods keep faith with them. Swift's cottage likewise contains many examples of fidelity, the objects being faithful to their material natures or locations, like the roasting-jack that adheres to its inseparable companion by becoming a clock when the chimney becomes a steeple. But the attribution of spiritual affections to jacks, chairs, and chimneys overturns Ovidian fidelity so boldly that the reader is conditioned to be cynical, to see fidelity and the conquest of time as rooted in inertial matter.

The metamorphosis of Swift's Philemon and Baucis follows, in narrative and in rhetorical development, that of the objects in the house. When asked 'what he fancy'd most', Philemon makes no bones about his motives:

> my House is grown so Fine,
> Methinks, I still wou'd call it mine:
> I'm Old, and fain wou'd live at Ease,
> Make me the *Parson*, if you please. (110, 113–16)

Possessive vanity and easy living being the sources of his piety, his achievements as a cleric are equally material. They are triumphs

---

[1] For the sloth of the snail, see entries S579 and S581–S583 in Morris Palmer Tilley, *A Dictionary of the Proverbs in England in the Sixteenth and Seventeenth Centuries* (Ann Arbor, 1950). Aristotle (*Historia Animalium*, lib. iv, cap. iv) and Pliny (*Historia Naturalis*, lib. ix, cap. xxxii) discuss the eyelessness of the snail as do such seventeenth-century scholars as G. J. Vossius and Sir Thomas Browne (*De Theologia Gentili . . .*, lib. iv, cap. xii; *Pseudodoxia Epidemica*, Book iii, ch. 20). Three-quarters of a century after Swift's poem the problem was still moot, as indicated by the brief discussion under 'Snail' in Rees's edition of Chambers's *Cyclopaedia*, iv (London, 1783).

of memory and cant: his sermons are filched, his parishioners are indifferently Christians and pigs (i.e., the sources of baptismal fees and tithes), his mechanical orthodoxy remains uninformed by reason or culture (127–36). Once again, Swift's revisions show his development of his theme. Originally, Philemon had spoken to the saints in 'complementall Style' and had become a demure sycophant given to drinking and smuggling (M 158, 171–80). Yet, amusing as that portrait was, it was inconsistent with the kind of metamorphosis upon which Swift was expanding. It presented a Philemon who had in fact changed, while Swift wanted one who had not, who was merely a newly 'furbish'd' (P 137) version of the old man. The revised version makes him speak to the saints 'in homely Stile', and lowers him from an active hypocrite to a dull rustic, consistent with his material past in his lengthened 'Grazier's Coat' and 'Pudding-sleeves' (P 112, 118–20). Baucis's metamorphosis, which is not included in the incomplete manuscript version, continues the 'Farce' (138). Again, her changes are changes in dress and title: she has new colberteen, satin, and lace in her costume; she rejects 'Goody' for 'Madam'; and although Swift's catalogue of her new splendour quickly dips to anticlimax with 'Grogram Gown'—grogram being a homelier material than any in the ascending trio of colberteen, satin, and lace[1]—she wins the undiscriminating admiration of her husband, just as the dubiously altered house had done. For the first time in 'Baucis and Philemon' we are told that man and wife are happy, not in poverty and virtue like Ovid's couple (viii. 633–4), but in their 'Change of Life' (149).

Since Swift's Baucis and Philemon seem to expect an immortality of changeless material bliss, they do not ask to die together. Their fidelity is imposed upon them by fate or natural procedure rather than by volition. Indeed, at the very arboreal moment that should sanctify their fidelity, infidelity rushes into Philemon's mind:

> *Baucis* hastily cry'd out;
> My Dear, I see your Forehead sprout:

[1] The superiority of lace over colberteen is indicated by Swift's description, in 'Cadenus and Vanessa', of the rustic Vanessa's being mocked because she 'Scarce knows what Diff'rence is between | Rich *Flanders* Lace and Colberteen' (416–17; *Poems*, ii. 700). For the comparative lowness of grogram, see the *O.E.D.* entry, with quotations from Addison and William Thompson.

Sprout, quoth the Man, What's this you tell us?
I hope you don't believe me Jealous.   (155-8)

He becomes a plant while only half sure that he is not becoming
a horned beast. With this sort of rhetorical preparation, Swift
could not permit the couple to become an oak and a linden, as in
Ovid. The linden, or lime, is a pleasant sweet-scented shade tree,
'*ad mille usus petenda*', according to Pliny; the oak symbolized
British naval power, and (as used by the Tories) the British
monarchy itself.[1] Swift's resolution is brilliant: he converts
Baucis and Philemon to yews. The yew commonly grows in
churchyards, and so fits in with the narrative. Since its berries
are poisonous, it is an equivocal tree, and represents both death
and resurrection, which is exactly appropriate for Philemon and
Baucis at this point in the narrative. Finally, it is an emblem of
sadness, which, when reinforced by the poem's brusqueness—
'Description would but tire my Muse: | In Short they both were
turn'd to *Yews*' (163-4)—prepares the proper tone for the end of
the tale.[2]

A reader may resent the harshness of that end, partly because
it is not funny, thus depriving him of the laughter he has come
to expect, and partly because the ruthlessness of its logic seems
unnecessarily vindictive.[3] Formally, however, Swift has worked
out his poem with impeccable skill. The material eternity to

[1] Pliny, *Hist. Nat.*, lib. xviii, cap. xxviii. J. H. Plumb mentions the Tories'
use of oak boughs as electioneering emblems 'to recall their part in the
Restoration'—*Sir Robert Walpole, The King's Minister* (Boston, 1961), p. 322 n.

[2] The characteristics of the yew are to be found in the *O.E.D.* entry, in
Browne's *Hydrotaphia* (ch. iv), in Brand's *Popular Antiquities* (ii. 159-64),
and in Ovid himself, *Met.* iv. 432-3: 'Est via declivis funesta nubila taxo:|
Ducit ad infernas per muta silentia sedes.'

[3] Professor Jessie Rhodes Chambers, to whom I am variously indebted,
has kindly pointed out to me several ballad analogues to Swift's ending, in
all of which someone or something—at times a parson—destroys memorial
plants that spring from dead lovers' hearts. See Francis Child, *English and
Scottish Popular Ballads*, Ballads 74A, and 85A and B. If in fact the mowing of
these vegetable mementos was a common folk-theme, the end of 'Baucis and
Philemon' may be somewhat lighter than it seems, and may represent a reversion of the old couple to their proper level of peasantry. They do, after
all, celebrate ballad heroes on their walls (93-6), so that the condition of
ballad hero is a legitimate aspiration for them, an ironic version of Ovidian
myth, just as the ballads are an ironic version of the myth's typological parallel,
Biblical history, in the poem.

which Philemon and Baucis have been devoted turns out to be as transitory as materiality must be in the real world: the couple suffer a final metamorphosis to firewood and lumber. Philemon, who had sprouted at the top and grown roots at the bottom through divine benediction, ends up stunted at the top and stubbed at the bottom through earthly agents (156–62, 177–8). Baucis, who doted on clothing, now shelters animals as part of a barn. Fate overturns the earlier dispensation, subjecting the worldly man and the carnal woman—if I may use those blatant terms *faute de mieux*—to proper judgement. In some sense, the justice of the procedure becomes an ironic recommendation of that divine justice that Ovid and the story of Lot had embodied.

Swift's logic here is not, of course, really a logic of individual rewards and punishments. For that, he would have had to give us far more sense of Baucis and Philemon as moral agents. Instead, he has lessened their degree of moral choice and has deprived them of the moral context that Ovid sets forth in the gods and the churlish neighbours. Everything in Swift has dwindled to an unthinking materiality, which this poem makes into its universe of discourse. Baucis and Philemon are merely parts of a spiritual landscape, not exemplary but representative. In these terms, one can understand how Ovid's eternity immanent within a sylvan nature suffers translation into a series of country parsons, all as irreligious as Philemon. Not only are these men blindly materialistic in treating any tree simply as a tree, not only do they mock the saints' earlier act of justice by their acts of impiety in this supposedly purged place, but they also muddle their religion with their husbandry: as parson Swift would have known, one was allowed to chop down churchyard trees only to repair a chancel.[1] For Philemon's successors, the barn and the chancel are equivalents, just as Philemon had equated babies and pigs. That 'Good-man *Dobson*' should point out the parsons' handiwork 'On *Sundays*, after Ev'ning Prayer' (165, 169) fits this ironic world as neatly as does the fact that the destruction of Philemon should have been caused by his fidelity (175–8).

Perhaps, after this discussion, to return to Swift's (and Addison's) changes may be anticlimactic. One can hardly doubt that the intricate imitation that Swift published justifies in every

[1] See Edmund Gibson, *Codex Juris Ecclesiastici Anglicani*, Tit. ix, cap. x, 35 Edw. I, Cap. 4.

regard its author's tact and skill; that imitation could not have
grown from the beginning that Swift had originally written. He
had started out with a simple mockery of Ovid's (or Dryden's)
tenderness and righteousness, following the Ovidian burlesques
of the Restoration, their anti-idealism, their anachronism, their
gaminess, their realism that reached down to the trivial.[1] That
is the obvious direction of the opening of the manuscript version,
with its racy puns and raucous villagers, with its permissible
diffusion of the reader's attention over a range of comic particulars. Such a technique may be successful in depicting a state of
mind, as in the hack's digressions in *A Tale of a Tub*; in a narrative
like this one it denies any thematic focus. Furthermore, through its
vivid energy, the original opening would have drawn attention
to the neighbours and the 'Saints', which would have offered
Baucis and Philemon a moral context, and thus have eroded or
destroyed the world of discourse that I have described above.
For similar rhetorical reasons, Philemon could never have
remained the cheerfully hospitable peasant associated with bacon
fritters and beer, homely earthenware, and exhortations to 'Eat,
Honest Friends, and never spare'. If he had, the poem would
have had to turn on the corruption of simplicity, and that would
have contravened Swift's theme of stasis through metamorphosis.
The temporal treatment of that theme—the slow and indefinite
drifting forward in time for a mock universality—would have
suffered serious injury if the villagers had been allowed their
aggressively contemporary speech; besides, an easy contempor-
aneity, both because it was conventional in the Ovidian burlesque
and because it had been used for non-thematic purposes (like
vivacity), also would have detracted from the peculiar significance of Christianizing this myth as a parable of divine justice.
Addison could have alleged numerous reasons, then, for pruning
'Baucis and Philemon', and one can see why Swift, whose inclinations always ran to moral satire rather than to impudent
stylistic burlesque, would have paid attention.

No one would deny that some messy poems are better than some

---

[1] These burlesques are discussed by Albert H. West, *L'Influence française
dans la poésie burlesque en Angleterre* (Paris, 1931); see in particular pp. 85–8.
See also Bush, *Renaissance Tradition*, 288–305, and the incidental discussions
of Restoration burlesque in Richmond P. Bond, *English Burlesque Poetry,
1700–1750* (Cambridge, Mass., 1932).

neatly plotted poems; and even if, to get to the point at hand, one prefers the published version of 'Baucis and Philemon' to that in manuscript, one can hardly help regretting that rowdy unsalvageable charm had to make way for the relevant sobriety and acidity. What is illegitimate is to slough off the changes on to a genteel or jealous Atticus, a counsellor who wanted to make 'Baucis and Philemon' into one of the 'lays of artful Addison, coldly correct'. The changes are those of a man—or two men—of trenchant literary and satiric intelligence. As the finished poem emerged from their discussions, it proved to be a happy exploitation of themes that had kept and were to keep a firm hold on Swift's interests. That of materialism and false spirituality is too obvious to be more than mentioned. That of the play between stasis and transformation—a theme that Ricardo Quintana, discussing 'The Rape of the Lock', has identified as Ovidian[1]— is kindred to the play between the rigid personality and the shifting situation which marks Swift's brilliant use of the 'persona' in other works. As in 'Baucis and Philemon', a variety of perspectives often becomes Swift's means of revealing moral inadequacy in all its nakedness and grotesqueness.[2] As in 'Baucis and Philemon', our freedom in our multiple points of view makes us aware of the limits of the Swiftian creatures that we observe, so much so that Swift's parables purge us through working upon our cognition rather than—as in Ovid—our implicit sympathy for other men. Thus a work like *Gulliver's Travels*, with its shifting time-references, its manipulation of the 'persona' as agent or as butt of the satire, its boldly material fantasy to establish logical worlds of illogical discourse, its use of allusions or burlesque to validate

[1] In ' "The Rape of the Lock" as a Comedy of Continuity', *A Review of English Literature* vii (1966), 9–19.

[2] Compare Martin Price's comment that 'the astonishing vigor of *A Tale of a Tub* comes of its remarkable range, its bland equation of various intellectual activities, and its steady reduction of all of them to a few simple principles of physical compulsion and mechanical causation. We are left with a world where, because the order of the mind has been rendered powerless, the order of the flesh can claim for itself the name of charity and offer a debased parody of its forms' (*To the Palace of Wisdom* (Garden City, New York, 1965), pp. 215–16). Behind both *A Tale* and 'Baucis and Philemon' religion and learning stand as parodied and at the same time as monitory ideals—it is for this reason that one can hardly overstress the Ovidian background of the poem, which serves a function analogous to the history of Christianity in *A Tale*.

a fictional reality—a work like *Gulliver's Travels* belongs quite clearly to the same craftsman who wrote and revised 'Baucis and Philemon'. As Jupiter, the master of metamorphoses, Swift seems to have profited from the company of an eloquent, if hardly mercurial, Addison: he emerged from the masquerade more sublimely himself than ever.

II

'THE LADY'S DRESSING-ROOM' EXPLICATED BY A CONTEMPORARY

By ROBERT HALSBAND

SINCE its publication in 1732 'The Lady's Dressing-Room' has aroused spirited comment. Although in our own day its interpretation has moved into the realm of psychiatry and man's fate,[1] in its own time it was dealt with in terms of morality, taste, and decorum. To some people the 'excremental vision' was—and is—an excruciating nightmare; and just as 'The Lady's Dressing-Room' made Mrs. Pilkington's mother vomit, so the unbuttoned fantasy-fiction of a Norman Mailer can nauseate the tender sensibilities of readers today.

Certainly Swift himself knew that his poem might arouse disapproval. For with mock-modesty he complained to Pope that the poem had been printed from 'a stolen Copy', a statement contradicted by his modern editor.[2] Besides, after the poem was published he probably wrote (in the same year) 'A Modest Defence of a Late Poem . . .', in which he defends, without benefit of irony, the moral seriousness of the '*Hibernian Bard*, upon the Article of *Decency* . . .'.[3] Would he have bothered to defend his poem unless he foresaw that it would be attacked?

And, to be sure, soon after its publication the poem elicited three replies. These anonymous pamphlets are important to an understanding of Swift's ideas by setting them in the context of their own time. Any fruitful study of Swift must begin at such a

---

[1] For an outline of this interpretation see Milton Voigt, *Swift and the Twentieth Century* (1964), pp. 161–2. More specifically on 'The Lady's Dressing-Room', see Maurice Johnson, *The Sin of Wit* (1950), pp. 116–19.

[2] Swift, *Corr.*, ed. Sir Harold Williams (1963–5), iv. 31; *Poems*, ed. Sir Harold Williams (1937), ii. 524.

[3] *Prose*, ed. H. Davis, v (1962), 227–40.

point. What adds interest to these replies is that one of them—
it can definitely be stated—was written by an important literary
figure.

The Gentleman's Study, in Answer to the Lady's Dressing-Room
was published the same year as Swift's poem, and answers it
by the obvious parallel of displaying the filth and squalor that
could be found in a man's study. Both poems were then answered
in turn by *Chloe Surpriz'd*, whose long subtitle reads: 'or, The
Second Part of the Lady's Dressing-Room. To which are added,
Thoughts upon Reading the Lady's Dressing-Room, and the
Gentleman's Study. The former wrote by D—N S—T, the latter
by Miss W—' (London and Dublin, 1732).[1] The pamphlet actually
consists of three separate parts. In the first, Chloe the prude is
warned by Father Time to be humble and charitable. The author
of 'Thoughts' briefly points out that since both male and female
exhibit the physical attributes of animals, the old bachelor and the
old maid should wed and then contend as to 'who excell most in
Dirt'. The pamphlet concludes with 'An Epigram upon the Lady's
Dressing-Room':

> What, the D— look in Closestools instead of the Bible!
> And write on poor *Caelia* so dirty a Libel;
> How well must he preach the Word of the Lord,
> Whose Texts are a Shift, stinking Toes, and a T—d?

But the most vigorous reply to Swift's poem did not appear
until two years later, in February 1734, when T. Cooper issued
an anonymous eight-page pamphlet entitled *The Dean's Provocation
For Writing the Lady's Dressing-Room*.[2] (It is printed below.)
What adds great interest to the verse is that its author was Lady
Mary Wortley Montagu. For it exists among her manuscripts in
two autograph drafts, one very heavily revised and the other a
fair copy with the conclusion missing.[3] The title that she put at the

---

[1] Listed in H. Teerink, *Bibliography of Swift*, ed. A. H. Scouten (1963),
p. 354. Copies of both pamphlets are in the British Museum.

[2] Teerink–Scouten (loc. cit.) does not locate any copy; it can be found in
the British Museum and the Bodleian. Both the *Gentleman's Magazine* and the
London Magazine list it in Feb. 1734.

[3] Harrowby MSS., vol. 81 (owned by the Earl of Harrowby). Although the
pamphlet is listed in the standard Swift bibliography and Lady Mary's drafts
were known to me, their confrontation can be credited to Miss Isobel
Grundy.

top of her drafts, slightly different from the printed one, is: 'The Reasons that induc'd Dr. S. to write a Poem call'd the Ladys Dressing room'. Lady Mary's customary form was the heroic couplet; here, however, she very cleverly imitates the metre, diction, and tone of Swift's own poem. Although her main burden is an attack on Swift for his misogyny, she also glances at his political friend (twenty years before), Lord Oxford, and his poetical one, Alexander Pope. The exact circumstances of publication are unknown, but Lady Mary probably arranged for it. For unlike the other replies, which are wretchedly printed in flimsy little pamphlets, hers is a stately folio set in handsome type, not unlike her *Verses to the Imitator of Horace* (1733) and her *Answer* (1733) to the *Elegy to a Young Lady* by James Hammond.

Although Swift and Lady Mary evidently never met in person, they must have been aware of each other when he was residing in London, in the years preceding the death of Queen Anne. Lady Mary, a generation his junior, was then a young lady on the marriage market, involved in a clandestine courtship with Edward Wortley Montagu. (In 1710 Swift wrote to Stella that he had spent an evening with Wortley and Addison 'over a bottle of Irish wine'.[1]) Through her father, the Marquess of Dorchester, a member of the Kit-Cat Club, Lady Mary frequented the Whigs, and abhorred Tories of all persuasions.

During his exile in Ireland Swift returned to England in 1726 and stayed with Pope, a neighbour of Lady Mary's at Twickenham, but by then she and Pope were on cool if not frigid terms. Soon after *Gulliver's Travels* was published, she remarked to her sister that it was 'the united Work of a dignify'd clergyman, an Eminent Physician, and the first poet of the Age, and very wonderfull it is, God knows'. She suspected 'some very powerfull Motive' behind the great veneration, warmth, and affection shown to the Houyhnhnms.[2] A few years later she was impelled to protest to the eminent physician himself, Dr. Arbuthnot, that she had not written a lampoon containing an attack on Swift and Vanessa: '. . . I never had any acquaintance with Dr Swift, [and] am an utter stranger to all his affairs, and even his person, which I never saw to my knowledge. . . ..'[3]

---

[1] *Journal to Stella*, ed. Sir Harold Williams (1948), i. 65.
[2] [Nov. 1726], *Complete Letters*, ed. R. Halsband (1965–7), ii. 71–2.
[3] [Oct. 1729], ibid. ii. 92.

As an expatriate in Italy in the 1750s Lady Mary fully expressed her loathing of Swift in private letters to her daughter. In his *Tale of a Tub* he had argued and laughed religion out of the world, she wrote—an opinion very similar to that of Sarah, Duchess of Marlborough (in 1713).[1] His love of flattery, his vain and trifling character, his ridiculing both 'Law and Decency' were so reprehensible, she wrote, that they could only be explained by his being mad.[2] She even compared him to Caligula, who preferred his horse to the highest honours in the state, and who did not disguise his misanthropy. (Does this not imply an interpretation of Book IV of *Gulliver*?) More concisely, she gave her opinion that he had 'set at defiance all Decency, Truth, or Reason...'.[3] If her animosity to Swift had a pattern, it ranged from political disapproval in the years of his London power, through the distaste engendered by her controversy with Pope, and finally, in her old age—when she suffered from hardening of her aristocratic prejudices—to a contempt for his low birth; it entitled him, she wrote, to be a link-boy.[4]

If these opinions were general and subjective, Lady Mary's attack in *The Dean's Provocation* is specific and objective. It may seem paradoxical to attack a writer for coarseness and obscenity by using terms as coarse and obscene; perhaps she believed in fighting fire with fire. Many years after Swift published his poem, his cousin Mrs. Whiteway teased him with the ironical compliment that he had gained the hearts of all women with *The Lady's Dressing-Room*.[5] One woman, at least, remained unwon—Lady Mary. Her answer proves it.

> The Doctor, in a clean starch'd Band,
> A Golden Snuff-box in his Hand,[6]
> With Care his Diamond Ring displays,
> And artful shows its various Rays;

[1] David Green, *Sarah Duchess of Marlborough* (1967), pp. 184-5 (also p. 162).
[2] 1754, *Complete Letters*, iii. 56, 57.
[3] 1758, ibid. iii. 158.
[4] Ibid. iii. 57.
[5] Swift, *Corr.* iv. 445.
[6] In his will Swift listed a 'Tortoise Shell Snuff Box, richly lined and inlaid with Gold' as well as seven gold rings (*Prose*, ed. H. Davis, xiii (1959), 153). Lady Mary's statement that she had never seen Swift was not made under oath, and need not be strictly true.

While grave, he stalks down — Street,
His dearest — to meet.
    Long had he waited for this Hour,
Nor gain'd Admittance to the Bow'r;
Had jok'd, and punn'd, and swore, and writ,
Try'd all his Gallantry and Wit;
Had told her oft what part he bore,
In OXFORD's Schemes in Days of yore;[1]
But Bawdy, Politicks, nor Satyr,
Could touch this dull hard-hearted Creature.
    JENNY, her Maid, could taste a Rhyme,
And griev'd to see him lose his time,
Had kindly whisper'd in his Ear,
For twice two Pounds you enter here;
My Lady vows without that Sum,
It is in vain you write or come.
    The destin'd Off'ring now he brought,
And in a Paradise of Thought;
With a low Bow approach'd the Dame,
Who smiling heard him preach his Flame.
His Gold she took (such Proofs as these
Convince most unbelieving Shees)
And in her Trunk rose up to lock it,
(Too wise to trust it in her Pocket)
And then return'd with blushing Grace,
Expects the Doctor's warm Embrace.
    And now this is the proper Place,
When Morals stare me in the Face;
And for the sake of fine Expression,
I'm forc'd to make a small Digression.
    Alas! for wretched Human-kind,
With Wisdom mad, with Learning blind,
The Ox thinks he's for Saddle fit,
(As long ago Friend *Horace* writ;)[2]
And Men their Talents still mistaking,
The Stutterer fancys his is speaking.
    With Admiration oft we see,
Hard Features heighten'd by Toupet;
The Beau affects the Politician,
Wit is the Citizen's Ambition;
Poor P— Philosophy displays on,
With so much Rhyme and little Reason;

---

[1] Robert Harley, Earl of Oxford.   [2] *Epistles*, i. xiv. 43–4.

But tho' he preaches ne'er so long,
That *all is right*, his Head is wrong.[1]
None strive to know their proper Merit,
But strain for Wisdom, Beauty, Spirit.
   Nature to ev'ry thing alive,
Points out the Path to shine or thrive,
But Man, vain Man, who grasps the whole,
Shows in all Heads a Touch of Fool;
Who lose the Praise that is their due,
While they've th'Impossible in view.
   [So have I seen the injudicious Heir,
To add one Window, the whole House impair.]
   Instinct the Hound does better teach,
Who never undertook to preach;
The frighted Hare from Dogs does run,
But not attempts to bear a Gun—
   Here many noble Thoughts occur,
But I Prolixity abhor;
And will pursue th'instructive Tale,
To show the Wise in some things fail.
   The Rev'rend Lover, with surprise, ⎫
Peeps in her Bubbies and her Eyes, ⎬
And kisses both—and tries—and tries— ⎭
The Ev'ning in this hellish Play,
Besides his Guineas thrown away;
Provok'd the Priest to that degree,
He swore, *The Fault is not in me.*
Your damn'd Close-stool so near my Nose,
Your dirty Smock, and stinking Toes,
Would make a *Hercules* as tame,
As any Beau that you can name.
   The Nymph grown furious, roar'd, by G—d,
The Blame lies all in Sixty odd;
And scornful, pointing to the Door,
Sai'd, *Fumbler see my Face no more.*
With all my Heart, I'll go away,
But nothing done, I'll nothing pay;
Give back the Money—how, cry'd she,
Would you palm such a Cheat on me?
I've lock'd it in the Trunk stands there,
Go break it open if you dare;
For poor four Pounds to roar and bellow,

Pope's *Essay on Man* was issued from Feb. 1733 to Jan. 1734.

Why sure you want some new Prunella?[1]
What if your Verses have not sold,
Must therefore I return your Gold?
Perhaps you have no better Luck in
The Knack of Rhyming than of ——
I won't give back one single Crown,
To wash your Band, or turn your Gown.
   I'll be reveng'd [,] you sawcy Quean,
(Replys the disap[p]ointed Dean)
I'll so describe your *Dressing-Room*,
The very *Irish* shall not come;
She answer'd short, I'm glad you'll write,
You'll furnish Paper when I Sh—e.

FINIS

[1] This invented name for a prostitute is an obvious pun on the worsted cloth used for clergymen's gowns. Only one month previously Pope had used it in the *Essay on Man*, iv. 204.

12

THE STYLE OF SOUND: THE LITERARY VALUE OF POPE'S VERSIFICATION

By IRVIN EHRENPREIS

IN the academic criticism of poetry no standard of merit seems accepted more instinctively than the accommodation of sound to sense. If a poet makes his metre suggestive of his meaning, he is bound to be praised. A particular feature commonly admired is what might be called 'local expressiveness', or the apparent matching of rhythms and sounds within a line or couplet to the meaning of the words themselves. This well-defined accomplishment I distinguish from a general decorum or propriety of style, such as the use of sharp stresses for the speech of an angry man, or the adoption of a leisurely stanza for a quiet verse tale. It is not, in other words, a broad congruence of style with character or action. Instead, it is the more localized effect, such as the crowding of heavy consonants into a line about climbing a hill, or a re-petitious series of vowels in a line about echoes.

The judicial exaltation of these devices goes along with the unexamined presumption that they do not undermine other literary merits—i.e., that they happily enrich the texture of a poem regardless of its genre or mode. Whether a passage happens to be narrative or expository, eulogistic or insulting, dignified or comic, we seem implicitly advised that expressive or imitative effects can only add positive value. Unobtrusively, they have taken over the position once held by purely musical qualities, and they still surpass in prestige those qualities of dramatic speech which have got wider and wider appreciation in the last twenty years. From local expressiveness flow theoretical benefits to the rhetoric, the beauty, and the truth of a poem.

Of course, the vaguer sort of pervasively decorous versifica-tion hardly escapes the notice of learned observers. If a poem modulates ingeniously from a rich, slow pattern of vowels and pauses to a dry, irregular pattern, when a boy's death is followed by a mourner's despair, most critics rejoice with analytic praise. So deep is the identification of this aspect of style with self-evident value that the workaday critic is satisfied merely to demonstrate the devices, without considering whether they may not deserve more blame than approval. Once the phenomena are visible, their merit is settled. Rarely does one find a line drawn between better and worse types of expressive or imitative technique.

Pope has received unusual applause for such accomplishments. In the *Pastorals* Warton found little to recommend besides their 'correct and musical versification'. R. K. Root celebrated the 'infinite metrical riches within the little room of twenty syllables'.[1] More recent scholars and critics have carried the examination of Pope's 'style of sound' to the point of electronic microscopy.

Yet I find that, except in a few masterpieces, Pope made large sacrifices in order to secure his beauties; and I suspect it must always be so. For instance, a devotion to expressive effects relieves an author from more profound demands of structure, whether narrative or expository. A series of discrete items lends itself to aural refinements as a well-told story or coherent argument does not. In the *Ode for Musick*, the *Essay on Criticism*, and the *Dunciad* we see instructive examples of this principle. Throughout a passage like

> Dreadful gleams,
> Dismal screams,
> Fires that glow,
> Shrieks of woe,
> Sullen moans,
> Hollow groans . . .[2]

the order of details is not only insignificant but also grotesque. If the sharply contrasted vowels and heavy pauses do indeed suggest the cries and pangs of souls in Hades, the poet's indifference to any other considerations makes the lines sound like a deliberately inane parody. In another part of the *Ode for*

---

[1] Joseph Warton, *Essay on Pope* (London, 1806), i. 9. Robert K. Root, *The Poetical Career of Alexander Pope* (Princeton, 1938), p. 50.

[2] Quotations from Pope come from the texts in the relevant volumes of the Twickenham edition; but I have followed the poet's use of capitals and italics only where they have the modern significance.

Musick, as Warton pointed out, the metrical form is hilariously incongruous: Orpheus has rescued Eurydice, and Pope says,

> Thus song could prevail
> O'er death and o'er Hell,
> A conquest how hard and how glorious?
> Though Fate had fast bound her
> With Styx nine times round her,
> Yet musick and love were victorious.

The choice and treatment of the feet suggest triumph and release, either through the shifts from short to long lines, or else through the sonority and vigour of the suddenly feminine rhymes—the first feminine rhymes in the poem. But of course, the rhythms are so quick, heavy, and abrupt that they suggest not solemn rejoicing but farce. In the fifth stanza a progression of images is hinted at: from the inanimate, through plant-life, to human beings. Yet the poet's obsession with vowels, rhymes, and pauses makes the choice of details seem pointlessly capricious: streams, winds, flowers; souls, meads, bowers; heroes, youths, Eurydice. Again Pope has sacrificed the pull of narrative or exposition to the advantage, for his narrow purpose, of a disorderly collection of specimens.[1]

In the *Essay on Criticism* the famous 'echo to the sense' passage is less deplorable, mainly because it is explicitly illustrative, and the poet does not pretend to supply a structure of persuasive rhetoric. If the passage were short, it would still be oppressive, since the effects are coarse and showy. But only a comic design could redeem the length of forty lines consecrated to a display of easy art. Johnson's complaint may be irrelevant when he says in effect that most impressions of sound conveying sense are imaginary; yet I find it significant that he quotes as 'one of the most successful attempts' two couplets not by Pope but by Broome.[2] If one supposes *r* to be an effortful noise, it requires little genius to crowd a line with *r*s—though even in his youth Pope knew enough to avoid excessive alliteration here. The

---

[1] The musical setting may have compensated for the effects I find; but of course this poem, like Dryden's similar poems, was published by the author; they have been praised by modern critics as independent literary works. Handel's operas illustrate what a great composer can do with puerile materials.

[2] *Lives of the English Poets*, ed. G. B. Hill (Oxford, 1905), iii. 231.

alexandrine snake and the line about monosyllables sink lower
yet; and for all their fluent precision and idiomatic effectiveness,
they only serve as crashingly obvious examples. Contrariwise,
some couplets in the passage exhibit not local expressiveness but
a more subtle decorum of sound; and these allow Pope's true
gifts to appear:

> praise the easy vigor of a line,
> Where Denham's strength and Waller's sweetness join.

Even taking such moments into account, I think the disjunctive,
miscellaneous nature of the images deprives the passage of real
grace and charm. Not that all my complaints together can relegate
this long paragraph to the same level as the *Ode for Musick*.
There are too many agreeable subtleties in it, such as the elegant
transitions from point to point, or the natural grouping of
observations within the whole sequence, or the gradual approach
to the brilliant, climactic ending. It represents a step up.

For the most magnificent sacrifice of coherence to local expressiveness we can look at the last stage of Pope's career. In
the *Dunciad* of 1743, when Dulness watches the breeding of new
theatrical entertainments, Pope delivers ten couplets with almost
no anchorage (i. 59–78): Zembla's fruits could change places
with Barca's flowers if it were not for the rhyme; 'hoary hills'
and 'painted vallies' are equally reversible. The vocabulary of
'how', 'here', and 'there' calls our attention to the floating inter-
changeability of the parts:

> How tragedy and comedy embrace;
> How farce and epic get a jumbled race. . . .

The entire passage of twenty lines fits no better where Pope
left it than it would two paragraphs earlier with

> Hence hymning Tyburn's elegiac lines,
> Hence Journals, Medley's, Merc'ries, Magazines.

It's no good reflecting that Pope means to describe chaos and
chaos is disorderly. We can do with a very short evocation of
simple disorder. What the artist has to produce is a shapely
expression of unshapely material, just as he must contrive to make
boredom interesting. But again and again the *Dunciad* breaks
up into lists of specimens, like the catalogue of Cibber's books,
or the file of scribblers falling asleep (ii. 411–14):

> At last Centlivre felt her voice to fail,
> Motteux himself unfinish'd left his tale,
> Boyer the state, and Law the stage gave o'er,
> Morgan and Mandeville could prate no more. . . .

It would be misleading to imply that a single motive could account for the atomization of the *Dunciad*. Pope had many witty turns he wished to show off in the poem, and most of them fit more easily into a collection of detached lines than a tightly organized march of ideas. Among the tricks of the last quotation above is the ripple of names growing out from a centre: first one name to a line, then two, and then three—'Norton, from Daniel and Ostraea sprung'. Another refinement is the matching of the rhyme-words 'o'er' and 'more' to the names Boyer, Morgan, and Norton. Often in the poem we notice how much Pope loves the effect of anticlimax at the end of a parade of apparently similar items; so at the beginning of Part III he lists some products of false inspiration (ll. 9–12):

> Hence the fool's paradise, the statesman's scheme,
> The air-built castle, and the golden dream,
> The maid's romantic wish, the chemist's flame,
> And poet's vision of eternal fame.

Ironically bowing in his own direction, Pope ends the sequence with humorous bathos. Clearly, such accomplishments—and I have only sampled the many varieties—discourage an author from trying to establish a large, unified design.[1]

If the poet wished to reverse the tendency, he might crowd his expressive features into a few climactic lines and lighten the use of them in the others. For Pope such a solution is difficult. In too many of his works he tries to build the structure on general moral principles, and he tries to derive these principles from groups of concrete instances. Normally the instances lend themselves to expressive versification better than the inferences, since the latter, being more or less abstract, leave a poet little to copy through sound. As a result, the versification of the preliminary

---

[1] One might argue that local expressiveness can itself be a means of giving form to sections of a poem, without regard to the progress of an argument, a narrative, a descriptive plan, or any other scheme derived from meaning. Those who find such a form to be a satisfactory literary structure will feel unmoved by my analyses.

matter often distracts the reader from a would-be drum-rolling conclusion.

The *Essay on Man* repeatedly fails us in this way. We remember bits like the illustration of the five senses, with the balance of sharp and dull vowels in

> The mole's dim curtain, and the lynx's beam . . .

or the subtle combination of pauses, *sostenuto* rhythm, and trailing alliteration in

> The spider's touch, how exquisitely fine!
> Feels at each thread, and lives along the line. . . . (i. 212, 217–18)

But who can state the hollow doctrine they lead to?[1] It is for such reasons that the *Essay on Man*, though hardly successful in any of its four epistles, grows weakest in the last. Concepts like happiness and humility must be embodied in particular, realized persons before they can challenge the true art of a poet like Pope. But for most of his fourth *Epistle* he treats them either abstractly or through fleeting allusions to individuals:

> To sigh for ribbands if thou art so silly,
> Mark how they grace Lord Umbra or Sir Billy:
> Is yellow dirt the passion of thy life?
> Look but on Gripus, or on Gripus' wife. . . . (iv. 277–80)

There are not enough lines of character here for a poet to draw parallels in sound. The final paragraph, with its developed contrast between Bolingbroke and his dedicator, does supply a fair opportunity; and Pope rises to it in a celebrated image:

> Oh! while along the stream of Time thy name
> Expanded flies, and gathers all its fame,
> Say, shall my little bark attendant sail,
> Pursue the triumph, and partake the gale?

Thanks to the long vowels closed by *m* or *n*, the first of these couplets moves in a broad, sustained advance, while the *t*s and short vowels of the second give it a lighter, quicker movement. Pope thus creates a delicate equivalent of the difference between the noble peer and the thin, small poet. Unfortunately, the plan of the *Essay* forces him to shift at the very end from this

---

[1] Recent expositions of the poem, I know, might contest my use of the epithet 'hollow'. None the less, I would adhere to it, supported by the view of Dr. Johnson and by many modern scholars and critics.

charming picture to a set of chilling maxims about social love and all that. The pull of the 'little bark' therefore undermines the thumpery of those ultimate six lines; and instead of securing the climax he desired, the poet declines into an unintentional bathos.

For an even more radical disturbance of an intended structure by a triumph in the wrong part, the much-laboured *Epistle to Bathurst* is available. Professor Brower has already suggested that the poet's heart was not in the apparent argument of this theodicy, and I agree.[1] Ironically, although the explicit declaration of positive doctrine is artfully placed and skilfully versified, its vapidity sinks it in comparison with what should be a less stirring paragraph. Certainly, the character of the Man of Ross ought to dazzle the reader. To no section of the *Epistle* can we better apply Pope's often-quoted words about the whole, viz., 'I never took more care in my life of any poem.'[2]

We can trace the twenty couplets (ll. 251–90) about Kyrle to a dramatic crest in the lines on his income.

> 'Oh say, what sums that gen'rous hand supply?
> What mines, to swell that boundless charity?'
> Of debts, and taxes, wife and children clear,
> This man possest—five hundred pounds a year.
> Blush, grandeur, blush! proud courts, withdraw your blaze!
> Ye little stars! hide your diminish'd rays.

With 'Blush, grandeur,' etc., the rhythm makes a bold shift obviously meant to convey the shock of the facts presented. Only three syllables in that lines are unstressed; the line is impeded by ponderous sounds and syntactic pauses. Add the prevalence of liquids and sibilants, and the modulation of vowels leading to the high note of *blaze*; then add the change from declarative statement to apostrophe. Together, such effects make a brilliant tonal contrast to the routine language and rhythm of the preceding lines. The rest of the couplet is less elaborate but still rich. On our way to these ingenuities we meet one instance after another of more subdued local expressiveness. The 'Vaga' echoes; the Severn sounds hoarse; a 'heav'n-directed spire' rises in a pyrrhic foot and a series of *i*s. Even Kyrle's title of 'Man of Ross' is converted to expressive purposes as babes lisp it in a sibilant line.

[1] Reuben A. Brower, *Alexander Pope. The Poetry of Allusion* (Oxford, 1959), pp. 257–60.

[2] Joseph Spence, *Anecdotes*, ed. S. Singer (London, 1820), p. 312.

Yet with all these precious elements Pope has manufactured a disappointment. The character of Buckingham, in less than half the number of the lines on John Kyrle, has remained the poetic zenith of the third *Moral Essay*. To this degree the character of Buckingham has been ruinous to the rhetorical structure of the whole poem: it outshines both the positive moral ideal and the laborious tale of Sir Balaam, which concludes the work and ought to provide a sort of negative climax.

It would take a brave man to argue that the versification of the portrait of 'great Villiers' surpassed that of Kyrle. In the later paragraph the turn comes with line 305, as Pope moves from Buckingham dying to the memory of the favourite's 'life of pleasure'. Before and after the change Pope's style is essentially the same: stichomythic, with strong caesuras, a profusion of monosyllables, and a steady beat of heavy iambics. The energy of the passage, the violence of the language, suggest the force of the speaker's emotion. In any local sense I find little expressiveness. Fascinating variety; magnificent suspense (from the periodic opening to the snowballing fragments of history recalled); an impulsive drive from the immediate present to a remote past, and then, by a quick process of detailed change, back to the present again. I find immense biographical appeal and ingenious rhetorical order, but not great expressiveness.

My deep appreciation of the devices I have been examining should be quite evident. If I find fault, it is in reaction against the often unqualified approval one meets of this aspect of Pope's genius. Surely a distinction has to be drawn between the finer and coarser forms his power takes. That is, if we consider imitative or expressive versification even as such, with no regard to its impingement on the other elements of a poem, some kinds must deserve less praise than others.

There also remains a self-contradiction in the usual approach, in so far as it separates art from truth and encourages us to admire techniques without regard to the validity of the meaning supporting them. After all, expressiveness exists and can properly be judged solely in relation to the sense imitated by the sound. Purely musical variation or sonority, of the kind Samuel Say adored in *Paradise Lost*, may perhaps be independent of meaning —though I doubt it. But expressive versification has no other mode of life. The comparatively dry style of Wordsworth in the

Prelude always operates as a magical counterpoint to the profundity of the experience he deals with. The rich style of Pope fails when he tries to make it screen the shallowness of his argument.

With these principles in mind, I place the 'echo to the sense' passage of the *Essay on Criticism* near the bottom of Pope's scale, not only for being coarse but also because the meaning of each illustration has no striking connection with its impact. Whether the alexandrine were a snake or a rope, whether Ajax or Sisyphus struggled with the rock, whether Camilla or Achilles skimmed along the main, would make no difference to the reader. Only when Timotheus comes on, and we approach Pope's praise of Dryden, does the choice of name or image grow cogent.

Windsor Forest, though an unsatisfactory whole,[1] has few things so obvious as this passage. When Pope describes the desolation left by William the Conqueror, he rises to a furious mingling of rage with description:

> The levell'd towns with weeds lie cover'd o'er,
> The hollow winds thro' naked temples roar;
> Round broken columns clasping ivy twin'd;
> O'er heaps of ruin stalk'd the stately hind;
> The fox obscene to gaping tombs retires,
> And savage howlings fill the sacred quires.

Centred within a fifty-line paragraph, these couplets convey with apparent spontaneity both the poet's passion and the scene that provokes it. Thanks to their very regularity and weight, the accented vowels sound thunderously indignant. One may speculate that, the details being more appropriate to the sixteenth century than to the eleventh, Pope was able to sympathize with the victims of the Reformation more truly than with those of the Normans.[2] But whether or not this is so, it remains clear that the close of the passage, which should sound rich and triumphant, fails to come near the strength of these lines. I don't mean to rehearse my account of how local expressiveness can upset larger patterns; but judging the scene of desolation in itself, I have two

---

[1] Once again, I follow what might be called the orthodox judgement of men like Dr. Johnson and George Sherburn, although I appreciate the force of other accounts of the structure of the poem.

[2] Cf. note to line 68 of *Windsor Forest* in Pope, *Pastoral Poetry and An Essay on Criticism*, ed. E. Audra and Aubrey Williams (London, 1961), p. 156.

comments to offer. First, we are drawn to interpret it as covertly anti-Reformation, because it does not fit even the vague impression we have of William I's reign. By treating the New Forest as if it were all England and by representing a few abandoned churches as if they were Christianity, Pope himself encourages us to look elsewhere. So the versification is too powerful for the ostensible subject. Secondly, if the description is to suggest ruin, it cannot be fortunate that the opulence of sound and rhythm connotes something grander and more interesting than the 'teeming grain' and 'ripen'd fields' with which the forest is contrasted. Instead of evoking a waste land, the versification hints at fulfilment.

Windsor Forest includes many such self-contradictions. The flight and death of the pheasant ought to sound pathetic, but they are far more engrossing than the military episode just before them, and the reader's main feeling must be something like satisfaction. In the death of the larks a similar incongruity obtrudes itself, for the dazzling polish of the couplet extinguishes the pathos.

> Oft as the mounting larks their notes prepare,
> They fall, and leave their little lives in air.

Charmed by the liquids, we ignore the creatures' fate. Because the poet renders the event only too well, he seems untrue to its meaning. When Lodona undergoes metamorphosis 'in a soft, silver stream dissolv'd away', the flaw runs deeper: we not only miss the intended pathos but also return to the over-expressive manner of the *Essay on Criticism*.

I think we may generalize—or perhaps speculate—that a direct, unaffected private emotion is the hardest to convey through a locally expressive style. It is for 'sincere' tenderness, spontaneous admiration, delivered as the inner feeling of the poet himself, that *ars celare artem* becomes essential. The less distance there must be between author and reader, the more 'natural' the style should appear. In dramatic or deliberately mannered works, as in pastiche, the poet is removed far enough for obviously artful effects to be welcome; the same rule holds for passages of comedy and ridicule, where the poet is separating both the reader and himself from the subject of the poem.

So it seems natural that Pope's short pieces should rarely

suffer from the faults I have been examining. Their brevity leaves small room for fragmentation and eliminates the collision of large and small patterns. Their subject is too narrow for many changes of tone; consequently, false tone becomes more avoidable. Many of Pope's short poems reveal a perfection that most of his long poems lack. All the more is it regrettable that academic criticism has laid so much weight on the big works.

In the *Epistle to Miss Blount with the Works of Voiture*—a short poem with an air of candour—we do not find much to call local expressiveness. Instead, there is an absolute sureness of touch from beginning to end. The poet wishes to sound graceful and melodious, but above all he must sound honest. Therefore, he works toward a subtle, general fitting of style to subject and mood. In a couplet like

> Ah quit not the free innocence of life
> For the dull glory of a virtuous wife!

the impetus and irregularity of the rhythm delicately convey the unscreened movement of the speaker's sentiments. The couplets with no pause between lines have a parallel effect:

> Let the strict life of graver mortals be
> A long, exact, and serious comedy. . . .

Throughout the poem the seesaw of false regulations and unconstrained virtue seems reflected by the fragile interplay of regular and irregular verse:

> Love, rais'd on beauty, will like that decay,
> Our hearts may bear its slender chains a day. . . .

In this couplet the first line has two strong pauses, and only three of its syllables are clearly unaccented: it runs downhill toward *decay*. The other line has a light, steady beat appropriate to *slender chain*.

If I am right, we may surely trust Spence's report of Pope as saying, 'There is scarce any work of mine in which the versification was more laboured than in my pastorals.'[1] The appeal of the *Pastorals* depends on our recognizing the conscious element of pastiche in their composition. We need not identify the allusions, but we must know that the poem is systematically conventional, that the poet is polishing themes, images, and phrases he

---

[1] Spence, *Anecdotes*, p. 312.

received from a line of predecessors. Once we understand these primary facts, we can enjoy the brilliant versifying as a revelation of musical and expressive powers. Warton defined the principal merit of the *Pastorals* as 'correct and musical versification; musical, to a degree of which rhyme could hardly be thought capable'.[1] I think this judgement naturally suits a poem in which the author keeps himself at several carefully measured paces from the reader. The extraordinary evenness of surface in the *Pastorals*, the use of the same high finish and rich tones everywhere, seems correct for the same reasons. In these poems such essentials of design as narrative, persuasion, suspense, and climax hardly exist. The poet expects us to supply the thread of love intrigue; he provides the jewelled eulogies and sonorous laments. Significantly, Pope inscribed his favourite *Pastoral* to the memory of a woman he never knew.

> No grateful dews descend from ev'ning skies,
> Nor morning odours from the flow'rs arise.
> No rich perfumes refresh the fruitful field,
> Nor fragrant herbs their native incense yield.

A pack of lies, of course, but who cares? The almost uniform regularity of feet, broken by a single pyrrhic substitution, frames a lush variety of vowels and a stream of *f*s with one or two *p*s or *v*s. Altogether, the sensuosities rejected by the meaning are amply affirmed by the versification; and the reader could hardly ask for more.

Pope's translations belong in a category near the *Pastorals*. In them, too, he can take the large structure for granted, as derived from famous models; and he also remains coolly separated from his own audience by the intervention of the original author. The expressive effects, whether local or general, are welcome because their ground is clear and fixed. But when Pope advances to the imitations, a new and widely admired feat becomes normal. This is his free use of colloquial inflexions within the heroic couplet. So many critics have praised the accomplishment that I may only nod along with them. But even while agreeing that the range of Pope's work gains immensely from the incorporation of a true speaking voice, I have some observations. For one thing, apart from the *Epistle to Dr. Arbuthnot*, Pope's supreme masterpieces

[1] Warton, *Essay*, pp. 9–10.

—like the *Rape of the Lock* and the *Second Moral Essay*—make very restrained use of the inflexions of common speech. For another, contrary to what is often implied, this was not something Pope had to learn late in his career. The *Epistle to Henry Cromwell*, written in 1707, is a brilliant example of the style. What happened is that Pope discovered how variously he could use it, especially as a starting-point for modulating to the steepest height.

Using versification as a guide, I think we must conclude that Pope composed his greatest works when he invented a comprehensive structure that could hold—without contradictions or incongruities—the whole range of his expressive devices. The *Epistle to Dr. Arbuthnot* is such a poem; the *Rape of the Lock* is another; the *Second Moral Essay* is a third. They have all received loving attention from the poet's admirers, and need no appreciation from me. In all of them Pope can shine freely without sacrificing climaxes to rival attractions. He can handle paragraphs as solid units and yet subordinate them to a larger action or rhetorical design. He can be his most artful while sounding spontaneous. When the Baron cuts Belinda's lock, Pope introduces a feminine rhyme to signalize the catastrophe, and starts the second line of the couplet with a pyrrhic foot so that the gap will be obvious. But he also places this supremely important action at the centre of the poem; and because the mode of the work is sympathetic comedy, he profits from the humorous connotation of feminine rhymes. In the *Second Moral Essay* the entrance of Mrs. Blount (l. 249) occasions a transformation of the metre from staccato violence, crackling with *p*s, *t*s and strong pauses, to the sustained dignity of hardly broken lines drawn out with *m*s, *b*s, and open vowels. But this ingenious modulation, the most elaborate in the poem, also accompanies the main shift of interest—from the long examination of vicious women to the portrait of the virtuous Lady. Thus the intensity of the poet's feeling resides in the structure, versification, and meaning at once. Such poems cannot be overpraised.

Yet in judging versification, we can hardly expect all rational standards to be met at the same time (though many critics seem to assume this ought to happen). What wins by one measure may fail by another. We praise a poet for reconciling the syntax of speech to the demands of metre. We praise him again for using sound and rhythm expressively. We also praise him—or at least we used to—for fulfilling gracefully and musically the rules of an established pattern. Can a single style ignore none of these ideals? And yet more standards may flutter as the climate of taste changes. Saintsbury particularly commended Sackville's pleasing variations in phrase and pause; John Thompson sneers at such a 'purely sonorous variety' and turns to praise Dolman for suiting his metrical pattern to his language and fulfilling a 'dramatic intention'.[1] If we accept this criterion, we judge versification by its appropriateness to the speaker of the lines. But if we follow Saintsbury, we judge by general rules of pleasing musicality, which are neither dramatic, nor locally expressive, nor closely related to the movement of natural speech.

My own opinion is that sheer musicality is now underestimated, and the relation between good verse and colloquial speech is exaggerated. To me, dramatic propriety seems only a minor feature of excellent versification—as it also is in prose so different as the King James Bible and the novels of Henry James. In the drama as such, different speakers may require different styles; and in any poem a shift from one speaker to another may be nicely evinced by rhythm and sound. But in non-dramatic poetry the writer's tone, the general colour of an episode or description, the dignity or triviality of a subject, should be overriding features. Beyond these lie the requirements of literary genre—the need, say, for a conventional love-song to sound different from an epitaph. It is while holding such views that I have tried to examine the merits of Pope's versification.

It would be hard to overstate my admiration for Pope's genius. No other poet from the birth of Prior to the death of Cowper so fully repays the closest attention to his style. But I have tried to suggest that the enticements of local expressiveness could distract Pope from important structural demands; that the liveliness of his most expressive passages sometimes weakens the power of others that should sound more significant; and that for certain purposes a softening of his expressive powers might have been desirable.

If Pope himself is to blame for the term 'correctness' as the mark of his literary achievement, we need not share that youthful opinion. But it is probably accurate to say that his failures, such as the 'Man of Ross' passage, are ultimately failures of decorum.

[1] *The Founding of English Metre* (New York, 1961), pp. 55, 56–61.

At least, I think we interpret both 'correctness' and 'decorum' most helpfully as appropriateness of style; and if we employ this sense of the words, we can state Pope's fundamental problem as the discovery of subjects or arguments suited to his many styles. Versification then becomes not a good or bad thing in itself but the element of Pope's style that most subtly indicates when he is doing his finest work.

13

ASPECTS OF SENTIMENTALISM IN EIGHTEENTH-CENTURY LITERATURE

By ARTHUR FRIEDMAN

IN his well-known 'Essay on the Theatre; or, a Comparison between Laughing and Sentimental Comedy' Oliver Goldsmith talks about two quite different aspects of sentimental comedy, and the distinction he makes seems useful for a more general consideration of sentimentalism in eighteenth-century literature. On the one hand, Goldsmith describes the kind of characters that appear in sentimental comedy:

> In these Plays almost all the Characters are good, and exceedingly generous; they are lavish enough of their *Tin* Money on the Stage, and though they want Humour, have abundance of Sentiment and Feeling. If they happen to have Faults or Foibles, the Spectator is taught not only to pardon, but to applaud them, in consideration of the goodness of their hearts. . . .[1]

On the other hand, Goldsmith characterizes the drama by its effect upon the audience (this is 'Weeping Sentimental Comedy'), which in turn is produced by the kind of incident or action represented: 'in describing Low or Middle Life' sentimental comedy gives 'a detail of its Calamities' or an 'Exhibition of Human Distress';[2] in it 'the virtues of Private Life are exhibited, rather than the Vices exposed; and the Distresses, rather than the Faults of Mankind, make our interest in the piece'.[3] Since these two aspects of sentimentalism do not necessarily appear in combination in plays and novels of the eighteenth century, they may well be discussed separately.

---

[1] *Collected Works of Oliver Goldsmith* (Oxford, 1966), iii. 212.
[2] Ibid., p. 210.
[3] Ibid., p. 212.

I

In sentimental comedy, Goldsmith tells us, 'almost all the Characters are good', and he describes their goodness in just the terms that we might anticipate from a prior knowledge of the doctrine of sentimentalism.[1] The virtue of the characters is stated first in terms of their benevolence : they are 'exceedingly generous; they are lavish enough of their *Tin* Money on the Stage'. They are men of feeling: they 'have abundance of Sentiment and Feeling'. They are good-natured men : we are asked to forgive their faults 'in consideration of the goodness of their hearts'.

We can see how the sentimental doctrine is used as the basis for evaluating the moral disposition of characters by considering one of the comedies Goldsmith probably had in mind in writing 'An Essay on the Theatre'—Richard Cumberland's *The West Indian*.[2] The hero is named Belcour to suggest the goodness of his heart, and at his first appearance he tells of his feelings of humanity : 'every child of sorrow is my brother; while I have hands to hold, therefore, I will hold them open to mankind' (I. v). Goldsmith tells us that such characters are 'lavish enough of their *Tin* Money on the Stage'; and Belcour upon hearing of the needs of Captain Dudley, a complete stranger, presents him with £200 (II. vii). Goldsmith complains that if the benevolent characters 'have Faults or Foibles, the Spectator is taught not only to pardon, but to applaud them, in consideration of the goodness of their hearts'; at the end of the play his father can say in easily forgiving Belcour his misdeeds : 'I have discovered through the veil of some irregularities, a heart beaming with benevolence, an animated nature, fallible indeed, but not incorrigible.'

In sentimental works such as this we find it easier to forgive

---

[1] The best analysis of sentimentalism, to which I am greatly indebted, is still R. S. Crane's 'Suggestions toward a Genealogy of the "Man of Feeling" ', *ELH* i (1934), 205–30, reprinted in his *The Idea of the Humanities and Other Essays* (Chicago, 1967), i. 188–213.

[2] In writing *Retaliation* a year after his 'Essay on the Theatre' Goldsmith described the characters in Cumberland's plays in much the same terms as those he had used of the characters in sentimental comedy (the parallels are given in *Collected Works*, iv. 355–6). When Goldsmith wrote, *The West Indian* was Cumberland's most successful play, and in some ways his most sentimental. Cumberland, without knowing the authorship of 'An Essay on the Theatre', thought it directed particularly against his comedy *The Fashionable Lovers* (see his *Memoirs* (1807), i. 379–80).

the good-natured heroes their faults when they are placed in contrast with hypocrites who pretend to more conventional virtues. Thus in *The West Indian* Belcour's 'uncommon benevolence' appears even more striking when opposed to the heartlessness of Lady Rusport. 'So much for the virtues of a puritan,' one of the characters says about her; 'out upon it, her heart is flint; yet that woman, . . . without one worthy particle in her composition, would . . . as soon set her foot in a pest-house, as in a play-house' (I. vi). Or, as another character says directly to her, 'You preach, and you pray, and you turn up your eyes, and all the while you're as hard-hearted as a hyena. . . . By my soul there isn't in the whole creation so savage an animal as a human creature without pity' (II. xi). Again, we find it easier to forgive the good-natured Tom Jones his 'follies and vices more than enough to repent and to be ashamed of' (XVIII. x), when we contrast him with his half-brother Blifil, whose hypocrisy extends even further than that of Lady Rusport, in that he pretends to benevolence, indeed even to 'the most amiable of human weaknesses'—'Compassion for those who do not deserve it' (XVIII. v). Similarly, to give a final example, in *The School for Scandal* Charles Surface, who 'in the midst of folly and dissipation, has still, as our immortal bard expresses it, "a tear for pity, and a hand open as day, for melting charity"' (III. i), is contrasted with his hypocritical brother Joseph, who has 'as much speculative benevolence as any private gentleman in the kingdom, though he is seldom so sensual as to indulge himself in the exercise of it' (V. i). Here and in the other comic works mentioned our pleasure in the resolution comes not only from seeing the good-natured hero rewarded by the favour of an uncle or a father and by the hand of the heroine; it comes also to a very considerable extent from having the hypocrite, long successful, finally exposed.

The use of the sentimental doctrine as a standard for judging the moral worth of characters may appear in 'weeping comedy' or in tragedy, but benevolent heroes do not in themselves make works pathetic or tragic. The three works briefly referred to— *The West Indian*, *Tom Jones*, and *The School for Scandal*—are all productive of laughter rather than tears, though the first of them is included in anthologies and discussed in histories of the drama as an example of sentimental comedy.

For a play or novel to be anti-sentimental in its use of characters it would be necessary to reverse the moral distinctions, and either (1) make selfishness and hardness of heart the signs of virtue or (2) make benevolence and good nature not admirable but ridiculous. I know of no anti-sentimental work of the first kind; a good example of the second kind is Goldsmith's first comedy.

Throughout his early career as a writer Goldsmith was pretty constantly concerned with portraying in his characters the dangers of excessive benevolence,[1] and this interest culminated in his picture of the title character in *The Good Natur'd Man*. Honeywood is a man of consummate benevolence, but his good nature is held up not for commendation but to ridicule: '. . . . he loves all the world; that is his fault', we are told at the beginning of the play, and again: 'He calls his extravagance, generosity; and his trusting every body, universal benevolence.' He gives away all he has to anybody that asks it 'or that does not ask it', and then makes valueless promises. When at the end he finds he has become contemptible to others he becomes contemptible to himself, and in an attempt to reform he resolves, 'it shall be my study to reserve my pity for real distress; my friendship for true merit'. This, then, is Goldsmith's attack on the doctrine of good nature, but it is worth noting that it is not so thoroughgoing an attack as at first it may seem. The hero's uncle, Sir William Honeywood, who is instrumental in bringing about his reformation, says about him at the beginning: 'What a pity it is . . . that any man's good will to others should produce so much neglect of himself, as to require correction. Yet, we must touch his weaknesses with a delicate hand. There are some faults so nearly allied to excellence, that we can scarce weed out the vice without eradicating the virtue.' And at the end Sir William can say: 'I saw with regret those splendid errors, that still took name from some neighbouring duty. Your charity, that was but injustice; your benevolence, that was but weakness; and your friendship but credulity.' In these passages at least Goldsmith seems to be saying that he is attacking not the sentimental virtues but the faults that resemble them.

II

The second expression that sentimentalism takes in eighteenth-century literature appears not in the moral disposition of the

---

[1] See *Collected Works*, v. 3.

characters but in the effect upon the reader or spectator (Gold-smith describes sentimental comedy as causing weeping rather than laughter), which is produced by a certain kind of incidents ('Exhibition of Human Distress'). The underlying assumption, only occasionally enunciated by authors, is that truly good-natured men, genuine men of feeling, will receive more pleasure, while viewing a play or reading a novel, from weeping for the distresses of the virtuous than from laughing at human faults or foibles. The really benevolent man (with Pope) will find

> The broadest mirth unfeeling Folly wears,
> Less pleasing far than Virtue's very tears.[1]

One of the clearest defences of weeping comedy appears in the Preface to Sir Richard Steele's *The Conscious Lovers*. In answer to the criticism that the serious parts of the play, and particularly the scene between Indiana and her father near the end, are 'no subjects for comedy', Steele has this to say:

... anything that has its foundation in happiness and success must be allowed to be the object of comedy; and sure it must be an improve-ment of it to introduce a joy too exquisite for laughter, that can have no spring but in delight, which is the case of this young lady. I must, therefore, contend that the tears which were shed on that occasion flowed from reason and good sense, and that men ought not to be laughed at for weeping till we come to a more clear notion of what is to be imputed to the hardness of the head and the softness of the heart. ... To be apt to give way to the impressions of humanity is the excel-lence of a right disposition and the natural working of a well-turned spirit.

What kind of incident or plot is likely to cause the good-natured audience 'to give way to the impressions of humanity'? Goldsmith, we remember, tells us that 'the virtues of Private Life are ex-hibited ...; and the Distresses, rather than the Faults of Mankind, make our interest in the piece'. John Dennis in his criticism of *The Conscious Lovers* similarly finds that the 'downright tragical' catastrophe of the play comes from the suffering of a *virtuous* heroine:

... the Scene of the Discovery in the *Conscious Lovers* is truly Tragical. *Indiana* was strictly virtuous: She had indeed conceiv'd a violent Pas-sion for *Bevil*, but all young People in full Health are liable to such

An Essay on Man, iv. 319–20.

a Passion, and perhaps the most sensible and the most virtuous are more than others liable: But besides, that she kept this Passion within the Bounds of Honour, it was the natural Effect of her Esteem for her Benefactor, and of her Gratitude, that is, of her Virtue. These considerations render'd her Case deplorable, and the Catastrophe downright tragical, which of a Comedy ought to be the most comical Part, for the same Reason that it ought to be the most tragical Part of a Tragedy.[1]

It would seem then that we can define a sentimental incident or a sentimental plot as one designed to produce tears by showing the sufferings of the virtuous. (Of course this luxury of woe in the audience may prepare the way for, or give place to, other emotions of sorrow or joy.)

The eighteenth-century plays that Goldsmith would apparently include under his designation of 'Weeping Sentimental Comedy' were not designed to produce tears throughout; indeed all of them, as far as I know, limit themselves to a very few sentimental scenes. In *The Conscious Lovers*, for example, Indiana, though appearing mildly pathetic elsewhere, is made to suffer only in the concluding scene of the play (the scene defended by Steele and attacked by Dennis). Here the heroine can cry out, 'What have I to do but sigh and weep, to rave, run wild, a lunatic in chains, or, hid in darkness, mutter in distracted starts my strange, strange story!' and she can 'demand of fate, "Why—why was I born to such variety of sorrows?" ' It is this frenzy of suffering, however, that leads immediately to the discovery of her long-lost father and the consequent union with the man she loves. Similarly, in comedies such as Edward Moore's *The Foundling* or Richard Cumberland's *The Fashionable Lover* (the play Cumberland thought Goldsmith 'particularly points his observations at' in 'An Essay on the Theatre'[2]) the heroines may invite our tears during a few scenes where, like Indiana, they appear as reviled and rejected orphans, but in due course their fathers turn up to produce a happy ending.

As opposed to the sentimental incidents or scenes in the plays just considered, it seems possible to have in comic novels what may be called sentimental plots. Perhaps as good an example as any of such a novel is Goldsmith's *Vicar of Wakefield*, where the

---

[1] *Remarks on a Play Call'd The Conscious Lovers* (1723), p. 8.
[2] See p. 248, n. 2 above.

plot is largely designed to lead to the sufferings of the Primrose family, and where in the last third of the work their sufferings are aggravated before being suddenly relieved. Thus when their misfortunes have been raised to the highest pitch at the beginning of Chapter XXX, Olivia, having been lured into an apparently false marriage, has withered and supposedly died; the Vicar, in a debtor's prison, is at the point of death from a burn he received when his home was destroyed by fire; Sophia has been abducted, and one can only fear the worst for her; and George, the eldest son, is in chains, facing a 'vile death' for having sent a challenge to the betrayer of the family's honour. A plot such as this will supposedly give a double pleasure to the good-natured reader: during the complication of distress he will enjoy being able 'to give way to the impressions of humanity', and at the resolution he will rejoice in the happiness of the virtuous characters with whom he has suffered. And he is able to luxuriate in his tears in *The Vicar of Wakefield*, as in any genuinely comic novel with a sentimental plot, because he can never really doubt that in the end all the characters will get pretty much what they deserve. Goldsmith accomplishes this effect in part by a variety of narrative devices, one of the most important of which is the revelation to the reader of Mr. Burchell's identity as early as Chapter III, so that his final appearance as a kind of *deus ex machina* is constantly anticipated. Perhaps even more important for the comic effect is the manner in which the novel is narrated. It is written as by the Vicar, and by the end of the first chapter we cannot possibly fail to know from the mere tone of his voice that, whatever misfortunes he may have to relate, he cannot conceivably be telling a tale that is to end in misery for his family and himself.

A serious novel[1] with a sentimental plot and a happy ending offers a somewhat different problem. In Richardson's *Pamela*, a good example of this class of novel, the reader will not know from the beginning with anything approaching complete certainty (except perhaps from the sub-title) whether or not the

---

[1] By a serious novel or play I mean one where a fortunate or unfortunate outcome does not seem clearly determined from the outset. For the category of 'serious' as distinguished from 'tragic' and 'comic', and for *Pamela* as an example of a serious work, I am indebted to Sheldon Sacks, *Fiction and the Shape of Belief: A Study of Henry Fielding, with Glances at Swift, Johnson, and Richardson* (Berkeley, 1964), particularly pp. 22–4.

heroine's suffering in the cause of virtue will eventually be appropriately rewarded; and, if he is a man of feeling, he is likely to be
much more profoundly moved than by a comic work, where the
suffering of the innocent is made to appear throughout as a
condition of their future happiness, or at most as only a temporary
obstacle to it. As a result, the good-natured reader is likely to
feel more intense relief and positive pleasure at the happy outcome in a serious sentimental novel than in a comic one: readers
of *Pamela* are said to have rung church-bells in honour of the
marriage of the heroine, but it is doubtful whether readers of
The Vicar of Wakefield were in the least tempted to ring bells even
for the double wedding of the Primrose children. The sentimental
plot, showing the suffering of the virtuous, thus fits very well
into the serious work with a happy ending. But what conceivable
pleasure could a benevolent man receive from a sentimental plot
in a tragic work or in a serious work with an unhappy ending?

III

Aristotle might have been talking about sentimental plots in
tragedy when in the *Poetics* he says: '. . . . there are three forms of
Plot to be avoided. (1) A good man must not be seen passing from
happiness to misery. . . . The first situation is not fear-inspiring or
piteous, but simply odious to us' (1452[b]). On the other hand, we
do have eighteenth-century tragic or serious works[1] showing
the virtuous passing from happiness to misery, and some of these
works were exceptionally popular. What devices could authors
use to make such works pleasurable rather than 'simply odious
to us'?

The Tragedy of Jane Shore by Nicholas Rowe is an instructive
example to begin with. First, there can obviously be no question
about the heroine's suffering. In the last scene we see her at a
time when she has walked the streets in 'solemn penance' for two
days and has 'not eat these three days'; in the midst of this misery
she is reviled and rejected by Alicia, 'her friend, the partner of
her heart'; and the minute before she expires she sees her long-
lost husband, who has just forgiven her, dragged off to prison.

[1] In the final section of my paper I call the first two works discussed
'tragedies', without attempting to decide whether they might not better be
called serious works with unhappy endings.

Second, in spite of the sinfulness of her past life (and even here there is some ambiguity as to whether Jane willingly became the mistress of Edward IV or whether 'the king by force possessed her person'), there can be little doubt that she is now a completely virtuous person. She is truly penitent for her past sins and shows herself resolute in virtue by her rejection of Lord Hastings. On the positive side, she is, as one might expect, a person of extraordinary benevolence. Good nature is made a standard for judging the excellence of characters when Jane blesses Bellmour for courting 'the offices of soft humanity' by clothing the naked and feeding 'the crying orphan' and mixing his 'pitying tears with those that weep' (I. ii); a little later in the same scene Alicia praises Jane for her 'gentle deeds of mercy':

> . . . the poor, the pris'ner,
> The fatherless, the friendless, and the widow,
> Who daily own the bounty of thy hand,
> Shall cry to heav'n, and pull a blessing on thee;

and Jane, in her only moment of boastfulness, can tell Gloster that she never forgot 'the widows' want, and orphans' cry' or failed to call 'the poor to take his portion with me' (IV. i). Finally, she displays in the last scene of the play a consummate virtue in forgiving Alicia's cruelty and calling upon 'gracious heaven' to look upon her former friend in mercy and not to 'visit her for any wrong to me'.

Rowe makes this superlative heroine undergo extraordinary suffering, and it is necessary to see how he was able to make her tragedy if not pleasant at least bearable. Perhaps most important, he was willing, while portraying Jane as completely virtuous, to suggest that she was not wholly undeserving of punishment. Although her misfortunes are made to result from the malice of Alicia and Gloster, and not her past life (except in the remote sense that her tragedy would never have occurred if she had been willing or able to stay at home with her husband), still there is always the underlying assumption that a sinner, however penitent, should not expect to avoid all punishment. Even during her final intense suffering Jane does not feel that she is being treated unjustly:

> Yet, yet endure, nor murmur, O my soul!
> For are not thy transgressions great and numberless?

And the final speech, while not clearly relevant to the action of the play, was perhaps in part designed to persuade us that Jane's tragedy could be properly moving, since it was morally understandable and consequently not simply odious:

> Let those who view this sad example know
> What fate attends the broken marriage vow;
> And teach their children in succeeding times,
> No common vengeance waits upon these crimes,
> When such severe repentance could not save,
> From want, from shame, and an untimely grave.

Rowe also makes a much more fundamental change in the very nature of tragedy. Many people would agree with Aristotle that tragedy should show a change from happiness to misery; Rowe's tragedy, however, shows much more nearly the heroine's fall from grief and resignation to suffering and death. But Rowe's innovation is much more radical than this. At the beginning Jane is 'sunk in grief, and pining with despair' (I. i) because of her repentance for her past life of sin. When her husband, disguised as Dumont, assures her that

> Assisting angels shall conduct your steps,
> Bring you to bliss, and crown your end with peace,

she replies that her 'painful heart will . . . never know a moment's peace till then' (II. i). When her punishment is ordered, she can thus address God, her 'most righteous judge':

> For my past crimes my forfeit life receive;
> No pity for my sufferings here I crave,
> And only hope forgiveness in the grave (IV. i).

During her final suffering she begs from heaven 'that mercy man denied her here'; and we cannot doubt that she will be granted the plea made with her dying breath: 'Oh, mercy, heav'n!' When eternal rewards are thus introduced, what at first seemed to be human tragedy now appears as divine comedy. For what Christian can fail to rejoice in the passage of a penitent sinner from grief and despair through suffering and death to eternal happiness? And what good-natured man can fail to enjoy lending a virtuous woman his sympathetic tears during her suffering along the way?

At first it may appear far-fetched to consider George Lillo's

The London Merchant as a tragedy with a sentimental plot, for it would seem that a hero who is a fornicator, a thief, and a murderer can hardly be considered virtuous. Lillo, however, performs the amazing task of carrying George Barnwell on his downward path quite untouched by any of the awful things he does; after murdering his uncle he is still pretty much the kind, generous, simple lad who could never do harm to anyone that he was at the beginning. The author accomplishes this improbable feat in part by pushing George against his will into committing his evil deeds, and by making him repent immediately after each one. Again, George has bad luck: when he wishes to confess his first slip to Thorowgood, his master refuses out of mercy to let him proceed; after resolving not to murder his uncle and throwing away his pistol, he is startled into stabbing him. And when he is persuaded by Millwood's false story to rob his master, he is puzzled by the fact that good motives seem to lead to bad actions:

What have I done! Were my resolutions founded on reason and sincerely made, why then has heaven suffered me to fall? I sought not the occasion; and if my heart deceives me not, compassion and generosity were my motives. Is virtue inconsistent with itself, or are vice and virtue only empty names? Or do they depend on accidents, beyond our power to produce or to prevent . . .? But why should I attempt to reason? All is confusion, horror, and remorse (II. ii).

Perhaps the most important determinant of our feelings concerning George Barnwell is the attitude of the paragon Thorowgood toward him. Thorowgood from the beginning is sympathetic toward the plight of youth and willing to forgive youthful mistakes: 'When we consider the frail condition of humanity,' he says, 'it may raise our pity, not our wonder, that youth should go astray when reason, weak at the best opposed to inclination, scarce formed and wholly unassisted by experience, faintly contends, or willingly becomes the slave of sense' (II. i). And after George's complete downfall Thorowgood shows only compassion and understanding. 'How should an unexperienced youth escape her snares?' he asks after seeing Millwood (IV. ii). 'With pity and compassion let us judge him!' he adds a little later; '. . . perhaps, had we like him been tried, like him we had fallen too' (V. i). George has fallen, then, because his reason is 'scarce formed and wholly unassisted by experience'. But how can reason ever be assisted by experience, if experience means giving up the use of reason to become the slave of sense? 'Many, less virtuously disposed than Barnwell was, have never fallen in the manner he has done', Thorowgood says, and asks, 'may not such owe their safety rather to Providence than to themselves?' (v. i). But if George's downfall has come not from any deficiency in virtue but from a whim of Providence, will not the play seem to us, in Aristotle's words, 'simply odious'? It is our answers to these questions that will reveal the distinctive characteristics of the play.

The answer to the first question is that our reason may learn from the experience of others as well as our own. If George had only had before him the example of an innocent lad ensnared by an evil woman, then he would not have fallen prey to Millwood. But since he has fallen, his sad example will prevent the fall of future youth. And Providence has not acted by whim; rather it has chosen the virtuous George Barnwell as a sacrifice, and in the penultimate scene of the play he shows that he has come to understand his place in the divine scheme:

Though short my span of life, and few my days, yet count my crimes for years, and I have lived whole ages. Thus justice, in compassion to mankind, cuts off a wretch like me, by one such example to secure thousands from future ruin. Justice and mercy are in heaven the same: its utmost severity is mercy to the whole, thereby to cure man's folly and presumption, which else would render even infinite mercy vain and ineffectual.

When George's fall is recognized as part of heaven's plan, it is easier to understand how he can go through his sordid experiences without seeming to be touched by them. And since he has fallen a sacrifice to the greater good, he is assured of an eternal reward. Of course, he must go through the form of 'true repentance, the only preparatory, the certain way to everlasting peace', before joy and gratitude take the place of despair (v. ii), but Millwood appears certainly right in her statement about him (though, George thinks, perhaps not about herself): 'I was doomed, before the world began, to endless pains, and thou to joys eternal' (v. iii). To gain his eternal salvation he has been made to suffer much; and his death on the gallows leaves us, as it does the characters who witness it, with 'Bleeding hearts and weeping eyes'. But while we are weeping we know that George is safely in heaven, and Christian tragedy thus takes on some of the characteristics of sentimental comedy.

The two examples of sentimental tragedy just discussed, though not without interest, have no great literary value; perhaps they suffer from the limitations of the dramatic form in which they are cast, or perhaps a sentimental plot is merely not appropriate for a genuinely tragic work. The last work to be considered in which a sentimental plot is softened by Christian doctrine, *Clarissa*, is one of the masterpieces of our literature; and its superiority results in part from Richardson's skill in incorporating a serious action in an extended prose narrative. (That the action of *Clarissa* is serious rather than inevitably tragic from the beginning is apparent from the agitation of its first readers, while it was appearing, as to whether it would end happily or unhappily.)

Nothing need be said to recall the virtuous heroine's suffering, but we may look briefly at her death to see how Richardson made it possible for his good-natured readers to shed tears of grief not unmixed with joy. Clarissa clearly indicates that she does not consider the misfortunes leading up to her death as meaningless; rather her period of suffering has given her an opportunity to make herself worthy of 'an heavenly crown *hereafter*': 'It is not so hard to die, as I believed it to be!—The Preparation is the difficulty—I bless God, I have had time for That—The rest is worse to beholders, than to me!—I am all blessed hope—Hope itself.'[1] Clarissa can consequently trust that others in their last hour can be 'happy as I am'; and her end is all that a Christian could hope for:

. . . she spoke faltering and inwardly,—Bless—bless—bless—you All—And now—And now—[holding up her almost lifeless hands for the last time] Come—O come—Blessed Lord—JESUS!

And with these words, the last but half-pronounced, expired: Such a smile, such a charming serenity overspreading her sweet face at the instant, as seemed to manifest her eternal happiness already begun (viii. 5).

Whether or not most of Richardson's first readers were pleased with this ending we do not know; but he tells us in a Postscript

[1] *Clarissa* (The Shakespeare Head edition of the Novels of Samuel Richardson, Oxford, 1930), viii. 3. I shall include further references to this edition in my text. In all cases, bracketed passages in the quotations are Richardson's.

to the novel that in the course of its publication he had received 'many anonymous Letters, in which the Writers differently expressed their wishes with regard to the apprehended catastrophe', and that 'Most of those directed to him by the gentler Sex, turned in favour of what they called a *Fortunate Ending*' (vii. 306). The sentimental pleasure these female readers expected to gain from such a work is excellently described by Richardson: 'And how was this happy ending to be brought about? Why, by this very easy and trite expedient; to wit, by reforming Lovelace, and marrying him to Clarissa—Not, however, abating her one of her trials, nor any of her suffering [for the sake of the sport her distresses would give to the *tender-hearted* reader as she went along] the last outrage excepted . . .' (viii. 307). In refusing to accede to his female readers' request for a serious work with a happy ending, Richardson was resolved, he says with perhaps some exaggeration, 'to attempt something that never yet had been done': 'He considered, that the Tragic poets have . . . seldom made their heroes true objects of pity . . .: And still more rarely have made them in their deaths look forward to a *future Hope*' (viii. 308). By thus introducing into his novel 'the great doctrines of Christianity' he has observed a higher kind of poetic justice, in rewarding the virtuous so that 'the very Balaams of the world should not forbear to wish that their latter end might be like that of the Heroine' (viii. 309). Or, as Richardson says even more emphatically a little later: '. . . who that are in earnest in their profession of Christianity, but will rather envy than regret the triumphant death of CLARISSA; whose piety, from her *early childhood*; whose diffusive charity; whose steady virtue; whose Christian humility; whose forgiving spirit; whose meekness, and resignation, HEAVEN *only* could reward?' (viii. 319). Richardson can consequently feel 'well justified by the *Christian System*, in deferring to extricate suffering Virtue to the time in which it will meet with the *Completion* of its Reward' (viii. 309).

We have interesting testimony from one of the author's friends concerning the success of the Christian catastrophe of *Clarissa*. Edward Moore, in a letter to Richardson of 23 December 1748,[1] defends the heroine's death, of which he thinks the author has

---

[1] The original of the letter is in the Forster Collection at the Victoria and Albert Museum. I am indebted to Mr. Anthony Amberg for bringing the letter to my attention and permitting me to use his transcript of it.

offered a hardly adequate vindication in his Postscript. The defence must be made, Moore asserts, by appealing to 'the Feeling of the Sensible Reader'. Although no one, he says, wants Clarissa's life preserved after her rape, this 'Outrage' is itself necessary, since it is only 'the greatest of all Trials' which she has suffered that 'could have made her the most finished of all Characters'. If, like most heroines, she had been afraid of death, or 'if, after the Manner of Tragedy, in a mad fit of Despair she had laid violent Hands on herself, and by an Act of Guilt had finished a Life of Misery', then her end could have been called unhappy. But the end of Clarissa is very different: '. . . where the Mind is raised by Calamity above the Pleasures of this World, and so prepared by it for the Happiness of Another; at the same time too, so totally excluded from all Hope of Comfort here, and so desirous of Death, both as a Relief and a Reward; it is then that I can see Clarissa in her Shroud, and exult in the Loss of her.' Moore goes on to defend his argument by the tears he has shed 'thro' the whole Narrative of her Death':

. . . whoever will take the Trouble to question his own Feelings, will learn that Joy has a much greater Share in his Tears than Sorrow. The Distresses of a Lear, however undeserved or strongly painted, will affect an Audience with no other Passion than Terror; and if Clarissa, innocent as she was, had lingered in Torments and died without Hope, the Reader had been frozen and not melted. It is her noble Forgiveness of Injuries, her Humanity, her Friendship, her Sweetness of Mind, and above all the Praises which are bestowed upon her, that compell Tears, and not that we have lost her.

If Moore was able thus to shed tears of joy at the release by death of the angelic Clarissa, he must indeed have found the novel the perfection of sentimental fiction.

14

THE VOICES OF HENRY
FIELDING: STYLE IN
TOM JONES

By HENRY KNIGHT MILLER

I SUPPOSE that these days one can argue that Henry Fielding is the 'real' hero of *Tom Jones* without fluttering many dovecotes. We have become accustomed to think of the omniscient (or semi-omniscient) narrator as answering, in some significant respects, to the idea of a 'character' in prose fiction, as possessing individual qualities to which the reader responds and which he can assess. It is true that the status of the narrator-as-character may be conceived to reside in a dimension somewhat different from that of *his* characters; but for the 'proper reader' his existence is none the less a potent empirical fact, and it is inextricably involved with the reader's response to the fictive world that the narrator presents.

The action of *Tom Jones* is intrinsically the action of Roman New Comedy and therefore 'comic' in that traditional sense, as Fielding's is also the 'comic vision' of a world not alien to man's best hopes. But ultimately, it is the *language* that must validate a comic world, make it felt as comic.[1] Dialogue is the traditional resource

---

[1] When the language of stage comedy ceases to perform (for a broad audience) its necessary function of identifying the kind of 'world' spectators are to set themselves to accept, as in modern productions of Plautus or Ben Jonson (or even Shakespeare), the defect must be made up through inventive, even farcical, 'stage-business'—which is always, in principle, justified; for the wrong psychological 'set' in addressing oneself to the world of comedy can be totally disastrous. Shakespeare's clear awareness of this requirement is seen in the care with which he handles his opening scenes: we know where we are, despite the potentially 'tragic' possibilities of oppressive father and stubborn daughter in the opening of *A Midsummer Night's Dream*, when Lysander suggests: 'You have her father's love, Demetrius, | Let me have Hermia's; do you marry him.'

of the comic dramatist; and Fielding (in *Tom Jones*) ranks easily
with Plautus and Terence, Shakespeare and Ben Jonson, as a
master of dialogue and of the comic characters given body by that
means. The comic romance, however, has yet another resource
and therefore another dimension: for in prose fiction the narrator,
as well as the characters, can function to define the comic world,
to evoke the peculiar multi-valued response that is of the essence
of comedy. He too makes use of dialogue: but it is a dialogue
with the reader.[1]

As Professor Hospers has observed, literature, the written
word, suffers (in its possibilities of implication) by comparison
with the spoken word, wherein we have not only the speaker's
'spoken utterance to go by but all the other cues such as his
facial expression and gestures and tone of voice and the environ-
mental circumstances accompanying the utterance'.[2] When, however, the narrator is present to our consciousness *as* narrator, as
another actor in the action, this insufficiency is minimized; for
he may offer us a variety of cues or 'signals' that, in effect, supply
the tone and gestures, etc., that give such richness of implication
to the directly spoken word. Where the narrator is present to
our consciousness, as in *Tom Jones*, every event is apprehended at
a level of complexity that must possess at least two dimensions
(often, of course, more): viz., the fictive event or predication, as
such, and the implications surrounding it because of the cognitive-
emotive envelope in which it is presented by the narrator and
hence experienced by the reader. (This stinks very much of jargon,
but I am not sure how else to put it.)

We are not, in *Tom Jones*, thereby deprived of the inalienable
right of drawing our *own* implications (moral, aesthetic, or other)
from the action and the assertions; but it is true that we are subjected to a gentle pressure in the direction of belief, in its largest
sense, that the narrator represents. Thus Fielding behaves (under
one aspect) as a rhetorician, presenting an *interpretation* of experience along with the raw experience, rather than as a reporter

---

[1] The relationship of Fielding's comic method to the *Vetus Comoedia*
appears most obviously, of course, when he mimics the *parabasis* of Aristophanes by performing as his own Chorus (e.g. III. vii, 'In which the Author
himself makes his Appearance on the Stage'). This has been noted in the best
of brief introductions to *Tom Jones*: Irvin Ehrenpreis, *Fielding: 'Tom Jones'*
(London, 1964), p. 8.

[2] 'Implied Truths in Literature', *JAAC* xix (1960), 41.

setting down neutral facts.[1] This means, both historically and aesthetically, that Fielding has nearer affiliations with Renaissance literature than with, say, Arnold Bennett. Fielding's is, indeed, a 'true history'; but he writes in a tradition that offers history (the local and particular) the option of elevating itself through language and through an interpretative rhetoric to the condition of poetry (the universal and general). This is the tradition of Cervantes and of Sidney's *Arcadia*, not the more familiar (to us) tradition of the 'realistic' novel.

My present concern, however, is not (precisely) Fielding as rhetorician, but 'Fielding' as a character in his own romance— which involves a nice philosophical distinction: for the belief that we accord a rhetorician (an actual human being) is one thing, the 'belief' that we grant to a fictional character is another. This is not to invoke the (by now, perhaps tiresome) concept of a 'persona'.[2] Henry Fielding presented himself as the historical personage Henry Fielding, in narrating *Tom Jones*, with such references as that to the little parlour in which he was writing his romance (xiii. i), and the direct address to contemporaries who might

[1] The critical language of Fielding's day would have described the interpretative function of style (perhaps inadequately) as 'embellishments'. But my essential distinction is his: 'Without Interruptions of this Kind, the best Narrative of plain Matter of Fact must overpower every Reader; for nothing but the everlasting Watchfulness, which *Homer* hath ascribed to *Jove* himself, can be Proof against a News Paper of many Volumes' (iv. i). Or, as one of the shrewdest modern analysts of Fielding's style has put it:

The perspective of irony is invaluable because of a danger inherent in the basic impulse of the novel to immerge in contemporary reality; for reality seen from so close is likely to be a shapeless mass of clamorous particulars which can easily subvert both moral intelligence and esthetic lucidity. This is clearly one basis for Fielding's objection to the whole method of *Pamela*, for his repeated insistence, *contra* Richardson, that a novelist must exercise the highest degree of selectivity and the finest narrative tact (Robert Alter, 'Fielding and the Uses of Style', *Novel*, i (1967), 57).

See also Mr. Alter's good discussion in *Rogue's Progress* (Cambridge, 1964), pp. 80–105.

[2] Cf. Irvin Ehrenpreis, 'Personae', in *Restoration and Eighteenth-Century Literature* (McKillop Festschrift), ed. Carroll Camden (Chicago, 1963), pp. 25–37. I find myself in sympathy with (what I take to be) Professor Ehrenpreis's aims in this witty and healthy Occamite corrective to critical misuse of a term that can relieve the author of all responsibility for what he posits. But he seems to me to err in identifying the use of the term with a rhetorical approach to literature: it is no part of classical, Renaissance, or Augustan rhetoric, however it may be used in contemporary rhetoric.

know him only by reputation: 'I question not but thou hast been told, among other Stories of me, that thou wast to travel with a very scurrilous Fellow: But whoever told thee so did me an Injury' (xviii. i).[1] Clearly, he intended the contemporary reader to identify the narrator of *Tom Jones* with the Henry Fielding who had been a successful comic dramatist, a political pamphleteer, a well-known wit, and (at the last) an important magistrate.

Hence, I do not argue that Fielding, as narrator, represents some 'detached expression of his creative sensibility', to use Prof. Ehrenpreis's phrase; he is Henry Fielding all right. But it remains true (though in what precise sense is a puzzle for philosophers) that the mode of being of a person in real life and that of a character in fiction are felt as different.[2] And if we are to argue that the person, Fielding, is a 'character', we plunge ourselves into this ontological puzzle.[3] If 'literature' (words presenting a fictive experience) is necessarily based upon and therefore ultimately continuous with, 'life' (human experience in the world),[4] this puzzle need produce no insuperable practical problems for criticism; for so the historical personage, Fielding, must be construed as in some way continuous with the narrator, Fielding

[1] All citations from *Tom Jones* are from the third edition (1749).

[2] I suppose 'modern' discussion of the question may be said to begin with the symposium 'Imaginary Objects', in the *Proceedings of the Aristotelian Society*, Supplementary Volume xii (1933); but see also the earlier paper by Bertrand Russell, 'On Denoting', *Mind*, xiv (1905), 479–93. For some relevant additional bibliography see Monroe C. Beardsley, *Aesthetics* (N.Y., 1958), pp. 70–3; and also 391 ff., 440 ff.

[3] It seems arguable, even outside fiction, however, that the man who writes his autobiography has made of himself a 'character', if not in the fictional sense, yet in the sense that he has produced a crystallized portrait which differs from the flux of tendencies and traits that is the living being.

[4] I really mean 'prose fiction' here, rather than 'literature'; because it is possible that the Crocean disciple could indeed unearth a lyric poem that is a self-contained aesthetic entity with no reference whatsoever to the actual world or to actual experience. But I should suppose such cases to be rare; and they cannot be taken to pose a norm for literature. We may conceive a 'non-objective' literature analogous to painting or music: but our experience of it is that, at the first evocative *word*, there is an inescapable reference back to human life. On the other hand, I by no means intend to deny that 'A work of art always involves the imaginative transformation of the given' (to seize upon a handy statement, from a thoughtful essay: Dorothy Walsh, 'The Cognitive Content of Art', in *The Problems of Aesthetics*, ed. Eliseo Vivas and Murray Krieger (N.Y., 1962), p. 607).

—even if not so palpably for us as for a reader in 1749. But by virtue of taking on the character of narrator, he has also confined himself to a particular role and function, he has (as it were) bracketed off certain particular aspects of his total actual character that are to be emphasized and that become 'fixed' for all time in the unchanging world of his completed fiction.[1] The *difference* between this kind of 'character' and the purely fictive character is that we may (or so I should argue) legitimately import material from our knowledge about the 'real' Henry Fielding to a discussion of the narrator of *Tom Jones*; in other words, he is not 'fixed' in the sense that Hamlet (or Tom Jones) is fixed: he himself insists upon his tie to the actual world. The *likeness*, however, to a fictive character, lies in the fact that Fielding has encapsulated himself within the confines of a literary structure, has made of himself a part of that total aesthetic construct—and an essential, an indispensable part. Hence what he narrates or argues can be conceived under the aspect of two quite different (but *not* mutually exclusive) modes: as a statement or predication made by the historical Henry Fielding, which is then (subject to reasonable analysis and interpretation) capable of being construed as part of his intellectual biography; but also as a calculated element of a total structure of fictive predications, assertions, and representations.[2] And to hold to either one of these critical modes, to the absolute exclusion of the other, seems to me a falsification of our broadest experience of literature. A work of literature is *both* continuous with life *and* an object of aesthetic concern, not either/or.

Emphasis may, however, legitimately be placed upon one or the other mode of construing a work of literature, without necessarily implying that the mode the analyst is presently working in must be the only 'proper' approach. *My* present intention is merely to consider a minute aspect of the question that I have propounded: I wish to comment very briefly upon some of the Voices that Fielding the narrator-character employs, both to

[1] Though still, of course, subject to interpretation—as the 'fixed' character of Hamlet (there are no additional outside facts bearing on Hamlet's biography that can be brought to bear) is, nevertheless, still very much subject to interpretation.

[2] This is not exactly analogous to the case of the writer who, in creating fiction, makes essential and obvious use of his own experience, like Charlotte Brontë or Ernest Hemingway; but there *is* an analogy in the fact that this 'literal' experience is transformed into a functioning part of a fictive construct.

convey 'force and vivacity' (in Hume's phrase) to his comic fiction, and to convey—and embody—*meaning* through manipulation of language, that is, through style.

It should be clear from this that in viewing Fielding as the 'actual' hero (the mind in which we are interested) in *Tom Jones*, I do not aim at the sense of a 'romantic' expression of individual personality. As Miss Tuve has observed of the Renaissance poet, he 'is in command certainly, but he is master rather than center of his work'.[1] Fielding is the focus of interest, not because he displays for our delectation the intimate operations of a self-absorbed psyche, but rather because he has a unique view of objective reality, and what one is interested in (or, at least, what I find myself interested in) is that reality, as seen through the narrator's eyes, as conceived, vivified, and integrated by his superb command of language. It is *reality* that is central, though an interpreted reality; it is not the personality of the poet.

The reality that Henry Fielding confronted was a complex reality, and to give it its fullest resonance required a complex mode of presentation. Fielding's 'mixed style' (to borrow Professor Lutwack's term)[2] is a compound of many voices; and, essentially, the art of the many-voiced in narrative is the art of *prosopopoeia*, of reproducing or 'counterfeiting' modes of speech. (Technically, 'prosopopoeia', in its broadest sense, would also include 'counterfeiting' modes of action, or indeed, characters and dialogue; but these are not my present concern.) This term,

---

[1] Rosemond Tuve, *Elizabethan and Metaphysical Imagery* (Chicago, 1947), p. 244.

[2] Leonard Lutwack, 'Mixed and Uniform Prose Styles in the Novel', *JAAC* xviii (1960), 350–7. Professor Lutwack argues that the 'mixed style' is the ideal vehicle for the writer who is motivated by the spirit of irony and parody and who finds it impossible to remain committed to a single vision of reality. A mixture of styles has the effect of making the reader pass through a succession of contradictory and ambiguous attitudes; it offers no sure stylistic norm by which the reader may orient himself permanently to the fiction and to the point of view of the author. He is conditioned to expect to change his position of witness as the style changes. Instead of being assimilative, the mixed style method is mimetic, or imitative of the inherent qualities of things and of the diverse attitudes with which reality may be viewed (p. 357).

My disagreement with some of the details of this provocative statement, as they apply to Fielding, will (I trust) emerge in the course of my argument. On the two styles: one thinks again of the Fox and the Hedgehog of Archilochus. Fielding is among the Foxes.

borrowed from Renaissance rhetoric,[1] seems to me useful in its denotation and implications, because inclusive of the idea behind the concept of 'persona' (viz., a feigned speaker), but also as retaining the primary sense that it is the artist *himself* who is speaking, though in a feigned voice suitable to his purposes.[2] Thus Fielding's many-voiced 'prosopopoeia' is that of the 'real' Henry Fielding, and we do not lose touch with him; but we are also aware that, as narrator, he can put on many guises, mimic many voices, to give us the peculiar 'feel' of a situation, to invoke an attitude, to create ironies or incongruities between matter and manner, to convey implicit meaning, or to encompass a multitude of other fictive ends (only a few of which will be treated here).

Fielding inherited one determinant of voice in the tradition of 'decorum' (appropriate levels of style) that provided conventions for creating diversified effect through variations in diction and syntax. He could also draw upon an associated theory of 'genres' for established *tones* appropriate to various moods and modes: poetic elevation (pastoral and epic), moral elevation (sermon and essay), the ironic and satiric (various forms of satire), and so on. Again (a related point), he could parody or burlesque regnant genres or the styles of earlier literary works, assimilating particular experiences to a previous literary assessment of experience, for comic effect, or for the kind of extension that is inherent in relating the particular to the general, the individual to the tradition. Fielding's implicit and explicit use of allusion is, as Reuben Brower has effectively demonstrated for Pope, 'a resource equivalent to symbolic metaphor and elaborate imagery'.[3] He also had at hand (and delighted in) a set of special jargons—medical, legal,

---

[1] 'Prosopopoeia' was used very broadly, in the Renaissance, as a synonym for mimesis, prosopographia, ethopoeia, and dialogismus (see Marvin Herrick, *Comic Theory in the Sixteenth Century* (Urbana, Illinois, 1964), p. 21). Richard Sherry's *Treatise of the Figures of Grammer and Rhetorike* (1555), for instance, listed six kinds of 'prosopopoeia': characterismus, prosopographia, ethopoeia, pathopoeia, sermocinatio, and mimesis (ibid., p. 134).

[2] Swift's Gulliver seems to me a perfect instance of the artistic exploitaation of 'prosopopoeia': he is neither to be identified with Swift nor to be construed as a 'consistent' character (the two basic errors of most 'modern' criticism of *Gulliver's Travels*). He is rather the tool of the author, given whatever voices accord with Swift's purposes—and these obviously are larger than mere narration or an uncommitted 'realism'.

[3] Reuben Arthur Brower, *Alexander Pope: The Poetry of Allusion* (Oxford, 1959), p. viii.

hunting—that could be employed not only as a characterizing agency in dialogue, but also by the narrator himself, to create a technical–mechanical garment for human actions (which Bergson would see as the very definition of the laughable).

And finally (for my purposes, at least), Fielding as narrator often takes on the voice of one of his hypothetical readers, in an individual kind of mimetic 'prosopopoeia' that renders or assesses experience in terms that are not those of his 'normal' voice, but rather of the Institutional Moralist or an Impressionable Young Lady—or in terms that may very well be Fielding's (the Skeptic or the Sentimentalist), but that are only an aspect of the whole man, though given an independent voice. This seems to me in some regards the most interesting of these varied possibilities of voice and I shall spend more time upon it than upon the others.

I

We may begin with the most elemental of the stylistic devices by which Fielding could 'signal' the reader to recognize some departure from his norm, and therefore to make a delicate shift in expectations, 'set', mode of apprehension and of judgement. (Fielding was by no means merely joking when he admonished his reader, 'thou art highly mistaken if thou dost imagine that we intended, when we begun this great Work, to leave thy Sagacity nothing to do' (XI. ix).) This basic device is the principle of 'decorum', or fit levels of style, that gave to the artists born under its fortunate aspect so great a variety of modes of expressive communication and made possible the subtleties of playing off 'manner' against 'matter' to create complex meanings not readily accessible to a single-levelled style.[1] And, as always, the comic writer had open to him the additional complexities of a calculated indecorum, incongruity, or illogic.[2]

---

[1] Cf. Rosemond Tuve: 'We read poetry on the understanding that a poet will not "use one order of speech for all persons"—e.g., for those different persons: himself as sardonic commentator, himself as serious reasoner, himself as ardent lover' (*Elizabethan and Metaphysical Imagery*, p. 210).

[2] On this important matter see my *Essays on Fielding's Miscellanies* (Princeton, 1961), pp. 272–91. I have also there dealt with Fielding's 'basic' style, in terms somewhat more technical than in the present essay (e.g., pp. 143–64).

By Fielding's time, it is true, the whole tradition of literary 'decorum' was becoming somewhat academic, old-fashioned, like the hierarchical conceptions that it mirrored; and it is one of the measures of his separation from his own age, his attachment to an earlier day, that he should have held so tenaciously to the tradition. If the very language and syntax ('nervous and masculine' Mason would have called them)[1] that he chose for his 'basic' style were consciously archaic, or at least, old-fashioned, so too were the scrupulously observed levels of that style. Fielding's practice displays a fourth level, supplementing the familiar classical Renaissance triad of the plain, the grand, and the middle styles (whose respective purposes were, as Quintilian has it, '*docendi, movendi, delectandi officium*', to instruct, to move, to please)[2] —namely, an 'elegant' version of the middle style, less highly figured than the grand (or sublime) but more consciously balanced and ordered than the ordinary middle: this 'elegant' middle is the style of the introductory essays of *Tom Jones*. There were, as well, variants of each of these levels—for example, as we shall see, there is more than one 'sublime'.

The significance of these distinctions for Fielding's comic romance is that the narrator has at his call voices appropriate to all the demands of a fictive world. There is the plain style for crisp direct narration: 'Our Company were now arrived within a Mile of *Highgate*, when the Stranger turned short upon *Jones*, and pulling out a Pistol, demanded that little Bank Note which *Partridge* had mentioned' (xII. xiv). For more involved narration and low-key commentary the middle style is appropriate: 'Logicians sometimes prove too much by an Argument, and Politicians often over-reach themselves in a Scheme. Thus had it like to have happened to Mrs. *Honour*, who instead of recovering the rest of her Clothes, had like to have stopped even those she had on her Back from escaping: For the Squire no sooner heard of her having abused his Sister than he swore twenty Oaths he would send her to *Bridewell*' (vII. ix). The 'elegant' middle style served for significant commentary inviting a tone of moral elevation, such as one finds in most of the introductory essays and in Fielding's interpolated commentary (of which I shall speak again

---

[1] Cf. John Mason, *An Essay on the Power and Harmony of Prosaic Numbers* (1749), pp. 58–9, commenting on Sir William Temple.

[2] *Institutio Oratoria*, xii. 10. 59.

under the next heading). And finally, the grand or sublime style offered a celebratory mode that by its inherent nature identified an occasion as a Special Occasion. Each of these levels of style could, moreover, be parodied or inverted or undercut to produce a meaningful comic assessment of their inherent stylistic claims for the subject; and much might be said about the infinite variety of choices and manipulations that this fourfold (or eightfold) schema provides, in its permutations and combinations. But, studious of brevity, I move on.

II

When Fielding reaches the point where he is to introduce his heroine (IV. ii), he faces a special case of the general matter of tone in a comic romance. It is patent that his heroine must be conceived as charming and desirable, that we must be invited to see her as surrounded by a consequential aura; but, in the frame of comedy, she must also be flesh-and-blood, a woman not too good for human nature's daily repast. She is to be a partner in the dance of young love: and we are to see this delightful phenomenon precisely in the light in which one of Fielding's obvious masters in the mode saw it in his own romance-comedies, as eternally delicious and eternally funny (though the latter—in Shakespeare, in Fielding, or in fact—only to the amused and tolerant onlooker, scarcely to the principals). In part, Fielding achieves the required double vision through Shakespeare's basic device of incongruous contrast, the transposition of the same theme to another key (Longaville's sighing sonnet followed by Biron's: 'This is the liver-vein, which makes flesh a deity, | A green goose a goddess; pure, pure idolatry . . .').[1] Thus Fielding's 'sublime' overture, introducing his heroine, is directly followed by a detailed description that begins flatly: '*Sophia* then, the only Daughter of Mr. *western*, was a middle-sized Woman; but rather inclining to tall' (IV. ii). The description, it is true, proceeds with just fervour to catalogue the beauties of her 'outside' ('the blazon of sweet beauty's best, | Of hand, of foot, of lip, of eye, of brow')[2] and of her mind; but we have nevertheless been brought down to earth.

There is a more subtle principle at work, however; for, the

---

[1] *Love's Labour's Lost*, IV. iii. 74-5.   [2] Shakespeare, Sonnet 106.

'short Hint of what we can do in the Sublime' is, itself, a qualified sublime, in two senses.[1] First, it employs not the truly grand style of the epic sublime, but rather the elevation of the Virgilian eclogue and the amiable blandishment of the Ovidian sublime, of the light and caressing elegy (*blanditias elegosque levis*),[2] which, though quite appropriate to the subject (of course) is somewhat less than lofty—its figures and exclamations had (with Virgil's) for generations been found proper to the pastoral mode and the celebration of pastoral love. A qualified sublime, nevertheless; and, secondly, there is a gentle mockery of the elevation in such interpolations as : 'the Charms of which call forth the lovely *Flora* . . . when on the first of *June*, her Birth-day . . .', or (perhaps) the somewhat incongruous juxtaposition of 'feather'd Choristers' with solid Handel.

For all this, however (and to ignore the qualifications is to be inexcusably reductive), we are clearly in the presence of panegyric, that most ancient of traditions;[3] and, besides the explicit allusions in the descriptive section (calling upon Suckling, Donne, and Horace), Fielding's language in the whole passage evokes reminiscences of earlier celebrations of loveliness in Shakespeare, in Spenser's *Epithalamion*, in Sidney's *Arcadia*, and even in *Paradise Lost* (not to mention the peerless Dulcinea del Toboso).[4] Hints and echoes only; but Fielding is summoning up a traditional language, that is still evocative for the literate, to bathe his heroine in the reflected light of several centuries of inspired praise for beauty. The *style*, in all its complexity, makes the point : Sophia is merely a human being; but, seen through the eyes of love, she is, like all such fortunate creatures, a very paragon. This is truth :

[1] Fielding's comic temperament was not really comfortable with the self-convinced sublime. Cf. his remark in the Preface to *The Tragedy of Tragedies* (1731) : 'What can be so proper for Tragedy as a Set of big sounding Words, so contrived together, as to convey no Meaning; which I shall one Day or other prove to be the Sublime of Longinus' (ed. J. T. Hillhouse, 1918, p. 84).

[2] Ovid, *Amores*, ii. i. 21.

[3] The particular convention associated with the introduction of one's heroine is illustrated in Lord Lansdowne's 'The Progress of Beauty', when he comes to celebrate Mary of Esté : 'And now, my Muse, a nobler Flight prepare, | And sing so loud that Heaven and Earth may hear . . .' (*Genuine Works*, 1736, i. 58).

[4] See Sidney's celebration of Urania (*Arcadia*, i. i) and of Philoclea (i. xiii); Milton's description of Eve, viii. 510 ff., and cf. also v. 1–25.

but it is through the subtle modulations of style that it is *felt* as truth.

If this is the voice of 'poetic elevation', the other voice, of 'moral elevation' (perhaps an unhappy term for today's readers, who may prefer to substitute the word that we reverence: 'seriousness'), is the voice of the essayist and the theologian who surround their fictive *exempla* with a meaningful world of interpretation. Both poetic and moral elevation obviously function to dignify a 'low' form—prose fiction, as well as comedy—, but this is a merely utilitarian consideration.[1] Within the terms of the narrative itself, the voice of moral seriousness—like other voices —invites a different order of attention, it has a different 'requiredness', as the Gestaltists would say. This is not only *signalled* by the style (the elegant middle), it is verified by the style: for the balance and antithesis of syntactic schemata and the increased incidence of figure and allusion carry their own testimony to the exalted world of order upon which the moral seriousness depends, and from which alone it acquires its compelling character. It is this order of moral truth that provides both a context and a measure of significance for the characters' actions and attitudes. In Fielding's fictive world the comedy (at the level of language and at the level of action) has always an implicit double reference: not only are language and action joyfully humorous in themselves, as a mirror of the incongruities and paradoxes of the human scene, but there is a profoundly serious comedy in the confrontation of this contingent order with a universal moral order that transcends it. The contingent is exhibited in all its delightful fullness and variety (and Fielding's many voices give us an equal variety of attitudes toward it); but the narrator's presence also makes us conscious of a pervading realm of value that is both above, and inclusive of, the merely human and the merely social. The laughter that arises from the disjunctions between these two equally (though differently) valid realms of value—the human and the suprahuman, the profane and the sacred—is thoughtful laughter,

[1] Every artist doubtless faces local and cultural problems of one sort or another; but the genuine necessity that Fielding confronted, of dignifying both a 'low' genre (comedy) and a 'low' medium (prose fiction), is sometimes forgotten. He had, of course, no way of knowing that what Renaissance and eighteenth-century aesthetics called 'low' (in style, genre, and medium) would become the one standard voice of succeeding centuries (any more than Milton could know that his would be the last effective heroic poem in English).

wise and humane, for it encompasses a full sense both of man's uniqueness and of man's fundamental incompleteness. Only man —that animal with free choice—can generate such hilarious complications from elementary drives; and only man can perceive the comedy (and tragedy) of the chasm between what he is and what he might be. Fielding's comedy, in its detailed texture (laughing comedy), issues from the failures of intersection between the two worlds; but in its larger structure (the comic vision), from an ultimate sense of completion in the ardent image of the two worlds harmonized.

An example of sober dignity: Fielding says

Mr. *Jones* had Somewhat about him, which, though I think Writers are not thoroughly agreed in its Name, doth certainly inhabit some human Breasts; whose Use is not so properly to distinguish Right from Wrong, as to prompt and incite them to the former, and to restrain and with-hold them from the latter.

. . . To give a higher Idea of the Principle I mean, as well as one more familiar to the present Age; it may be considered as sitting on its Throne in the Mind, like the LORD HIGH CHANCELLOR of this Kingdom in his Court; where it presides, governs, directs judges, acquits and condemns according to Merit and Justice, with a Knowledge which nothing escapes, a Penetration which nothing can deceive, and an Integrity which nothing can corrupt (IV. vi).

This is the voice of moral elevation: its stylistic qualities underscore and support the explicit observations. Implicitly, the style presents us with the assured logic of experience and tradition: it validates, in its own balance, sequences, and repetitive emphasis, the message of moral order that is its overt content. More locally, Fielding's figure of the Conscience as Lord Chancellor places that 'faculty' in an hierarchical metaphor which is a monad of the larger hierarchical order that he conceives the world to exhibit— and which his comic world ultimately reflects.

Fielding can modulate freely from moral seriousness to (equally *serious*) humour, without engendering a sense of strain, because he has a soundly established base of easy dignity as the norm of discourse. Though susceptible of many modulations (and brief excursions, as on Squire Western: 'He was indeed, according to the vulgar Phrase, whistled drunk' (XII. ii)), this norm provides a permanent focus of expectation, like the analogous iambic beat of blank verse; and the many individual voices or tones that it is

capable of assuming may modify, but do not destroy, the underlying and durable stability of the norm. Just so, in the total world
of Fielding's comic romance, of which his style is mirror, the
ambivalencies and incongruities of the contingent world of man
and society may obscure but cannot destroy the perpetual certainty of the ordered world of Providence.[1]

III

The literary tradition offered Fielding a variety of expressive
possibilities that could be brought under the control of the
narrator's voice, yet continue to carry their traditional aura. His
use of parody and allusion ranges from such large-scale effects as
the '*Battle sung by the Muse in the* Homerican *Stile*' (IV. viii) to such
(apparently) off-hand citations as Horace on barbers (II. iv) or the
moroseness of Aristotle's view of women (II. vii). Few indeed of
the several hundred explicit and implicit echoes of earlier writers,
classical and English, fail to have precise function in their context—but that is matter for another day; I shall confine myself to
a pair of instances involving 'voice'.

The voice of the Homeric muse, which regales us with its epic
account of Molly Seagrim's stand in the churchyard against her
envious attackers, is the voice of an immemorial bard celebrating
immemorial events. And, although it is quite true that the contrast between authorial manner and the 'low' matter with which
he has to deal generates the mock-heroic, it is also true that the
familiar resonances of the heroic voice *elevate* the contest and
lift it from merely another country-churchyard brawl to *The*
Country-Churchyard Brawl, an eminence it yet holds. For, of
course, the notable paradox of the mock-heroic voice (in Cervantes, in Pope, in Fielding, in Joyce) is that at the same time that
it diminishes its matter by increasing the disjunction between
subject and style, it also strangely aggrandizes its matter, because
the style itself carries the implicit meaning: 'Hark, this is *important*.'[2] Thus the mean encounter of a motley band of bumpkins

---

[1] Cf. the concluding section of my essay, 'Some Functions of Rhetoric in
Tom Jones', *PQ* xlv (1966), 209–35; and see, in this volume, the very full
treatment by Martin C. Battestin.

[2] Cf. Herrick, *Comic Theory in the Sixteenth Century*, pp. 190 ff. (on 'Ampli-
ficatio') and pp. 205–6 (on 'Meiosis').

becomes assimilated to the heroic battles on the plains of Troy or the fields of Latium: it is removed from the realm of the merely 'real' (the only existence that a reportorial style could give it) to the realm of timeless conflicts celebrated by ageless bards. It enters the world, not of the 'mythical', but of the legendary; and a virulent local conflict is rendered not as just *this* conflict but as an emblem and type of the rural brawl from the beginning of time.

But perhaps the most remarkable of Fielding's epic echoes[1] is that simile, the 'period of a mile', which occurs when Jones and Molly Seagrim have been '(to use the Language of Sportsmen) *found sitting*' by Thwackum and Blifil:

> As in the Season of RUTTING (an uncouth Phrase, by which the Vulgar denote that gentle Dalliance, which in the well-wooded Forest of *Hampshire*, passes between Lovers of the Ferine Kind) if while the lofty crested Stag meditates the amorous Sport, a Couple of Puppies, or any other Beasts of hostile Note, should wander so near the Temple of *Venus Ferina*, that the fair Hind should shrink from the Place, touched with that Somewhat, either of Fear or Frolic, of Nicety or Skittishness, with which Nature hath bedecked all Females, or hath, at least, instructed them how themselves to put on; lest, through the Indelicacy of Males, the *Samean* Mysteries should be pryed into by unhallowed Eyes: For at the Celebration of these Rites, the female Priestess cries out with her in *Virgil*, (who was then, probably, hard at Work on such Celebration). . . . If, I say, while these sacred Rites, which are in common to *Genus omne Animantium*, are in Agitation between the Stag and his Mistress, any hostile Beasts should venture too near, on the first Hint given by the frightened Hind, fierce and tremendous rushes forth the Stag to the Entrance of the Thicket; there stands he Centinel over his Love, stamps the Ground with his Foot, and with his Horns brandished aloft in Air, proudly provokes the apprehended Foe to Combat (v. xi).

This single period (though technically perhaps two 'sentences') is an amazing *tour de force*, syntactically and contextually. But, however analyzed, its significance as implicit commentary upon Jones's and Molly's 'retirement' remains the same. The syntactic qualifications (and qualifications of qualifications) are matched at the level of style by the contrast of elevated diction with abrupt

---

[1] Or, more properly, georgic echoes, considering the topic (see Virgil's *Third Georgic*). Fielding's task, indeed, would have been seen as analogous to Virgil's: '*et angustis hunc addere rebus honorem*' (iii. 290), to raise his low matter to a high estate.

plunges into vulgar phrase, and, at the level of explicit statement, by the lofty celebration of the rites of 'Venus Ferina' and the sceptical afterthoughts parenthetically inserted. And, contextually, we are not allowed to forget that this noble simile of rutting animals (to maintain Fielding's paradox) is introduced as an *interpretation* of the surface situation: Jones's drunken retirement into the grove with Molly, full on the heels of his elevated (pastoral) declaration of undying love for Sophia. 'Some of my Readers may be inclined to think this Event unnatural. However, the Fact is true . . .' (v. x).

Fielding is writing a 'true history' of human nature as it is. And deplorable though the fact may be, man partakes of the order of nature and will sometimes find that his highest (and most sincerely adored) ideals prove unbraced in the confrontation with his animal needs. So with Jones. But neither the voice of the Moralist nor the voice of the Forgiving Father ('To say the Truth, in a Court of Justice, Drunkenness must not be an Excuse, yet in a Court of Conscience it is greatly so' (v. x)) would totally serve Fielding here; and all the ambivalencies involved in pronouncing judgement upon a drunken young man who has behaved like a natural animal—without totally destroying sympathy for him or reducing him to the level of the *merely* animal—all these ambivalencies and oscillations of moral attitude are conveyed in the syntactic involutions, the struggle of diction, the skirmish between celebration of the natural and reduction to the merely natural, that Fielding's dynamic 'period of a mile' sustains.

IV

Quite as much as Molière, Henry Fielding loved the pompous and exotic ring of professional jargon: the medical man's 'the Aliment will not be concreted, nor assimilated into Chyle, and so will corrode the vascular Orifices, and thus will aggravate the febrific Symptoms' (viii. iii); the lawyer's Coke upon Lyttelton; the hunter's: 'Soho! Puss is not far off. Here's her Form, upon my Soul; I believe I may cry *stole away*' (v. xii).

The value of such jargons as a characterizing device is almost secondary, one can feel, to the pleasure the author experienced in their sheer rolling volume of sound. I am not, however, to speak of dialogue here, but only of the narrator's own use of the voices of jargon: for just as Partridge puts on one style as appropriate to his role of Barber and another for his role of Surgeon, so Fielding the narrator finds it decorous to assume, for particular events, the jargon-voice appropriate to the context.

An allusion to Bridget's wedding calls forth the formulaic voice of the newspaper-announcement: 'the Celebration of the Nuptials between Captain *Blifil* and Miss *Bridget Allworthy*, a young Lady of great Beauty, Merit, and Fortune . . .' (II. ii).[1] A reference to Black George's poaching assumes the stately jargon of the law: 'This Hare he had basely and barbarously knocked on the Head, against the Laws of the Land'—and, Fielding adds, 'no less against the Laws of Sportsmen' (III. x). To convey in a phrase the sense of Squire Western and his sister as mighty opposites combined in a formidable union against the peace of poor Sophia, Fielding does not disdain to purloin some jargon from Mrs. Western herself: 'Here then a League was struck (to borrow a Phrase from the Lady) between the contending Parties . . .' (XV. vi). Or the maxims of publicans are cited (VIII. vii), not only to disclose to us 'the grand Mysteries of their Trade', but to provide a 'professional' context for the oncoming events at Upton. The interrelationship of soldiers on the march and the inns at which they are quartered—a reiterated and significant collocation in itself, for Fielding's plot—is summed up in a military phrase, when Fielding describes the Landlady's fears at a disturbance in the night: 'the Apprehensions of the latter were much greater, lest her Spoons and Tankards should be upon the March, without having received any such Orders from her' (VII. xiv).

In each of these instances Fielding not only conveys an attitude toward his materials by assuming the jargon-voice of a particular profession or activity (there is a notable discrepancy between Black George's action of knocking a hare on the head and the monumental language of the law that judges that transgression);

---

[1] Besides giving a deadly cast of mere formality to the topic, the placement of this wedding announcement is subtle: in context, it holds off the collocation of 'EIGHT Months after' and 'delivered of a fine Boy'; but it also emphasizes the nuptials, lingers over that event, and then follows it without pause by: 'was Miss *Bridget*, by Reason of a Fright, delivered of a fine Boy'. (These remarks by no means exhaust the compressed beauties of this bland pronouncement. It will be noticed that the conventions of eighteenth-century typography conspire with Fielding here by placing 'eight' in bold capitals.)

he also creates a comic dimension in which human behaviour is caricatured by being frozen in the mechanical postures of a specialized language that reduces the infinite variability and vitality of the human scene to the conventions of its own narrow taxonomy of experience.

Fielding also exploits the possibilities of technical idiom in the multitude of occasional metaphors or 'allegories' that give colour and dilated significance to the activities and events of his comic romance. This is not strictly a matter of 'voice' (as I conceive it), however, and I shall mention only one brief instance. When he comments upon Lady Bellaston's feeling for Jones, it is in these terms: 'She was indeed well convinced that *Sophia* possessed the first Place in *Jones*'s Affections; and yet, haughty and amorous as this Lady was, she submitted at last to bear the second Place; or to express it more properly in a legal Phrase, was contented with the Possession of that of which another Woman had the Reversion' (xiv. ii). Not only does the legal analogy give precision to the description: nothing could better have insinuated the wholly practical and instrumental nature of Jones's role as the town-lady's inamorato—the ignoble role of (in the expressive phrase of a sensitive and precise critic) 'an ambulatory dildo'.[1]

V

The narrator's 'basic' middle-style voice is, of course, the norm. Fielding is telling the story and we feel quite sure that we can depend upon him: he establishes very early both the nature of his knowledge and power and its limitations, in a 'true history' raised to the level of an art-form. The central fact of his narrative, however, is that it is *heard* (as opposed to 'overheard', the reigning assumption of middle-class lyric poetry and the 'realistic' novel) —it addresses itself to an audience. Hence Fielding's awareness of the hypothetical 'reader' is at the centre of his awareness of literary technique.

That 'reader', however, may take many shapes: he is multiform; and this, too, is a fact that Fielding the narrator must take into

---

[1] Robert Alter, 'Fielding and the Uses of Style', p. 54 (in reference to Square's function *vis-à-vis* Molly Seagrim).

account. The reaction to any given event, however shaped and directed by the narrator, will still depend upon the qualities peculiar to any given reader (in addition to the assumed fundamental humanness that links all readers—*and* the narrator—together, and that makes any literature of general reference possible). It is this idiosyncratic response of the individual reader that Fielding frequently appeals to, in assuming (for the moment) the voice and point-of-view of such a hypothetical personage to provide a different perspective on 'reality' from that offered by his normal voice.

Thus when Fielding brings his young hero on the stage, the point of view taken is that of the Institutional Moralist. The mimesis is not total: that is to say we are perfectly aware that it is still Fielding's voice we hear; but he has assumed the tone and demeanour of one who looks sadly upon the imperfect world of man and sadly shakes his head (what we may call the 'tch-tch syndrome'): 'it was the universal Opinion of all Mr. *Allworthy's* Family, that he was certainly born to be hanged'.

Indeed, I am sorry to say, there was too much Reason for this Conjecture. The Lad having, from his earliest Years, discovered a Propensity to many Vices, and especially to one, which hath as direct a Tendency as any other to that Fate, which we have just now observed to have been prophetically denounced against him. He had been already convicted of three Robberies, *viz.* of robbing an Orchard, of stealing a Duck out of a Farmer's Yard, and of picking Master *Blifil's* Pocket of a Ball (III. ii).

Of course, the triviality of the offences makes implicit appeal to that general root-humanity which Fielding must assume for his style to work at all: in a world where such offences could genuinely be given profound weight, there would be no quarrel between the matter and the manner, and no ironic qualification of the institutional moralist's head-shaking. The major premiss of *Tom Jones*, in so far as its subject is Youth, is precisely the assumption common to a significant body of comic literature (and not to it alone) that Youth is to be forgiven much in its 'testing out' of the official values of its culture,[1] and that high spirits are not necessarily to be equated with moral turpitude. The type of mind that I have designated as that of the 'institutional moralist' has always

---

[1] Hence the numerous images of court-room, the trial, the judgement, associated with Jones throughout the tale.

existed and made its stern judgement upon this lax state of affairs; and Fielding gives this fact full cognizance.[1] But there has always existed, too, the opposing voice, the appeal (variously phrased) to life, vitality, the blood, whatever, as against the claims of social order and propriety. The central theme of New Comedy, this conflict of the Sons against the Fathers (as it has been metaphorically expressed), has remained at the heart of comedy in the Western tradition, and it is, of course, at the heart of Fielding's comic romance. What he has done, in the introduction of his hero, is to establish through the very style of that introduction the opposed worlds of values that will obtain throughout the narrative. And the ambivalent position of Henry Fielding in this conflict is equally well conveyed; for if he is not quite the institutional moralist (as we soon understand without equivocation when we see the 'bad' young man 'contented to be flead rather than betray his Friend, or break the Promise he had made' (III. ii)—an implicit appeal to a more comprehensive moral judgement), neither is he *merely* a romantic celebrant of Youth as its own sufficient excuse. Fielding's attitude is more complex than that; and the complexity is inherent in the stylistic voice that introduces his young hero to us.

In a somewhat less solemn vein, we may note that Fielding takes cognizance also of that notable and novel phenomenon of his time: the Female Reader. He will sometimes address himself directly to this fair audience, as when he points the 'moral' of Sophia's missing Tom because of unlucky minutes spent in choosing a proper ribbon—'A most unfortunate Accident, from which my fair Readers will not fail to draw a very wholesome Lesson. And here I strictly forbid all Male Critics to intermeddle with a Circumstance, which I have recounted only for the Sake of the Ladies, and upon which they only are at Liberty to comment' (VI. vi). But more than this, he will also enter mimetically into the voice and point-of-view of one or another of his (presumed) female audience; as, for example, the polite Town-Lady:

[1] Not sufficiently, however, for the Institutional Moralist himself, in the person of Sir John Hawkins, who declared that *Tom Jones* was 'a book seemingly intended to sap the foundation of that morality which it is the duty of parents and all public instructors to inculcate in the minds of young people, by teaching that virtue upon principle is imposture, that generous qualities alone constitute true worth, and that a young man may love and be loved, and at the same time associate with the loosest women' (*The Life of Samuel Johnson, LL.D.*, 1787, pp. 214-15).

'She was of that Species of Women, whom you rather commend for good Qualities than Beauty, and who are generally called by their own Sex, very good Sort of Women—as good a Sort of Woman, Madam, as you would wish to know' (i. ii); or (casually): 'the next Morning, before the Sun, she huddled on her Cloaths, and at a very unfashionable, unseasonable, unvisitable Hour went to Lady *Bellaston*' (xiii. iii). Or the voice of the Prude: 'Indeed she was so far from regretting Want of Beauty, that she never mention'd that Perfection (if it can be called one) without Contempt' (i. ii), where the parenthesis supports the Bridget Allworthys against fairer neighbours—as does the sober narrative report: 'Mrs. *Deborah* approved all these Sentiments, and the Dialogue concluded with a general bitter Invective against Beauty, and with many compassionate Considerations for all honest, plain Girls, who are deluded by the wicked Arts of deceitful Men' (i. viii).[1] If it were not ungallant, one might call another instance of the female voice 'moral nit-picking'; as when Fielding comments upon Mrs. Fitzpatrick's refusal to accept a bed in the Irish peer's mansion:

> Some Readers will perhaps condemn this extraordinary Delicacy, as I may call it, of Virtue, as too nice and scrupulous; but we must make Allowances for her Situation, which must be owned to have been very ticklish; and when we consider the Malice of censorious Tongues, we must allow, if it was a Fault, the Fault was an Excess on the right Side, and which every Woman who is in the self-same Situation will do well to imitate [and so forth] (xi. x).

More amiable is the voice which the narrator assumes to describe (and embody) for us Sophia's reflections upon Jones's 'symptoms' of love:

> Thus his Backwardness, his Shunning her, his Coldness and his Silence, were the forwardest, the most diligent, the warmest, and most eloquent Advocates; and wrought so violently on her sensible and tender Heart, that she soon felt for him all those gentle Sensations which are consistent with a virtuous and elevated female Mind— In short, all which Esteem, Gratitude and Pity, can inspire in such, towards an agreeable Man—Indeed, all which the nicest Delicacy

---

[1] In another context, Bridget is supported, rather, by the voice of the mature woman of the world, in her 'reasonable Passion' for Captain Blifil: 'Nor did she go pining and moping about the House, like a puny foolish Girl, ignorant of her Distemper . . .' (i. xi).

can allow—In a word,—she was in Love with him to Distraction (v. vi).

If these mimetic voices are clearly distinguishable from the narrator's 'normal' voice—and achieve their effect from this very fact—there are some other cases that are rather more problematic. Of these we may consider two: the Skeptic and the Sentimentalist. They present something of a crux for my 'theory' of prosopo-poeia; and my argument would essentially be this: that, unlike the voice of the Young Lady, or the Prude, or the Institutional Moralist, in which an implicit distinction exists between the narrator and the voice that he ventriloquizes, we have in the Skeptic and the Sentimentalist an aspect of the Narrator (of Henry Fielding) himself—but *only*, it should be added, an aspect.

The range of tones and points-of-view that Fielding employs to narrate his comic romance may be thought of as constituting a continuum, one pole of which would represent the historical Henry Fielding, the narrator, and the opposite pole that kind of Reader (say, the Prude) who may be thought of as occupying a position at the greatest distance of mind from Fielding. Other readers (and other voices) would approach more or less nearly to the 'normal' Fielding; and, as I have argued, much of the complexity and the pleasure of *Tom Jones* arises from the felt distinction between the narrator's point of view and the point of view implicit in the style of one or another mimetic voice. But when we come to such 'voices' as that of the Skeptic and the Sentimentalist, we face a special problem. For both internal evidence (the *style* of sceptical or worldly pronouncements is not notably different from that of other interpolated commentary; and there is no stylistic evidence to suggest that scenes of 'sentiment' are to be inverted and received as ironical) and external evidence (that is, the evidence that we can import from other works in which Fielding displays sceptical or sentimental tendencies) would suggest that Henry Fielding, like most of us, enjoyed moods of sceptical, or even bitter, reflection upon human fallibility, as well as enjoying moods of amiable reflection upon human possibility. These are aspects of the man; and I should agree with Professor Ehrenpreis that to inject some sceptical *persona* or sentimental *persona* into the argument brings small illumination.

Henry Fielding was a man who could say flatly that knaves and fools found better acceptance than the 'good and amiable' as literary characters, because supported by the ill-nature of mankind (viii. i); or that 'the Examples of all Ages shew us that Mankind in general desire Power only to do Harm' (xii. xii); or that 'Friendship makes us warmly espouse the Interest of others; but is very cold to the Gratification of their Passions' (v. iii). Although (he says) we learn by rote to despise outside, and to value more solid, charms, 'yet I have always observed at the approach of consummate Beauty, that these more solid Charms only shine with that Kind of Lustre which the Stars have after the Rising of the Sun' (xvi. ix). In the same chapter in which he attacks the sect of sceptical philosophers who 'deduced our best Actions from Pride', he himself observes (not the same thing: this is not my point): 'Predominant Vanity is, I am afraid, too much concerned here. This is one Instance of that Adulation which we bestow on our own Minds, and this almost universally. For there is scarce any Man, how much soever he may despise the Character of a Flatterer, but will condescend in the meanest Manner to flatter himself' (vi. i).

These are, by any definition, sceptical observations, reflecting a genuine dubiety about the goodness, trustworthiness, objectivity, etc., of human kind. Fielding is (of course) not a total sceptic, because he never doubts the ultimate *worth* of humankind: but he is far from being a naïve admirer of his species, and the sceptical note is a genuine aspect of Fielding himself (the 'I' of the narration). It is the vein of iron that gives validity to his ultimate optimism; because it provides a context in which that optimism can be seen as fully earned, in confrontation with and in total recognition of the contrary evidence that must press itself upon any intelligent observer. Fielding accepts the fallibility of man, sometimes resignedly, sometimes bitterly, and he gives full voice to the sceptical doubts that the spectacle of man's folly and inanity can engender. But this spectacle does not lead him into doleful whimperings on the hopelessness of the human condition: for him it is *a* reality to be assimilated and transcended, not *the* reality to be acquiesced in and defeated by. But as a part of reality, the doubts of the sceptical voice find a place in the range of voices that interpret for us the world of Tom Jones and the world of man.

The sentimental voice is (alas) no less genuine, as an aspect of Henry Fielding's literary consciousness. It is the voice and the mode most nearly reflecting a local and contemporary phenomenon; and, as is usually the case with such fashions, it has not worn well. An effort of the historical imagination may enable us to recreate intellectually some appreciation of a context in which the exploitation of pathos as a means of linking one's soul sympathetically with other souls (signalled by a mild heightening of style, diluted from the tragic stage, and by a special diction of emotive terms)—a context in which such a mode, along with other aspects of the then new and radical middle-class sensibility, can be understood to have been quite entirely as exciting to the eighteenth century[1] as the new sensibility of 'proletarian' writers undoubtedly is to our own era. But, as this instance would suggest, we do have a new diction, a new set of signals, for emotive response and involvement (that a future age will scornfully dismiss as 'sentimental'), and Fielding's scenes of calculated pathos are no more successful for us than are those of his lesser contemporaries and the long train of successors, when the 'melodious tear' was put into mass production.[2]

Without aiming at anything other than an ostensive definition of 'sentimentality' (I shall *point* at examples), I may perhaps be allowed a speculation or two upon those scenes which are normally labelled 'sentimental' in *Tom Jones*—primarily, the revelation of Nancy's unhappy burden and Jones's argument with Nightingale to convince him that he should marry her (xiv. vi, vii), and the description of Anderson's desperate little family, rescued by Jones's ten guineas (xiii. viii, x). It is noteworthy, first of all, that in both scenes Fielding allows the dialogue of his characters to create the 'pathetic' atmosphere, and that the narrator himself (though he approves their overflowing hearts) does not venture into the diction of pathos. Indeed, having presented us with Jones's extraordinary generosity following upon Mrs. Miller's moving tale, the narrator's contribution is as follows: 'I have in

[1] Lady Bradshaigh wrote to Richardson in 1749: 'Pray, Sir, give me leave to ask you . . . what, in your opinion, is the meaning of the word *sentimental*, so much in vogue amongst the polite, both in town and country. . . . Every thing clever and agreeable is comprehended in that word; but [I] am convinced a wrong interpretation is given, because it is impossible every thing clever and agreeable can be so common as this word' (*The Correspondence of Samuel Richardson*, ed. A. L. Barbauld, 1804, iv. 282–3).

[2] Cf. Ernest Dilworth, *The Unsentimental Journey of Laurence Sterne* (N.Y., 1948), p. 4.

Truth observed, and shall never have a better Opportunity than at present to communicate my Observation, that the World are in general divided into two Opinions concerning Charity . . .'; which clearly marks a return to the unheightened norm of tone. (The two opinions are, I may add, that charity is voluntary and meritorious or that it is a duty; and Fielding concludes: 'To reconcile these different Opinions is not in my Power. I shall only add, that the Givers are generally of the former Sentiment, and the Receivers are almost universally inclined to the latter' (XIII. viii).)

So, too, in commenting upon Nightingale's situation after the violation of poor Nancy, the narrator, although he gives us a benevolent 'sentiment', does not move very far from the even tone of his normal commentary:

> The Good or Evil we confer on others, very often, I believe, recoils on ourselves. For as Men of a benign Disposition enjoy their own Acts of Beneficence, equally with those to whom they are done, so there are scarce any Natures so entirely diabolical, as to be capable of doing Injuries, without paying themselves some Pangs, for the Ruin which they bring on their fellow Creatures (XIV. vii).

This may be contrasted with Jones's deliberate rhetoric of pathos: 'And do not the warm, rapturous Sensations, which we feel from the Consciousness of an honest, noble, generous, benevolent Action, convey more Delight to the Mind, than the undeserved Praise of Millions?' (XIV. vii). The clear difference in tone marks the degree of relative detachment that Fielding the narrator maintains in these scenes in which his actors are so deeply involved.

I am not trying to take Fielding off the hook. He is responsible for the actions and speeches of his characters, and those actions and speeches are, by present definition, 'sentimental'. Indeed, that they have a palpable intent upon our emotions is signalized by the importation of the Little Child, who had already become a standard signal of the presence of pathos: thus, poor Nancy must have a little sister, Betsy, who will say: 'I was always afraid to die; because I must have left my Mamma, and my Sister; but I am not afraid of going any where with those I love' (XIV. vi). It is perhaps a narrowing of emotional range that leads us no longer to be moved by such speeches; the generations that could respond to the Pathetic Child have presumably been succeeded by those who are more given to feel (in a sentiment attributed, I believe, to Oscar Wilde) that the Man has *no heart* who can read the death of Little Nell, without laughing.

But my present point is simply that although Fielding indeed exploits dramatic pathos in *Tom Jones*, there is no narrative *voice* of sentimentalism, as there is a voice of scepticism. The narrator himself very seldom slips into the fashionable diction and rhetoric of Sensibility. I do not wish (not at this point, anyway) to edge over into extended sociological commentary; but it does seem to me evident that Fielding employs the dramatic heightening of pathos precisely at those points where he could feel that public sentiment was in something of a state of flux and required the reinforcement of a heightened rhetoric. That a man should feel responsibility for a violated girl when that girl came of humble stock was something rather new: an aristocratic ethos had seen such girls as fair game (after all, no blood-line was involved). Clearly, then, the individual worth of the humble girl had to be validated on a different kind of ground; and, for several generations, it was to be validated primarily by an appeal to emotion.

The other instance, the poor family of the amateur highwayman, Anderson, offers more patent evidence of an ambivalence in Fielding's attitude, once again signalized by his turning to an emotional validation, where explicit appeal to publicly shared moral evaluations would have been chancy. When Jones permits the highwayman to escape, the narrator observes: 'Our Readers will probably be divided in their Opinions concerning this Action; some may applaud it perhaps as an Act of extraordinary Humanity, while those of a more saturnine Temper will consider it as a Want of Regard to that Justice which every Man owes his Country. *Partridge* certainly saw it in that Light . . .' (xII. xiv). In the 'good' world of *Tom Jones*, Partridge is wrong;[1] and, after we have later been exposed to the overflowing heart of a regenerate Anderson ('My little Boy is recovered; my Wife is out of Danger, and I am happy'), the narrator tells us that Jones

proceeded to Lady *Bellaston*'s, greatly exulting in the Happiness which he had procured to this poor Family; nor could he forbear reflecting without Horror on the dreadful Consequences which must have

[1] As, indeed, is Allworthy: ' "Child", cries *Allworthy*, "you carry this forgiving Temper too far. Such mistaken Mercy is not only Weakness, but borders on Injustice, and is very pernicious to Society, as it encourages Vice" ' (xvIII. xi; cf. also III. vi).

attended them, had he listened rather to the Voice of strict Justice, than to that of Mercy when he was attacked on the high Road (XIII. x).

But in 1751, speaking as a magistrate, Fielding would take precisely the opposite view:

the principal Duty which every Man owes, is to his Country, for the Safety and Good of which all Laws are established; and therefore his Country requires of him to contribute all that in him lies to the due Execution of those Laws. Robbery is an Offence not only against the Party robbed, but against the Public, who are therefore entitled to Prosecution; and he who prevents or stifles such the Prosecution, is no longer an innocent Man, but guilty of a high Offence against the Public Good.[1]

Clearly, not only Fielding's readers, but Fielding himself proved 'divided' in opinion on this matter; and it is my point that precisely at such junctures the Sentimentalist in Fielding is likely to make an appearance, with a rhetoric of the Heart that signalizes the disquieting need for a kind of moral validation that sober reflection and public standards could not fully supply.

I have perhaps given more space to this element than it requires, for the sentimental does not really bulk large in *Tom Jones* (happy endings, contrary to the opinion of some, are not in themselves sentimental), and I should not wish to give it disproportionate weight. As I have suggested, there is no consistently sentimental voice adopted by the narrator that could be set against the sceptical voice that maintains an attitude of gentle irony toward the characters and events, a multi-valued assessment of experience that is, in fact, the very reverse of sentimentalism, because it invites detachment as well as involvement.

[1] *Enquiry into the Causes of the Late Increase of Robbers* (1751), p. 108.

15

'TOM JONES': THE ARGUMENT OF DESIGN

By MARTIN C. BATTESTIN

FROM a certain point of view—the one I shall take in this essay—
Tom Jones (1749) is at once the last and the consummate literary
achievement of England's Augustan Age: an age whose cast of
mind saw the moral drama of the individual life enacted within
a frame of cosmic and social Order, conceived in the then still
compatible terms of Christian humanism and Newtonian science,
and whose view of art, conditioned by the principles of neo-Aristo-
telian aesthetics, saw the poem as fundamentally mimetic of this
universal Design. For the Augustan writer—for Gay or Pope, let
us say—the poem was a highly finished artefact: a 'product', as
Northrop Frye has put it, rather than a 'process'.[1] The philosophical and aesthetic assumptions of the age are perhaps most
explicitly and memorably expressed in Pope's complementary
poems, the *Essay on Criticism* (1711) and the *Essay on Man* (1733–4),
in which the neo-classical concepts of Nature and of the poetic
imitation of her are set forth in couplets as finely wrought and
balanced as the poet's universe itself. These assumptions, moreover, are the implicit affirmation behind the ironic correspondences
and desperate paradoxes of *The New Dunciad* (1742), in which the
triumph of Dulness is seen as a dark apocalypse, a grotesque
parody of classical and Christian ideals of Order and of Art. As
a rationale for literature, however, these ideals are perhaps
more appropriate to comedy than to Pope's favourite mode of
satire, because the cosmic system they assume and celebrate is
ultimately benign—comic in the profoundest sense. It is a universe
not only full and various, but regular, created by a just and benevolent Deity whose genial Providence governs all contingencies,

[1] See Frye, 'Towards Defining an Age of Sensibility', *ELH* xxiii (1956),
144–52.

comprehends every catastrophe, from the bursting of a world to the fall of a sparrow. This creation, as opposed to the one with which we are familiar, is characterized not only by Energy, but by Order.

The idea is perhaps most succinctly stated in these familiar lines from the best philosophical poem of the age:

> All Nature is but Art, unknown to thee;
> All Chance, Direction, which thou canst not see;
> All Discord, Harmony, not understood;
> All partial Evil, universal Good. . . .[1]

Significantly for our present purposes, for Fielding, as for many of his contemporaries, Pope was '*the inimitable Author of* the Essay on Man', who '*taught me a System of Philosophy in* English *Numbers*'.[2] Although, to be sure, Fielding had other teachers besides Pope—from Plato and Cicero to Locke and the Latitudinarians—there is, as we shall see, an essential agreement between the doctrine of the *Essay on Man* and the meaning of Fielding's masterpiece. As a comic novel—that is, as a fictional imitation of Life, of Nature—*Tom Jones* stands as an elaborate paradigm of those correlative tenets of the Augustan world view: the belief in the *existence of* Order in the great frame of the universe, and in the *necessity for* Order in the private soul. Its special triumph as a work of art is that it does not merely declare these values explicitly in the narrator's commentary and in the dialogue, but embodies them formally in the structure of its periods and its plot, in the function of its narrator, and in the emblematic significance of many of its scenes and principal characters. The meaning of *Tom Jones* is, in other words, inseparable from its form and rhetorical texture: the novel itself is the symbol of its author's universe.

To state this proposition in other, more schematic terms, the meaning of *Tom Jones* turns upon the presentation of two major and complementary themes: these are, I would suggest, the doctrines of Providence with respect to the macrocosm and of Prudence, the analogous rational virtue within the microcosm, man. Together with charity and good-nature, always the essential

---

[1] *An Essay on Man*, i. 289–92.

[2] From Fielding's Preface to his own and William Young's translation of Aristophanes' *Plutus, the God of Riches* (1742), p. x.

and indispensable qualifications of Fielding's moral men, Providence and Prudence define the specific ethos of *Tom Jones*. These concepts are what Fielding particularly intended when he declared in his Dedication to George Lyttelton that he had written his novel with 'the Cause of Religion and Virtue' firmly in mind.[1] One reason why *Tom Jones* is the salient example of literary art in Augustan England is that Art, in a fundamental and philosophic sense, is its subject: thus the Creation and that Providence which presides over it are, according to the language of traditional Christian theology, 'the Art of God'; and Prudence, as Cicero had insisted in a phrase Fielding was to borrow in *Amelia* (i. i), is 'the Art of Life'. For all its generous exuberance and cheerful, bumptious energy, *Tom Jones* is the celebration of the rational values of Art, of the controlling intelligence which creates Order out of Chaos and which alone gives meaning to vitality, making it a source of wonder and of joy.

Although Fielding's twin themes are closely (even etymologically)[2] related and should therefore be treated together, the practicalities of space have obliged me, for the time being, to separate them. Elsewhere I have discussed the meaning of Prudence in the novel;[3] here I wish to consider the correlative doctrine of Providence, the argument of the book's design.

I. THE MEANING OF DESIGN

The relationship between Fielding (or, if we prefer, the narrator or 'implied author', Fielding's 'second self')[4] and his book *Tom Jones* has more than once been likened to God's providential supervision and superintendence of His creation. 'Such a literary *providence*, if we may use such a word,' declared Thackeray in

[1] Quotations from *Tom Jones* are from the fourth edition, 1749 (title-page reads 1750), 4 vols.

[2] For the derivation of *prudentia* from *providentia*, see the *O.E.D.* under 'prudence'. Cf. Joseph Spence in *Polymetis* (1747), p. 138: 'The Romans seem to have called this [prudence] indifferently by the name of Prudentia, or Providentia; the reason of which may be gathered from Cicero's derivation of the word Prudentia.' In a note, Spence quotes from *De Oratore* as follows: 'Sapientis est providere; ex quo sapientia est appellata prudentia.'

[3] See 'Fielding's Definition of Wisdom: Some Functions of Ambiguity and Emblem in *Tom Jones*', *ELH* xxxv (1968), 188–217.

[4] See Wayne C. Booth, *The Rhetoric of Fiction* (Chicago, 1961), pp. 71 ff.

admiration at Fielding's artful conduct of his story, 'is not to be seen in any other work of fiction.'¹ More recent critics have urged the same analogy, Wayne Booth among them, for whom the idea of Providence becomes a way of describing the unique *effect* of Fielding's narrator: not so much the sense we have of his presiding over and manipulating the action of the book (to which Thackeray had reference), but more especially the sense we have of the narrator's 'voice', the expression of an eminently urbane, judicious, and benevolent intelligence, himself the principal 'character' of the novel, who more than any other *within* the world of his book—more even than Allworthy—provides us with a moral 'norm' and centre, conditioning our attitudes toward and judgement of his people, benignly reassuring us about their ultimate fates, even, finally, redeeming 'Tom's world of hypocrites and fools'.² That Fielding's example should have given currency to the term 'omniscient' author is more appropriate, perhaps, than we have thought. What Thackeray and Booth regard as a useful analogy for describing the effect of the narrative in *Tom Jones* is with Fielding himself a deliberate metaphor: the author-narrator of *Tom Jones* stands in relation to the world of his novel as the divine Author and His Providence to the 'Book of Creation'— not like Joyce's artist or his God, 'invisible, refined out of existence, indifferent, paring his fingernails',³ but rather very much interested and involved.

With its genial and omniscient author, its intricate yet symmetrical design, its inevitable comic denouement, *Tom Jones* offers itself as the paradigm in art of cosmic Justice and Order, at once the mirror and embodiment of its author's Christian vision of life. In the opening chapter Fielding declares that he has chosen 'no other than HUMAN NATURE' as his subject—its whole range and variety, from the 'more plain and simple Manner in which it is found in the Country' to all the 'Affectation and Vice which Courts and Cities afford'. To invoke his own figure, he was setting out to purvey the feast of life, or, as he had earlier remarked of Cervantes' achievement in *Don Quixote*, to present

---

¹ Review of Roscoe's edition of Fielding's *Works*, in *The Times*, 2 Sept. 1840; quoted in F. Homes Dudden, *Henry Fielding: His Life, Works, and Times* (Oxford, 1952), ii. 616.

² Booth, p. 217.

³ *A Portrait of the Artist as a Young Man* (New York, 1957), p. 215.

'the History of the World in general'.[1] Several passages in *Tom Jones* encourage this interpretation: that Fielding consciously understood his task as an author to be the creation, by aesthetic and rhetorical means, of a symbolic 'world' which would faithfully represent the nature of that actual world which God created and providentially controls. The narrator himself repeatedly calls attention to the very characteristic of his plot which critics, according to their prejudices, have either lauded or deplored: namely, that intricate concatenation of little trivial events which either bring his characters together or keep them apart and which lead, finally, to the comic resolution of every difficulty. Such, for example, are Sophia's snatching from the fire the muff which Tom had cherished, thereby revealing her love for him (v. iv); or Partridge's failing to see Mrs. Waters at Upton, when he might thus have prevented Tom's apparently incestuous affair (ix. iii–iv). 'Instances of this Kind', the narrator remarks of the latter unlucky situation, 'we may frequently observe in Life, where the greatest Events are produced by a nice Train of little Circumstances; and more than one Example of this may be discovered by the accurate Eye, in this our History' (xviii. ii). Similarly, in commenting upon the episode of the muff, he had earlier compared the mechanism of his plot to the great machine of the universe itself, invoking a favourite metaphor of the rationalist divines :[2] 'The World may indeed be considered as a vast Machine,

---

[1] *Joseph Andrews* (1742), iii. i. Quotations from this novel are from the Wesleyan Edition, ed. Battestin (Oxford, 1967).

[2] The metaphor of the universe as a vast and intricate machine implying the existence of God, the supreme Artificer, was a commonplace in the period. With the passage in *Tom Jones*, for example, compare John Spencer, *A Discourse Concerning Prodigies* (1665), sig. (A): '*to shew how many wheels in some great Engine, move in subordination to the production of some great work, were* [*not*] *to obscure and eclipse the art of the Artificer*'. See also Henry More, *Divine Dialogues* (2nd edn., 1713), Dialogue II, p. 117; John Ray, *The Wisdom of God Manifested in the Works of the Creation* (5th edn., 1709), pp. 32–3; Isaac Barrow, Sermon VI, 'The Being of God Proved from the Frame of the World', *Works* (5th edn., 1741), ii. 75; John Tillotson, Sermon CXXXVII, 'The Wisdom of God in the Creation of the World', *Works* (1757), viii. 138; Samuel Clarke, Sermon I, 'Of Faith in God', *Works* (1738), i. 6, and 'A Discourse Concerning the Unchangeable Obligations of Natural Religion', ibid. ii. 647–8; Richard Kingston, *A Discourse on Divine Providence* (1702), pp. 48–50; and William Sherlock, *A Discourse Concerning the Divine Providence* (9th edn., 1747), pp. 10–11.

in which the great Wheels are originally set in Motion by those which are very minute, and almost imperceptible to any but the strongest Eyes' (v. iv). In passages like these the controlling analogy between the two creations, that of the comic novelist and that of the Deity, is implied throughout the book; but in the introductory chapter to Book X Fielding declares it explicitly, albeit with a decorous apology for the brashness of the comparison. In language echoing such works as Cudworth's *True Intellectual System of the Universe* (1678) and Pope's *Essay on Man*, Fielding applies to his own book a metaphorical compliment which his friend John Upton had reserved for the supreme achievement of Shakespeare:[1]

First, then, we warn thee not too hastily to condemn any of the Incidents in this our History, as impertinent and foreign to our main Design, because thou dost not immediately conceive in what Manner such Incident may conduce to that Design. This Work may, indeed, be considered as a great Creation of our own; and for a little Reptile of a Critic to presume to find Fault with any of its Parts, without knowing the Manner in which the Whole is connected, and before he comes to the final Catastrophe, is a most presumptuous Absurdity. The Allusion and Metaphor we have here made use of, we must acknowledge to be infinitely too great for our Occasion; but there is, indeed, no other, which is at all adequate to express the Difference between an Author of the first Rate, and a Critic of the lowest.

What Fielding has here done—and what he intended throughout *Tom Jones* to be the basic point and symbol of the novel—is to invert the terms of a familiar analogy, as old at least as Plotinus: God is to His creation as the poet to his poem. Those qualities which we have already remarked in the novel—the intrusive, genial, omniscient narrator; the shaped periods and logical syntax

[1] In *Critical Observations on Shakespeare* (1746) Upton advised literary critics that the best artists understand the principles of subordination and relationship, keeping in mind the whole design and not just the part. He then anticipates Fielding's analogy between the two artists, human and divine:

And were it not a degree of prophanation, I might here mention the great Designer, who has flung some things into such strong shades, that 'tis no wonder so much gloominess and melancholy is raised in rude and undisciplined minds, the sublime Maker, who has set this universe before us as a book; yet what superficial readers are we in this volume of nature? Here I am certain we must become good men, before we become good critics, and the first step to wisdom is humility. (2nd edn., 1748), pp. 134–5.

of the prose;[1] the intricate yet symmetrical structure; the final distribution of rewards and punishments—make *Tom Jones* the image and emblem of its author's universe, as the universe had been understood by countless philosophers and divines of the Christian humanist tradition. On one level, the design of *Tom Jones is* the argument of the novel; and this argument is, in sum, the affirmation of Providence—a just and benign, all-knowing and all-powerful Intelligence which orders and directs the affairs of men toward a last, just close. The usual form of the analogy may be seen in Cudworth, who compares the design of the creation to that of a dramatic poem:

But they, who, because judgment is not presently executed upon the ungodly, blame the management of things as faulty, and Providence as defective, are like such spectators of a dramatick poem, as when wicked and injurious persons are brought upon the stage, for a while swaggering and triumphing, impatiently cry out against the dramatist, and presently condemn the plot; whereas, if they would but expect the winding up of things, and stay till the last close, they should then see them come off with shame and sufficient punishment. The evolution of the world, as *Plotinus* calls it, is . . . a *truer poem* . . . [and] God Almighty is that skilful dramatist, who always connecteth [our actions and His designs] into good coherent sense, and will at last make it appear, that a thread of exact justice did run through all, and that rewards and punishments are measured out in geometrical proportion.[2]

To cite only one other of many possible examples, the same analogy was developed by Samuel Boyse in *Deity* (1740), a poem on the attributes of God which Fielding praised and quoted at some length, both in *The Champion* (12 February 1739/40) and in *Tom Jones* (VII. i). For Boyse, celebrating God's Providence in the lines Fielding quoted, the world is 'the vast theatre of time' in which God's creatures 'Perform the parts thy PROVIDENCE assign'd, | Their pride, their passions to thy ends inclin'd' (viii. 617, 621–2).

---

[1] For an excellent analysis of the way in which Fielding's rhetoric and syntax attest a world of order see Henry Knight Miller, 'Some Functions of Rhetoric in *Tom Jones*', *PQ* xlv (1966), esp. pp. 227–35.

[2] Ralph Cudworth, *The True Intellectual System of the Universe*, (2nd edn., 1743), ii. 879–80. A copy of the 1678 edition of this work was in Fielding's library. On Fielding's probable use of Cudworth in *Amelia* see Ralph W. Rader, *MLN* lxxi (1956), 336–8.

The theatre—or for that matter the 'comic Epic-Poem in Prose' —was a fit emblem of the world, because it was, as Fielding observed earlier in this same chapter, 'nothing more than a Representation, or, as *Aristotle* calls it, an Imitation of what really exists' (vii. i). The fundamental problem for the critic, of course, is the definition of that Nature which the poet has attempted to imitate. What, in other words, is the *poet's* understanding of 'what really exists'? For Fielding, as for Pope and a hundred philosophers and divines of the eighteenth century, Nature was 'the Art of God': its characteristics were Order and Design, symmetry and proportion; its Author the great Artificer who supervised its operation and presided over the most trivial acts of His creatures, conducting them at last to that final catastrophe at which the divine analogue of poetic justice would be meted out to all. Again, Cudworth may be allowed to summarize this relationship between the two artists, human and divine, the one creating Nature, the other imitating and reflecting that creation. Nature, like the written word, is the visible sign of its Author's mind, the 'living stamp or signature of the divine wisdom';[1] as 'the *orderly, regular and artificial frame* of things in the universe',[2] she is 'the stamp or impress of that infallibly omniscient art, of the divine understanding, which is the very law and rule of what is simply the best in every thing'.[3] As Cudworth and others glossed Aristotle for a later, Christian age, the function of the poet was thus to imitate the perfect art of Nature: 'when art is said to imitate nature, the meaning thereof is, that imperfect human art imitates that perfect art of nature, which is really no other than the divine art itself; as before *Aristotle*, *Plato* had declared in his Sophist, in these words . . . *Those things, which are said to be done by nature, are indeed done by divine art.*'[4]

Before we proceed to consider the relevance of this abstract

---

[1] Cudworth, i. 157.　　　　　　　　　　[2] Cudworth, i. 154.
[3] Cudworth, i. 156.
[4] Cudworth, i. 157. Cf. the review of an unpublished work on hermeticism, carried in Dodsley's *Museum: or, The Literary and Historical Register*, no. xxxiii (20 June 1747), iii. 257. Book I of this work, entitled 'Of Nature and Art', is summarized by the reviewer: 'the Author observes, that what we stile Nature may with great Strictness and Propriety be consider'd as the Art or Wisdom of God; and that what we call Art, is no more than the Imitation of the Wisdom of God, so far as it can be reached or imitated by the limited Nature of Man'.

notion to the fact of *Tom Jones*, we must examine it more precisely and explore its significance as a basic principle of Augustan aesthetics—one which may be seen, for example, in the delicate formalism of Gay's poetry and in the nice symmetry and exquisite tensions of Pope's couplets.[1] The notion is this: since Nature is herself the supreme artefact—harmonious, symmetrical, skilfully contrived and designed to express the divine Idea—the artist who imitates her will reflect and embody this comely order in his own creation. The very form of the poem—or of the painting, the building, the cantata—thus assumes a symbolic, even an ontological significance. Form *is* meaning. This is the burden of countless poems, essays, homilies which either celebrate the beauty of the creation in terms of the analogy of art, or, conversely, formulate a system of aesthetics by reference to the inherent order of the creation. The two terms of the analogy were inextricably connected in Augustan thought: order in art and in the world—the one implied the other. For Tillotson, for example, 'this vast curious engine of the world' argues for the existence of 'the great artificer' behind it, just as the human artefact—the poem, picture, or building—implies the poet, painter, or architect:[2]

As any curious work, or rare engine doth argue the wit of the artificer; so the variety, and order, and regularity, and fitness of the works of GOD, argue the infinite wisdom of him who made them; a work so beautiful and magnificent, such a stately pile as heaven and earth is, so curious in the several pieces of it, so harmonious in all its parts, every part so fitted to the service of the whole, and each part for the service of another; is not this a plain argument that there was infinite wisdom in the contrivance of this frame?[3]

The point, indeed, was a commonplace among the divines of the seventeenth and eighteenth centuries—with John Ray, Isaac Barrow, Robert South, Samuel Clarke, and many others who

---

[1] Cf. my article, 'Menalcas' Song: The Meaning of Art and Artifice in Gay's Poetry', *JEGP* lxv (1966), 662–79. On the manner in which the structure of Pope's couplets may be said to reflect his view of cosmic order see Maynard Mack's Introduction in the anthology *Major British Writers* (N.Y., 1954), i. 659–60; and Earl Wasserman's essay on *Windsor Forest* in *The Subtler Language* (Baltimore, 1959), ch. iv.

[2] John Tillotson, Sermon CXXXVII, 'The Wisdom of God in the Creation of the World', *Works* (1757), viii. 136–8.

[3] Ibid. viii. 126.

celebrated the 'correspondence and symmetry',[1] the 'fulness and regularity',[2] the 'admirable Artifice and exact Proportion and Contrivance'[3] of the creation. For Barrow, 'Chance never writ a legible book; Chance never built a fair house; Chance never drew a neat picture'; and the world was a much more splendid work of art.[4] For Clarke, the Deity was '*That* Power, which in the frame and construction of the *natural* World, has adjusted all things by Weight and Measure: *That* Power, which with exquisite artifice has made every thing in the exactest harmony and proportion, to conspire regularly and uniformly towards accomplishing the best and wisest Ends, in compleating the beautiful Order and Fabrick of the *Material* Universe.'[5]

Since an artful design was thus the formal characteristic of Nature, the plastic expression of a wise and benevolent Creator, the business of the human artist was to reflect this fact in the symmetry and order of his own form, implying, as a consequence, the larger harmonies of the universe. The theories of the aestheticians and the critics were founded upon the assumptions of the philosophers and divines. In 'Soliloquy: or, Advice to an Author', for instance, Shaftesbury decried '*Gothick*' monstrosities in the designing arts, 'For HARMONY is Harmony *by Nature*. . . . So is *Symmetry* and *Proportion* founded still *in Nature*.'[6] For Dennis, since Nature 'is nothing but that Rule and Order, and Harmony, which we find in the visible Creation', so 'Poetry, which is an Imitation of Nature', must formally express these same qualities.[7]

[1] Barrow, Sermon VI, 'The Being of God Proved from the Frame of the World', *Works* (1741), ii. 69; see also Sermon XXXVI, 'Of the Goodness of God', ibid. iii. 289.

[2] South, Sermon XVIII, 'On the Mercy of God', *Sermons Preached upon Several Occasions* (1843), iii. 362.

[3] Clarke, 'A Discourse Concerning the Unchangeable Obligations of Natural Religion', *Works* (1738), ii. 647. See also 'A Demonstration of the Being and Attributes of God', ibid. ii. 546, 569–71; and Sermon I, 'Of Faith in God', ibid. i. 5–6.

[4] Sermon VI, *Works* (1741), ii. 68.

[5] Sermon XCV, 'The Shortness and Vanity of Humane Life', *Works* (1738), i. 601.

[6] Anthony Ashley Cooper, third Earl of Shaftesbury, *Characteristics* (5th edn., 1732), i. 353.

[7] John Dennis, *The Advancement and Reformation of Modern Poetry* (1701), in E. N. Hooker, ed., *The Critical Works of John Dennis* (Baltimore, 1939), i. 202.

One of the clearest statements of this principle—which is in fine the principle of expressive form—is a little-known poem by Isaac Hawkins Browne, entitled *An Essay on Design and Beauty*. For Browne, Design is the essential requisite of all art—'DESIGN, that Particle of heavenly Flame, | Soul of all BEAUTY.'[1] The poem is a useful compendium of terms and assumptions common in neo-classical aesthetics: the conception of art as artifice, the carefully fashioned and finished product of the human mind. The ultimate goal of the artist is seen as the achievement of 'lucid Order' (p. 7) and 'perfect Unity' (p. 8), wherein a 'Grateful Variety' (p. 7) is complemented and controlled by 'the Pow'rs of Symmetry . . . | Bright Emanation of Intelligence' (p. 10), and wherein part relates to part, harmoniously and proportionately, each 'directed to one common End' until 'the Relation centers in a Whole' (pp. 2–3). The rationale for this exaltation of design and artifice is essentially that which Cudworth had proposed—the notion that human art must emulate Nature, the perfect art of God:

> THE Love of Order, sure, from NATURE springs,
> A Taste adapted to the State of Things.
> NATURE the Power of Harmony displays,
> And Truth and Order shine thro' all her Ways.
>   WHO that this ample Theatre beholds,
> Where fair Proportion all her Charms unfolds;
> The Sun, the glorious Orbs that roll above,
> Measuring alternate Seasons as they move;
> Who but admires a Fabrick so complete?
> And from admiring, aims to imitate?
>   HENCE various Arts proceed; for human Wit
> But copies out the Plan by Nature writ.
> Truth of Design, which Nature's Works impart,
> Alike extends to every Work of Art;
> Where different Parts harmoniously agree,
> Together link'd in close Dependency;
> Supporting, and supported, in one Frame,
> Each has its several Use, and all the same.
> However various Ways they seem to tend,
> All are directed to one common End.
> Tho' wide dispers'd, yet in Proportion fall,
> Till the Relation centers in a Whole. (pp. 2–3)

[1] *An Essay on Design and Beauty* (Edinburgh, 1739), p. 1. (British Museum call number: 11632. cc. 2.)

In this period a recurrent theme of all discussions of form in art is that, however imperfect she may appear to the clouded vision of men, Nature is the supreme Artefact, fashioned, according to John Gilbert Cooper, author of *The Power of Harmony* (1745), on the first day, when God's 'plastic word' dispelled 'dark Chaos . . . | And elemental Discord', bringing all creation into 'one harmonious plan' (pp. 10–11). This poem, a verse essay on the relation of beauty in Nature, morality, and art, asserts that the function of art is to comfort men, who are lost in this fallen, sublunary world, 'this vale of error' (p. 12), by reminding them of 'the plan | Of Nature' (p. 15), the 'UNIVERSAL HARMONY' (p. 48), which the Deity created and sustains. This is

> th'effect divine
> Of emulative Art, where human skill
> Steals with a Promethéan hand the fire
> Of Heav'n, to imitate cœlestial pow'r. (p. 20)

It is not surprising, then, that through Burlington's influence and example the early years of the eighteenth century saw the revival of interest in the pure geometrical forms of Palladian architecture, whose buildings embody those exact proportions and that symmetrical balance which were thought to inhere in the great frame of Nature. In the Preface to the fourth book of his *Architecture*, Palladio himself had espoused the doctrine of design and expressive form which underlies Augustan art in general, and—as I wish to suggest—the art of Fielding's masterpiece in particular:

IF Labour and Industry are to be laid out upon any Fabrick, to the end that in all its parts it should have the exactest symmetry and proportion, this, without the least doubt, is to be practis'd in those Temples, wherein the most gracious and all-powerful God, the Creator and Giver of all things, ought to be ador'd by us. . . . [God] being the chiefest good and perfection, it is highly agreeable, that all things dedicated to him should be brought to the greatest perfection we are capable to give them. And indeed, when we consider this beautiful Machine of the World, with how many marvellous Ornaments it is replenish'd, how the Heavens by their continual rounds change the Seasons according to the necessities of Men, and preserve themselves by the sweetest harmony and temperament of their motion: we cannot doubt, but that as these little Temples we raise, ought to bear a resemblance to that immense one of his infinite goodness, which by his bare word was perfectly compleated; so we are bound to beautify them with all the ornaments we possibly can, and to build them in such a manner and with such proportions, that all the parts together may fill the eyes of the beholders with the most pleasing harmony, and that each of them separately may conveniently answer the use for which it was design'd.[1]

This rather devious excursion into the theory of design in the Augustan period—a theory based, as we have seen, upon the mutually dependent assumptions of theology and aesthetics—has brought us, I believe, a little closer to our immediate objective, the meaning of *form* in *Tom Jones*. Form, a sense of significant design, is one of Fielding's chief contributions to the art of the novel. Even in *Joseph Andrews* character and action were made to imply a dimension of meaning larger than their literal reality: the twin heroes of that novel—representatives of the cardinal Christian virtues of chastity and charity—embark on a pilgrimage which leads them away from the City of this World toward a life of simplicity and love in a better country.[2] In *Tom Jones* Fielding fully realized the possibilities of the symbolic form he had tentatively explored in his first novel. As we have seen, he was setting out to represent in art the feast of life, the 'History' and emblem of the world in little. Since *design*—not merely fullness, but regularity; not merely variety, but symmetry, proportion, relationship —was the characteristic of that world, his own fiction would embody, and therefore symbolically assert, that principle of life.

Although critics have acknowledged, even marvelled at, the balanced architecture of *Tom Jones*, they have failed to grasp its value as symbol of the book's total philosophical meaning. Here, for example, is the one major inadequacy of R. S. Crane's

---

[1] See Giacomo Leoni, *The Architecture of A. Palladio; In Four Books* (2nd edn., 1721), ii. 41–2. See also Isaac Ware's translation, dedicated to Burlington (1738), p. 79. On the Palladian idea that in architecture the form of the building should imitate the harmonious design of the macrocosm see Rudolf Wittkower, *Architectural Principles in the Age of Humanism* (London, 1967), pp. 22–3. This doctrine is based on the Pythagorean and neo-Platonic notion that proportion in the arts is essentially musical, since musical harmony is expressive of the laws of cosmic order. Though this was a fundamental assumption of Renaissance aesthetics, Wittkower demonstrates that it survived into the early decades of the eighteenth century (Part IV, Section 7).

[2] See Battestin, *The Moral Basis of Fielding's Art* (Middletown, Conn., 1959; 2nd printing, 1964), esp. ch. vi.

otherwise brilliant and illuminating anatomy of the plot of *Tom Jones*.[1] Though Professor Crane defined the organic interrelationship of character and action in the novel, he ignored an equally essential fact of the book's structure: Fielding's schematic arrangement of his materials according to principles which may best be described not in literary terms—not, that is, in terms of the interaction of the characters and the probable sequence of events (though these are, of course, fundamental considerations)—but in terms of contemporary aesthetics. It is awkward that the theory of literature so strenuously espoused by the Chicago critics should have found its chief example in an author whose greatest work contradicts an essential axiom of that theory: namely, that meaning and form in fiction are determined exclusively from *within* the work by the developing organic interrelationship of character, thought, and action which, in one sense, *is* the novel.[2] This is true enough if we are to consider only the literal level of the narrative; but in *Tom Jones*—as in countless other novels from Richardson to Joyce and Faulkner—meaning and even the shape of the action are in large part determined by certain extrinsic, non-organic principles which may be generally termed *figurative* or *analogical*. Characters, scenes, the action itself—while maintaining an autonomous 'reality' within the world of the novel—may owe their conception to some ulterior, abstract intention of the author. When the abstraction becomes so obtrusive that it dispels the illusion of reality in a fiction, we no longer have a novel, but an allegory or parable. The two levels of meaning may, however, and often *do*, exist concomitantly, character and action preserving their literal identity and integrity, while at the same time implying values more universal and conceptual. Thus, by means of such devices as allusion and analogy, Fielding could shape an entire episode in his novel— Tom Jones's encounter with the gypsy king—into a complex political parable;[3] or, by means of certain emblematic techniques in the presentation of Sophia Western and in the description of

---

[1] See 'The Concept of Plot and the Plot of *Tom Jones*', in Crane, ed., *Critics and Criticism Ancient and Modern* (Chicago, 1952), pp. 616–47. The essay is reprinted in Battestin, ed., *'Tom Jones': A Collection of Critical Essays*, Twentieth-Century Interpretations (Englewood Cliffs, N.J., 1968).

[2] See, for example, Sheldon Sacks, *Fiction and the Shape of Belief* (Berkeley and Los Angeles, 1964).

[3] See Battestin, 'Tom Jones and "His *Egyptian* Majesty": Fielding's Parable of Government', *PMLA* lxxxii (1967), 68–77.

his hero's ascent of Mazard Hill, he could imply a broadly allegorical significance in the story of Tom Jones's pursuit of his mistress.[1]

This same principle of ulteriority affects the structure of the novel. Design is the matrix of plot in *Tom Jones*; it is the primary (if not the only) determinative factor in the structure of the book. The elements of the plot have been organized within an artificial and schematic framework imposed upon them from without. Nothing inherent in Fielding's *story* necessitated the geometrical arrangement of its parts according to what may be called the Palladian[2] principles of proportion, balance, and symmetry. To speak of the 'architecture' of *Tom Jones* is not merely a gratuitous critical elegancy; on one significant level, Fielding's novel demands to be considered in terms of this analogy. The same axioms that determined the form of Ralph Allen's 'stately House' at Prior Park or Lord Pembroke's bridge at Wilton[3] have, in a sense, determined the form of *Tom Jones*. Thus, as is well known, the novel is divided into three equal parts of six books: Parts I and III, containing the adventures in Somerset and in London, comprise the twin 'stationary' bases of the structure; Part II, serving as a sort of arch between the two, carries the reader, together with Fielding's hero and heroine, from Paradise Hall and its immediate environs to the Great City. The adventures at Upton, where the lines of the plot converge and separate again, stand as the keystone of the arch in the mathematical centre of the novel, and are balanced on either side by the narratives of the Man of the Hill and Mrs. Fitzpatrick, the one serving as a foil to the character and story of Jones, the other performing the same function for Sophia.

---

[1] See p. 291, n. 3.

[2] Dorothy Van Ghent seems to have been the first critic to compare the structural design of *Tom Jones* to that of a 'Palladian palace': see *The English Novel: Form and Function* (New York, 1953), p. 80. See also Frederick W. Hilles, 'Art and Artifice in *Tom Jones*', in Maynard Mack and Ian Gregor, eds., *Imagined Worlds: Essays on Some English Novels and Novelists in Honour of John Butt* (London, 1968), pp. 91–110. To demonstrate the 'Palladian' structure of *Tom Jones*, Professor Hilles offers a 'ground plan' of the novel based on John Wood's original design for Prior Park (p. 95).

[3] The phrase describing Allen's mansion is Joseph Andrews's (III. vi); earlier in that novel Fielding himself had referred to it as a 'Palace' (III. i), and he praised it again in *A Journey from This World to the Next* (I. v). Both Prior Park and Wilton are among the estates complimented in *Tom Jones* (XI. ix).

There is, of course, more than one way to account for such a balanced and proportionate arrangement of parts: 'every thing that is perfect and regular', declared Robert South, 'is a credit and a glory to itself, as well as to its author';[1] and in his widely read work, *Reflections on Aristotle's Treatise of Poesy*, René Rapin insisted that 'the *Design*' of an heroic poem, like that of a great painting or palace, must evince a '*Proportion* and *Symmetry* of Parts'.[2] There is a pleasure, pure and simple, in the apprehension of harmony. But the Palladian design of *Tom Jones* has a deeper, more functional significance. Like the Order of the 'great Creation' to which Fielding compared his book, the symmetrical frame of *Tom Jones* becomes apparent only after we have 'come to the final Catastrophe' and have broadened our perspective, stepping back from the consideration of the part to comprehend the plan of the whole. In this sense the design of *Tom Jones* is an essential aspect of Fielding's imitation of 'what really exists', the emblem of a similar pattern in the cosmic architecture of Nature, a similar artistry in the Book of Creation.

II. FORTUNE AND PROVIDENCE

Design, as we have seen, implies an artificer. The assertion of Order and Harmony in the Creation entails the correlative belief in God's superintending Providence: as Pope has it, Nature is Art; Chance, Direction. Whereas the *Essay on Man* declares this doctrine discursively, a fundamental purpose of *Tom Jones* is to *demonstrate* it in the dramatic and representational mode of a comic fiction, which is—at least as Fielding practised the form— the symbolic imitation and epitome of life. Just as the methods of historical criticism have helped to clarify the meaning of design in *Tom Jones*, enabling us to grasp the full implication of Aristotle for the Augustan artist, so they may help us to come to terms with the vexed question of 'probability' in Fielding's plot—as, indeed, in such other eighteenth-century fictions as *The Vicar of Wakefield* and *Roderick Random*.

Fielding declares in *Tom Jones* (VIII. i) that the true province of

[1] Sermon XVIII, *Sermons* (1843), iii. 363.
[2] Rapin, *Whole Critical Works* (3rd edn., 1731), ii. 150; see also ii. 151–3, 195–7.

the novelist is the 'probable', not the 'marvellous', even averring that he would rather see his hero hang than rescue him by unnatural means (XVII. i). But few critics have taken him seriously. In response to Coleridge's famous dictum that, together with *Oedipus Tyrannus* and *The Alchemist*, *Tom Jones* has one of the most perfect plots in literature, Austin Dobson long ago protested that

progress and animation alone will not make a perfect plot, unless probability be superadded. And though it cannot be said that Fielding disregards probability, he certainly strains it considerably. Money is conveniently lost and found; the naïvest coincidences continually occur; people turn up in the nick of time at the exact spot required, and develop the most needful (but entirely casual) relations with the characters.[1]

Although Professor Crane has gone far toward demonstrating that the action of *Tom Jones* may be seen as an 'intricate scheme of probabilities', yet his inclusion of so many 'accidents of Fortune' within this scheme does indeed strain, as Dobson put it, the definition of what is 'probable'.[2] Certainly Fielding's practice in the novel seems often to belie his professions. What, we may well wonder, is perfect and probable about a plot which depends for its complication and happy resolution upon such a remarkable series of chance encounters and fortunate discoveries? Fleeing from her father's house, Sophia happens upon the one person who can direct her along the road that Tom has taken. Tom happens to find himself in that isolated region where both the Man of the Hill and Mrs. Waters are threatened by ruffians, and so is able to rescue them. Having been seduced by this rustic Circe, he later discovers that she is (as he has been told) his mother! Disconsolate when he learns that Sophia knows of his infidelity and has spurned him, he resolves to lose his life in defence of Hanover, but his plans are changed when he chances to fall into the same road his mistress has taken and chances to meet a beggar who has found the pocket-book she inadvertently dropped. Later, languishing in prison, he finds that he has not, after all, committed incest and that Mr. Fitzpatrick has not, after all, died of his wounds. Indeed, the incidence of such happy casualties in Fielding's plot has led critics deeper and more recent than Dobson to

[1] Dobson, *Fielding* (London, 1907), p. 126. Cf. Dudden, ii. 621–2.
[2] See *Critics and Criticism*, p. 624.

pronounce 'Fortune' the sovereign deity of *Tom Jones*,[1] 'Fantasy' the wishful refuge of its author.[2] Fielding *knew* the hard realities and tragic consequences of life, wherein handsome young men, however good-natured, are ruined by knaves and hanged for their indiscretions; but his sanguine humour was forever compelling him to turn the nightmare of actuality into a cheerful dream of Eden: something like this is the drift of too many modern readers.

What I wish here to suggest is that the fortunate contingencies and surprising turns which affect the course of events in *Tom Jones* are neither the awkward shifts of incompetency nor the pleasant fantasies of romance; rather, they have an essential function in the expression of Fielding's Christian vision of life. As the general frame and architecture of *Tom Jones* is the emblem of Design in the macrocosm, so the narrative itself is the demonstration of Providence, the cause and agent of that Design. Unlike Defoe or Richardson, Fielding rejected the methods of 'formal realism'[3] for a mode which verges on the symbolic and allegorical: his characters and actions, though they have a life and integrity of their own, frequently demand to be read as tokens of a reality larger than themselves; his novels may be seen as artful and highly schematic paradigms of the human condition. For Fielding, and for the great majority of his contemporaries, no assumption about the world, and about man's place in the world, was more fundamental than the doctrine of a personal and particular Providence: 'the belief of this', Tillotson had insisted, 'is the great foundation of religion'.[4] This is the theme of countless discourses and homilies, most of which base their arguments on the discernible Order in the natural world and on the precepts of scripture. If we are to understand the significance of certain crucial recurrent themes in *Tom Jones*—the question of *probability* in the action of the novel and of *fortune* as it affects the lives of the characters—it will be useful to consider the doctrine of Providence as it appears in such representative authors as William Sherlock, whose *Discourse Concerning the Divine Providence* (1694) was a standard treatise

[1] See Van Ghent, *The English Novel*, pp. 78–80.
[2] See Morris Golden, *Fielding's Moral Psychology* (n.p., 1966), ch. vi.
[3] See Ian Watt, *The Rise of the Novel* (Berkeley and Los Angeles, 1957).
[4] Sermon CXXXVIII, 'The Wisdom of God in his Providence', *Works* (1757), viii. 145.

on the subject, and those influential divines, Barrow, South, Tillotson, and Clarke, whose works Fielding is known to have read and admired.[1]

Deriving ultimately from Aristotle and Horace, the critical principle of 'probability' was first systematically applied to the novel by Fielding himself in *Tom Jones* (VIII. i), and—with the notable exception of the literature of the absurd—it has remained a basic operative principle with critics and novelists alike. Unlike the writer of romance, the novelist must decline the favours of gods from machines; his plot must work itself out by means of the natural interaction of the characters, the plausible and inevitable sequence of cause and effect. Fielding presents the doctrine most clearly in the prefatory chapter to Book XVII, as he considers the difficulties of extricating his hero from 'the Calamities in which he is at present involved, owing to his Imprudence':

> This I faithfully promise, that notwithstanding any Affection, which we may be supposed to have for this Rogue, whom we have unfortunately made our Heroe, we will lend him none of that supernatural Assistance with which we are entrusted, upon Condition that we use it only on very important Occasions. If he doth not therefore find some natural Means of fairly extricating himself from all his Distresses, we will do no Violence to the Truth and Dignity of History for his Sake; for we had rather relate that he was hanged at *Tyburn* (which may very probably be the Case) than forfeit our Integrity, or shock the Faith of our Reader.

Yet what is 'natural' or 'probable' about the extraordinary chain of events by which Jones is redeemed from prison and reconciled to his friend and mistress, his 'crimes' undone, his enemies exposed, his true identity revealed? As we have seen, the 'faith' of more than one reader has been 'shocked' by the apparent contrivance of Fielding's story. In another sense, however, the reader's faith—both in the ingenuity and kindly art of the author (his wonderful ability to make everything come right in the end) and in a corresponding benignity and design in the world he is imitating —is confirmed and substantiated by this very contrivance. Though Fielding spurned the good offices of the *deus ex machina*, he warmly affirmed the benevolent Providence of the god *in* the machine, that 'vast Machine' to which he had earlier compared the world.

---

[1] See Battestin, *The Moral Basis of Fielding's Art*, pp. 159, n. 1, and 161, n. 28.

He could do so, moreover, without violating the critical principle he had himself laid down. In a universe ultimately 'comic' and Christian, the occurrence of what William Turner called '*the Most Remarkable Providences, both of Judgment and Mercy*'[1] was both natural and probable. To write a novel—at least a comic novel—and fail to imply them would be, in effect, to misrepresent the creation, to belie 'what really exists'.

Consider, for example, Tillotson's analysis in his sermon, 'Success not always Answerable to the Probability of Second Causes': though 'prudence', that virtue which Tom Jones so notably lacked, is necessary in human life, since 'GOD generally permits things to take their natural course, and to fall out according to the power and probability of second causes',[2] yet 'GOD hath reserved to himself a power and liberty to interpose, and to cross as he pleases, the usual course of things; to awaken men to the consideration of him, and a continual dependance upon him; and to teach us to ascribe those things to his wise disposal, which, if we never saw any change, we should be apt to impute to blind necessity.'[3] When prudence fails—prudence, which is the judicious weighing of means to accomplish a desired end according to the probability of second causes—then we must 'look above and beyond these to a superior cause which over-rules, and steers, and stops, as he pleases, all the motions and activity of second causes. . . . For the providence of GOD doth many times step in to divert the most probable event of things, and to turn it quite another way: and whenever he pleaseth to do so, the most strong and likely means do fall lame, or stumble, or by some accident or other come short of their end.'[4] This, too, is the burden of Samuel Clarke's sermon, 'The Event of Things not always answerable to Second Causes': 'the *Providence of God*, by means of *natural Causes*, which are all entirely of *His* appointment, and *Instruments only* in *His* hand; does often for wise reasons in his government of the World, disappoint the most probable expectations.'[5] With characteristic shrewdness, Robert South, whose wit Fielding could on occasion prefer to that of Congreve,[6] managed his own

---

[1] Turner, *A Compleat History of the Most Remarkable Providences, both of Judgment and Mercy, Which have Hapned in this Present Age* (1697).

[2] Sermon XXXVI, *Works* (1757), iii. 40.   [3] Ibid. iii. 27.

[4] Ibid. iii. 29.   [5] Sermon XCVIII, *Works* (1738), i. 620.

[6] See the *Covent-Garden Journal*, no. 18 (3 Mar. 1752).

extreme formulation of this doctrine. In his sermon, 'On the Mercy of God', he presents a sort of Sartrean universe, wherein the accidental and adventitious are the rule rather than the exception: paradoxically, the improbable is the probable. Only the benevolent supervention of God prevents human life from being a monstrous succession of unpredictable calamities:

. . . how many are the casual unforeseen dangers, that the hand of Providence rescues [men] from! How many little things carry in them the causes of death! and how often are men that have escaped, amazed that they were not destroyed! Which shows that there is an eye that still watches over them, that always sees, though it is not seen; that knows their strengths and their weaknesses; where they are safe, and where they may be struck; and in how many respects they lie open to the invasion of a sad accident. . . . In a word, every man lives by a perpetual deliverance; a deliverance, which for the unlikelihood of it he could not expect, and for his own unworthiness, I am sure, he could not deserve.[1]

In another well-known sermon, 'All Contingencies under the Direction of God's Providence', South further insists that what men call Fortune and Chance are in fact nothing more than agents of God's wise government of the world, affecting everything that happens to us down even to the casting of lots.[2]

The idea of Fortune is, indeed, a controlling theme in *Tom Jones*. It affects every stage in the hero's life from his birth to his imprisonment to his final redemption and marriage. To Allworthy, Tom is 'a Child sent by Fortune to my Care' (XVIII. iii). Before accepting his own responsibility for the calamities which have befallen him, Tom exclaims against the fickle goddess who has tormented him: 'Sure . . . Fortune will never have done with me, 'till she hath driven me to Distraction' (XVIII. ii). As we have remarked, the direction of Fielding's plot is frequently determined by the most unlikely coincidences, to which the narrator calls our attention in wry tribute to the goddess who 'seldom doth Things by Halves' (v. x). As we follow what Professor Crane has called the 'intricate scheme of probabilities' leading through complication to final resolution, we are never allowed to forget another, equally significant aspect of the plot: that it is Fielding who is contriving the circumstances and manipulating the characters,

[1] Sermon XVIII, *Sermons* (1843), iii. 365–6.
[2] Sermon VIII, ibid. i. 121–36.

violating the rules of probability in a deliberate and self-conscious manner, introducing into his own story an element of the improbable analogous to those unexpected and inexplicable occurrences in the actual world which come under the category of 'luck'. It is 'Fortune', who, 'having diverted herself, according to Custom, with two or three Frolicks, at last disposed all Matters to the Advantage of' Sophia as she plans to flee her father's house (VII. ix). It is 'luck' which brings her to the same town and inn from which Jones had started on his journey, and which causes her to stumble on the same guide who had conducted him toward Bristol (x. ix). It is the 'lucky Circumstance' of Western's arrival in the nick of time that prevents Lord Fellamar's rape of Sophia (xv. v). It is 'Fortune', who, 'after so many Disappointments', brings Tom and Sophia together again in Lady Bellaston's house (XIII. xi), and 'Fortune' again who appears 'an utter Enemy' to their marriage (xv. x). As he introduces his hero's ill-timed visit to Mr. Nightingale, the narrator summarizes this theme in the novel:

> Notwithstanding the Sentiment of the *Roman* Satirist, which denies the Divinity of *Fortune*, and the Opinion of *Seneca* to the same Purpose; *Cicero*, who was, I believe, a wiser Man than either of them, expressly holds the contrary; and certain it is, there are some Incidents in Life so very strange and unaccountable, that it seems to require more than human Skill and Foresight in producing them (XIV. viii).

As Tillotson, as well as Cicero, was aware, there are limits to the efficacy of human prudence, an unpredictable and *apparently* irrational shape to circumstances.

Nowhere in the novel is this point more clearly and deliberately made than in the sequence of events which befall Fielding's hero immediately after Upton. Aware that his indiscretion with Mrs. Waters is known to Sophia, who has consequently abandoned him in dismay and indignation, Jones sets out from the inn convinced that his love is hopeless and resolved to give his life in the war against the Jacobites. Fortune, however, intervenes to change his purpose and lead him in pursuit of his mistress. The operation of Chance in human affairs is first demonstrated, appropriately enough, at a crossroads. Western, arriving at this junction in his efforts to overtake his daughter, 'at last gave the Direction of his Pursuit to Fortune, and struck directly into the *Worcester* Road', which leads him away from Sophia (XII. ii); confronted with the same choice, Jones, still determined to join the King's forces, 'immediately struck into the different Road from that which the Squire had taken, and, by mere Chance, pursued the very same thro' which *Sophia* had before passed' (xii. iii). Reaching another cross-way, Jones and Partridge there encounter an illiterate beggar who, in travelling the same road Sophia had taken, happened to find the little pocket-book containing a £100 bank-note which she had accidentally dropped. This chance discovery provides Jones both with a motive to pursue Sophia and with the guide he needs to resolve the difficulty of the crossroads. Of this fortunate coincidence—and a later one equally lucky—Partridge points the obvious moral: '"two such Accidents could never have happened to direct him after his Mistress, if Providence had not designed to bring them together at last." And this [the narrator observes] was the first Time that *Jones* lent any Attention to the superstitious Doctrines of his Companion' (xii. viii).

The episode of the beggar at the crossroads serves as a sort of parable of the doctrine of Providence which Fielding affirms throughout *Tom Jones*. Finding himself by chance in that remote place where the Man of the Hill is threatened by thieves, Jones comes to the rescue and acknowledges himself to be the instrument of God: '"Be thankful then," cries *Jones*, "to that Providence to which you owe your Deliverance"' (viii. x). As he takes his leave of the Old Man, Jones's 'providential Appearance' (ix. vii) at the scene of Northerton's attempted murder of Mrs. Waters enables him to perform a similar office, no less pious than gallant, by rescuing the damsel from distress, and confessing himself 'highly pleased with the extraordinary Accident which had sent him thither for her Relief, where it was so improbable she should find any; adding, that Heaven seemed to have designed him as the happy Instrument of her Protection' (ix. ii). Such 'extraordinary accidents' and happy improbabilities are not so much a convenience to Fielding the author, providing him with easy escapes from the difficulties of his plot, as they are a calculated demonstration of providential care and design in the world. Most of these coincidences in *Tom Jones* are so gratuitous that an author of Fielding's inventive skill could easily have avoided them: Jones's rescue of the Old Man, for example, serves no real function either in advancing the plot or in allowing the two characters to meet, since Jones and Partridge have already settled themselves in the

Old Man's house before the attack occurs; and there were a score of devices more probable than the chance encounter with a lucky beggar at a crossroads which Fielding might have used to put his hero on the trail of Sophia. Jones in the first case and the beggar in the second are agents not only of their author in administering the narrative, but also of that higher Providence for which, within the symbolic microcosm of the novel, the author stands as surrogate. Fielding's contrivances imply those of the Deity.

The theme of Providence is—somewhat paradoxically it may seem to us—enforced by those recurrent, intrusive references to Fortune that we have earlier remarked. For the modern reader the two concepts appear contradictory; for Fielding and his contemporaries, however, they were two ways of conveying the same idea, of acknowledging that 'more than human Skill and Foresight' which alone could produce the 'strange and unaccountable' casualties of life. Fortune (or Chance) was, indeed, no more than a figure of speech, a convenient vulgarism, enabling one to talk of Providence while avoiding the note of pious sobriety—a note well lost in the pages of a comic novel. 'As to *Chance*,' declared Samuel Clarke, "'tis evident That is nothing but a *mere Word*, or an *abstract Notion* in our manner of conceiving things. It has no real Being; it is Nothing, and can *do* nothing.'[1] Or again, in his sermon 'The Event of Things not always answerable to Second Causes', Clarke denounces the Epicurean notion that Chance, not Design, governs the world: 'We may observe, that what men vulgarly call *Chance* or unforeseen *Accident*, is in Scripture always declared to be the *determinate Counsel and Providence of God*. What careless and inconsiderate men ascribe in common Speech to *Chance* or *Fortune*; that is, to *nothing at all*, but a mere empty word, signifying only their *Ignorance* of the true Causes of things; this the Scripture teaches *Us* to ascribe to the all-seeing and all-directing Providence of God.'[2] Perhaps the most illuminating gloss on the theme of Fortune and Providence in *Tom Jones*, however, is found in William Sherlock's *Discourse Concerning the Divine Providence*, a work popular enough to have gone through nine editions by 1747. Sherlock's third chapter, '*Concerning God's* Governing Providence', anticipates Fielding's parable of the lost-and-found banknote, using the same example to illustrate the dominion of Fortune

---

[1] Sermon I, 'Of Faith in God', *Works* (1738), i. 6.
[2] Sermon XCVIII, ibid. i. 619.

over the affairs of men and the dominion of Providence over Fortune:

... Let us consider God's Government of accidental Causes, or what we call Chance and Accident, which has a large Empire over human Affairs: Not that Chance and Accident can do any Thing, properly speaking; for whatever is done, has some proper and natural Cause which does it; but what we call Accidental Causes, is rather such an Accidental Concurrence of different Causes, as produces unexpected and undesigned Effects; as when one Man by Accident loses a Purse of Gold, and another Man walking in the Fields without any such Expectation, by as great an Accident finds it. And how much of the Good and Evil that happens to us in this World, is owing to such undesigned, surprizing, accidental Events, every Man must know, who has made any Observations on his own, or other Mens Lives and Fortunes. ... *Time and Chance*, some favourable Junctures, and unseen Accidents, are more powerful than all human Strength, or Art, or Skill.

Now what an ill State were Mankind in, did not a wise and merciful Hand govern what we call Chance and Fortune? How can God govern the World, or dispose Mens Lives and Fortunes without governing Chance, all unseen, unknown, and surprizing Events, which disappoint the Counsels of the Wise, and in a Moment unavoidably change the whole Scene of Human Affairs? Upon what little unexpected Things do the Fortunes of Men, of Families, of whole Kingdoms turn? And unless these little unexpected Things are governed by God, some of the greatest Changes in the World are exempted from his Care and Providence.

This is Reason enough to believe, That if God governs the World, he governs Chance and Fortune; that the most unexpected Events, how casual soever they appear to us, are foreseen and ordered by God.

Such events as these are the properest Objects of God's Care and Government; because they are very great Instruments of Providence; many times the greatest Things are done by them, and they are the most visible Demonstration of a superior Wisdom and Power which governs the World. ... [1]

As Sherlock postulates and Fielding in *Tom Jones* dramatizes, a lost purse, a dropped pocket-book—however adventitious they may appear—find a place in God's benevolent ordering of things.

Sherlock also anticipates Fielding in defining the relationship between Fortune and human foresight, Providence and Prudence

---

[1] Sherlock, *A Discourse Concerning the Divine Providence* (9th edn., 1747), pp. 40–2.

—the one sustaining the frame of the world and guiding the affairs of men according to the dictates of perfect Wisdom, the other imitating the example of this divine wisdom, however fallibly, in the sphere of the individual life. As the passage opens, we may recall Fielding's allusion to Cicero:

The Heathens made Fortune a Goddess, and attributed the Government of all Things to her. . . . Whereby they only signified the Government of Providence in all casual and fortuitous Events; and if Providence governs any Thing, it must govern Chance, which governs almost all Things else, and which none but God can govern. As far as Human Prudence and Foresight reaches, God expects we should take care of ourselves; and if we will not, he suffers us to reap the Fruits of our own Folly; but when we cannot take care of ourselves, we have reason to expect and hope, that God will take care of us. In other Cases, human Prudence and Industry must concur with the Divine Providence: In Matters of Chance and Accident, Providence must act alone, and do all itself, for we know nothing of it; so that all the Arguments for Providence, do most strongly conclude for God's Government of all casual Events.[1]

Though God allows scope for the voluntary acts of men—who, in so far as they conduct themselves virtuously, with charity and prudence, have fulfilled their duty to their neighbours and themselves—He none the less controls the whole Creation with unerring wisdom and omniscience, ordering even the bungling and malicious deeds of human beings within the fabric of His wise design. As Clarke expressed it, "'tis impossible but he must actually direct and appoint every particular thing and circumstance that is in the World or ever shall be, excepting only what by his own pleasure he puts under the Power and Choice of subordinate Free Agents'.[2] 'Nor is there *in Nature* Any *Other Efficient* or proper *Cause* of any Event . . . but only the *Free Will of rational and intelligent* Creatures, acting within the Sphere of their limited Faculties; and the *Supreme Power of God*, directing, by his omnipresent Providence . . . the inanimate Motions of the whole material and unintelligent World.'[3] Within *Tom Jones* both these assumptions about reality are accommodated: on the one hand, we may trace,

[1] Sherlock, *A Discourse Concerning the Divine Providence*, p. 43.
[2] Clarke, 'A Discourse Concerning the Unchangeable Obligations of Natural Religion', *Works* (1738), ii. 602.
[3] Sermon XCVIII, 'The Event of Things not always answerable to Second Causes', ibid. i. 619–20.

with Professor Crane, what might be termed the 'naturalistic' determination of events through the probable and predictable interaction of the characters; yet, on the other hand, we are aware of what seems best described as the 'artificial' determination of events through the arbitrary and quite improbable contrivances of the author, who presides like Providence over the world of the novel, distant yet very much involved, omniscient and all-powerful, arranging the elements and circumstances of his story according to a preconceived scheme as symmetrical and benevolent as the Design of that larger Creation he mirrors.

The shape of Fielding's narrative in *Tom Jones* and his choice of a narrative method may thus be seen as, in a sense, inevitable: the perfect vehicles for his theme. This theme, the assertion of Design and Providence in the world, is indeed the basis of Fielding's comic vision. It echoes in his writings from *The Champion* to that refutation of Bolingbroke which he died too soon to finish. God was always for him 'the only true, great Ruler of the Universe, who is a Being of infinite Justice',[1] a Being 'supremely wise and good', who was concerned to reward the virtuous and punish the guilty,[2] and 'in whose Power is the Disposition of all Things'.[3] He could scoff at those atheists and freethinkers who, like Epicurus or Mandeville, preferred to believe against the dictates of reason 'that this vast regular Frame of the Universe, and all the artful and cunning Machines therein were the Effects of Chance, of an irregular Dance of Atoms'.[4] Such perfection in the works of Nature, he declared in another leader, was 'infinitely superior to all the little Quackery, and impotent Imitation of Art'.[5] But always for Fielding this nice Design in the Creation implied the continuing care of the Artificer, whose hand controlled the fates of nations and of individual men: in *The Jacobite's Journal* (19 March 1748) he printed with approval a letter from a correspondent who observed that it was God's 'good and all-directing Providence' which had freed England from Stuart tyranny and established her Constitution; and a similar conviction informs his little chronicle of divine retribution, *Examples of the*

---

[1] The *Champion* (8 Jan. 1739/40). Quotations from this journal are from the 1743 reprint.
[2] The *Champion* (4 Mar. 1739/40).   [3] The *True Patriot* (24 Dec. 1745).
[4] The *Champion* (22 Jan. 1739/40).   [5] The *Champion* (4 Mar. 1739/40).

Interposition of Providence in the Detection and Punishment of Murder (1752). What Fielding himself affirms is, moreover, reiterated by the good men and women of his fiction, who express their trust in Providence in their adversity or their gratitude to God for their timely deliverances. Appropriately enough, it is Parson Adams who best summarizes this doctrine when, echoing Tillotson and a score of other divines,[1] he admonishes Joseph Andrews in affliction: with Joseph we are reminded that 'no Accident happens to us without the Divine Permission', that 'the same Power which made us, rules over us, and we are absolutely at his Disposal'; but, while acknowledging God's omnipotence, we may take comfort in the knowledge that every accident, every event, is 'ultimately directed' to some benevolent purpose (III. xi). In Fielding's last novel it is Amelia who echoes the parson's faith, acknowledging 'that Divine Will and Pleasure, without whose Permission at least, no Human Accident can happen' (VIII. iv).[2]

As in the world at large, the 'ultimate direction' of events in *Tom Jones*—and, indeed, in all Fielding's novels—is a comic apocalypse: that last, improbable, joyous catastrophe in which true identities are discovered, the innocent redeemed, an unerring justice meted out to one and all. To use South's fine phrase, the 'perpetual deliverance' of Fielding's characters from rape, murder, imprisonment, disgrace, is the essential pattern of his fiction—a pattern culminating in the final distribution of poetic justice. Yet one of the absurdities which Fielding found in *Pamela* was Richardson's insistence that virtue was rewarded and vice punished in this world: 'A very wholesome and comfortable Doctrine,' Fielding remarked in *Tom Jones* (xv. i), 'and to which we have but one Objection, namely, That it is not true.' Why, one may well ask, should the happy conclusion of Fielding's own fiction be considered any less intellectually reprehensible than that of *Pamela*? The answer, I believe, is implicit in what we have been saying so far about the relation of form to meaning in *Tom Jones*. Whereas Richardson offers *Pamela* to us as a literal transcription

---

[1] With Adams's remarks compare, especially, Tillotson's Sermon CXXXVIII, 'The Wisdom of God in His Providence', *Works* (1757), viii. 140–60.

[2] For an excellent discussion of theme of Fortune and Providence in *Amelia* see D. S. Thomas, 'Fortune and the Passions in Fielding's *Amelia*', *MLR* lx (1965), 176–87.

of reality, Fielding's intention is ultimately symbolic. In the Preface to *Joseph Andrews* Fielding saw the business of the comic novelist, as he saw that of his friend Hogarth, the 'Comic History-Painter', as 'the exactest copying of Nature'; but he meant this in an Aristotelian, not a Baconian, sense. He would have agreed with Imlac that the poet was not concerned to number the streaks of the tulip; his subject was 'not Men, but Manners; not an Individual, but a Species'.[1] Richardson's eye is on the fact, Fielding's on the abstraction which the fact implies. The happy ending of *Pamela* is unacceptable because the novel asks to be taken as a faithful (even in a pious sense) representation of actuality. Fielding's fiction makes no such claim. Ultimately he asks us to consider not Tom Jones, but 'HUMAN NATURE', not so much the story of his hero's fall and redemption as that rational and benign scheme of things which the story and its witty, genial author imply. *Tom Jones* asks to be taken as a work of Art, as paradigm and emblem of that wise Design which Pope celebrated, and in terms of which, 'partial Evil', however real, however terrible, may be seen as 'universal Good'. Given this assumption of an order and meaning to life, there must be, as Samuel Clarke put it, a

final vindication of the Honour and Laws of God in the proportionable reward of the best, or punishment of the worst of Men. And consequently 'tis certain and necessary . . . there must at some time or other be such a Revolution and Renovation of Things, such a *future State* of existence of the same Persons, as that by an exact distribution of Rewards or Punishments therein, all the present Disorders and Inequalities may be set right; and that the whole Scheme of Providence, which to us who judge of it by only one small Portion of it, seems now so inexplicable and much confused; may appear at its consummation, to be a Design worthy of Infinite Wisdom, Justice and Goodness.[2]

Within the microcosm of the novel, this is precisely the function of Fielding's comic denouements, at which, miraculously, every difficulty is swept away, every inequity redressed. What appeared confusion, both in the conduct of the story and in the lives of the characters, is, after all, a wise design: the mighty maze is not without a plan. And a principal instrument of this revelation is

[1] *Joseph Andrews* (III. i.). For Imlac's 'Dissertation upon Poetry' see Johnson's *Rasselas* (1759), ch. x.

[2] Clarke, 'A Discourse Concerning the Unchangeable Obligations of Natural Religion', *Works* (1738), ii. 597–8.

an astonishing sequence of what Fielding calls 'those strange Chances, whence very good and grave Men have concluded that Providence often interposes in the Discovery of the most secret Villainy' (xviii. iii). Sharing Allworthy's admiration at the 'wonderful Means' by which mysteries have been dispelled and justice has triumphed, the reader may wish to apply to Fielding himself what the good squire exclaims of the Deity: 'Good Heavens! Well! the Lord disposeth all Things' (xviii. vii).

In the deliberate, philosophic use of coincidence, if in no other respect, Fielding reminds us of no one so much as Thomas Hardy —though, to be sure, the intentions of the two novelists are antithetical. Whereas the grotesque improbabilities of Hardy's plots are meant to mirror a universe hostile, or at best indifferent, to man, Fielding's happy turns and fortunate encounters reflect a very different, appropriately Augustan world. His contrivances, as we have remarked, imply those of the Deity. Fielding was not, of course, alone among his contemporaries in enforcing this analogy. As Richard Tyre has shown, it was a fundamental argument with such critics as John Dennis, for whom poetic justice in the drama was necessary as the reflection of 'meaning, order, and coherence' in the universe.[1] Neither Dennis nor Fielding was blind to the tragic circumstances of life, but both conceived the function of art to be the imitation of a reality more comprehensive and rational than our limited experience could disclose: 'Poetick Justice', Dennis observed, 'would be a Jest if it were not an Image of the Divine, and if it did not consequently suppose the Being of a God and Providence.'[2] A similar rationale, I believe, underlies that extraordinary series of calamities and fortunate restorations which modern critics have deplored in the plot of Goldsmith's Christian fable, *The Vicar of Wakefield*; and Smollett, too—though in a much more arbitrary and perfunctory fashion—attempts to justify the preposterous turns and discoveries of *Roderick Random* by attributing them all to the marvellous workings of Providence.[3] Written from a comparable belief in a Christian universe, such works as *Troilus and Criseyde*, *Paradise Lost*, and *Clarissa* attempt to reconcile the tragedy of existence

---

[1] See Richard H. Tyre, 'Versions of Poetic Justice in the Early Eighteenth Century', *SP* liv (1957), 34.

[2] Dennis, *The Usefulness of the Stage* (1698), in Hooker, ed., *Critical Works*, i. 183.   [3] See, especially, chs. lxvi–lxvii.

with the consoling doctrine of the Church by resorting, variously, to a final apotheosis of the hero or to the reassurances of a ministering angel.

Happily, no such solution is possible or necessary to the comic novelist. As the example of Smollett in *Roderick Random*, or of Osborne in the film of *Tom Jones*,[1] makes clear, nothing, of course, is less artistically satisfying than a happy ending incoherently imposed on a story, whereby chance medley at a stroke becomes a wedding feast. The marriage of Tom and Sophia, however, is the *telos* of Fielding's novel, standing in the same relation to the world of *Tom Jones* as that 'Great Day' toward which life itself was tending, 'when', as Clarke expressed it, 'the Reasons of things and the whole Counsel of God shall be more perfectly disclosed'.[2] *Tom Jones* has been cherished for many reasons, but its special triumph is as a work of art: the form of the novel—its symmetry of design; the artful contrivance of its plot; the intrusive, omniscient narrator; and that final, miraculous resolution of every complication—is the expression and emblem of its author's coherent, Christian vision of life.

[1] See Battestin, 'Osborne's *Tom Jones*: Adapting a Classic', *The Virginia Quarterly Review*, xlii (1966), 383.

[2] Sermon XCV, 'The Shortness and Vanity of Humane Life', *Works* (1738), i. 602.

16

CHRISTOPHER SMART AND THE EARL OF NORTHUMBERLAND

By CHARLES RYSKAMP

CHRISTOPHER SMART's attempts to win some sort of patronage from the Earl of Northumberland emphasize the irony and pathos of the poet's life and the difficulty in the middle of the eighteenth century of finding any certain financial reward for writing. Poor Kit Smart and the Distressed Poet have become clichés of literary and social history. But this poet's life—although again much remains obscure and unaccountable—and the general situation of financial success or failure for English writers about 1750 may be better understood by looking at the events which link Smart and the Northumberland family.

Almost everyone who has considered authorship and publishing at this time has recognized that it was a period of transition, when the old rewards of patronage were rapidly declining, when subscription might still prove successful, but when proper payments and something like royalties would only occasionally happen. The great expansion of the reading public and the development of the publisher, as opposed to the bookseller, gradually eliminated collective or individual patronage. This was noticed by the literary observers of Smart's own day. Goldsmith, for instance, wrote in his Letter LXXXIV, later collected in *The Citizen of the World*: 'At present the few poets of England no longer depend on the Great for subsistence, they have now no other patrons but the public. . . .' That was at least beginning to be true. Macaulay's opinion of the gains of authors in the age of Johnson was also nearly right: 'Literature had ceased to flourish under the patronage of the great, and had not begun to flourish under the patronage of the public' ('Samuel Johnson', *Encyclopædia Britannica*, 1856). Most notably, of course, patronage had been denounced by Dr. Johnson himself; but it continued to tantalize authors, and it was certainly not yet dead during his life.

After a century and a half, historians of publishing (men like A. S. Collins, F. A. Mumby, and Harry Ransom) have described more fully the confusion of attempts in the eighteenth century to find a less precarious system of financial reward for authorship. Christopher Smart's position was as perilous as that of any writer in the 1750s and 1760s. What makes him an especially dramatic example is that he not only tried every way then known of gaining remuneration for his writing, but at times seems to have combined the various possibilities in a single publishing venture. The desperate concentration of his attempts marks their difference from those of Grub Street or of established authors. Smart also used all methods of advertising his poetry, including some devices which appear to be unique. Puffing one's own writing was common throughout the century. Boswell, naturally enough, wrote anonymous advertisements of his books; even the diffident William Cowper could be an ambitious advocate of his own undertaking, and announce it to the world.[1] But Smart's schemes are closer to the methods of those making personal appearances on a late-night television show. He tried to sell his work through personal plugging.

The reasons for Smart's insistent appeals and advertising lie frequently in his own extravagance. 'During the far greater part of his life he was wholly inattentive to œconomy; and by this negligence lost first his fortune and then his credit.'[2] He was always in debt and died in a debtors' prison. When a student and Fellow of Pembroke College, Cambridge, he had many bills outstanding, and the same was true of the years in London. His heavy drinking must have taken a good part of his money, and so would his fine clothes. One must not see Christopher Smart either in a madhouse or as the emaciated model for Hogarth's famous picture of 'The Distressed Poet'—in a garret with crumbling walls and squalid, tattered clothing thrown about, a dunning milkmaid badgering him and his penniless wife and bawling child. The true portrait of Smart is the one which hangs in the Hall of Pembroke

---

[1] Cowper sent a long letter, signed 'A Well-Wisher To the New Translation', to the *Public Advertiser* (printed 18 May 1786), which puffed his translation of Homer and his own attempts to reform English verse. This was at the time his 'Proposals for Printing by Subscription a new Translation of . . . Homer' were published.

[2] [Christopher Hunter, Smart's nephew], 'The Life of Christopher Smart', *The Poems of . . . Smart* (Reading, 1791), i. xxix.

College, where his fat paunch is not hidden but is the centre of the picture, and it is covered by one of the shiniest, most splendid waistcoats in English portraiture. The library and the exuberant drapery in the background are also rich and fine. That is the way Smart lived, and drank, and entertained his friends. And got into debt.

In an excellent article on 'The Rewards of Authorship in the Eighteenth Century' Mr. Harry Ransom has written: 'It is undeniable that Grub Street, the hackney writer's garret, and the bailiff waiting below stairs are true remembrances of authorship in those times; but so, too, are flowered waistcoats and plum-colored breeches bought with the income of songs and stories. . . .'[1] Smart's waistcoat was probably bought with just such an income, but unfortunately the coat, the drink, his rooms, all were beyond his means, and so he was driven to more hack work, more schemes, more 'puffs'. By 1750 a poet really could not expect that a dedication to royalty or to a nobleman would bring a generous financial reward.[2] But some of Smart's dedications are rather obvious solicitations for such a reward or for favour. The nobleman's influence might bring the poet to the attention of the reading public. If not money, then recognition, a position of greater importance which would bring him more money. This seems to be the expectation, for example, of Smart's Dedication to the Earl of Middlesex of his *Poems on Several Occasions* (1752). Subscription had replaced patronage as the acceptable form of remuneration; yet, despite Smart's success in accumulating over 700 subscribers for the volume, he could not avoid, nor afford to neglect, the almost hopelessly out-of-date and now servile method of the past. None the less, he was, so far as we know, unrewarded.

The year 1755 was a particularly unsuccessful one for Smart. Few poems were published; his periodical work and theatrical presentations were almost non-existent. By December he must have been desperate, for he now had a wife and two daughters to support. He then had an occasion which provided opportunities for improving his position in every way.

On 15 May the Earl of Northumberland, the President of the

---

[1] *Studies in English* (University of Texas, 1938), pp. 47–8.
[2] See A. S. Collins, *Authorship in the Days of Johnson* (London, 1927), pp. 180–3. 'By 1780 dedications had become merely a graceful and expected introduction to a work' (p. 183).

Middlesex Hospital, had laid the first stone of the new hospital building in Marylebone Fields.[1] On 5 December he 'gave a grand Entertainment to upwards of an hundred Gentlemen and Governors of the Middlesex Hospital on Account of his Lady's Birth-Day': there was a dinner at Northumberland House and afterwards a benefit performance at the Theatre Royal, Covent Garden.[2] The Earl and Countess of Northumberland were acclaimed and sought after because of their vast wealth, their interest in literature and art, as well as their position at the centre of social and political life in England. Part of the entertainment on 5 December was a performance of Steele's *The Conscious Lovers*, with a special Prologue and Epilogue, the Epilogue written by Christopher Smart. Why he was chosen is not known, but we can find at least a slight connection with some of the principal figures of that evening. The Countess had subscribed to his *Poems on Several Occasions* of 1752. So had Edward ('Ned') Shuter, probably the greatest comic actor of the day, who spoke Smart's Epilogue. Shuter did not act in *The Conscious Lovers*, but he was Scapin in *The Cheats of Scapin*, the other play performed that evening.[3] Smart's Epilogue and the second play were much more appropriate to Shuter's style than was Steele's didactic and sentimental comedy.

This is Smart's Epilogue as it was printed in the *Public Advertiser* for 19 December 1755 where it appeared with the Prologue by Mr. Boyce spoken by Mrs. Woffington 'at the Theatre Royal in Covent-Garden, to the Play of *The Conscious Lovers*, e[n]acted Dec. 5, for the Benefit of the *Middlesex-Hospital* for sick and lame Patients and Married Lying-in Women'. The Prologue and Epilogue were preceded by a note which said that 'the Governors of the Middlesex Hospital, having obtained Leave of the Authors of the underwritten Prologue and Epilogue to publish them, thought it would be an agreeable Entertainment to the Readers'.

---

[1] *Gentleman's Magazine*, xxv (May 1755), 233. Hugh Smithson (1715–86) had in 1750 become Earl of Northumberland and assumed the name and arms of Percy. In 1766 he was created Duke of Northumberland.

[2] *Whitehall Evening Post*, 4–6 Dec. 1755 and *Public Advertiser*, 8 Dec. 1755.

[3] *The London Stage, 1660–1800*, vol. iv, part ii, ed. G. W. Stone (Carbondale, Ill., 1962), 500, 513.

EPILOGUE, wrote by C. SMART, M.A.

On the same Occasion;

Spoken by Mr. SHUTER, in the Character of a MAN-MIDWIFE.

Enters with a Child.

Whoe'er begot thee has no Cause to blush:
Thou'rt a brave chopping Boy (*Child Cries*) nay, hush, hush, hush.
A Workman, faith! a Man of rare Discretion,
A Friend to Britain, and to our Profession;
With Face so chubby, and with Looks so glad,
O rare roast Beef of England—here's a Lad!

Shews him to the Company.

(*Child makes a Noise again*)

Nay if you once begin to puke and cough,
Go to the Nurse. Within, here, take him off.
Well, Heav'n be prais'd, it is a peopling Age,
Thanks to the Bar, the Army, and the Stage;
The Nation prospers by such joyous Souls,
Hence smoaks my Table, hence my Chariot rolls.
Tho' some snug Jobs from Surgery may spring,
Man-Midwifry, Man-Midwifry's the Thing.
Lean should I be, e'en as my own Anatomy,
By mere Cathartics and by plain Phlebotomy.
Well, besides Gain, besides the Pow'r to please,
Besides the Music (*shakes a Purse*) of such Birds as these,
It is a Joy refin'd, unmix'd, and pure,
To hear the Praises of the grateful Poor.
This Day comes honest Taffy to my House,
'Cot pless hur, hur has sav'd hur Poy and Spouse,
'Hur sav'd my Gwinnifrid, or Death had swallow'd hur,
'Tho' Creat crand-creat-crand-crand Child of Cadwallador.'
Cries Patrick Touzl'em, 'I am bound to pray,
'You've sav'd my Sue in your same Physic Way,
'And further shall I thank you Yesterday.'
Then Sawney came, and thank'd me for my Love,
(I very readily excus'd his Glove)
He bless'd the Mon, e'en by St. Andrew's Cross,
'Who'd cur'd his bonny Bearn and blithsome Lass.'
    But Merriment and Mimickry apart,
Thanks to each bounteous Hand, and gen'rous Heart,
Of those, who tenderly take Pity's Part;
Who in good-natur'd Acts can sweetly grieve,
Swift to lament, but swifter to relieve.

> Thanks to the lovely fair Ones, Types of Heav'n,
> Who raise, and beautify, the Bounty giv'n;
> But chief to *him, in whom Distress confides,
> Who o'er this noble Plan so gloriously presides.
>   * The Earl of Northumberland.

The Epilogue appeared alone as a special leader in the *Whitehall Evening Post* for 18–20 December 1755, which was most uncommon in this newspaper, and, in fact, not common in any newspaper of the time. (The only verbal variation was 'thou art' in line two of the poem.) Smart's poem was again printed in the December issues of the *Gentleman's Magazine* (xxv. 567) and the *London Magazine* (xxiv. 592). These reprints were probably not so much owing to Smart's interest as to the common practice of the day, when poetry in particular was freely taken from one journal and reprinted without authorization in another. For whatever reason, Smart had had an unusual amount of publicity, but he continued to keep his work in the public eye. In the Appendix to Volume xxiv of the *London Magazine* (p. 626), there was the following announcement:

> *In Justice to the ingenious Author of the* Epilogue, *in our* Mag. *of December, p.* 592, *we insert the following Correction and additional Lines, which he has favoured us with.*

> Line 9. Well heav'n be prais'd, it is a peopling age,
> Thanks to the bar, the pulpit and the stage;
> But not to th'army—that's not worth a farthing,
> The Captains go too much to Covent-Garden,
> Spoil many a girl,—but seldom make a mother,
> They foil us one way,—but [*shakes a box of pills*] we have them
>   t'other.

The Epilogue was reprinted a few months later, in April 1756, in *A Collection of Pretty Poems for the Amusement of Children Six Foot High* (pp. 37–9), a miscellany almost certainly edited by Smart.[1]

One might well ask why there should be so much publicity for poetry of this quality. No one can claim that the Epilogue has extraordinary merit; only a handful of Smart's occasional verse has any distinction whatsoever. No poet more completely proved

---

[1] See Arthur Sherbo, 'Survival in Grub-Street: Another Essay in Attribution', *BNYPL* lxiv (Mar. 1960), 152. I have profited also from Professor Sherbo's biography, *Christopher Smart: Scholar of the University* (East Lansing, 1967), published after I had written this article.

that 'great wits are sure to madness near allied'. The difference between Smart's great poetry, written out of madness and apocalyptic vision, and his occasional poems is almost absolute. Nevertheless, although the specific reasons for the repeated attention to the jingling Epilogue are not known, they may be guessed. Smart's letters reveal how carefully he directed his booksellers in the way they were to advertise his books and as to how frequently they should announce them. Now he was undoubtedly again directing his own publicity.

Smart would have wished to impress the Earl of Northumberland, who was as powerful as any peer in literary, social, and political circles; and Northumberland was reported to be a generous patron. The grand entertainment of 5 December united one of his favourite charities and his wife's birthday, a most opportune moment for the destitute poet to find patronage. But, as we have seen, Smart did not dare to hazard his possible rewards by taking only one way.

The Middlesex Hospital was principally for lying-in women. This gave Smart a chance to bring on Shuter as a man midwife, a role which bore no relationship to the preceding play. As a matter of fact, Smart's Epilogue was in direct contradiction to the original Epilogue (written by Leonard Welsted), which was altogether in keeping with the didactic purposes of *The Conscious Lovers*: to present a pattern for the life of a Christian gentleman. Welsted's Epilogue, intended to be spoken by the actress playing Indiana in the comedy, began:

> Our author, whom entreaties cannot move,
> Spite of the dear coquetry that you love,
> Swears he'll not frustrate (so he plainly means)
> By a loose Epilogue, his decent scenes.

Smart's Epilogue, appropriate to the acting abilities of Shuter and the nature of the benefit, also served to puff his favourite money-raising schemes during the years 1750–60. These were *The Midwife: or, Old Woman's Magazine* (1750–3, with selections printed later), which Smart edited under the pseudonym of 'Mrs. Mary Midnight' (a slang expression for a midwife), and the closely related entertainments, 'The Old Woman's Oratory . . . conducted by Mrs. Midnight, Author of the Midwife, and her Family'. Both were farcical, simple-minded, and good-humoured productions which achieved great popularity. 'The Old Woman's Oratory' consisted of what might now be called vaudeville acts. During 1752 and 1753 this low buffoonery was the rage of London, and 'Mrs. Midnight' became closely identified with Smart. In 1755 the theatrical use of a man midwife would still call to mind Smart's wild farces, but by that year the printed pieces and the public entertainments no longer created the same kind of excited talk, and by no means the same kind of income. Smart could not resist a chance of puffing what nevertheless must have seemed to be his best sources of financial reward. (It should not be forgotten that it was most important to get the poet's name before the public just now, because in December J. Newbery published in two volumes the work that Smart laboured over for months: *The Works of Horace, Translated Literally into English Prose*.)[1] As a consequence, in this Epilogue we have a rather strange amalgam of personal publicity and farcical humour with his plea to the Earl of Northumberland, 'in whom Distress confides'.

During the next years Smart tried similar schemes to raise money by publicizing his work: by advertising and puffing; by dedications, proposals, subscriptions. This was true before and after his confinement in St. Luke's Hospital and in Mr. Potter's Madhouse (off and on from 1757 to 1763). When he was released he did not join his wife and children in Reading; he took a lodging in Westminster. We know his precise address from a letter of January 1764 to a Welsh friend, Paul Panton.[2] The letter, like almost every one of Smart's, is about money or subscriptions (or advertising).

Janry 10th 1764.

Dear Sir /

Being about to put my book to the press forthwith I desire the favour you wou'd immediately send me the names of such subscribers as you have been so kind as to procure & make their payments by your Agent in Town, who probably will subscribe himself, if you will be

[1] The title-page reads '1756', but the translation was announced in the monthly catalogue of books for December 1755 in the *Gentleman's Magazine* (p. 574) and the *London Magazine* (p. 629).

[2] Paul Panton (1731–97) of Plâs Gwyn, Anglesey, and Holywell, Flintshire: see Cecil Price, 'Six Letters by Christopher Smart', *RES* N.S. viii (May 1957), 144–8. The letter of 10 Jan. 1764 is printed from the original manuscript in the collection of Mr. Robert H. Taylor, Princeton, New Jersey.

so good as to desire him. I am now at Mrs Barwell's in Park Street Westminster.

> Your most obliged
> & affectionate friend
> & Serv!
> Christopher Smart.

The address is important to us if we are to have a fair picture of Smart at this time. He might still be a Grub-Street poet, in that he continued to do hack work and was certainly a needy author. But he did not live in Grub-Street surroundings. It is difficult to imagine a more charming place in London than Park Street (now Queen Anne's Gate). It is today the most beautiful eighteenth-century street in London. This is how it was described in 1755: '. . . a handsome open Square, with very good Houses, well inhabited, especially that Side that fronts St. *James's-park*, having a delightful Prospect therein, with the Conveniency of Doors out of their Gardens into the same; and here is a very fine Cock-pit, called the King's Cock-pit, well resorted unto'.[1] The short street was like a square, with the Royal Cockpit at one end and at the other a high wall, with a niche containing a statue of Queen Anne. The park had a canal in the middle filled with ducks and every kind of aquatic fowl; there were walks of trees, wide meadows with tame stags, fallow deer, and cows at noon and evening from which milk was drawn on the spot and served for a penny a mug.[2] Mrs. Barwell's house was the third house from the Cockpit on the north side of Park Street; its garden adjoined the park, as can easily be seen in Kip's large 'Perspective View of the City of London, Westminster, and St. James's Park' (1710).[3]

[1] John Stow, *A Survey of . . . London and Westminster* (6th edn., London, 1755), ii. 643.

[2] See Hugh Phillips, *Mid-Georgian London* (London, 1964), pp. 26, 40, 265–6.

[3] According to the ratebooks of the Absey Division of St. Margaret's Parish she occupied this house from 1753 to 1773. In the latter year the seven houses on the north side of Park Street were torn down (they had been built in 1705) and seven new houses built. It cannot be proved that the site of any of the new houses was identical with that of those demolished. But it would seem that Mrs. Barwell's house was replaced with one occupied by John Pettiward, Esq., at 5 Park Street, subsequently 18 Queen Anne's Gate. The ratebooks indicate that the Hon. William Wyndham, who had helped to manage for the House of Commons the impeachment of Warren Hastings, lived here from 1796 to 1800. And they record an Eleanor Barwell at a house

It was at Mrs. Barwell's house that Dr. John Hawkesworth visited Smart and reported to Mrs. Hunter, one of Smart's sisters: 'He is with very decent people, in a house most delightfully situated with a terras that overlooks St. James's Park, and a door into it.'[1]

Smart's nephew, Christopher Hunter, said that his uncle conducted his affairs 'for some time with sufficient prudence. He was maintained partly by his literary occupations, and partly by the generosity of his friends; receiving among other benefactions fifty pounds a year from the Treasury; but by whose interest, as I do not certainly know, I will not hazard a conjecture.'[2] But such a pleasant lodging in as fine a location as this must have been an expensive undertaking for Smart. And, as before, he had to raise more money.

In April 1763 'Proposals for Printing, by subscription, A New Translation of the Psalms of David' were advertised at the end of Smart's *Song to David*. He solicited subscribers, and, as we have seen in the letter above, by 10 January 1764 he expected to send his book to the press 'forthwith'. It was not published, however, until August 1765. In the meantime, during 1763 two small collections of his poetry were published, *Poems* (July) and *Poems on Several Occasions* (by November). By September 1764 there was another collection of poems, more important for our purposes: *Ode to the Right Honourable the Earl of Northumberland, on his being appointed Lord Lieutenant of Ireland, Presented on the Birth-day of Lord Warkworth. With some other pieces.*[3] In this volume there are two or three of Smart's finest lyrics, including 'On a Bed of Guernsey Lilies'. The 'Advertisement' to the *Ode* is a curious attempt at gaining favour, or at avoiding displeasure:

Though the following Piece was in a degree received at a certain place, and something handsome done (according to custom) yet such

in Great Queen Street (subsequently Old Queen Street, leading into Queen Anne's Gate) in 1774, and at another house in the same street from 1775 to 1788. (Information from G. F. Osborn, Reference Librarian and Archivist, City of Westminster Public Libraries; *Survey of London*, vol. x (1926), especially pp. 73–4, 78–81, 89–90; Phillips, p. 26.)

[1] Hunter, 'The Life of Christopher Smart', p. xxv. Hawkesworth's letter is dated October 1764.

[2] Hunter, pp. xxii–xxiii.

[3] It was listed in the monthly catalogue for September 1764 in the *Monthly Review*, xxxi. 231.

was the modesty of the excellent person to whom it was addressed, that the Printing of it was so far from being approved of, that very positive injunctions were given to the contrary.

The Author therefore was content to have the Manuscript handed about amongst his friends for their private entertainment, determining at all events to abide by his obedience.—But at length having the honour to communicate it to a great and worthy friend, who has been for some years in the country, he persuaded him to make it public, urging that the suppression would in a degree be a loss to letters; and as for any blame about the matter, he was ready to take that upon himself. This is an honourable Gentleman who has a most profound respect to my Lord Lieutenant, and whose commands were not likely to be resisted, as they were given with equal authority and benevolence, and in the true spirit of an Englishman, born to encounter opposition and triumph over difficulty.

Without much trouble, we may again guess at Smart's plan in publishing these verses and, in effect, dedicating the collection to the Earl of Northumberland. As before, a birthday is celebrated: the twenty-first birthday of the heir, Hugh Lord Warkworth, afterwards second Duke of Northumberland, was on 14 August 1763; but this time there was an even more significant occasion: the appointment of the Earl of Northumberland as Lord Lieutenant of Ireland (20 April 1763). In December 1758 the *Gentleman's Magazine* had published Smart's poem, 'The English Bull Dog, Dutch Mastiff, and Quail', with a note which read: 'The following Fable, which has been handed about in private, was written by the ingenious Mr. Christopher Smart, late of Pembroke Hall, Cambridge, when his Grace the Duke of Devonshire (then Lord Hartington) was appointed Lord Lieutenant of Ireland.'[1] No doubt, then, in 1764 Smart was repeating his attempt to win favour from a new Lord Lieutenant, who had at his disposal many posts in the Irish Government. The powerful interest of this position was widely known. Goldsmith's ballad, *Edwin and Angelina . . . Printed for the amusement of the Countess of Northumberland*, written in the same year, was interpreted as a gesture in the hope of an Irish post. But Goldsmith rejected Northumberland's offer to do something for him.[2] In Smart's case we do not know of any offer or reward, beyond the first 'something handsome' which

---

[1] *Gentleman's Magazine*, xxviii. 594.

[2] Collins, *Authorship*, p. 197; Temple Scott, *Oliver Goldsmith Bibliographically and Biographically Considered* (N.Y., 1928), pp. 148 ff.

was done. And, as before, he did not dare to let his expectations rest on patronage. At the end of the *Ode* were printed Smart's 'Proposals for . . . the Psalms'. It is pleasant to know that the Countess of Northumberland at least subscribed to this (as did Ned Shuter).

The conclusion to this story of patronage and subscription, frustration and distress, is even sadder. As friends and subscribers dropped away, and all possibility of patronage disappeared, Christopher Smart had to turn to charity. Garrick and others had arranged a benefit for Smart at Drury Lane early in the year 1759, when he was confined in the madhouse. Ten years later he could look for grants of £10 from the Trustees of Lord Crewe.[1] But primarily Smart depended upon an 'annual Subscription of a guinea or two yearly amongst my friends' which had been proposed by William Mason of Pembroke. Smart wrote about this to Paul Panton: 'Sundry gentlemen have come in to this good-naturd Scheme, which was none of my own devising. . . .'[2] Most of his letters until the spring or summer of 1769, when he moved to Chelsea (in April of the following year it was to the debtors' prison),[3] are reminders or requests for payment of the subscription:

> It is now the anniversary of Mason's kind plan in my favour, which I humbly take the liberty of reminding you of—You subscribed two guineas last year & promised to continue it—If every man, that had much more cause to use me kindly had been possessed of your generous sentiments, I should have been well enough off with regard to circumstances—I pray God bless you & many happy years attend you![4]

Or a note like this to George Colman (and presumably one like it to Garrick) which said merely, 'I find myself reduced by the necessity of the case again to tax such of my friends as are disposed to do me the honour of their names'; and then a postscript of congratulation on the very successful new play, *The Clandestine Marriage*, by Colman and Garrick.[5] All these letters from 1764 to

---

[1] Christopher Devlin, *Poor Kit Smart* (London, 1961), pp. 101, 182.

[2] 22 Jan. 1767: Price, 'Six Letters', p. 145.

[3] Devlin, pp. 181, 189.

[4] To Panton, 4 Jan. 1768: Price, 'Six Letters', p. 147.

[5] 27 Feb. 1766: *Posthumous Letters, from Various Celebrated Men* (London, 1820), p. 90. The letter to Garrick of the same date and from the same place, 'St. James's Park, next door to the Cock Pit', has disappeared. It was once in

1769 are from 'St. James's Park next door to the Cockpit' or from 'Storey's Gate Coffee House St. James's Park'. This Coffee House was at the bottom of Great George Street, where Storey's Gate led into the park at the end of Bird-Cage Walk.[1] It was a walk of a minute or two from Mrs. Barwell's house, where, presumably, Smart continued to live until financial difficulties made it impossible to keep these lodgings.

It would be a great advantage to us if we knew this story from the point of view of the Northumberland family.[2] Perhaps there was no story at all for them to tell. The *Dictionary of National Biography*, quoting Louis Dutens's *Memoirs of a Traveller*, adds this about Northumberland: '. . . although his expenditure was unexampled in his time, he was not generous, but passed for being so owing to his judicious manner of bestowing favours'. Christopher Smart was not a judicious risk. As his nephew wrote: 'The civilities shewn him by persons greatly his superiors in rank and character, either induced him to expect mines of wealth, from the exertion of his talents; or encouraged him to think himself exempted from attention to common obligations.'[3] This, with his other failings, helped to create one of the most pathetic and ironic careers among the lives of the English poets.

the collection of William Upcott: *Catalogue of the Autograph Room, entirely filled with the collection of Mr. William Upcott . . .*, Liverpool Mechanics' Institution, June and July 1844, p. 21.

  [1] Bryant Lillywhite, *London Coffee Houses* (London, 1963), pp. 553–4.

  [2] The Duke of Northumberland, K.G., has been most helpful in searching for records at Syon House and Alnwick Castle, but no papers appear to have survived to give information relating to Smart and the Northumberland family.

  [3] Hunter, p. xxix.

17

JOHNSON AND THE SOCIETY
OF ARTISTS

By JAMES L. CLIFFORD

VERY little is known about Samuel Johnson's day-to-day existence in the early 1760s. Except for the receipt of a pension from the King in the summer of 1762 and for a trip to Devonshire with Reynolds in the same year, there were few memorable events until he met Boswell in May 1763. Later, his biographer found it difficult to fill up these years with much that was specific, except for some poetical praise from Arthur Murphy, a few long letters, and the listing of various minor pieces of hack writing. Among the latter were a formal address and a Preface which Johnson apparently drafted for a group of artists who were struggling for recognition. Unfortunately, however, Boswell did not describe the events which led up to their composition, being unaware of the extent of Johnson's involvement in the affairs of these artists.

Happily, we now know more about this episode. Although some of the evidence has been in print, and is known to art historians,[1] the material has not been much used by literary scholars. No biography of Johnson discusses it. He is usually assumed to have had little interest in the visual arts. For these reasons, then, it may be worth while to bring together the whole story, as it is recorded in the surviving minutes of the artists'

[1] For example, see John Pye, *Patronage of British Art* (1845), pp. 91–109; Algernon Graves, *The Society of Artists of Great Britain* (1907), pp. 303–6; 'The Papers of the Society of Artists of Great Britain', *The Sixth Volume of the Walpole Society, 1917–1918* (Oxford, 1918), pp. 113–30; Derek Hudson and Kenneth W. Luckhurst, *The Royal Society of Arts, 1754–1954* (1954), pp. 36–9; E. K. Waterhouse, *Three Decades of British Art, 1740–1770* (American Philosophical Society, vol. lxiii, 1965). Waterhouse supposes that Reynolds was the behind-the-scenes manipulator of the artists' committee, using Hayman as his cover.

meetings, now preserved in the library of the Royal Academy of Arts in Piccadilly, London.[1] The assembling in one place of all the miscellaneous evidence, along with the unsolved problems, should make possible some reasonable guesses.

Until the mid eighteenth century the ordinary British creative artist had no satisfactory place in society.[2] Only the outstanding genius could achieve financial security. The others, without any regular means of exhibiting their work, found life uncertain and hard. To be sure, there had been a few attempts to form private institutions for art instruction, such as Kneller's and the St. Martin's Lane Academy, but the craving persisted for a Royal Academy following the example of the French. In 1755 a number of leading artists formed themselves into a committee and published a statement of their aims. Because of various rivalries, however, nothing came of the project.

In the 1740s the new Foundling Hospital had been presented with a number of fine paintings, which were hung in its public rooms, where they were easily seen. As these were much admired, it was natural that there should be talk about the desirability of a more extensive gathering of the work of all kinds of creative artists, including the best work of the famous and the little known alike.

On 5 November 1759, at the Foundling Hospital, proposals were initiated for some definite action, and a week later, on the 12th, at a gathering at the Turk's Head Tavern in Gerrard Street, Soho, a committee was selected to set in motion arrangements for the first extensive public exhibition ever to be held in London. The committee, which included Joshua Reynolds, William Chambers, Richard Wilson, Joseph Wilton, and Francis Hayman, was composed of six painters, two sculptors, two architects, two engravers, one seal-cutter, one chaser, one medallist, and a secretary, Francis Milner Newton. It was he who kept the minutes of the subsequent meetings.

On 1 December, at the first real meeting of the committee,

[1] Early portions were printed by the Walpole Society, op. cit. I quote from the original minutes, with the help of the Librarian, Mr. Sidney C. Hutchison, and the kind permission of the President and Council of the Royal Academy of Arts.

[2] See Rudolf Wittkower in *Man Versus Society in Eighteenth-Century Britain*, ed. J. L. Clifford (1968), pp. 70–84, and other authorities mentioned on p. 333, n. 1.

Francis Hayman was elected Chairman, but little business was done. The most pressing problem was that of finding an available room large enough to hold all the paintings, sculptures, and other art objects to be shown. At the next meeting, then, three weeks later, this and other practical details were discussed. One obvious solution was to request the use of the spacious room in the Strand belonging to the well-established Society for the Encouragement of Arts, Manufactures, and Commerce (hereafter called the Society of Arts, although it is known today as the Royal Society of Arts). But to do so would require a formal petition, and the practical artists, who may have been quite sure of their ability to handle a brush or chisel, were not quite so certain of their skill in letter-writing. And so the matter lagged.

At the fourth meeting, on 19 January 1760, however, someone among the thirteen who attended made a proposal. Why not ask the help of a professional writer? And he obviously had someone in mind—a man who was friendly with members of the group, was known to be in sympathy with their aspirations for greater public recognition, and was noted for his skill in fashioning memorable phrases. Thus the Secretary recorded: 'Resolved—That Mr Johnson may have the Form of a Letter drawn up by this Society to correct, in order to be sent to the Society for the Encouragement of Arts &c to sollicite the Use of their Room for the Exhibition.' Unfortunately, Reynolds, who may well have initiated the idea, was not actually present at this meeting, and again there was no speedy action. Two weeks later, on 2 February, however, with Reynolds in attendance, another resolution was passed: 'Resolved—That this Committee do meet on Saturday next the 9th Instant to peruse the Letter given to Mr Johnson for his Correction & appoint the Time & manner of sending it to the Society for the Encouragement of Arts &c.' Still, it was not until 26 February that what had been prepared was ready to show to the group. On that day there was another meeting, attended by Reynolds. Newton, the Secretary, recorded:

Resolved—That the following Letter with the Plan inclosed be sent to the society for the Encouragement of Arts &c & that it be Signed by Mr Hayman as Chairman & that it be directed to the Sec^ry of the Society.

The Artists of this City having resolved to raise a Sum for Purposed [*sic*] of Charity by the Annual Exhibition of their Works entreat the Society to allow them the Use of their Room from the 7th of April to the 19th This Favour they consider as very important. The Publick concurrence of the Society will give to a new Practice that Countenance which Novelty must always need, and the Arts will gain Dignity from the Protection of those whom the World has already learned to respect.

I am Sir

Your most Humble Servt

F. Hayman Chairman

The Plan Inclosed

It has been lamented, that notwithstanding the general Disposition to encourage Artists, now prevailing in this Nation, many Men whose Abilitys and Attainments might justly raise them to Distinction languish in Obscurity; there being no certain or establish'd Method, by which, Regard may be modestly solicited, or the Publick Eye attracted to merit.

A Proposal was therefore made to the Artists at their annual Meeting on St. Luke's Day 1759, that every Painter, Sculptor, Architect, Engraver, Enchaser, Seal Cutter & Medalist should exhibit Once a Year at a Place appointed, a Specimen of his Art, that the Judges & Patrons of Merit may have at Once under their View the present State of the Arts in England. Elegance & Ingenuity are most valuable when they contribute to the Purposes of Virtue; it is therefore resolved, that the just advantage of this Exhibition shall be destined to the support of those Artists, whose Age, Infirmities or other lawful Hindrances suffer them to be no longer Candidates for Praise. A shilling shall be taken at the Door from every One that enters, and the sum so collected, shall be placed in the Hands of Trustees chosen by the Artists, and publickly declared in the Daily Papers.

Elsewhere I have described the difficulty of identifying a long succession of references to 'Mr. Johnson' which appear about this same time in the unpublished diary of Thomas Hollis.[1] Some of them we are certain must refer to Samuel Johnson, while others definitely represent other men. Any doubt as to which 'Mr. Johnson' was involved in fashioning these communications for the committee of artists must be dispelled for most readers by the rhythms of the concluding sentence of the letter, and by the writer's insistence that 'Elegance & Ingenuity are most valuable when they contribute to the Purposes of Virtue'. Indeed, it is

[1] 'Some Problems of Johnson's Obscure Middle Years', *Johnson, Boswell and Their Circle: Essays Presented to L. F. Powell* (1965), pp. 101–6.

unlikely that much of the original draft remained intact. If Reynolds and others supplied the factual details, the general wording must surely be Samuel Johnson's.

It should be remembered that Johnson was himself a member of the Society of Arts, though he was slightly in arrears with his dues.[1] He had been elected to membership on 1 December 1756, having been proposed by James Stuart (later known as 'Athenian Stuart', because of his advocacy of Greek architecture). In March 1757 Johnson paid the rather high annual fee of two guineas, and he paid again in November 1758 (for the year 1757). But because of straitened circumstances he paid nothing for the years 1758 and 1759. He was, then, in the spring of 1760 two years behind. But on 25 March, after paying four guineas, he was again in good standing. The reason usually given for this revival of interest was Johnson's desire to support the application for membership of Robert Dossie, but the continuing negotiations over the proposed exhibition may also have been involved.

One would like to think that when the matter was considered by the Society of Arts, Johnson, even though in arrears with dues, attended the general meeting and listened to his own resonant phrases read out by the Secretary. Unfortunately his name is not included in the list of those present on 3 March 1760.[2] Even had he been in good standing, he might conscientiously have stayed away while others were considering his letter. On the other hand, Reynolds and Hayman do appear to have acted for both sides.

Negotiations now moved fairly rapidly. As soon as the letter was received by the Society of Arts, it was referred to a large special committee including Garrick, Reynolds, and Hayman. Although this committee reported favourably to the Society, this meant only general acceptance of the artists' proposal. Quite obviously the Society was not merely lending its rooms; it intended to be in active control of all proceedings. The Society was determined not to allow any charge for admission, and also insisted on postponing the date two weeks. Having no choice at

---

[1] 'Dr. Johnson and His Friends at the Society of Arts', *Journal of the Society of Arts*, xlviii (12 Oct. 1900), 829–31; and John L. Abbott, 'Dr. Johnson and the Society', *Journal of the Royal Society of Arts &c.*, cxv (Apr., May 1967), 395–400, 486–91. See also F. R. Lewis in *TLS*, 25 June 1938, p. 433.

[2] I owe this information to Mr. David Allan, Curator-Librarian of the Royal Society of Arts in London.

this late date, the artists had to accept or give up the whole project.

Finally, on 21 April the exhibition opened, and was a great success. Sixty-nine artists were represented, with 131 works. There were large crowds, at times even unruly ones, and windows were broken. One estimate of the total attendance went as high as over 20,000 people.[1] Partly to circumvent the Society of Arts' ban on an admission fee, the artists charged sixpence for each catalogue, and since over 6,000 were sold, when it was all over the artists felt financially secure. They gladly voted various payments to people who had helped with arrangements—half a guinea for one man, ten for another and his son, one for another, four for someone else, and a handsome piece of plate for the Secretary. Then at the end of the minutes for the meeting of 12 May comes the entry: 'Order'd That Thanks be return'd to Mr Johnson for his great assistance to the Committee of Artists & that Mr Reynolds return the same.' At the time, Johnson's finances being what they were, a few guineas might have been more welcome than the formal thanks. But at least the action would seem to indicate that Johnson's help involved more than the mere rewriting of the letter of request.

He may possibly also have drafted the formal letter of thanks sent to the Secretary of the Society of Arts in mid May, although the style is hardly distinctive.

Sir—

> You are requested by the Artists whose Works appeared in the late Exhibition to return their sincerest Thanks to the Society for the Use of their Room and the Honour of their Patronage. Whatever improvement the Arts of Elegance shall receive from the honest Emulation which publick Notice may excite will be justly ascribed to those by whose Example the Public has been influenced.

This first exhibition having been so successful, it was natural that the artists should think of arranging a second. The following November, meetings began again. On the 14th a new committee was elected, and on the 25th Hayman was re-elected Chairman. Following this the group passed a series of resolutions:

> Resolved—That Application be made to the Society for the Encouragement of Arts &c for the Use of their Room. That the

[1] See Hudson and Luckhurst, op. cit., and the minutes of the committee printed in *The Sixth Volume of the Walpole Society*.

Exhibition be the begining of June in order that the Pictures offer'd for the Premiums may be removed. The Artists having found great Inconvenience in lying under the Imputation of loosing those Premiums for which they were not Candidates.

Great Inconvenience having been found by Inferior People crowding last Year.

Resolved—That the Catalogue be a shilling & that no Person be admitted without taking one, the same to serve as a Ticket.

Resolved—That the above Minutes be the substance of the Letter to be sent to the Society. Mr Reynolds is desired to request Mr Johnson to continue his good Offices to the Artists.[1]

That Mr. Johnson was so inclined appears from the minutes of the next meeting of the committee on 8 December 1760. At this time the Secretary recorded:

Mr Chairman reported that he had received the Draught of a Letter from Mr Johnson as requested last Meeting, as follows—

Sir—

The favour conferred last Year on the Artists by the Society has encouraged them to solicite the use of their Room for a second Exhibition.

This request may now be granted with less inconvenience to the Society, as the Exhibition will be defered to June a Month in which the Meetings of the Society are more rare than in the Winter; the Artists being desirous that the Pictures drawn for the prize should be removed, lest any Man should a second time suffer the disgrace of having lost that which he never sought.

The Exhibition of last Year was crowded and incommoded by the intrusion of great Numbers whose Stations and education made them no proper Judges of Statuary or Painting, and who were made idle and tumultuous by the opportunity of a shew.

It is now therefore intended that the Catalogues shall be sold for a shilling each and none allowed to enter without a Catalogue which may serve as a Ticket for admission.

These regulations which have been very deliberately formed will be doubtless thought expedient and useful, and the Artists flatter themselves that the improvement of National taste which will be promoted by comparing the Works of different Performers is not unworthy of the care of the Society.

I am . . .

[1] Just what the 'Good Offices' had been is not completely clear. This may even refer to the projected 'Address to the King' referred to later. On the surface it would appear to allude to the writing of another letter to the Society of Arts.

Here, in this juxtaposition of the original resolutions passed by the committee with the letter made from them, can be seen a perfect demonstration of the way Johnson worked. From the lame half sentences, the awkward phrases and unexpressed assumptions of the minutes which had been submitted to him, Johnson fashioned a formal letter, dignified but to the point. The mixed-up explanation of the choice of June for the exhibition has been turned into a moral issue—'lest any Man should a second time suffer the disgrace of having lost that which he never sought' —and the reminder of last year's 'inconvenience' caused by 'inferior' people crowding the rooms is elaborated in the memorable third paragraph of the letter. Although the basic ideas are the same, a new element had been added. Here is The Rambler seeing all human actions as moral choices or social dilemmas.

About this time Johnson also helped some of the artists in another project. Early in November, following the accession of George III, there had been drafted great numbers of formal addresses to the throne. Every town and county, organization and group, wished to carry up to St. James's some expression of their enthusiastic welcome to the new Sovereign. Consequently, through the last weeks of 1760 the *London Gazette* and other newspapers were packed with these addresses. In the minutes of the committee of artists there is no mention at all of any plan to join in this mass outburst of loyalty, yet evidently something must have been done by a representative selection of the same individuals. All that we know definitely is that in the *London Gazette* for 6–10 January 1761, on the first page, there appeared the following:

St. James's, January 10. The following Address of the Painters, Sculptors, and Architects, has been presented to His Majesty by the Right Honourable the Earl of Holdernesse, one of His Majesty's Principal Secretaries of State: Which Address His Majesty was pleased to receive very graciously

To the King's most Excellent Majesty.

May it please your Majesty.
Amidst the general Emulation of Loyalty with which all Orders of your Majesty's Subjects have testified their Duty, Zeal, and Veneration, to receive this humble Address from those who must owe, in a particular Manner, their Success and Eminence to Royal Notice.

Your Majesty's early Patronage of the politer Arts has given the

Painters, Sculptors, and Architects, Confidence to express, in your Royal Presence, their Sorrow for the Death of their late gracious Sovereign, and their Joy for your Majesty's Accession to the Throne. It is our Happiness to live in the Age, when our Arts may hope for new Advances towards Perfection, assisted by the Favour of a British King, of a Monarch no less judicious to distinguish, than powerful to reward: who knows the Usefulness and Value of that Skill, which delights the Eye with Beauty, but not corrupts the Manners by unlawful Passions, and which has been hitherto learned in Foreign Countries, for Want of sufficient Encouragement in our own.

The present Felicity of your Majesty, who rules over a People, blessed at the same Time with the Triumphs of Conquest, and the Plenty of Peace, leaves us nothing to desire but its long Continuance. May You live many Years to reform our Manners, and regulate our Taste; to make the Arts of Elegance subservient to Virtue and Religion; to bestow Happiness upon us, and teach us to enjoy it.[1]

Boswell later asserted that this address was written by Samuel Johnson, though the source of his information was never given.[2] He obviously had good authority, for the piece was included in a manuscript list of 'The Publications, Fugitive Pieces, etc. of Mr. Samuel Johnson', which still survives in the Yale collection. Dated September 1772, it brings together various ascriptions originally given to Boswell by Thomas Percy and further additions received from other people.[3] The 'Address' appears among the latter, but here and in later manuscript lists the exact informant is never identified, nor is there ever any indication as to where the piece had first appeared in print.[4]

---

[1] The 'Address' also appeared in the *Daily Advertiser* for Monday 12 Jan. 1761, p. 1. In the *London Gazette* for 31 Jan.–3 Feb. appeared an address from the Society for the Encouragement of Arts, etc., but there is no evidence that Johnson had anything to do with it.

[2] *Life*, i. 352; W. P. Courtney and D. Nichol Smith, *A Bibliography of Samuel Johnson* (1925), p. 99, etc.

[3] Yale University, Boswell Papers, Cat. No. M 148. A copy was sent to Garrick in a letter of 10 Sept. 1772 (Cat. No. L 560), requesting corrections and additions. In this list no mention is made of where the piece had been published, although items above and below do carry such information. See also *Life*, iii. 321. I am deeply indebted to Mrs. Marion Pottle, who has searched through all the Boswell Papers and sent me what is relevant to this matter.

[4] Three other manuscript lists of Johnson's works made by Boswell may be found in Cat. M 147, in Cat. M 149, and in L 1095 (a letter to Isaac Reed of 21 Apr. 1790). Boswell sent Reed his list, which included the

When he came to draft the first version of the *Life*, Boswell merely stated: 'In 1760 I have discovered nothing written by him but an Address of the Painters to George III on his accession to the throne of these kingdoms.' In the printed first edition, however, he complicated matters by adding a dagger (†), which he explained elsewhere was used to indicate works identified through internal evidence.[1] Possibly all this means is that early in his friendship with Johnson he had been told by someone else of this bit of ghost-writing for the artists, but had never talked to Johnson about it. Yet because the piece sounded so Johnsonian he had no real doubt about its authenticity.

For some reason this 'Address' was never included in any of the authorized collected editions of Johnson's works, and consequently has not been much discussed by scholars. Still, there seems to be no reason to question the accuracy of Boswell's ascription. The balanced clauses in the third paragraph, the emphasis on art which pleases but does not corrupt, and the final insistence on its subservience to virtue and religion—all this has a characteristic ring. One might guess that the same procedure had been followed as before. Reynolds, or another of his friends, came to Johnson with a rough sketch of the main points to be made. After some general discussion, the sheet was left with him for consideration. He then reworked the sentences and added the moral sentiments. The final result, perhaps picked up some time later, while partly a mixture of styles, is overwhelmingly Johnsonian.

When was it written? Boswell merely says '1760', although it first appeared in print in early 1761. It is impossible for us to add much more than that, for, unfortunately, there is no clear indication of the length of time which normally passed between the composition of such addresses and their presentation at Court. All we can know definitely is the date when they were made public in the newspapers, which would appear to have been shortly after their presentation at St. James's. To be sure, some of the addresses do contain dates indicating when they had been

'Address', asking for comments and corrections. In returning the list, Reed passed over this item with no comment.

[1] For Boswell's explanation of his use of asterisk and dagger in ascribing Johnson's writings, see *Life*, i. 112, n. 4. A dagger attached to a work, however, need not preclude the existence of other external evidence. Apparently it means that Johnson had not definitely admitted authorship.

formally voted by the official body involved, and these sometimes go back as far as a month. The address from the painters, sculptors, and architects, unfortunately, contains no date, except 10 January 1761, when it was released by the Court officials. As a result, everything else must be pure speculation. Still, the chances are strong that it was composed some time during the preceding December.

The piece stirred up at least one reaction—'A Copy of Verses, Occasioned By seeing in the Gazette, An Address Humbly Presented to His Majesty by the Painters, Sculptors, and Architects', which appeared anonymously in the *London Evening Post* of 10–13 January 1761, and in the *Public Advertiser* of 14 January (and possibly other papers). Horace Walpole cut out a copy, without making any attempt to identify the author, or to comment on the style.[1] The likelihood of our doing any better seems remote. Actually, it makes little difference, for the quality of the verses is not outstanding, and the poet apparently had not read the 'Address' with any care. A few lines should be enough to indicate their quality.

> To their lov'd monarch, Albion's potent king,
> While grateful subjects freedom's tribute bring;
> His reign, with heart and voice united, greet,
> Their lives and fortunes off'ring at his feet:
> From Greece, where Genius vanquish'd freedom's foes,
> Where Painting, Sculpture, Architecture rose,
> Behold! tho' late, as humbly in the rear,
> A pleasing group, the sister arts appear:
> Adorn'd with ev'ry charm the graces claim,
> Alike their number, diff'ring but in name.

One can find scarcely any connection between the 'Address' and the 'Verses', and no similarity of points of view. The writing of the 'Verses' was merely suggested by the fact that an address had finally been produced by the artists, and not by any of the ideas expressed. Johnson's moral seriousness was apparently completely lost on at least one reader.

As to plans by the committee of artists for the next exhibition, various differences arose, one of the most difficult being their proposal to charge a shilling for each catalogue and to make this

---

[1] *Anecdotes of Painting in England 1760–1795* . . . *Collected by Horace Walpole*, vol. v, edited by F. W. Hilles and Philip B. Daghlian (1937), pp. 1–3.

serve as an entrance fee. The Society of Arts was still determined that admission should be free. The result was an impasse, since the artists, too, were adamant. Consequently Reynolds and James Paine were appointed a committee of two to search for another place. Throughout February nothing happened. There were two meetings, but no action of any kind. It was not until 4 March that an agreement with Mr. Cock, the auctioneer, was reported, for the use of his room in Spring Gardens during the month of May. Evidently the rent of £40 was considered of less importance than the right to run the exhibition in the way they wanted.

Once the decision had been made, there were frequent advertisements in the papers addressed to possible exhibitors and to the public.[1] A general meeting of all concerned was held on 7 April, and arrangements made to receive all pieces of art to be shown by the 27th. The exhibition, which ran from Saturday 9 May to Saturday the 30th, and was open each weekday from seven in the morning to seven at night, was again a huge success.

In all the later planning—with discussions of newspaper publicity and a frontispiece for the catalogue—there is no evidence that Johnson was in any way involved.

But this was not the end of his help for the artists. The next autumn, in November 1761, discussions began again, this time planning the third annual exhibition. Although there were the usual arguments about a suitable place, Johnson's writing skill was apparently not needed for any of the negotiations. During the early winter the inconclusive meetings continued. Even as late as March the room had not been definitely chosen. Finally, by the middle of the month one of Cock's big rooms in Spring Gardens had again been engaged, and various decisions made concerning the catalogue. At this time Johnson once again comes on to the stage, but just how, and in what guise, is not completely clear.

For a biographer the juxtaposition of bits of evidence is always suggestive, and in this instance it may be worth while to put together the plain facts as they appear in the minutes of the artists' group and in Reynolds' engagement book for 1762.[2] For 15 March

---

[1] For example, see *Daily Advertiser*, 7 Mar., 21 Apr., 5 May 1761. There were almost daily advertisements from 12 May to the closing of the exhibition on the 30th.

[2] Reynolds's engagement book for 1762 is now in the library of the Royal Academy in London. For information concerning the catalogue and for the

Reynolds noted that at 2 p.m. he was to see 'Mr Johnson'. Then the next day, the 16th, at a meeting of the artists which Reynolds attended, the Secretary recorded 'A Motion being made & seconded that Mr Johnson be requested to give a Motto for the Catalogue & that Mr Hayman make a Design agreeable thereto.' On the 18th Reynolds saw 'Mr Johnson' again. Twelve days later, at a meeting of the committee, there was some discussion of the design, but nothing concerning the motto. Indeed, in later meetings of the committee there never was any discussion of the classical quotation to be chosen by Johnson, though the catalogue, when it appeared, did carry a line from Martial—'*Aurea si Tuleris Dona, Minora Feres.*'[1]

On 12 April Reynolds noted that he had an engagement at 1 p.m. with 'Mr Johnson', but at a meeting of the committee the next day nothing was reported. Finally, on the 20th, at another meeting, the secretary's minutes record 'Mr. Reynolds having presented a Preface which was agreed to & ordered to be printed'. Instead of merely bringing in a motto, Reynolds produced something of much greater importance.

Of course, one must admit that there is no conclusive evidence that the 'Mr Johnson' in Reynolds' notebook was Samuel. It might have been any one of a number of other Johnsons. Nor can we be certain whether the entries represent appointments for portrait sittings, or social visits.[2] The former would appear to be the more likely, since at this time Reynolds was chary of taking away any daylight time from painting. If it was merely a business or social visit, the hours are odd. On the other hand, there is no evidence that Reynolds at the time was painting the portrait of anyone named Johnson. Thus, in the light of what we know, it does seem probable that the person the artist was seeing was Samuel Johnson, and that the meetings were at least partly connected with the affairs of the committee of artists.

Since the question of the authorship of the Preface which Reynolds brought in has been discussed elsewhere in some detail,[3]

text of the Preface see Allen T. Hazen, *Samuel Johnson's Prefaces and Dedications* (1937), pp. 200–5.

[1] Ibid.

[2] In attempting to interpret entries in Reynolds's notebook, and elsewhere in this investigation, I have relied heavily on the advice of Professor F. W. Hilles.

[3] See Hazen, op. cit., and an exchange of letters in *The Times*, London,

there is no need here to do more than sum up the principal points at issue. Most scholars today accept the Preface as the composition of Samuel Johnson, but at least one art historian has attempted to ascribe it to Reynolds.[1] Certainly the closest contemporary evidence would seem to point to Reynolds. The entry in the minutes mentions no one else, and there are no later qualifications. On the other hand, in 1773 the Preface was reprinted by Thomas Davies in volume ii of a three-volume set of *Miscellaneous and Fugitive Pieces*, most of them by Johnson. It was there sandwiched in between the Preface to Shakespeare and the Preface to the *London Chronicle*, both of which have always been accepted as by Johnson.[2] And in a full review of these volumes in the *Gentleman's Magazine* the Society of Artists Preface for 1762 was specifically referred to as 'by Dr. Johnson'.[3] Since in 1774 Johnson still retained some connection with the *Gentleman's Magazine*, it is difficult to see how the reviewer could speak with such confidence if he did not have convincing evidence from someone who knew the truth. The fact that Thomas Tyers, in annotating his copy of Davies's volumes, has nothing to say about this piece is not significant, since he leaves similarly blank many of Johnson's best-known works.[4]

This Preface was included in volume xiv of Johnson's *Works* in 1789, four years before Reynolds's death.[5] Boswell accepted the attribution in the *Life*; Malone, who was Reynolds's executor, and editor of his literary works, accepted the fact; and Northcote in his *Life of Reynolds* categorically stated that the piece was by Johnson.[6] There is no evidence that Reynolds himself ever claimed to have been even partly responsible. Furthermore, the Preface sounds like Johnson. The style, the tone, the rhythms are Johnsonian. Thus,

between W. T. Whitley and L. F. Powell, 22 Jan., 5, 14, 27 Feb. 1934. See also F. W. Hilles, *The Literary Career of Sir Joshua Reynolds* (1936), pp. 24–5.

[1] Used as conclusive evidence by W. T. Whitley in *Artists and Their Friends in England, 1700–1799* (1928), i. 178–9.

[2] See Powell, op. cit., and Hazen, op. cit. The Preface was not entered in the List of Contents, a fact that caused it to be overlooked by scholars.

[3] *Gentleman's Magazine*, xliv (Nov. 1774), 525.

[4] Tyers's annotated copy is now in the British Museum, although it is not specifically catalogued as his.

[5] The volume was probably edited by Isaac Reed, who was a careful and knowledgeable worker.

[6] James Northcote, *The Life of Sir Joshua Reynolds* (2nd edn., 1818) i. 100–2.

despite the lack of conclusive proof, the question does appear to be settled. If Reynolds may have made the original suggestion, and the two men together have sketched out what was to be said, it was Johnson who did the actual writing. As a literary work, the Preface is Johnson's, and there's an end on't.

Despite the fact that the piece is fairly well known, I should like to quote at least one passage. In some circles there had been criticism of the earlier exhibitions, as being motivated by avarice and false vanity on the part of the contesting artists. In answer to this, Johnson readily admits that 'all who offer themselves to criticism are desirous of praise', but he goes on to insist that

this desire is not only innocent but virtuous, while it is undebased by artifice and unpolluted by envy; and of envy or artifice these men can never be accused, who, already enjoying all the honours and profits of their profession, are content to stand candidates for public notice, with genius yet unexperienced, and diligence yet unrewarded; who, without any hope of encreasing their own reputation or interest, expose their names and their works only that they may furnish an opportunity of appearance to the young, the diffident, and the neglected. The purpose of this Exhibition is not to enrich the Artists, but to advance the Art; the eminent are not flatter'd with preference, nor the obscure insulted with contempt; whoever hopes to deserve public favour is here invited to display his merit.[1]

One question still remains. Did all this work for the artists mean that Johnson himself had undergone any change of heart? Near-sighted as he was, and unable to see anything clearly at a distance, he had never been noted for any overt admiration for the visual arts. It is easy to document his obvious lack of interest in paintings. There is the well-known story of his visit, with Boswell and Reynolds, to the home of Richard Owen Cambridge in Twickenham. As soon as they had been welcomed by their host, Johnson 'ran eagerly to one side of the room, intent on poring over the backs of the books. Sir Joshua observed, (aside,) "He runs to the books, as I do to the pictures: but I have the advantage. I can see much more of the pictures than he can of the books." '[2] And there are other accounts of Johnson's candid admission of how little paintings meant to him.

In the early 1760s, had Reynolds, temporarily at least, won him

[1] Hazen, op. cit.

[2] *Life*, ii. 364–5 (18 Apr. 1775). See also Boswell papers at Yale.

over? The new evidence hardly justifies such a conclusion. Although he was happy to help his friends in a practical way, the successful exhibitions had not brought any change in his fundamental position. He could see few basic moral values in mere visual representation. Thus after the first two exhibitions he commented to his friend Baretti in far-off Milan, when giving him the news of London, and describing the artists' success and Reynolds' pre-eminence: 'This exhibition has filled the heads of the Artists and lovers of art. Surely life, if it be not long, is tedious, since we are forced to call in the assistance of so many trifles to rid us of our time, of that time which never can return.'[1]

Yet this is not to suggest any essentially divided opinion or hypocrisy on Johnson's part. He was fully in support of the artists project. From the beginning it had been advertised as a philanthropic venture—the proceeds of the first exhibition had been designed to aid the elderly, indigent artists, though gradually this side of the business was pushed aside—and it did stress the independent recognition of serious-minded artisans who worked with their hands. Honest labour, which injured no one else, should be encouraged. Besides, the necessity for man to fill up the vacuity of life by every means possible was one of Johnson's recurrent themes. As one critic has recently put it, 'Johnson's basic metaphor for human experience is the empty receptacle which cannot tolerate its own emptiness.'[2] In man there is this every-present dichotomy—the 'inherent need of the mind to be filled with "objects of attention" and the elusive nature of the objects offered it by temporal experience'.

The aims of the Society of Artists may well have appeared to Johnson as one innocent means of filling up the vacuity of life. Whatever he thought of the objects to be exhibited, he was glad to help in any way he could.

[1] Letter, no. 138 (Chapman, i. 134).
[2] Arieh Sachs, *Passionate Intelligence: Imagination and Reason in the Work of Samuel Johnson* (1967), p. 3.

INDEX

PRINTED IN GREAT BRITAIN
AT THE UNIVERSITY PRESS, OXFORD
BY VIVIAN RIDLER
PRINTER TO THE UNIVERSITY